The **AFTERLIFE** *of*
REPRODUCTIVE SLAVERY

Alys Eve Weinbaum

The **AFTERLIFE** of
REPRODUCTIVE SLAVERY

Biocapitalism and Black Feminism's Philosophy of History

DUKE UNIVERSITY PRESS | DURHAM AND LONDON | 2019

Printed in the United States of America on
acid-free paper ∞
Designed by Julienne Alexander
Typeset in Quadraat Pro and Scala Sans Pro by
Westchester Publishing Services

Library of Congress Cataloging-in-Publication Data
Names: Weinbaum, Alys Eve, [date] author.
Title: The afterlife of reproductive slavery : biocapitalism
and Black feminism's philosophy of history / Alys Eve
Weinbaum.
Description: Durham : Duke University Press, 2019. |
Includes bibliographical references and index.
Identifiers: LCCN 2018035543 (print)
LCCN 2018047129 (ebook)
ISBN 9781478003281 (ebook)
ISBN 9781478001768 (hardcover : alk. paper)
ISBN 9781478002840 (pbk. : alk. paper)
Subjects: LCSH: Womanism—United States. | Human
reproduction—Political aspects—United States. |
Surrogate motherhood—United States—History. |
African American women—Social conditions—History. |
Women slaves—Atlantic Ocean Region. | Slavery—United
States—History. | Slavery—Atlantic Ocean Region.
Classification: LCC HT1523 (ebook) | LCC HT1523 .W44
2019 (print) | DDC 306.3/620973—dc23
LC record available at https://lccn.loc.gov/2018035543

Cover art: Senga Nengudi, *Performance Piece*, 1978. Nylon
mesh and artist Maren Hassinger. Pearl C. Woods Gallery, Los Angeles. Photo by Harmon Outlaw. Courtesy
of the artist; Thomas Erben Gallery, New York; and Lévy
Gorvy, New York, London.

CONTENTS

ACKNOWLEDGMENTS

I have carried the ideas that compose this book with me in numerous forms for so long that accumulated intellectual and personal debts stretch far back in time. It began as an idea for a project on contemporary reproductive cultures and politics that I ended up putting aside for a number of years when I instead opted to write a book on "the race/reproduction bind" that subtends modern transatlantic thought—a book whose central claims I needed to elaborate in order to arrive at the related arguments that I present here. It is thus with pleasure (if also a little worry about inadvertently leaving someone out) that I extend heartfelt thanks to those who have engaged in dialogue and debate as the traces of a long thought process congealed enough so that they might eventually be released into the world on the printed page.

The following individuals contributed to my thinking by reading and commenting on parts of this book in incipient and polished forms, by inviting me to present work in progress, by responding to presentations and queries, by collaborating on panels and roundtables, and, not least, by sharing their scholarship: Vanessa Agard-Jones, Camille Barbagallo, Dan Berger, Eileen Boris, Nick Bromell, Daphne Brooks, Stephanie Camp, Eva Cherniavsky, Melinda Cooper, Alexandra Deem, Brent Hayes Edwards, Jane Elliot, Keith Feldman, Tom Foster, Andrew Friedman, Susan Gilman, Thavolia Glymph, Sarah Haley, Gary Handwerk, Michael Hardt, Gillian Harkins, Saidiya Hartman, Habiba Ibrahim, Moon Ho Jung, Robin D. G. Kelley, Ranjana Khanna, Caleb Knapp, Leslie Larkin, Rachel Lee, Treva Lindsey, Lisa Lowe, Jodi Melamed, Jennifer Morgan, Fred Moten, Michelle Murphy, Zita Nunez, Priti Ramamurthy, Chandan Reddy, Sonnet Retman, David Roediger, Jey Saung, Nikhil Singh, Phillip Luke Sinitiere, Stephanie Smallwood, Mediha Sorma, Gayatri Chakravorty Spivak, Neferti Tadiar, Lynn Thomas, Emily Thuma, Kalindi Vora, Priscilla Wald, Catherine Waldby, Christina Walter, Sandy Weinbaum, and Elizabeth Wilson. I sincerely thank each of these individuals for their engagement; whether extensive or precise, sympathetic or critical, it has all contributed immeasurably to my understanding of this book's many audiences and its stakes.

I wrote this book while at the University of Washington, and it is thus to colleagues and friends in Seattle and a few located farther afield, but always in mind, to whom I must express my greatest gratitude. Habiba Ibrahim, Gillian Harkins, Chandan Reddy, and Sonnet Retman have in one form or another read and commented on all parts of this manuscript (sometimes reading the same parts multiple times). Each has helped me to grapple with problems and to hone my thinking. All the book's remaining flaws are entirely of my own making. For being a wonderful interlocutor on black feminism and a fellow traveler on the up-and-down road of departmental life, I thank Habiba. For always pushing me on the political implications of my readings and reading practice, I thank Gillian. For developing with me, over many years, a transformative understanding of Benjamin's philosophy of history—the understanding upon which several of this book's titular arguments turn—I thank Chandan. For helping me to hammer out crucial formulations about postracialism and blackness, and for commenting on the revised manuscript in its entirety, I thank Sonnet. I am fortunate to have these individuals as interlocutors; I am unbelievably lucky to count them among my closest friends. Though no longer here, Stephanie Camp generously shared her knowledge of women in slavery over many years and offered invaluable feedback on early drafts. She is dearly missed. Others at the university have offered indispensable support. I am honored to have Anis Bawarshi, Eva Cherniavsky, Gary Handwerk, Moon Ho Jung, Suhanthie Motha, Stephanie Smallwood, Kathleen Woodward, and, not least, my sage *mogas* Madeleine Yue Dong, Lynn Thomas, and Priti Ramamurthy as my colleagues. For walks, music, and talk that take me far away from writing and allow me to return to it with new eyes, I thank Annie Gage, Gretchen Yanover, and Marcia Robins. For sharing many meals over many years, and, not least, the quotidian wonder of watching tiny people become bigger people, I thank Sonnet Retman and Curtis Bonney. For being there to wander, talk shop, and endlessly digress, I thank Brent Hayes Edwards. For sharing a world beneath the ocean, I thank Phylleen Jackson. For welcoming me in with open arms, I thank Nicki Barbolak, Beth Raymond, and Steve Raymond. For just being, I thank Sandy Weinbaum and Shelly Weinbaum.

My students have been an important part of my life, and this book owes more to my time in the classroom than they could possibly know. I am grateful to numerous undergraduate students and especially to the graduate students in my first seminars on black women's neo-slave narratives and black feminism. Elizabeth Brown, Leanne Day, Leslie Larkin, Claire Naeun Lee, Christopher Patterson, Alice Pedersen, Sue Shon, Balbir Singh, and Maya Smorodinsky are among those whose response to my readings of texts treated in this book compelled me to think and think again. Three students have worked closely with me as research assistants. I am indebted to Alexandra Deem, Annie Dwyer, and Caleb Knapp for their meticulous labors and for exchange of ideas, related and unrelated to this book.

I wish to acknowledge those involved in production through Duke University Press. Courtney Berger has been an ideal editor. She has believed in this book from the start. At a particularly challenging moment she provided the encouragement that kept the revision process going. Editorial associate Sandra Korn, senior project editor Liz Smith, and book designer Julienne Alexander have been a pleasure to work with. I also extend my sincere thanks to the anonymous readers of the manuscript for thoughtful and challenging engagement. The book is stronger for their input. Above all, I wish to thank the final reader for the press, now known to me, Jennifer Morgan. My work on the afterlife of reproductive slavery would simply not have been possible without Jennifer's groundbreaking book on reproduction in slavery. I have been inspired by her, and I thank her not only for her clear understanding of the intellectual and political stakes of this book but also for sharing work in progress back and forth over the years.

As it happened, my deepest immersion in the worlds of surrogacy, human cloning, and the organ trade, in neo-slave narratives and speculative fictions that represent these biocapitalist processes of extraction, and in black feminist texts that reflect and refract them, coincided with the first decade of my daughter's life. Her arrival into the world not only transformed my research and writing habits but also profoundly reshaped my understanding of the complexity and beauty of reproductive labor in all its forms. It is to my amazing Amara, and to Matt Aalfs, who makes all good things seem possible, that I dedicate this book. Without the two of them in the world, writing books would be a far less meaningful undertaking.

Introduction

HUMAN REPRODUCTION
and the SLAVE EPISTEME

It is the enslavement of Blacks that enables us to imagine the commodification of human beings, and that makes the vision of fungible breeder women so real.

—DOROTHY ROBERTS, *KILLING THE BLACK BODY* (1997)

If slavery persists as an issue . . . it is not because of an anti-quarian obsession with bygone days or the burden of a too-long memory, but because black lives are still imperiled and deval-ued by a racial calculus and a political arithmetic that were en-trenched centuries ago. This is the afterlife of slavery.

—SAIDIYA HARTMAN, *LOSE YOUR MOTHER* (2007)

This book investigates Atlantic slavery's reflection in and refraction through the cultures and politics of human reproduction that characterize late twenty-first-century capitalism. Through close readings of a range of texts—literary and visual, contemporary and historical—I demonstrate that slavery, as prac-ticed in the Americas and Caribbean for roughly four hundred years, has a specifically reproductive afterlife. Slavery lives on as a thought system that is subtended by the persistence of what Saidiya Hartman calls "a racial calculus and a political arithmetic," and what I will refer to throughout this book as *the slave episteme* that was brewed up in the context of Atlantic slavery.[1] Like all thought systems, the slave episteme produces material effects over time. In rendering reproductive slavery thinkable it enables continued—albeit continuously recalibrated—forms of gendered and racialized exploitation of human reproductive labor as itself a commodity and as the source of human biological commodities and thus value. The slave episteme manifests in contemporary cultural production. In this book, I demonstrate how such cultural production mediates gendered and racialized capitalist processes that the slave episteme, in turn, subtends.

My argument is predicated on and posits the existence of a largely unacknowledged historical constellation. There are two periods in modern history during which in vivo reproductive labor power and reproductive products have been engineered for profit: during the four centuries of chattel slavery in the Americas and the Caribbean and now, again, in our present moment. And yet proof of neither historical repetition nor simple continuity is my primary aim. In contrast to studies of human trafficking and what is sometimes referred to as neoslavery, I do not amass empirical evidence or document resurgence of human enslavement. And I never argue that enslavement has proceeded in a linear fashion over time.[2] My argument is neither positivist nor teleological. Rather, I offer an epistemic argument about the afterlife of a thought system that renders human reproduction's devaluation and extraction *conceivable* in both senses of that biologically laden term. This is a story about the emergence of what Walter Benjamin has called "the time of the now"—in this case, a story about contemporary reproductive cultures and politics that exposes the epistemic conditions that will, if left uninterrogated and unchecked, continue to enable slavery's reproductive afterlife.[3] In telling a story about human reproduction in biocapitalism and thus about the episteme's endurance, my aspirations are modest. I hope to generate nothing more (and hopefully nothing less) than what Raymond Williams once referred to as an "extra edge of consciousness"—in this case, consciousness about the conflicts and contradictions that shape the time of the now, a time characterized, in part, by the reproductive afterlife of slavery.[4]

My argument begins by building on previous scholarship that has sought to convene a discussion of the long and intertwined histories of slavery and capitalism. Such scholarship argues that slavery is an urform of what the political scientist Cedric Robinson famously called "racial capitalism." As Robinson explained, slavery ought not be construed as historically prior to the emergence of capitalism proper; it is not part of a finite process of primitive accumulation. Rather, slavery is part of racial capitalism's ongoing work of racialized and gendered extraction.[5] In chapter 1, I treat Robinson's ideas and those of historians of slavery who have expanded upon them to demonstrate that slavery and capitalism are not and have never been antithetical or discrete

GOOD WRITING HERE

formations neatly arranged in temporal succession. As we shall see, accounts of the historical development of capitalism that were initially offered by Marx and Engels (and perpetuated by a legion of traditional Marxists) constitute an antiquated approach to capitalism that is myopically European and falsely teleological. In contrast to such an approach, I follow Robinson in arguing that slavery and capitalism were co-emergent and co-constitutive, and are continuously bound together in complex relations of historical reciprocity whose dynamics have changed over time. In the past, such relations produced the wealth of nations and empires. In the present, they subtend biocapitalism by shaping ideas about race and reproduction as these are manifest in the racialization and feminization of reproductive labor in contexts in which life itself is commodified.

In engaging with the concept of racial capitalism, I ally myself with the radical project that Robinson dubbed "black Marxism"—a way of thinking about the intersection of class formation and racial formation that Robinson regards as most fully realized in the writings of well-known black radicals such as W. E. B. Du Bois and C. L. R. James. At the same time, I challenge and expand Robinson's genealogy of black Marxism by calling our attention to its presumptive masculinism. Indeed, throughout this book I push against prevailing constructions of the black radical tradition in order to move understanding of this tradition in a new direction that encompasses black feminist thinkers whose writings, in multiple idioms, have not often been recognized as contributions to black Marxism but ought to be. Of special interest in the pages that follow are contributions by black feminists who began writing about enslaved women's insurgency against reproduction in bondage and the implications of this insurgency for substantive reproductive freedom in the 1970s, 1980s, and 1990s. With a focus on the unprecedented intensity of black feminist publication across these three decades—those that witnessed, not coincidentally, the rise of neoliberalism and the flourishing of biocapitalism—this book identifies and contributes to a distinctly black feminist philosophy of history.

I have coined this term to draw attention to a unique materialist and epistemic knowledge formation, expressed in multiple idioms, including history, theory, and literary fiction, that constellates the slave past and the biocapitalist present and thus examines the reproductive dimensions of racial capitalism as it has evolved over time. Although it is inaccurate to suggest that the masculinism of the black radical tradition is an express target of the black feminist writings that I treat throughout, the black feminist philosophy of history that I limn and contribute to must nonetheless be recognized as a powerful critique of Robinson's idea of the black radical tradition because of the way it consistently and persistently centers slave breeding in its discussion of both economic and cultural reproduction in slavery and beyond. This is something that the black radical texts written by the men who are elevated by Robinson (and many others) simply do not do.

Building on a dialogue about black women's writing initiated by literary scholars such as Hazel Carby, Barbara Christian, Valerie Smith, and Hortense Spillers (to name only a few), who were among the first to train our attention on representations of black motherhood in fictional writings by and about black women, I suggest that black feminists worked together to clear space for arguments about black motherhood but also for arguments specifically attentive to the issues of reproduction and sex in slavery.[6] In this way they keyed black feminism in its present moment of production to forms of female insurgency in the slave past, effectively linking their own knowledge production to knowledge produced in and through the actions of insurgent enslaved women. The upshot: black feminism has offered forward a profound and profoundly collective analysis of the forms of reproductive extraction that began to emerge in the 1970s, 1980s, and 1990s and, simultaneously, an understanding of how reproductive extraction and women's resistance to it in the present are connected to the forms of extraction that characterized Atlantic slavery as well as to the forms of racialized and gendered insurgency that sought to challenge slavery's reproduction.

Racial Capitalism and Biocapitalism

Today myriad forms of human biological life are objects of speculative investment and development. Ranging from the microscopic (stem cells, sperm, and oocytes) to the large and fleshy (organs and babies), life is routinely offered for sale in the global marketplace. As numerous journalists and social scientists have documented, nearly all parts of the human body can be purchased, as can an array of in vivo biological processes, including gestation and birth of human beings by so-called surrogates.[7] Precisely because so many aspects of contemporary capitalism involve commodification of in vivo labor and of human biological products, over the past decade scholars in science and technology studies have identified what they variously describe as "the tissue economy," "the bioeconomy," "lively capital," and, most succinctly, "biocapital."[8] In chapter 1, I treat the genealogy of the concept of *biocapitalism*, the titular concept used throughout this book, and highlight feminist contributions to its development. For present purposes, suffice it to note that I use biocapitalism to describe, by way of shorthand, the ascent of biotechnology, pharmaceuticals, genomics, and reprogenetics as primary areas of contemporary capitalist investment and expansion. Following other feminist scholars, in using *biocapitalism* I seek to stretch and retool the concept so that the otherwise implicit reproductive dimensions of the *bio* prefacing *capitalism* surface. I also seek to extend existing feminist approaches to biocapitalism by employing the concept to name the pervasive *sublation*—by which I mean the simultaneous *negation and preservation*—of the history of slavery and the practice of slave breeding by forms of capitalism that are involved, as is contemporary biocapitalism, in extraction of value from life itself. Along with other scholars, I argue that human biological commodities, especially reproductive labor power and its products, are required to maintain biocapitalism. To this I add that the perpetuation of the slave episteme is required to make biocapitalism go. As I will elaborate, slavery is epistemically central to biocapitalism even when biocapitalist processes and products do not immediately appear to depend upon slavery as antecedent. Chapters 4 and 5 and the epilogue, expand this claim through treatment of novels and films that mediate the rise of neoliberalism and the disavowal of the persistence of the slave episteme that is part and parcel of neoliberal celebrations of the freedom to consume reproductive processes and products.[9] As we shall see, when biocapitalism sublates slavery and neoliberalism celebrates consumer choice, cultural texts provide a window onto all that transpires. When read critically, such texts allow us to perceive biocapitalism's dependence on reproductive extraction, reproductive extraction's dependence on the persistence of the slave episteme, and, not least, the slave episteme's role in enabling conceptualization of human reproduction as a racializing process through which both labor and products are rendered alienable.[10]

Given my focus on what may initially appear to some readers to be two distinct historical formations—slavery and biocapitalism—I pause here to address any possible assumptions about the existence of an absolute distinction between the two. As feminists across the disciplines have shown, women's reproductive labor, broadly construed as the reproduction of workers and the relations of production, has powered dominant social and economic formations in diverse geographic locations. As scholars of antiquity reveal, nearly all forms of slavery, beginning with those practiced in the Ancient world, have involved sexual subjection and reproductive dispossession and have created distinct domestic and political regimes. As we know, in the Roman Empire slave women reproduced slaves for their masters and were often valued for their reproductive capabilities.[11] Indeed the doctrine of *partus sequitur ventrem* ("that which is brought forth follows the womb"), which determined the slave status of children born to enslaved women in the Americas and the Caribbean beginning in the seventeenth century, originated not in American colonial law, as is commonly thought, but rather in Roman law.[12]

As Marxist feminists such as Maria Mies and autonomist feminists such as Mariarosa Dalla Costa, Silvia Federici, and Leopoldina Fortunati have argued, demonization of women and attempts to wrest control of reproductive capacity from women was a precondition for capitalism's emergence.[13] Historians of domestic labor and homework such as Evelyn Nakano Glenn and Eileen Boris have shown in their now classic scholarship that since the advent of industrial capitalism, exploitation of women's reproductive labor has functioned as a form of continuous primitive accumulation.[14] In instances in which reproductive labor functions as paid labor (as opposed to unremunerated subsistence labor) it is racialized. Although the race, ethnicity, or nationality of the bodies tasked with this labor continues to change as trends in outsourcing shift, it is from poor women of color around the globe that reproductive work is most readily and frequently extracted. Today hyperexploitation of domestic laborers, care workers, and sex workers living in or migrating from the Global South is predicated on devaluation of reproductive labor and the inextricable process through which this labor is racialized.[15] In globalization, wages for all forms of reproductive labor are continuously driven down. For example, Rhacel Salazar Parreñas demonstrates that devaluation of women's work requires women from the Philippines to migrate abroad to receive livable wages, a practice that compounds the ongoing feminization of global poverty by forcing migrant laborers to rely on "care-chains" in which the children whom they leave behind must either be looked after by relatives or placed into the hands of women who are less mobile than their absent employers.[16]

Notably all of the feminist arguments about reproductive labor that I have mentioned explicitly or implicitly begin from Marx and Engels's watershed observation that capitalism relies on the reproduction of the relations of production, and on subsequent Marxist feminist observations about the manner in which the reproduction of the means of production—including the reproduction of the bodies that compose the labor force—is biologically, socially, culturally, and ideologically maintained through the domination and subjugation of women and women's reproductive labor. As should be clear, this book's argument would be impossible to envision were it not for the immensely rich Marxist and Marxist feminist traditions of engagement with reproductive labor over capitalism's longue durée and in the precapitalist past that preceded it.[17]

And yet the ideas about human reproductive labor that I examine here are also distinct. As I elaborate in greater detail in chapters 1 and 2, in which I discuss black feminist historical scholarship on slave breeding and black feminist legal scholarship on slave breeding's relationship to contemporary surrogacy, in biocapitalism the reproductive body creates surplus value in a manner that has epistemic precedent neither solely in industrial capitalism nor in the global service-based economy ushered in by post-Fordism and outsourcing. It also has precedent in chattel slavery as practiced in the Americas and the Caribbean. It was, after all, in the context of Atlantic slavery that, for the first time in history, in vivo reproductive labor was deemed alienable and slaves bred not only for use and prestige (as they were in the Ancient world) but also expressly for profit. As historians amply document, slave breeding in the Americas and the Caribbean was increasingly important to the maintenance of slavery as time wore on, and thus slave women's wombs were routinely treated as valuable objects and as sources of financial speculation. Most important for present purposes, after the 1807 closure of the Atlantic slave trade, slave breeding was pursued with urgency (it was now the only source of fresh slaves) and carefully calculated efficiency. Whereas previous feminist work has theorized the centrality to capitalism of reproductive labor and its dispossession, the forms of reproductive labor and dispossession that exist in contemporary biocapitalism recall—even as the afterlife of reproductive slavery is disavowed—the reproductive extraction that enabled reproduction of human biological commodities in black women's wombs. Put otherwise, while contemporary capitalism depends upon the exploitation of reproductive labor to sustain and create laborers (as have all forms of capitalism throughout history), biocapitalism also depends on the prior history of slave breeding as an epistemic condition of possibility. Although the historians whose work on reproduction in slavery I discuss at length in chapter 1 do not write about the implications of their research for the study of contemporary biocapitalism (notably, the concept had not yet been proposed when they wrote), black feminist legal scholars studying surrogacy recognized slave breeding as a conceptual antecedent for surrogacy, and thus also the fact that it is the slave episteme that renders the racialized capacity to reproduce human biological commodities thinkable across time.

Because this black feminist insight is so central to my argument, it is important to be clear at the outset on its scope and parameters. The black feminist argument that I take up and to which I add is *not* that biocapitalism and chattel slavery are the same or that they ought to be treated as analogical. The argument is that in all situations in which human biological life is commodified, processes of commodification must be understood as subtended by the long history of slave breeding as it was practiced in the Americas and Caribbean. When human biological life itself is commodified, reproductive labor is invariably conceptualized as a gendered process that can be undervalued and thus hyperexploited (this is the argument made by Marxist feminists outlined earlier). Simultaneously, when human reproduction is commodified it is as a *racializing process* that transforms reproductive labor and its products into commodities that may be alienated. As in slavery, commodities that may best be described as *(re)produced* are construed as alienable because they are conceptualized as "rightfully" separable from the bodies that (re)produced them. They do not "naturally" belong to these bodies. Historically the alienability of reproductive labor power and its products has been guaranteed by the racialized dehumanization that was slave breeding and the fungibility of the lively products that so-called breeding wenches (re)produced.

In the 1980s, when black feminists first analyzed the surrogacy arrangements that had begun to emerge in the United States, they began to theorize what I call the *surrogacy/slavery nexus*. Their insights were largely speculative. After all, at the time they wrote, surrogacy was not a widespread practice. It was only due to a few high-profile cases in which surrogates sought, and failed, to retain custody of the children to whom they had given birth that surrogacy became part of a national dialogue and the object of intense scrutiny by media pundits and academics alike. I discuss the two most important surrogacy cases, the so-called Baby M case (1986) and *Johnson v. Calvert* (1990), in chapter 1. Today the number of so-called surrobabies born each year remains relatively small. US agencies that attempt to track an unregulated and therefore elusive market estimate that although roughly 12 percent of all people in the United States (and many more globally) struggle with infertility, and three to four billion US dollars are spent annually on a full spectrum of infertility treatments, in 2015 only fifteen hundred of the 1.5 percent of babies born using assisted reproductive technologies (ARTs) were surrobabies.[18] Given these numbers, it would be foolish to argue that surrogacy ought to be studied because it is a statistically significant phenomenon or that the philosophical importance of black feminism's theorization of the surrogacy/slavery nexus rests on the pervasiveness of surrogacy as a practice. Instead my argument turns on acknowledgment of surrogacy's hold on the public imagination (in part, a function of the media's preoccupation with the surrogate industry and the sensationalizing of cases that go awry), on what this hold on the public imagination suggests about surrogacy's cultural significance, and on what it is that black feminist approaches to surrogacy enable us to understand about contemporary biocapitalism's relationship to racial capitalism that those analyses of surrogacy that do not contribute to elaboration of black feminism's philosophy of history cannot.

In building on and contributing to black feminism's analysis of the surrogacy/slavery nexus, this book intervenes into prevailing theories of racialization. To risk a necessarily reductive generalization, within critical race studies, critical ethnic studies, and black studies, race is most often theorized as a social construct that is mobilized and attached to individual bodies and populations as power is arrayed hierarchically in the service of the nation-state, capitalism, and other forms of racial hegemony. Depending on the political orientation of the analysis (and the disciplinary preoccupations of the analyst), race is neither regarded as a biological truth (though it may be parsed for how it is equated with phenotype and thus naturalized or for how it functions as a bio-social formation) nor as a genetically stable category (as amply confirmed by studies of the human genome which assert that race is not genetic).[19] Rather race is construed as a product of globalizing capitalism, regimes of racial nationalism (white racial nationalism and other forms of ethnic nationalism), colonialism, empire, or some combination of these.

In situating black feminist work on surrogacy as the fulcrum on which my analysis of human reproduction in biocapitalism pivots, I suggest that the race a priori ascribed to individuals and populations is often irrelevant to the extraction of value from in vivo reproductive labor and its products. This is a crucial point of departure from theorists of racialization who imagine that it is only racialized reproductive bodies that exist as racialized prior to their exploitation whose exploitation is racialized. Instead it is an argument predicated on the idea that so long as the performance of reproductive labor is construed as a *racializing process*—as it was in Atlantic slavery—laborers who engage in reproductive labor are racialized by their labor, and their racialization (via their labor) used as the pretext to further extract labor and products. Additionally, as we shall see in my discussion of speculative fiction in chapters 4 and 5, a focus on *reproduction as a process* rather than on the perceived or ascribed gender identity that belongs a priori to the reproductive laborer makes it possible to imagine worlds in which reproductive labor is no longer performed by bodies that are sexed as female. Just as it is the reproductive process that racializes reproductive labor and laborer, this same process can retroactively feminize a body that has not previously been gendered thus.

The proposed approach to reproductive labor and its racialization in biocapitalism makes sense given available information about the women who currently participate in surrogate arrangements. Although in recent years the comparatively high price of surrogacy in the United States has led to outsourcing of reproductive labor and therefore to the performance of surrogacy by poor women in India, Thailand, Mexico, and elsewhere, when surrogacy is performed in the United States—which at the time of writing remains the world's largest market for surrogate labor—it is predominantly performed by white women.[20] The existence of a global, multiracial surrogate labor force suggests that it is not primarily the ascribed or perceived racial identity of these women that racializes reproductive labor and renders labor and products alienable.

And yet this formulation also raises an irrepressible question: What happens to "blackness," as it functioned in Atlantic slavery, in the context of contemporary surrogacy as it functions within biocapitalism? Put differently, how can we understand "blackness" as one but not the only modality through which we can trace the forwarding of the slave episteme into biocapitalism? Over the course of this book, and especially in chapter 1, in which I explore the racialization of surrogate labor even when the surrogate is not herself a recognizably black woman, I engage these complex questions from several vantage points. I calibrate my response to what can best be described as the *flickering off and on of blackness* (as what Saidiya Hartman calls "the racial calculus and political arithmetic entrenched centuries ago") in the context of an emergent neoliberal hegemony that sometimes successfully, and at other times unsuccessfully, disavows, and thus seeks to erase from view, the historical processes of racialization on which reproductive extraction relies. These are of course the processes of racialization, buttressed by the doctrine of partus sequitur ventrem, that transformed enslaved reproductive laborers into racialized "black" bodies from whom both labor and children could be stolen.[21]

As alluded to earlier, the verb *to sublate* is especially germane and instructive for the present argument. As a philosophical term, it has been most fully developed by Hegel, subsequent Hegelian philosophers, and Marxist theorists. In their usage, as opposed to the colloquial usage, it is not synonymous with that which has disappeared or been repressed. It is instead an active verb that describes the seemingly paradoxical movement by which ways of being in the world (Hegel) and systems of power such as feudalism or capitalism (Marx) are simultaneously *negated* and *preserved* by historical forces that transform the status quo by transcending it over time. In certain strands of Marxist theory, the term has been used to describe processes that challenge and reshape hegemony, not by toppling it in one fell swoop but rather by taking up new positions of power within an ongoing struggle for dominance. The bourgeois revolutions that led to the birth of industrial capitalism are the most well-known example of this dialectical process of sublation. The proletarian revolution that Marx believed would eventuate in the end of the system of private property as we know it is perhaps the most anticipated example of sublation as a dialectical process. The *Oxford English Dictionary* neatly captures the Marxist idea of sublation in one of its definitional quotations: "It is the actualization of the system that makes it rational, and *sublates* its past history into a rationally-necessary moment of the whole."[22] To return to the question of blackness and what I describe as its flickering off and on in our contemporary moment with these ideas about sublation in mind, I venture the following formulation: biocapitalism sublates slavery by producing the *flickering off and on of blackness*. This is especially so in the context of neoliberalism. Neoliberalism requires that forms of racial power rooted in slavery be understood as antiquated and thus disavowed as irrelevant, even though they have been not only negated but also preserved. Borrowing and tweaking the definitional quotation from the OED, we might say that blackness flickers off and on in our neoliberal present because biocapitalism is a form of racial capitalism that sublates the history of slavery by rendering it a "rationally-necessary moment of the whole," even though this rationally necessary moment must be systematically disavowed for the system to function smoothly.

In advancing this argument, I do not mean to suggest that other histories are not also sublated (that is, negated and preserved) and then disavowed in contemporary biocapitalism. It is imperative to recognize the afterlife of Euro-American colonialism and imperialism when treating surrogacy, especially when surrogate labor is performed by women residing in former colonies such as India, which was until recently the world's second largest surrogacy market. Nor do I wish to downplay the impact of postcolonial theory on my thinking about reproduction.[23] Rather this book, which is resolutely based in a US archive, treats the slave episteme rather than what might be referred to as a colonial or imperial episteme in order to underscore the importance of slave breeding as a historical phenomenon of epistemic importance precisely because slavery and its reproductive afterlife have not been taken up by other scholars of contemporary reproductive labor and its outsourcing, and, just as important, because slavery has not been treated in scholarship on biocapitalism, the larger area of scholarly inquiry into which all work on surrogacy fits.[24]

In arguing that the racialization of reproductive laborers skews neither "black" nor "white" in any simple sense and does not solely or necessarily depend on the ascribed or perceived blackness of the bodies tasked with performing reproductive labor, this book's argument resonates with recent critiques of biopower offered by black studies scholars who have pointed out that racialization is a form of dehumanization that operates in context-specific ways depending on the biopolitical organization of the population in question. Theorists such as Achille Mbembe and Alexander Weheliye, for instance, observe that it is imperative to recognize slavery and colonialism as biopolitical formations (something neither of the two most famous theorists of biopower, Michel Foucault and Giorgio Agamben, acknowledge) and also that blackness is not the only racial cut or caesura (to use Foucault's original term) that is capable of creating the distinction upon which biopower depends: that between individuals and populations entitled to full humanity and those who are denied it; those who are made to live, and those who can be killed with impunity.[25] For Mbembe and Weheliye, being "human" invariably equates with being white or European; however, those who are racialized as less than human are never exclusively black. Indeed both theorists refuse to create hierarchies of oppression among the individuals and populations they discuss, including South Africans, African-descended slaves, historically colonized populations, Palestinians, Jews, Roma, and queers. As Weheliye explains, "If racialization is understood not as a biological or cultural descriptor but as a conglomerate of sociopolitical relations that discipline humanity into full human, not-quite-human, and nonhuman, then blackness designates a changing system of unequal power structures that apportion and delimit which humans can lay claim to full human status and which cannot."[26] As in the present analysis of biocapitalism, in their analyses of biopower, theorists regard blackness as a foundational form of racialized dehumanization, but never as the only form that racialized dehumanization takes. Inspired by the agility and flexibility of this work, I argue that it is a mistake to explore the endurance of the slave episteme solely by looking for the visible "blackness" of the laborer. Instead we must look for the processes through which reproductive labor and products are racialized, how these processes of racialization are recalibrated over time, and, thus too, at those processes through which racialization is disavowed and prior histories of racialized dehumanization erased from view.

The conventional, positivist approach to understanding the racialization of labor risks positing race as a biological and thus empirically verifiable identity that preexists the labor process. As the historians of labor David Roediger, Theodore Allen, and Moon-Ho Jung have shown, the labor that individuals and collectivities engage in or are forced to perform racializes labor, renders the labor performed as a racializing process, and transforms the laborer into an individual who may, as a consequence of his or her place in the division of labor, be identified as "white," "black," or "Asian," or, as the case may be, as a "coolie" or a "nigger."[27] Just as static theorizations of race as a pregiven identity are too rigid to account for historical processes of racial formation in industrial capitalism, they are too rigid to account for current biopolitical and biocapitalist realities. On the one hand, such rigid ideas about race foreclose awareness of the historical relationships among racial slavery, colonialism, and empire—the relationships that enabled the development of the global capitalist modernity we have inherited. On the other hand, they foreclose consideration of the flickering off and on of blackness in contemporary neoliberalism and thus of the ways in which market-driven reproductive practices and politics build upon, disavow, and erase racialized historical violence. In sum, they foreclose our ability to see that labor processes create observable racial formations and not the other way around.

One last caveat is required. In venturing the argument about the reproductive afterlife of slavery I do not wish to imply that the slave episteme determines the totality of social and economic relations in contemporary biocapitalism. The history of slave breeding and the persistence of the slave episteme that four hundred years of slave breeding left in its wake necessarily but not exclusively shape contemporary social and economic relations. At the risk of being both too obvious and redundant, biocapitalism relies on *reproduction as a racializing process* that creates human biological commodities and itself functions as a commodity. This is a process that is powered by the slave episteme that was inherited from Atlantic slavery, itself an economic formation that was world shaping, even though its implementation, in the form of plantation slavery, was geographically restricted. As the black feminist legal scholar Dorothy Roberts observes, "It is the enslavement of Blacks that enables us to imagine the commodification of human beings, and that makes the vision of fungible breeder women so real."[28] Translating Roberts's deceptively straightforward insight into the conceptual language developed thus far, it is the prior existence of slave breeding as a racializing process that today makes the vision of breeder women and surrobabies a reality. The history of racial slavery may not be the exclusive antecedent of contemporary biocapitalism—such an argument is reductive. However, if scholarship on biocapitalism looks at the commodification of life itself from the vantage point of contemporary surrogacy and thus from the vantage point of breeding as labor and children as products, it becomes clear that slavery is a "necessary moment of the whole" that has been sublated, and is today quite often disavowed.

As with any argument about epistemic endurance, the present argument has implications for knowledge production about the past and present, the relationship between the two, and how we imagine the future. If biocapitalism functions by sublating slavery, it behooves us to recognize that we cannot fully comprehend biocapitalism unless we examine its relationship to slavery as a way of knowing and being in the world. Reciprocally we cannot come to terms with the history of the present unless we recognize that slavery was not only a racial capitalist formation (as Robinson and others argue) but also an emergent biocapitalist formation, as I argue. When we recognize that biocapitalism constitutes a new naming and framing of the reproductive extraction upon which slavery turned, we are also compelled to consider that such a new naming and framing requires revision of how we understand the impact of the past on the present and on a future yet to come.

Despite the advantages of what might be characterized as two-way epistemic traffic, it is noteworthy that the linkages between slavery and biocapitalism that interest me here have not been treated by other scholarship on capitalism's past or present formations. Most historians of slavery hew to historical archives and, unsurprisingly, eschew presentism. Most theorists of biocapitalism focus exclusively on the present and leave slavery out of the discussion. Both practices result in the narrowing of the temporal frame in a manner that buttresses arguments about biocapitalism's newness and occludes arguments about dialectical processes of sublation, and thus about constellation of past and present. In fact, save for the black feminist writings discussed throughout this book, the relationship of slave breeding to reproduction in contemporary capitalism has been entirely neglected.[29] I speculate about some of the reasons for this in chapter 1, in which I discuss feminist scholarship on biocapitalism. In the remaining chapters I respond to the conceptual aporia that is generated by demonstrating what a cultural studies approach focused on close reading of imaginative literary and visual texts can offer us when we seek to produce a counterhistory of the present that places the history of slavery and its reproductive afterlife front and center. In doing so I trace the workings of the slave episteme across a range of cultural texts and explore how each differently enables *critical speculative engagement* with slavery and its reproductive afterlife—a form of engagement that, I argue, is methodologically useful and politically necessary.[30]

Although the works of creative imagination, mainly novels and films, that I treat are not often read as works of philosophy, I argue that each contributes to black feminism's philosophy of history. Moreover I suggest that such works reveal the unique part played by *imagination* in accounting for slave women and other reproductive laborers as insurgent theorists of power, historical actors who considered how their choices, although individual and constrained by circumstance, might constitute resistance to sexual and reproductive extraction. While I leave a description of specific authors and texts until the chapter overview with which I close this introduction ("What Lies Ahead"), suffice it to note that what I am calling critical speculative engagement neither replaces nor substitutes for feminist historical work on women in slavery or for social scientific work on biocapitalism. Contributions of historians, anthropologists, sociologists, and ethnographers have been invaluable to development of my argument and are engaged throughout this book. Rather I focus on works of creative imagination and engage in critical speculation to supplement existing methodological approaches that are less able to track the work of the slave episteme. While the argument I advance is not empirically verifiable, I believe it is worth considering because it has the capacity to transform current understanding of the reproductive cultures and politics by which we are surrounded and the reproductive practices in which we participate.

In the first part of this book (chapters 1 through 3) I track the slave episteme as it appears in black feminist texts that highlight the reproductive dimensions of slavery. In these texts, many of which are novels referred to in genre criticism as neo-slave narratives, reproduction and sex in bondage are thematically and formally central. In placing these novels alongside black feminist nonfiction, I argue that, when taken together, all collectively elaborate a philosophy of history, one that takes up questions of reproductive extraction and reproductive insurgency in slavery and in the 1970s, 1980s, and 1990s—the three decades of black feminism's most robust production and publication. For instance, in chapter 3, I offer an extended reading of perhaps the most famous neo-slave narrative, Toni Morrison's *Beloved*. However, instead of situating *Beloved* as exceptional, I place it within a wider field of engagements with slave women's participation in what W. E. B. Du Bois called "the general strike" against slavery.[31] When contextualized thus, it becomes clear that Morrison was working alongside other black feminists with whom she sought to shake up received histories of slavery and of women's resistance to it, effectively contributing to a collective argument articulated across textual idioms.

In the second half of the book (chapters 4 and 5 and the epilogue) I engage in critical speculation somewhat differently. Here I treat the relationship of the slave past to the biocapitalist present through a reading of speculative fiction (sf)—fiction, I argue, that reveals to readers the relationship between today's reproductive scene and that which characterized four hundred years of slavery *even though racial slavery is not fully manifest on the surface of any of the texts in question.* In contrast to the late twentieth-century writings by black feminists that I treat in the first half of the book, the sf treated in the book's second half has been selected for consideration precisely because it appears superficially to be engaged in the *disavowal* of the history of slavery, and because it therefore mutates and in so doing distorts the representation of slavery in a manner that begs the question of the singularity of racial slavery. In other words, the sf selected provides a window onto biocapitalism's sublation of slavery, a process involving negation and preservation, and, as already discussed, disavowal and erasure.[32]

In sf from which racial slavery is absented from the textual surface—and thus in sf in which reproductive commodities are not imagined to be reproduced by enslaved black women, or even, as may be the case, by living beings sexed as female—it is nonetheless possible to demonstrate that the text in question meditates on the slave episteme. Indeed my purpose in treating speculative fictions that depict reproductive extraction but do not link it to slave breeding is to show that in neoliberalism, active textual engagement— what has often been referred to, in a nod to Benjamin, as reading against the grain—is imperative to discernment of biocapitalism's sublation of slavery and thus its simultaneous negation and preservation of slavery in our time.[33] In the texts of neoliberalism, disavowal of slavery can and should be read as symptomatic, as revelatory of the mechanisms by which biocapitalism sublates slavery and obscures from view the fact that the slave episteme subtends the neoliberal world that the texts in question depict and mediate. For this reason, when I read sf, my attention is trained on what Jacques Derrida has called the text's *démarche*—on the way in which each text enacts the disavowal of slavery that it can also be read to diagnose. For even when slavery disappears from the surface of a text, it is simultaneously preserved beneath it, where, I argue, it lies latent and waiting.[34]

In engaging in critical speculation, I follow scholars of slavery in embracing the possibility that knowledge about the slave past and the afterlife of slavery in the present may come to us through our interaction with unanticipated archives, genres, and textual idioms. The historian of slavery Jennifer Morgan observes, "To depend upon archival collaboration to rewrite the history of black life can route you back to the very negations at which you started."[35] For these reasons, I follow Hartman in embracing the idea that "critical fabulation" may be necessary if we are to summon "unverifiable truths" that would otherwise remain unavailable.[36] While Morgan and Hartman treat documents created in the slave past—for instance, plantation record books, slave laws, records from slave ships, and transcripts of trials in which slave women were criminalized for refusing sexual and reproductive violence against their persons—the "archives" I treat throughout this book comprise recent and contemporary texts that have been deemed too politically biased (too feminist and too black), too fantastical, too elliptical, or too multivalent to function as evidence in support of arguments about history, political economy, and relations of power by those seeking answers to the hard questions that besiege us. And yet it is precisely through engagement with such alternative archives of biocapitalism and neoliberalism that it becomes possible to perceive contemporary cultures and politics of reproduction as part and parcel of the afterlife of slavery and, too, to perceive the forms of disavowal that make it possible to offer for sale the array of reproductive commodities that are consumed by those who elect to reproduce genetically related progeny, biological kinship, and genealogy through the purchase of human biological commodities, in vivo reproductive labor, and its products. In sum, it is in a close reading of cultural texts that make a *proleptic* gesture by casting back into the slave past to reveal contemporary biocapitalism as enslaving, alongside a close reading of texts that make an *analeptic* gesture by reading the past through the lens of an imagined world yet to come, that it becomes possible to discern that four hundred years of slavery ought to be recognized as biocapitalist, and that contemporary biocapitalism ought to be recognized as a form of racial capitalism that is predicated, as was Atlantic slavery, on the racialized extraction of reproductive labor and its products. This is so even though the processes of racialization that are operative in contemporary biocapitalism do not skew black or white in the same way that they did during slavery, and even though processes of racialization are often distorted beyond superficial recognition or altogether disavowed.

Surrogacy as Heuristic Device

Historians argue that racial slavery in the Americas and the Caribbean entailed the simultaneous exploitation of women's productive and reproductive labor. On plantations women worked in the household and in the fields
and were used to reproduce biological commodities. When we examine the
contemporary reproductive horizon, the practice of surrogacy stands out as
structured by related forms of hybridized exploitation. In contemporary surrogacy arrangements, which are currently almost entirely gestational, surrogates, all of whom are already mothers with children of their own (and thus
engaged in conventional forms of reproductive labor such as housework and
childcare), carry and deliver a child (and, sometimes, multiples) whose genetic material belongs to others.[37] In most surrogacy arrangements, surrogates
are obligated, by contracts that are signed going in, to turn the children to
whom they give birth over to those who have paid to have them (re)produced.
Recognizing the relationship between women's work as breeding wenches
in the slave past and their work as surrogate mothers in the present, one
legal scholar writing about contemporary surrogacy observed, "All African
American slave women before the Civil War were surrogate mothers for their
owners, gestating and giving birth to children who would not belong to them
but became the property of their masters."[38]

Although this insight is shared by many black feminists living and writing in and about the United States, it has neither been understood as germane
by US courts that have adjudicated surrogacy disputes, nor been taken up by
scholars who treat surrogacy practiced elsewhere around the globe. Chapter 1
thus tells the heretofore untold story of how black feminist legal scholars
first theorized the historical relationship between slave breeding and contemporary surrogacy, considers how their contributions might be taken up
in contexts beyond the United States, and argues that surrogacy ought to be
regarded as a *heuristic device* that allows us to see that the history of slave breeding in the Atlantic world and the slave episteme that is its contemporary
echo ought not be left out of evolving discussions about biocapitalism and
outsourced or transnational reproduction. When engaged as a heuristic device, I argue, surrogacy makes visible relationships between the slave past
and the biocapitalist present that other approaches to surrogacy and biocapitalism have not. For surrogacy holds the key to unlocking the imbricated
workings of race and gender in biocapitalism and to revealing how the slave
episteme shapes contemporary cultures and politics of reproduction despite

neoliberal pieties about the irrelevance of the slave past to life in our market-saturated, consumer-oriented present.

Although it will by now be evident that my primary focus is on historical constellation, epistemic endurance, echoes and hauntings (all descriptions of the afterlife of reproductive slavery employed throughout this book), before moving on I wish to consider the question of *discontinuity* and thus the apparent distinction between women who reportedly choose to labor as surrogates (as is most often the way that surrogate arrangements are represented today), and those on whom surrogate labor was forced, as it was in racial slavery. To treat this apparent distinction, at various points in this book I examine the relationship of slave labor to wage labor, and thus the relationship of bondage to contract. In slavery in the Americas and the Caribbean, when women were compelled to labor by their masters and overseers they were forced to endure sexual and reproductive violence, and thus a specifically gendered version of what the sociologist Orlando Patterson calls "natal alienation" and what the literary scholar Hortense Spillers insists on describing as slave women's forced reproduction of their own kinlessness.[39] For these reasons, in chattel slavery reproductive extraction must be understood as specific. And yet, even as we acknowledge this, we must also foreground the intellectual and political dangers of overlooking the epistemic proximity between slave breeding and contractual reproductive labor and, thus, the dangers of failing to examine the afterlife of reproductive slavery because such an examination appears to wrench a unique historical experience out of context.

The division of slave and contract labor is predicated on a distinction that is part of (bio)capitalist ideology. For this reason, rather than begin from the assumption that surrogates freely choose to engage in contractual labor, I begin from an insight neatly if too implicitly encapsulated in Marx's quip that contract labor ought to be recognized as "wage slavery." In creating his oxymoron, Marx challenges us to consider wage or contract labor on a continuum with the labor performed by slaves. He suggests that entrance into wage labor, even when it appears to be freely chosen, is all too often necessitated by life-threatening material desperation and coercion. He argues, nowhere more plainly than in the *Communist Manifesto*, that the concept of freedom propagated within capitalism—and, I would add, within racial capitalism and thus biocapitalism—is the bourgeois freedom to own and dispose of property, including property in the self. This is a supposed freedom that Stephanie Smallwood, a historian of slavery, urges us to label "commodified freedom" as it does not allow those who possess it to exit the system that requires the commodification of things (and people regarded as things) in the first place.[40] Similarly the political theorist Carole Pateman connects the freedom to enter in to contract to slavery when, in her now classic treatise on "the sexual contract," she asserts that contract always creates relationships of command and obedience. The capitalist is situated by contract in the role of master, he who possesses the right to decide how the worker's labor is used and objectified. As Kathi Weeks observes in her assessment of Pateman's contribution, the relationship between capitalist-master and worker-slave "is not so much the byproduct of exploitation as its very precondition."[41]

The paradoxical character of the supposed "freedom of choice" that characterizes capitalism is especially evident when we consider the genealogy of liberalism and the predication of the universality of human rights on the exemption of slaves, the colonized, and indigenous peoples from possession of such rights and therefore from exercise of substantive freedom. In the course of theorizing the interlinked forms of violence that subtend liberalism, Lisa Lowe explains, "Social relations in the colonized Americas, Asia, and Africa were the condition of possibility for Western liberalism to think the universality of human freedom."[42] On the flip side of liberal freedom, Lowe continues, one finds racialized governance and political, economic, and social hierarchies deployed in the management of all peoples (she includes the enslaved, the colonized, and the indigenous) who have been and often continue to be thought of as less than human.[43] This paradox of liberalism becomes stark in the aftermath of manumission in the United States as one of the principal outcomes was resubjugation of the enslaved by new regimes of unfreedom. The historians Amy Dru Stanley and Sarah Haley, the black studies scholars Salamishah Tillet and Dennis Childs, and the sociologists Loïc Wacquant and Naomi Murakawa all concur (albeit from different disciplinary vantage points and in relation to varied institutions and archives): the emancipated were compelled to endure continued and frequently exacerbated forms of dehumanization through subjection to vagrancy laws that criminalized those unwilling to enter into wage labor; through incarceration on chain gangs on which death rates among leased convicts (male and female) were higher than they had been on the plantations on which slaves had formerly labored; and, not least, through the recruitment of former slaves into sharecropping and other forms of debt bondage and indenture that curtailed the capacity of putatively free individuals to exercise actual freedom of domicile or movement.[44]

Like freedmen and free women, many of today's reproductive laborers, especially those in the Global South, have little control over the circumstances in which they live, circumstances that compel them to alienate in vivo reproductive labor and its living products.[45] As all ethnographies of Indian surrogacy document, in this market as in other outsourced or transnational reproductive markets, women who elect to engage in surrogacy do so in order to survive and to help their families to survive. Surrogacy pays for food, shelter, and clothing, and sometimes also for children's education or daughters' dowries. While some women elect surrogate labor over the other options available to them, others are pressured into it by in-laws and husbands. Either way, poor women are actively sought out by clinics and recruiters who work for the numerous international agencies that arrange surrogacy across national borders. Ethnographies detail that surrogates are housed in dormitories that separate them from their children and families; they are subjected to painful and often dangerous medical procedures and drug protocols; and, most important, they are required to give up the babies they gestate and to whom they give birth. In surrogacy arrangements maternity is fragmented into oocyte vendors (euphemistically called egg "donors"), gestators or birthers, and socializers, and legal contracts are drawn up and signed to enforce the surrogate's status as a nonmother, effectively restricting her to sale of her (re)productive labor and its products. Like the bills of sale that mandated that slave women reproduce their own kinlessness by rendering mother and child chattel, the contracts that are used in surrogacy ensure that the reproductive labor of the surrogate is alienable and fungible and that the children born to surrogates are treated as property belonging to others—that is, until the transfer of the baby-commodity to those who have paid for their (re)production. Although the media and surrogate agencies characterize outsourced surrogacy as a win-win situation for poor, enterprising women, the full weight of the legal establishment (and its ability to enforce contracts and protect consumer's genetic property) is imposed to ensure that surrogates surrender the products they have (re)produced to their supposed owners.

Although surrogacy exchanges in the United States are typically cloaked in a discourse of altruism in which both surrogate and consumer characterize surrogacy as "a labor of love," reproductive extraction is as amply evident in the United States as in India or elsewhere in the Global South.[46] In Baby M and *Johnson v. Calvert*, the watershed surrogacy disputes I examine in chapter 1, courts forcibly removed children from the surrogates (one white, one black and Native American) who gestated and gave birth to them and who sought to mother them rather than exchange them for payment. While it is rare for surrogates who breach contract by refusing to give up children to whom they have given birth to become known to the public either in the United States or abroad, the fact that even a few are known to have protested reproductive extraction and legally enforced kinlessness is not an aberration that we can afford to dismiss. Rather the existence of broken contracts and legal precedents must be regarded as an index of the persistent potential for surrogate insurgency and the violent measures that biocapitalism deems necessary to stave off crises that would otherwise disrupt its smooth functioning.

Unwittingly invoking and simultaneously disavowing the work of the slave episteme in contemporary surrogacy, in the early days of surrogacy prosurrogacy propaganda frequently cited the Old Testament figure of Hagar, the handmaid, as the first surrogate mother. In Judeo-Christian tradition, Hagar bore a child to Abraham when his wife, Sarah, appeared to be barren. By invoking Hagar's story, pro-surrogacy forces seek to provide religious and moral precedent for women to serve other women as surrogates, and thus to participate in what pundits such as Oprah Winfrey tout as a "beautiful" instance of "global sisterhood."[47] Instructively the fact that Hagar was neither Sarah's equal nor her sister goes unacknowledged when the biblical handmaid is trotted out in support of surrogacy. Hagar was a slave, as black feminist theologians underscore. And she was not just any slave. Hagar was an Egyptian who was forced under penalty of exile into the wilderness, to surrender her body for reproductive use and to part with her child. And she was also an insurgent slave. Hagar neither acceded to her assigned role as nonmother nor to Abraham's eventual disinheritance of her son. Instead she went rogue, found a way where there was no way, and eventually journeyed with Ishmael across the desert of Beersheba to freedom. For these reasons, as I discuss in greater detail in chapter 4, black feminist theologians elevate Hagar as a fugitive foremother who rose in struggle and today represents all women who refuse racialized sexual and reproductive dispossession.

Taking cues from black feminists, I treat contemporary surrogates and other reproductive laborers as Hagar's daughters. I do so in two distinct ways. First, as already discussed, I recognize that understanding of the slave episteme in biocapitalism necessitates treatment of surrogacy as a heuristic device that centers reproduction as a form of labor and as an in vivo commodity productive of other living commodities. Following in the footsteps of those discussed throughout this book—Hartman, Roberts, Spillers and

Darlene Clark Hine, Deborah Gray White, Angela Davis, Jennifer Morgan, and others—I take the slave woman and her experience in slavery not as an incidentally gendered standpoint but rather as *the point of reference* in constructing a story about the slave past and in imagining the relevance of this story for the present and future.[48] Second, in treating contemporary surrogates as Hagar's daughters, I recognize the importance of slave women's past insurgency not only because recognition reshapes received understandings of the history of slavery but also because it expresses what the historian Robin D. G. Kelley refers to as "freedom dreams"—dreams expressed in multiple idioms by those who have turned to slave women's lives to locate prior forms of refusal. As Kelley notes, freedom dreams are transformative of conventional understandings of human agency and resistance, and therefore of the connection of both "agency" and "resistance" to Marxist materialist mainstays such as "work," "worker," and "class consciousness." To conceive of freedom dreams in the past, Kelley elaborates, is to "recover ideas—visions fashioned mainly by those marginalized black activists who proposed a different way out of our contradictions." However, he cautions, the point of recovery is not to "wholly embrace . . . [past] ideas or strategies as the foundation for new movements." Rather it is to engage recovered ideas so that we may "tap the well of our own collective imaginations" and consider, under present circumstances, how we might conceive of "freedom" as unbound from free enterprise.[49]

In insisting on the relevance of black feminist analysis of and response to racial capitalism's current biocapitalist configuration, it is important to point out that many historians of feminism have considered black feminism somewhat differently than I do here. They have situated black feminism in the context of the long civil rights movement, the rise of Black Power, and the ascendance of dominant forms of (white) feminism. And they have cast black feminism as a negotiation of the sexism and masculinism and sometimes, though less often, the heterosexism of black nationalism, and as a response to the racism and classism of second wave feminism.[50] With their research into the frequently overlooked history of black feminist involvement in the reproductive rights movement, they have demonstrated how, beginning in the 1970s, black feminists, working alongside other antiracist activists, pressured the movement to expand its narrow focus on access to abortion to include the full spectrum of reproductive freedoms, including the freedom to elect when to bear children, the economic freedom to raise and care for them, and the freedom to call out sterilization abuse and refuse all forms of racist, sexist, and ultimately eugenic medical coercion.[51]

What historians have not considered is how black feminism articulated freedom dreams that were specifically if not always expressly keyed to the biocapitalist economy of the 1970s, 1980s, and 1990s—that is, to the form of capitalism that emerged as black feminists wrote. Consequently most have not read black feminism as a social and political formation that necessarily, but not always explicitly or self-consciously, mediates the conflicts and contradictions that characterized the exploitation of in vivo reproductive labor in black feminism's moment of production and publication. Relatedly, they do not read black feminism as constituting a philosophy of history that reflects and refracts the rise of biocapitalism and the forms of neoliberalism that emerged alongside it. In regarding the black feminism articulated across three decades as a philosophy of history, I underscore black feminism's contributions to a full-scale critique of racial capitalism and position it as an insurgent response to the question of human futurity in biocapitalism and neoliberalism. As already noted, chapter 1 does so by examining black feminist contributions to the scholarship on surrogacy. Chapter 2 does so by analyzing black feminist ideas about slave women's participation in a general strike against slavery. Chapter 3 does so by reading Morrison's *Beloved* as a manifesto for substantive sexual and reproductive freedom. Chapter 4 does so by demonstrating how Octavia Butler's black feminist sf of the late 1970s and 1980s constitutes a prescient meditation on the rise of neoliberalism and the racialized reproductive cultures and politics that it ushered in. In short, across this book's chapters I engage black feminism in and through its multiple idioms of expression to demonstrate how it has persistently and imaginatively mobilized the history and image of the slave past to challenge received understandings of this past and to recast the present in which the past is being recalled in a new light. For it is only when past and present are constellated that it becomes possible to imagine a more liberated future.

The suggestion that black feminism accesses the freedom dreams of enslaved women who refused or dreamed of refusing sexual and reproductive extraction is not meant to be triumphalist. Along with others, I am cautious of recuperative and frequently sanguine attempts to redeem a story of agency, solidarity, and liberation from a past so violent that it may well have foreclosed all three.[52] Alongside other scholars of black feminism, I too lament the sizable struggle involved in resurrection of black feminism as an intellectual and institutional intervention in the face of its neglect or overt dismissal.[53] For all of these reasons the second half of this book treats dystopian sf that rings out an alarm about the manner in which black feminist freedom dreams can be and have been incorporated, co-opted, or entirely eviscerated in the context of neoliberalism. Such sf mediates the same material conflicts and contradictions that animated black feminist production in the 1970s, 1980s, and 1990s, but instead of imagining reproductive refusal, it depicts futures so devastatingly bleak that it appears that acquiescence to racialized reproductive extraction has been and remains the only option. Through engagement with dystopian fictions—three by Butler (chapter 4), a novel by Kazuo Ishiguro (chapter 5), and Alfonso Cuarón's apocalyptic film *The Children of Men* (epilogue)—I argue that it is possible to put on display, and thus put up for critical inspection, the myriad obstacles to robust imagination of resistance and refusal, and therefore to achievement of substantive sexual and reproductive freedom. As we shall see, in such dystopian texts space for alternative imaginings comes under pressure as the reproductive laborer's freedom dreams are actively colonized by neoliberal economic imperatives and the proliferation of empty ideas about reproductive choice as an end in itself. And yet, as I hope is already apparent, I do not conclude this book with dystopian sf to suggest throwing in the towel. Rather I do so because I am just utopian enough to imagine that when dystopian sf is juxtaposed with black feminist manifestos for freedom that dare to imagine refusal of sexual and reproductive extraction, the boldness of black feminist freedom dreams will appear newly resonant. Although such freedom dreams are quickly becoming historically distant and fragile—keyed as they are to a prior moment of radical possibility that today can too often feel out of reach—they also strike me as urgent.

What Lies Ahead

Chapter 1 explores contemporary surrogacy, develops the idea of surrogacy as a heuristic device, and argues for recognition of the workings of the slave episteme in biocapitalism. I treat historical scholarship on women in slavery that reveals the centrality of reproductive extraction to the entire slave enterprise. Through examination of feminist contributions to debates about biocapitalism I examine what is yet to be gained by including an account of slave breeding in theories of the biocapitalist extraction of life itself. Most important, I engage feminist scholarship on surrogacy, explore feminist responses to the two most controversial surrogacy cases in US history, and detail the groundbreaking contributions of black feminist legal scholars who sought to theorize surrogate labor as a racializing process. In so doing, I explore how black feminists conceptualized what I call the surrogacy/slavery nexus—the dialectical relationship between past and present that characterizes black feminism's philosophy of history. In conclusion I speculate that attention to the surrogacy/slavery nexus can enrich our understanding of the forms of outsourced or transnational surrogacy that are available today.

Chapter 2 develops the argument about the importance of black feminism's philosophy of history for analysis of biocapitalism by expanding my previous discussion to include a wider range of black feminist texts, especially so-called neo-slave narratives. Reading across a range of meditations on women in slavery, I demonstrate how they collectively situate sexual and reproductive extraction at the center of their accounts of racial capitalism's transformation over time. I further argue that black feminists writing in the 1980s and 1990s did this by gendering the Du Boisian idea of the general strike against slavery and, in the process, positioning sexual and reproductive insurgency as central to slavery's overthrow. In so doing black feminism made a major though often unrecognized contribution to the black radical tradition, which has generally been construed as male. I conclude the chapter by suggesting that black women's neo-slave narratives be read as manifestos for freedom from sexual and reproductive dispossession in slavery and beyond, and, therefore, for recognition of black feminist neo-slave narratives as an indispensable component of not only black feminism's philosophy of history but also the black radical tradition.

Chapter 3 deepens the preceding argument about the importance of neo-slave narratives by treating the most famous black feminist neo-slave narrative published to date, Morrison's *Beloved*, and its retelling of the story of a fugitive slave mother who murdered her daughter to save her from enslavement. Through an extended close reading of *Beloved* I concretize the idea that critical speculative engagement is central to the project of constellating past and present and thus to development of black feminism's philosophy of history. In Morrison's case, the present—the 1970s and 1980s—is also the period that witnessed the ascent of the surrogate industry in the United States and the global biocapitalist economy of which surrogacy was to become a constitutive part. I conclude the chapter with a speculative provocation: although Morrison's protagonist, Sethe, is a figure heretofore exclusively linked to Margaret Garner, she ought to be linked to Joan Little, the young black woman who murdered the white prison guard who raped her in 1974. Throughout the 1970s and 1980s, Little was at the symbolic center of an interracial feminist mobilization against criminalization of women's violent refusal of sexual and reproductive exploitation. In juxtaposing Sethe's and Little's insurgency, *Beloved* advances the radical idea that insurgent violence can defy incorporation into hegemonic systems of understanding; and thus, together with the black feminists with whom Morrison was in dialogue, she ought to be seen as meditating on the place of violent insurgency in the fight for substantive sexual and reproductive freedom.

Chapter 4 commences the second major argument of the book, complicating our understanding of the struggle for freedom from reproductive exploitation in the context of neoliberalism through a reading of dystopian sf by Butler. While the black feminist neo-slave narratives treated in the previous two chapters explore insurgency against sexual and reproductive extraction, they do not account for neoliberalism's disavowal of slavery and ideological embrace of postracialism. In contrast, Butler's fictions, which were written alongside black feminist neo-slave narratives, offer an extended meditation on reader complicity in the perpetuation of the slave episteme through its disavowal. They do so by calling attention to racial and gender violence as by-products of the contemporary preoccupation, facilitated by the availability of reproductive technology, with pursuit of forms of kinship that are rooted in notions of racial or genetic relatedness. As Butler makes plain, such forms of kinship depend on forms of racialized reproductive extraction that ought to be pursued (through consumption of surrogacy and ARTs) with great caution. Building on Hartman's observation that "telling the story of women in slavery necessarily involves an intersection of the fictive and historical," or work in a "subjunctive tense" that ventures "toward another mode of writing," the chapter includes a discussion of Butler's work in a "subjunctive tense" through treatment of her use of the trope of time travel.[54] Through this trope, Butler illuminates how reproductive revolts have already been and will continue to be stymied by uncritical pursuit of forms of kinship that are rooted in racial or genetic connection.

Chapter 5 treats human cloning and the international trade in human bodily organs as part of the phenomenon of reproductive extraction in biocapitalism. I examine how and why cloning (a form of reproduction that sidelines the necessary contribution of the female body by transforming reproduction into a technological process performed by men) and the organ trade are routinely represented as bound. I read Ishiguro's 2005 novel *Never Let Me Go* and its portrait of clones bred to be organ donors as a story about disavowal of the afterlife of reproductive slavery in our time. And I explore how the form of Ishiguro's novel, its hallmark slow-reveal and unreliable first-person narration, provide readers with an experience of complicity in perpetuation of the slave episteme—in particular, of complicity with the racialized dehumanization of in vivo labor upon which the organ donation program that is depicted in the novel, like the forms of surrogacy depicted in Butler's work, depends. Although cloning is a form of reproduction that is generally construed as unmoored from the female body (notably, Ishiguro's clones appear to be motherless and are sterile), through engagement in critical speculation I argue that the slave mother and thus the slave episteme operate beneath the surface of the seemingly autochthonous world that the novel depicts. Consequently, Ishiguro's novel serves as a platform from which to consider how a neoliberal text that disavows the slave episteme might nonetheless be recognized as a contemporary slave narrative, albeit one that erases blackness as it calibrates itself to the neoliberal ideology of postracialism.

The epilogue examines fears that spring from our impending failure to rescue the human reproductive process from immanent destruction by disease and environmental catastrophe and explores how fantasies about universal human infertility—a crisis I call "the end of men"—lead to celebration of the black surrogate as the fount of human life on earth. This is an idea expressed in a spate of popular films, novels, and TV dramas. In concluding the book's argument about the importance of critical speculative engagement, I treat Cuarón's The Children of Men, a film in which humanity is saved from extinction by a black African prostitute-surrogate who appears, against all odds, to have conceived a miracle child, the last child to be born on earth. My reading of The Children of Men, a film often celebrated for its portrayal of a black Madonna as humanity's savior, demonstrates that even superficially progressive representations of racialized reproduction warrant scrutiny. In the film, all political factions vie for control over the black mother and her girl child; and, despite apparent differences, all factions fail to imagine rescue of human civilization through anything but racialized reproductive extraction. Insofar as it allows for apprehension of the endurance of the slave episteme, my reading of the film prods us to consider how we might exit the reproductive death spiral it represents. For, if we allows ourselves to be guided by black feminism's philosophy of history and refuse resolution of the immanent crisis of human futurity through racialized reproductive extraction, we might well be able to imagine heretofore unimagined ways to reproduce and sustain life on planet Earth.

Chapter One

The SURROGACY/SLAVERY NEXUS

Capital comes [into the world] dripping from head to toe, from every pore, with blood.

—KARL MARX, *CAPITAL, VOLUME 1* (1867)

The Africanist character [acts] as a surrogate. . . . Africanism is the vehicle by which the American self knows itself as not enslaved, but free; not repulsive, but desirable; not helpless, but licensed and powerful; not history-less, but historical; not damned, but innocent; not a blind accident of evolution, but a progressive fulfillment of destiny.

—TONI MORRISON, *PLAYING IN THE DARK* (1992)

When Marx wrote in the latter half of the nineteenth century about the birth of capitalism as a bloody bodily process he relied on the metaphor of childbirth to convey the violence of so-called primitive accumulation—the process by which the commons were seized, enclosed, and privatized, people subdued and forced to labor, and natural resources extracted from the land. As Marx argued, from a decidedly teleological standpoint, these three events needed to happen in order for European feudalism to give way to modern capitalism, and thus for capital to be born into the world "dripping from head to toe, from every pore, with blood."[1] Marx no doubt intended the metaphor of bloody birth to portend the violence of industrialization that he presciently predicted would come to characterize the second half of the nineteenth century and the first half of the twentieth century in much of Europe.

What Marx was clearly not thinking about was the richness and aptness of the childbirth metaphor in the contemporaneous context of slavery in the Americas and the Caribbean. And this was so despite the fact that Marx was no doubt aware of the sexual and reproductive dispossession that slavery entailed, and might have integrated an account of the relationship of nineteenth-century slavery and capitalism into his work had he been inclined to consider what subsequent scholars have called *racial capitalism*, or, more precisely still, *slave racial capitalism*.[2] Nor was Marx thinking about the uncanny relevance of his reproductively laden metaphor in the context of twenty-first-century capitalism—that is, in the context of *biocapitalism*.

In the former context—that of Atlantic slavery—the aptness of childbirth as the metaphor for production of surplus value has been examined by feminist historians of slavery who have centralized slave women's work as breeders of human commodities in the process of situating slavery as a global capitalist enterprise. I treat this scholarship at this chapter's outset and build on its insight into the dependence of the new world plantation system on the engineering of slave reproduction for profit. As we shall see, slavery increasingly relied upon slave breeding as time went on, especially after the outlawing of the transatlantic trade by the Slave Trade Act of 1807. In the latter context—that of biocapitalism—I demonstrate that "bloody birth" all too neatly describes one of the primary motors of capitalism's expansion over the past four decades. The chapter's second section thus treats scholarship on contemporary biocapitalism. Like slavery before it, biocapitalism relies on reproductive labor power and products. Indeed biological, often "bloody" processes and raw materials enable the scientific research and development that fuels profit in a global marketplace dominated by giant multinational corporations invested in the extraction of surplus value from the mining of life itself.

In this chapter's second epigraph, Toni Morrison reminds us that the idea of surrogacy resonates across American history and within the modern episteme. In *Playing in the Dark*, the literary theoretical work from which it is drawn, Morrison makes visible the inchoate or spectral "Africanist presence" whose textual figuration subtends white American literature and the production of the white American self.[3] As Morrison elaborates, whiteness was one of the most significant products of nineteenth-century American literature and of the national culture that it mediated. Through close reading of canonical nineteenth- and early twentieth-century texts, Morrison demonstrates how representation of black Africanism enabled the "birth" of white citizens who are invariably figured as protagonists whose arrival in the world, via the written page, constitutes the "fulfillment of destiny." At various points Morrison describes the Africanist presence as a specter or literary foil. At others, as in my epigraph, she describes it as a "surrogate" that sometimes literally and always metaphorically births and nurses whiteness, effectively facilitating reproduction of white racial hegemony. Although Morrison never mentions the actual work of reproductive surrogacy that was performed by all African slave women forced to gestate human chattel, her use of the term *surrogate* resonates with my discussion of slavery and biocapitalism. It implicates the racialized reproductive processes that fueled slavery (the biological acts of gestation, parturition, and nurture) in the production of hegemonic racial formations and modern capitalism alike. Put otherwise, by using *surrogacy* to describe the ideological work performed by the literary representation of blackness, Morrison brings into view the gendered and sexualized processes that enabled the creation of a capitalist world system predicated on sexual and reproductive dispossession and, in turn, on the reproduction of racialized subjects and social formations, including American citizenship, white racial nationalism, and a racialized division of labor.

Overall this chapter brings together the imbricated meanings of *bloody birth* and *surrogacy* that circulate in and through its paired epigraphs by treating the relationship between contemporary biocapitalism and slave racial capitalism as it has been theorized by black feminists engaged in debates about surrogacy. Along the way I treat historical scholarship on women in slavery that demonstrates that slave breeding depended upon processes of racialization that rendered the reproduction of the system of slavery possible. As black feminist writings on surrogacy show, these processes have been epistemically recalibrated to render conceivable the forms of reproductive extraction that exist in contemporary biocapitalism. The black feminism discussed here thus ought to be recognized as a sustained meditation on what I will henceforth call the *surrogacy/slavery nexus*—the constellation of past and present that allows for examination of the persistence of the slave episteme in contemporary biocapitalism. As the surrogacy/slavery nexus reveals, even after the official end of slavery in the late nineteenth century, the slave episteme continues to subtend the cultures and politics of reproduction, especially the practice of surrogacy as a form of contract labor.

Although slave labor and contract labor are conventionally understood as distinct, historians of the transition from bondage to contract in the nineteenth century demonstrate that the creation of a division between the two was an ideological mainstay of modern liberalism and of liberal discourses such as slave abolitionism and free market capitalism. The historian Amy Dru Stanley explains, "The antislavery claim of the nineteenth century was that abstract rights of freedom found concrete embodiment in the contracts of wage labor and marriage—that the negation of chattel status lay in owning oneself, in selling one's labor as a free market commodity, and in marrying and maintaining a home."[4] And yet, former slaves were unable to procure the self-sovereignty promised by entrance into labor and marriage contracts. Manumission, followed in short order by legal and political emancipation, placed the formerly enslaved into new forms of social and economic debt. Consequently, substantive freedom was perpetually deferred and emergent forms of subjection continuous with, as opposed to a departure from slavery, albeit retooled, as black labor was, for the era of supposed "freedom" that followed in slavery's wake.[5] As Stanley elaborates, "contract freedom" is a worldview that rests on principles of self-ownership, consent, and free and equal exchange, and yet it was only in theory that self-ownership was possible for the formerly enslaved. In practice freedmen and freed women were forced, coerced, or simply compelled by the need to survive to contract their labor. Black Codes, vagrancy laws, debt bondage, sharecropping, and chain gangs as well as other racialized forms of governance ensured that contract was little more than an obligation to officially translate slavery into the ruse of "free choice." Although former slaves were de jure entitled to their persons and ownership of their labor, they were de facto prohibited from acting as sovereign subjects within an economic system that they entered, by necessity, empty-handed.[6] Keeping this in mind, we ought to cautiously approach the idea that there is a decisive distinction between slave breeding and contract surrogacy. The liberal discourse that opposes one to the other and regards entrance into contract as antithetical to bondage persists in the present neo-liberal moment in which the purported freedom to choose among numerous unfreedoms is a perverse ideological mainstay of labor and consumer markets alike. In sum, I suggest that it makes most sense to regard labor performed by contemporary surrogates not as antithetical to slave breeding but rather in relation to, if never precisely synonymous with it.

This chapter is divided into four sections. The first treats critiques of traditional Marxism and historical approaches to slavery that clear space for theorization of slavery as both a form of racial capitalism and biocapitalism that powered globalization in the eighteenth and nineteenth centuries. As already noted, it also treats feminist historical scholarship on reproduction in slavery that helps me to make the connection between slave breeding and contemporary reproductive extraction. Although historians of slavery do not discuss contemporary surrogacy, I suggest that their work compels recognition of slave racial capitalism as a biocapitalist formation and, reciprocally, understanding of contemporary biocapitalism as a form of racial capitalism. The second section emphasizes this historical reciprocity as it turns to theories of biocapitalism published in recent years that do not but ought to place the history of slave breeding at the center of the discussion of reproductive extraction. For when slavery is brought in, reproductive labor can be understood as a racializing process that has a long history and that today continues to epistemically subtend extraction of value from in vivo labor and human biological products.

The third and longest section of the chapter tells the story of the feminist scholarship on surrogacy's evolution over two decades. It begins with discussion of contributions that emerged alongside the first legal cases involving US surrogates who breached contract in the 1980s and early 1990s. These early contributions did not adequately historicize surrogate labor. However, this all changed when black feminist legal scholars entered the discussion and connected slave women forced to reproduce their own kinlessness to surrogates forced to give up the children to whom they had given birth. And yet, despite black feminists' convincing intervention, the US legal system persisted in its effort to shore up the legality of surrogacy, favoring arguments about surrogate labor that erase the history of slavery as they secure contract and protect genetic property (regarded as personal property) and its transfer. This manifests in the verdicts reached in the two most well-known court rulings on surrogacy, that in the so-called Baby M case (1986–88) and that in Johnson v. Calvert (1990–93). In the former, the court's ruling opened the way for surrogate dehumanization; in the latter, it imposed the force of law to safeguard contract and create precedent for the transfer of genetic property in subsequent cases in which surrogates gestated unrelated genetic materials. As important, the ruling in the Johnson case instantiated a distinction between bondage and contract that sublated the history of slavery—the history that must be resurrected if we are to compass the work of the slave episteme. The chapter's final section speculates that the surrogacy/slavery nexus might yet enrich our understanding of outsourced and transnational reproductive labor.

Racial Capitalism and (Re)Production

As noted previously, the concept of racial capitalism can be attributed to the political scientist Cedric Robinson.[7] In his classic study, *Black Marxism: The Making of the Black Radical Tradition*, Robinson explicates writings by a range of black radical thinkers who were the first to recognize capitalism's racial dynamics, and writings by Marx and Engels in which inchoate ideas of race animate the social divisions that they characterized as precapitalist. In the traditional Marxist story of so-called primitive accumulation, Robinson demonstrates that an unselfconscious developmentalism morphs into racism. As Marx and Engels relate, old racialized processes of differentiation justifying dispossession are left behind as capitalism proper commences, replacing racial distinctions (Jews, Roma, and Slavs, for instance) with class distinctions. Summarizing the problem with this version of the story of capitalism's genesis—one that refuses to recognize that racialized social formations did not simply disappear but rather evolved over time to produce the modern world system—Robinson elaborates, Marx and Engels's conceit "was to presume that the theory of historical materialism explained history. . . . At worst, it merely rearranged history. And at its best . . . historical materialism still only encapsulated an analytical procedure which resonated with bourgeois Europe, merely one fraction of the world economy."[8] Because Marx and Engels neglected substantive discussion of colonialism, slavery, and genocide of indiginous populations and the global regions that sustained all three, in Robinson's view they also failed to recognize that racism not only imbricated these systems of expropriation but enabled their continuous recalibration and expansion.[9] "At base," Robinson concluded, "at its epistemological substratum, Marxism is a Western construction" (2) that is of little use when we seek to comprehend capitalism's global reach and impact and its racial character.

Rather than moving forward as if traditional Marxism were universally applicable outside of Western Europe, Robinson suggests shifting the "epistemological substratum" through embrace of the perspective offered by black Marxism and the black radical tradition of which it is a part. In this way, he argues, non-European material realities become foundational to theorization of capital's complex global movements, and the racial organization of these material realities and their transformation over time becomes visible. In an oft-quoted passage Robinson proffers the concept that has subsequently had so much staying power: "The development, organization, and expansion of capitalist society pursued essentially racial directions, so too did social ideology. As a material force, then, it could be expected that racialism would inevitably permeate the social structures emergent from capitalism. I have used the term 'racial capitalism' to refer to this development and to the subsequent structure as a historical agency" (2). In a reading of Robinson, Jodi Melamed observes that embrace of the concept of racial capitalism requires apprehension of the fact that "capital can only be capital when it is accumulating, and that it can only accumulate by producing and moving through relations of severe inequality among human groups."[10] Antinomies of accumulation (capitalists/workers, creditors/debtors, conquerors of land/the dispossessed, etc.) exist in excess of the historical "rearrangement of history" that Robinson attributes to Marx and Engels and are necessarily ongoing. Indeed for centuries capitalist expansion has required production of disposable humans and thus "unequal differentiation of human value" on a global scale.[11] Along with other engines of differentiation, racism creates the divisions of labor, credit, conquest, and, not least, the concepts of the "human" and the "less-than-human" that enable ongoing accumulation. In the twentieth and twenty-first centuries it is therefore necessary to pay attention not only to the recognizable features of white racial supremacy and imperial prowess that subtend capitalism but also to superficially (and often officially) race-neutral ideologies, such as liberal multiculturalism and neoliberal postracialism— ideologies that would appear to constitute "progress" but in fact shore up racial hegemony.[12] In chapters 4 and 5 I return to the problem of tracking the afterlife of racialized reproductive extraction in neoliberalism. In the present chapter, I begin by turning to a discussion of slavery in the seventeenth, eighteenth, and nineteenth centuries, for it is in the past that I locate antecedents for the epistemic endurances that most interested the black feminist scholars whose contributions I treat here.

Within what can be loosely labeled "the new slavery studies," Robinson's impress is apparent. In award-winning monographs by Edward Baptist, Walter Johnson, Stephanie Smallwood, and Moon-Ho Jung, among others, Atlantic slavery is treated as a global capitalist enterprise that functions through the production of what Robinson calls "racialisms."[13] In his study of the cotton kingdom and its importance to the emergence of US empire, Johnson condenses the insight by writing throughout about what he refers to as "slave racial capitalism."[14] This formulation, one I have adopted here, is useful in that it implies the coexistence of multiple modalities of racial capitalism as well as racial capitalism's ability to continuously recalibrate as required. It is thus a formulation that allows me to suggest that biocapitalism is one among many evolving forms of racial capitalism.[15] And yet it is not only the scholarship that is expressly focused on racial capitalism that informs the present argument. I am also deeply indebted to groundbreaking social histories of women in slavery by Deborah Gray White, Darlene Clark Hine, Marietta Morrissey, Barbara Bush, and a subsequent generation of historians including Stephanie Camp, Sharla Fett, and Thavolia Glymph that have homed in on the question of gender-specific economic exploitation.[16] Above all, two historical monographs, those by Hilary Beckles and Jennifer Morgan, afford me insight into the history of reproductive extraction in slavery. Both treat Atlantic slavery as a reproductive enterprise first and foremost, and both therefore offer the needed historical foundation for examination of the work of the slave episteme in biocapitalism.[17]

In *Natural Rebels: A Social History of Enslaved Black Women in Barbados*, Beckles treats slavery in the oldest and most lucrative of the sugar economies. His premise is that empiricist scholarship documented but could not explain why female slaves outnumbered male slaves in Barbados beginning in the late seventeenth century, and therefore could not recognize the fact that female slaves constituted "the main labor source of capital accumulation within the plantation economy" (2). Notably, Beckles regards his study of Barbadian slavery as pertinent "to the overall history of plantation America" because his findings attest to a larger truth: all slave women experienced slavery as producers and reproducers and were valued in both capacities everywhere. Beckles elaborates that the challenge he faced when he set out to write the history of enslaved women in Barbados was not the "absurd" one of "adding women to history" (5). It was the urgent challenge of restoring history to the slave women who constituted "the pivot" (as opposed to the tangent) around which the entire slave enterprise turned.

Beckles follows earlier scholars of Caribbean slavery in dividing slavery in Barbados into three distinct periods. During the first (1627–1730), planters clearly expressed a preference for male slaves. However, once the heavy work of land clearing was accomplished, women were imported to perform the same work as men.[18] In the second period (1730–90), planters came to realize that female labor was more manageable than male labor largely because the West and Central African women who were being imported to Barbados were already acculturated to agricultural work. Consequently in the second period women were increasingly imported. By the start of the third period (1790–1838) a new gender dynamic had begun to be firmly established. Planters worked women in field gangs and simultaneously invested in women's reproduction. Because this period encompassed the ending of the Atlantic slave trade, replacement of the labor force by the labor force through use of so-called breeding wenches became a necessity. This third period, characterized by intensified "creolization" of the slave population, increase in material and ideological valuation of female slaves, and systematic "stimulation" of female fertility, is the one that most interests me. As Beckles explains, in this period fertility was increased by offering slave women "concessions" that were targeted at the amelioration of the social, domestic, and labor conditions that militated against their participation in heterosexual sex and their care for and nourishment of resulting pregnancies. Although Beckles claims that he was unable to find empirical evidence of "selective" breeding (by which he presumably means the application of the principles of animal husbandry to human beings), his archive, which comprises slave management manuals and other sources providing evidence of plantation organization and administration, convincingly demonstrates that slave breeding was intentionally and carefully orchestrated. Planters understood that successful slave reproduction was the sole means by which the plantation labor supply could be replenished.[19]

Because of Barbadian planters' highly successful implementation of managerial strategies and incentives in the late eighteenth century, when the Slave Trade Act that officially ended the Atlantic trade was issued in 1807, Barbados was the only sugar colony no longer dependent on African imports. Whereas in the 1730s and 1740s at least half of the slaves born in Barbados died within one week, in the 1790s improved diet, lessened workload during pregnancy, fieldwork schedules more amenable to lactation, and monetary incentives for births together led to sharp declines in infant mortality. As Beckles observes, "The amelioration of the late eighteenth century can be defined as a system of thought and practice by which money that would have been otherwise spent on . . . buying unseasoned Africans was used to improve the lot of existing slaves in order to induce them to breed their replacements" (97). Nothing corroborates the shift to planter dependence on slave breeding more poignantly than the bookkeeping practices that Beckles describes. Planters routinely recorded increase in slaves alongside increase in cattle and horses. On late eighteenth- and nineteenth-century plantations all new births to breeding stock constituted capital gains (102).

Morgan's *Laboring Women: Reproduction and Gender in New World Slavery* richly expands on Beckles's study of Barbados by focusing on the ideological dimensions of reproductive enslavement throughout the new world. Through her treatment of the manner in which slave owners in the early English colonies in the West Indies and on the North American mainland required not only women's physical labor but also their "symbolic value in order to make sense of racial slavery," Morgan demonstrates that slave women's blackness was "produced by and produced their enslavability" (1) in a manner that resonates deeply with the arguments about reproductive labor as a racializing process advanced here. Morgan demonstrates that the idea of "enslavability" was keyed to reproductive capacity and thus to slave women's actual and imagined ability to create new slaves. Like Beckles, Morgan insists on the importance of her study of slave reproduction in specific sites to the study of Atlantic slavery tout court. Specific bodily experiences of slavery transcended geographic location. Female slaves were used for sex and breeding everywhere and thus everywhere experienced both sexual and reproductive slavery. Slave reproduction produced the wealth of a vast globalizing Euro-American empire, and, by necessity, it constituted a common experience "for enslaved women that interrupt[ed] the specificities of place" (2).

Through analysis of archives, including European travelers' accounts of black and Amerindian women in the sixteenth and seventeenth centuries, Morgan creates a genealogy of slave women as reproductive assets. She finds in accounts of first contact a series of consistently invoked rationalizations for the exploitation of black women's reproduction prior to their mass transport into the plantation system. In creating and circulating ideas about the black female bodies that were encountered by travelers as excessively fecund and simultaneously capable of hard labor, Europeans produced the moral and social distance that enabled the enslavement of those whose reproductive labor could be racialized and thus treated as the product of a less-than-human laborer. In written and pictorial representations, black and Amerindian women are envisioned as capable of "pain-free" or even "disinterested" delivery, and of strenuous toil immediately after giving birth to and while nursing their infants.[20] As Morgan demonstrates, the women that Europeans encountered were animalized through their depiction as a breed apart, as a breed descended from a bestial point of origin rather than from the Christian Eve.[21] Such representations maintained slavery over time. On the one hand, they undergirded the ideology that viewed African and Amerindian women as reproductive and productive laborers. On the other hand, they demonstrated that by contrast to white women's reproduction, these women's reproduction was a process that was alienable and fungible. Morgan concludes that ideological constructions of slave women's reproduction racialized and dehumanized slave women and their reproductive labor and facilitated their treatment as engines of value and as sites of economic speculation.[22]

Together Beckles and Morgan envision the long historical production of the enslaved reproductive body as a site for venture capitalism in the modern world.[23] In so doing their crucial intervention allows us to retroactively comprehend Atlantic slavery as a form of biocapitalism, and, simultaneously, points the way toward redress of the neglect of slavery in much of the scholarship on contemporary biocapitalism. Although scholars of the latter treat reproductive extraction, they neither recognize slave racial capitalism as a world shaping force nor engage with human reproductive labor as a racializing process that shapes the thought systems that subtend contemporary forms of reproductive extraction. In the next section I therefore bring together the two divergent scholarly inquiries—those on slave breeding and those on biocapitalism—in order to indicate what is gained by infusion of the history of slave racial capitalism into the account of contemporary biocapitalism and thus into our understanding of the reproductive extraction upon which it relies.

Biocapitalism and Slavery

The concept of biocapitalism first appeared in scholarship produced in the wake of the mapping of the human genome and has subsequently been taken up by feminist science and technology scholars. In his influential study *Biocapital: The Constitution of Postgenomic Life* (2006), the anthropologist Kaushik Sunder Rajan examines the transformation of capitalism by the advent of new biotechnologies in industries based in the genome sciences.[24] Though Sunder Rajan develops the term *biocapital* (as opposed to *biocapitalism*, the term I've adopted), and other scholars had, at the time he wrote, already employed related terminology, Sunder Rajan's was the first book-length study.[25] With the completion of the sequencing of the human genome in 2000, Sunder Rajan argued, genomic science began to catalyze major changes in the nature of capitalism, including increased speculation and financialization. Such changes were enabled by the transformation of life sciences into information sciences and by the maximization of surplus extraction based on the creation of information about the genome and speculation about the practical applications for this information. Through ethnographies of biotechnology, pharmaceutical, and genomic start-ups in India and the United States, Sunder Rajan explored biocapitalism's celebration of the medical benefits that genetic sequencing would ideally enable and argued that evolution of basic life science research into speculative informatics facilitated corporatization of the life sciences. As Sunder Rajan observed, in the wake of the mapping of the genome, biocapital and financial capital became mutually contingent on the "coproduction of the life sciences and political economic regimes" (4).[26]

The development of recombinant DNA technology is commonly regarded as a significant milestone in the advent of biocapital/ism, as it allowed researchers to cut up and join DNA molecules in the lab and assess the functionality of individual genes for the first time. Expansion of the biotech industry in the 1970s and 1980s is often expressly attributed to hype about new genetically based diagnostic and therapeutic products that accompanied the development of recombinant DNA technology. Characterizing relationships between capitalism and biotechnology in these decades as rapidly changing and future oriented, Sunder Rajan concludes that biocapital is "one vantage point from which to view the complexities of capitalism(s)"—a vantage point that is overdetermined by the rise of biotechnology industries, transnational pharmaceutical giants, and the financialization of both (7). Although Sunder Rajan rejects the idea that biocapital signifies "a distinct epochal phase of capitalism that leaves behind or radically ruptures capitalism as we have known it," he argues that biocapital is a "face" of capitalism that is so distinct that it requires its own moniker (10).

Given Sunder Rajan's focus on the relationship of biotechnological development to the rise of biocapital, it is striking that his book did not treat the reproductive biotechnologies that gained increased notice among his feminist colleagues during the period that interested him. Nor did he acknowledge that it was at this same time that human reproductive labor (which was a by-product of biotechnological research and development) was first offered for sale. Most notably, Sunder Rajan ignores in vitro fertilization (IVF), the biotechnology that made it possible for eggs to be extracted, fertilized outside the womb, and transferred back into it, and thus the biotechnology that made a market in gestational surrogacy possible. He also neglects the fact that IVF catalyzed the opening of a host of related markets in associated reprogenetic services that allow for selection, screening, and preservation of gametes.[27] This neglect is strange. After all, reproductive biotechnologies must have been on Sunder Rajan's radar. The research that interests him requires access to reproductively derived raw materials: oocytes, fertilized ova, and stem cells, among others. In fact a related point was made as early as 2001 by Sarah Franklin and Margaret Lock, feminist science and technology scholars who observed in their introduction to a collection of essays on contemporary changes in the biosciences that "shifts in the definition of biology-as-capital involve a prioritization of reproduction" precisely because reproduction was, at the time they were writing, quickly emerging as the "primary generator of wealth, agency, and value" in all biosciences that are dependent on research participants for what are often euphemistically referred to as "donations" or "gifts" of reproductively derived raw materials.[28] Though Sunder Rajan popularized the concept of biocapital, his book ultimately erased the reproductive dimension of biocapital/ism, obscuring the manner in which it is subtended by the female reproductive body, its processes, and the extraction of an entire range of reproductive products, including in vivo labor.[29]

In the immediate wake of Sunder Rajan's contribution, numerous feminist scholars expanded the epistemological possibilities of the concept of biocapital and proffered a new and robust conceptual vocabulary. In book-length studies by Catherine Waldby and Robert Mitchell (2006), Debora Spar (2006), Sarah Franklin (2007, 2013), Melinda Cooper (2008), Donna Dickenson (2008), Melinda Cooper and Catherine Waldby (2014), and Kalindi Vora (2015), to name the most influential, the reproductive dimensions of biocapitalism are not only foregrounded; they are mined.[30] In this insightful and corrective scholarship, discussion of the commodification of life necessarily encompasses reproduction, and each study treats one or more specific reproductive circuits of exchange. In developing their titular concept, "tissue economies," for instance, Waldby and Mitchell analyze embryonic stem cell banking and umbilical cord blood banking as forms of venture capital. In her work on the long history that led to the cloning of Dolly the sheep and her subsequent monograph on IVF, Franklin treats the commodification of reproductive medicine, tracing the marketization of reproductive and cloning technologies back to innovations in animal husbandry and forward to IVF's transformation of the structure and meaning of human kinship. In her popular book *The Baby Business*, Spar examines the "commerce of conception." In her crossover treatise on "body shopping," Dickenson, a biomedical ethicist, traverses the "global market in baby making," including markets in stem cells and oocytes. Formulating the concept of "life as surplus," Cooper examines the political economy of "life itself" in neoliberalism. Developing an analysis of the capitalization of "vital energy," Vora joins social scientists such as Arlie Russell Hochschild in examining the outsourcing of affective labor and intimate life in what Hochschild colloquially refers to as "market times." In their collaborative study, Cooper and Waldby develop the concept of "clinical labor," highlighting the radical reshaping of labor by the emergence of commodified in vivo processes such as oocyte production, gestation, reproduction of stem cells, and participation in clinical drug trials. By placing chapters on various reproductive markets amid chapters on bioinformatics, genomics, gene patenting, pharmaceutical development, and the trade in human tissues, organs, blood, and in vivo labor, these feminist scholars decisively demonstrate the inextricable relationship between human reproduction and biocapital/ism. In so doing they portend one of my key arguments: biocapitalism is *(re)productive* in that it obeys the logic of capitalist *production*—which is not to suggest that reproduction has been subsumed within production (the older Marxist feminist argument that I discussed in my introduction), but rather that reproduction is today a form of production, or better yet a form of *(re)production* that *(re)produces* surplus value.[31]

Although discussion of (re)production is not unprecedented, as I have just shown in my examination of historical work on slave breeding, discussion of Atlantic slavery and slave breeding is almost entirely absent from feminist scholarship on biocapitalism. There appear to be two reasons for this: this scholarship is focused on the present rather than the past, and, relatedly, it is only the extraction of gendered labor that is deemed germane to present circumstances. Consequently the work of the slave episteme and the insights of those black radical thinkers and feminist historians of slavery who argued that capitalism is always already racial capitalism and that slavery is foundationally reproductive and racializing of the labor process and laborer are sidelined or overlooked.

The problems that result from the neglect of slave breeding might be examined in any of the feminist studies of biocapitalism mentioned above, but I turn to Waldby and Cooper's collaboration because their argument is in many ways closest to my own. Waldby and Cooper point out, as do I, that theories of biocapitalism have been inattentive to specific forms of labor that subtend it, especially reproductive labor.[32] They insist on the centrality of "reproductivity" to the bioeconomy and attend to the centrality of "clinical labor" to circuits of global exchange. They offer two rationales for their development of the concept of clinical labor and their rejection of the old feminist standby "reproductive labor." Their new term expands reproduction to include provision of tissues and organs, effectively connecting all forms of labor that involve assumption of in vivo risk. And their focus on the outsourcing of risk allows them to connect reproductive laborers (surrogates and oocyte vendors) with the participants in clinical drug trials that are their focus in the second half of their book. Clinical labor additionally differentiates their contribution from earlier contributions keyed to a fordist model of production that posits the family and the reproductive labor that happens within it as private and thus separated from the public realm of work. Clinical labor, they argue, takes place in a world in which market deregulation and financialization rule everyday life. As they observe, in the new bioeconomy (as opposed to the old industrial economy) all labor is "deregulated, privatized, and made available for investment and speculative development," and "female reproductive biology" can therefore be said to undergo "complex rearticulation."[33]

In discussing capitalism's access to women's in vivo biology, Cooper and Waldby tentatively analogize clinical and slave labor. "In often surprising ways," they observe in a journal article on oocyte vending that preceded their treatment of the topic in their book, "the kinds of power struggles that today implicate the (re)reproductive body . . . bear striking similarities to the history of reproductive, sexual, and slave labor in early capitalism."[34] In their book they add an account of surrogacy in India and California to their earlier discussion of oocyte vending. However, although they allude to slave breeding a second time, they appear to do so mainly in order to dismiss it. Consequently, their analysis begs rather than treats the question of how contemporary biocapitalism might be constellated with slave racial capitalism and any other prior racial capitalist formation, and they do not offer an account of reproductive labor as racialized and racializing in past and present. Considering the capaciousness of the concept of clinical labor and the social scientific and largely positivist methodology it entails, it is possible to speculate about the reasons for the neglect of (slave) racial capitalism. On the one hand, when gestational labor is linked to the labor performed by participants in drug trials, the specific in vivo labor performed by the reproductive body can no longer be prioritized. On the other hand, when focus is on oocyte vendors and surrogates, many of whom are white women, it appears difficult for Cooper and Waldby to imagine that processes of racialization might nonetheless subtend the reproductive extraction in which these women are involved.

To examine processes of racialized reproductive extraction in biocapitalism, I have thus found it necessary to build on the insights of black feminist scholarship on slavery and surrogacy and to place black feminism's insight into the connections between the two into dialogue with existing feminist scholarship on biocapitalism. In the next section, I therefore tell the story of the feminist response to surrogacy in a manner that highlights black feminist contributions, especially after 1990, when the first gestational surrogate, a biracial black and Native American woman, sought custody of the child she delivered. Because the surrogacy cases I treat may be familiar to some readers, I should express my reasons for going back to these well-known cases: I do so not simply to rehearse them, but rather to radically reconstruct the intellectual history of engagement with them so that black feminisms' theorization of the surrogacy/slavery nexus becomes visible as a contribution to black feminism's philosophy of history, and, in turn, to the wider black radical tradition to which black feminism contributes.

Black Feminism and the Surrogacy/Slavery Nexus

The first surrogacy case to garner international media attention quickly became known as the "Baby M" case. In 1986 Mary Beth Whitehead, a white New Jersey mother of two, refused to turn over the child to whom she had given birth to the Sterns, the white professional couple with whom she had entered into contract.[35] With this act of refusal, Whitehead became the first surrogate to challenge the legal enforceability of contractual surrogacy arrangements in the United States.[36] During the two years that the case was under consideration by New Jersey state courts, numerous academics and pundits weighed in, some lionizing and others demonizing Whitehead. The case is invariably invoked as a touchstone in discussions of surrogacy in the United States, and most books on surrogacy begin with an account of it. What is most frequently recalled in the retelling is Whitehead's insurgent act, her dramatic flight into hiding with Baby M, and the case's practical (as opposed to its official) outcome: Whitehead lost custody of a child she had gestated, delivered, and bonded with during the first four months of life, during which time she cared for and breastfed it.[37]

In the focus on the case's practical outcome, what is forgotten is that the presiding judge at the state supreme court deemed the contract itself unenforceable. Judge Harvey Sorkow ruled that children cannot be promised to others prior to their birth (New Jersey state adoption law), and neither "baby-bartering" nor "baby-selling" is legal in the United States.[38] In other words, even though this particular surrogacy contract was not enforced, what persists in public memory, precisely because it has been naturalized and rendered commonsensical, is the idea that reproductive labor is alienable and fungible, and surrogates "unnatural" mothers—women legally entitled to payment for their labor but not to the products of that labor. Indeed, despite the court's ruling, in the wake of the Baby M case babies born to surrogates have been routinely placed in the legal custody of those who are called in the ethnographic literature on surrogacy (which, notably, often reuses rather than contests the language of the promotional literature on surrogacy) "intending parents," "prospective parents," "contracting parents," or "commissioning parents," but whom it is more instructive and accurate to refer to as the *consumers* of in vivo reproductive labor and its living products.[39]

As the media reportage on the Baby M case presaged, Judge Sorkow's ideas about "good" motherhood left a lasting impression. In his courtroom Sorkow made plain that he disapproved of Whitehead's parenting of her first two children (with whom he deemed her "over enmeshed") and openly condemned the actions Whitehead took as the legal dispute unfolded.[40] As Sorkow noted and the press quoted, Whitehead acted "irrationally" when she fled with her baby and went into hiding in her parents' home in Florida and when, on a recorded phone message, she threatened to kill Baby M and herself should she be forced to turn the child over to the Sterns.[41] According to Sorkow, and those whose now dominant views on surrogacy would appear to have been shaped by Sorkow's words rather than his ruling on the contract, Whitehead was "unreliable," "emotionally unbalanced," "irresponsible," "cruel," "manipulative," "exploitative," "deceitful," and both too poor and too "dangerous" to be a "good" mother.[42]

Though Sorkow was unable to connect the dots, the historical referent for the image of the anguished and desperate Whitehead fleeing with her baby the week after she had given birth to her was not lost on feminist commentators. Although Whitehead fled south from New Jersey to Florida, her fugitive act reminded more than one pundit of other flights to freedom embarked upon the century prior, although, of course, these other flights were taken in the opposite geographic direction. Lorraine Stone, tapping into liberalism's long-standing alliance with sentimentalism, observed that Whitehead's actions recalled the iconic escape of Eliza and her baby across the ice floes of the Ohio River as this treacherous journey was depicted by Harriet Beecher Stowe in *Uncle Tom's Cabin.* Just as Eliza sought to save her infant from being sold away, so too, Stone argued, did Whitehead. Instructively eliding the distinction between the two women, Stone wrote, "It does not matter that one was a mid-nineteenth century black slave and the other a late-twentieth century white woman who had unlawfully sold her right to her child prior to its conception and birth. Whatever their legalistic differences, both Eliza and Whitehead took flight for exactly the same reason: to avoid having their children snatched from their breasts. . . . Slave mothers sometimes killed their children, and themselves, to prevent such separations, as Mrs. Whitehead threatened to do."[43] For Stone and others, in transferring a child from the woman who gave birth to it to a second party the court's actions undercut its ruling, as its actions recalled a world, supposedly long gone, in which slave women reproduced living commodities for others. As the journalist Katha Pollitt mused in her widely circulated article in The Nation, "Judge Sorkow is surely the only person on earth who thinks [that] William Stern paid Mary Beth Whitehead $10,000 merely to conceive and carry a baby and not also to transfer that baby to him."[44] In the eyes of many, the case heralded the creation of a "breeder class" of women desperate enough to sell their reproductive labor and to allow brokers to sell off the human fruits of their labor.[45] In short, by awarding custody of Baby M to the Sterns, the court implicitly sanctioned a market in human in vivo labor and human commodities.[46] And yet, even as pundits appeared to recognize the all too familiar economic logic of reproductive extraction, the racialization of slave breeding went unexamined. The upshot: Feminists who initially argued against surrogacy by likening it to slavery replicated a problem that had plagued arguments put forth by white suffragettes in the nineteenth and early twentieth centuries. They invoked slavery to dramatize and deepen their arguments against women's exploitation, but they ignored the violent imbrication of sexism and racism in chattel slavery as practiced for roughly four hundred years.[47]

This all changed when black feminist legal scholars began to write on surrogacy. They immediately brought into the mix not only analogical reasoning but also a materialist and epistemic account of slave breeding.[48] In a watershed article, Anita Allen wrote, "Slave mothers had no legal claim of right or ownership over the natural children they had given birth to. Slave owners not only had ownership over slaves but owned their children too, and could buy and sell them to third parties without regard to the wishes of the natural mother. This phenomenon of American slavery thus resembles a de facto system of certain elements of surrogacy."[49] In contrast to Stone, who had analogized Whitehead to a fictional character driven by maternal despair (Stowe's Eliza), Allen dug into the archives in order to launch her analysis of the connection between surrogates and slaves as racialized reproductive laborers.[50] Comparing Whitehead to a free black child named Polly who was kidnapped and sold into slavery in Missouri, Allen materialized the relationship between surrogacy and slavery, paving the way for elaboration of the surrogacy/

slavery nexus.[51] As she related, when Polly grew up and became a mother, her young daughter was in turn enslaved according to *partus sequitur ventrem* (the legal doctrine previously discussed that required those born to slave women to follow the status of the mother), which was transformed into common law practice throughout the slave South, beginning in the second part of the seventeenth century.[52] When, after a failed escape attempt, Polly found a lawyer, she successfully sued for her own freedom and her right as a free woman to purchase her daughter. According to Allen, Polly's story was germane not only because of the shared affective experience of Polly and Whitehead ("Imagine" Allen urges her reader, "that Mary Beth Whitehead's . . . anguish at losing her daughter was not unlike Polly's" [145]) but also because Polly's reproductive dispossession was enforced by a legal system that regarded reproduction as a racializing process that rendered reproductive labor and its products alienable and fungible. Whitehead, a white woman who had entered "freely" into contract was de facto no more capable of pursuing justice on her own and her child's behalf than was Polly, who had been, along with her child, de jure enslaved. Surrogate and slave are linked by the experience of racialized dehumanization that is historically predicated on the racialization of reproductive labor as a process performed by slaves. As Allen explained, "Both women's sense of security—responsibility and identity—was connected to the children to whom they had given birth . . . but [whom they] had no [legal] right to parent" (145). Drawing a conclusion meant to inform public policy, Allen concluded that opposition to surrogacy, like opposition to slavery, ought to be grounded in awareness that "slavery had the effect of causing black women to become surrogate mothers on behalf of slave owners" (140) and thus of denying reproductive laborers the right to be recognized as the "rightful" mothers of the children to whom they have given birth.

Arguments akin to Allen's became increasingly frequent throughout the 1990s as black feminist legal scholars effectively shifted the ground upon which the debate about surrogacy was taking place.[53] In Dorothy Roberts's oft-cited book *Killing the Black Body: Race, Reproduction, and the Meaning of Liberty* (1997), she solidified the argument. Roberts boldly and presciently argued that anyone seeking to understand contemporary reproductive cultures and politics must begin by connecting present reproductive practices to the reproductive and sexual practices that were routine in the context of chattel slavery. Reiterating an insight made by many members of the black women's health movement who were (and remain) wary of mainstream feminism's narrow focus on abortion, Roberts professed, "I came to grasp the importance of women's reproductive autonomy, not from the mainstream abortion rights movement, but from studying the lives of slave women" (5). She continued, "The systematic, institutionalized denial of reproductive freedom has uniquely marked Black women's history in America" (4). To understand the emergence of "the new bio-underclass," it is therefore imperative to study so-called Jezebels and Mammies, Breeder Women and Fancy Girls—that is, the black enslaved women who functioned as the old bio-underclass. Coercion, exploitation, and regulation of sexuality and reproduction are not in any simple sense aspects of contemporary women's lives that carry over from slavery; however, the slave episteme enables contemporary forms of reproductive extraction. As Roberts put it, the history of reproduction in slavery decisively shapes the core "meaning of reproductive liberty" (6). In extending Roberts's argument, I suggest that the core "meaning of reproductive liberty" (or what I refer to as substantive sexual and reproductive freedom) is overdetermined by the history of slave racial capitalism. As Roberts concludes, it was "the brutal domination of slave women's procreation [that] laid the foundation for centuries of reproductive regulation that continues today" (23).

By discussing slave women as breeders at the start of her book and taking up contemporary surrogacy at the book's close, Roberts forcefully constellates the slave past and the present reproductive scene.[54] In fact the arc of *Killing the Black Body* neatly encapsulates the surrogacy/slavery nexus. Recognizing that slave mothers had no legal claim to their children and that masters had an *in futuro* interest in the breeding capacity of their slaves, Roberts lays the groundwork for a theory of "prenatal property" that is rooted in the history of slavery. This theory accommodates the incursion of property law into reproduction as implemented in the context of slavery in the form of partus sequitur ventrem, and the incursion of property law into surrogacy in the form of the contract between the breeder woman and the consumer of surrogacy. Instancing the practice in which pregnant slave women were forced to lie face down in depressions dug in the earth that could accommodate swollen bellies during whippings, Roberts locates the first maternal-fetal conflict and explores how it uncannily set the stage for contemporary constructions of this conflict, and thus for incarceration of drug-addicted pregnant women thought to have inflicted harm on fetuses, as well as for enforcement of a range of practices that supposedly protect "the unborn" while stripping women of the right to determine the fate of their pregnancies.[55] As Roberts observes, "Even without the benefit of perinatology and advanced medical technologies, slave owners perceived the Black fetus as a separate entity, that would produce future profits that could be parceled out" (41). Put in the terms of the present argument, Roberts recognized that advanced biotechnology is in no way necessary to creation of four centuries of slave racial capitalism; however, this does not militate against use of ARTs to calibrate the gendered and racialized division of labor that subtends contemporary biocapitalism and the market in reproductive labor and products.

In a subsequent law review article, Cheryl J. Sanders explains that work begun by Allen, Roberts, and others paved the way for the constellation of surrogacy and slavery. And yet, she observes, disavowal of racial slavery's relevance persists among those empowered to adjudicate the disputes over custody that have come before courts.[56] This becomes stunningly apparent when we review the history of the second surrogacy case to grab media attention, *Johnson v. Calvert*. While this 1990 case made its way through the California state court system to the state supreme court, it was widely acknowledged by black feminist legal scholars, and by the surrogate in question, Anna Johnson, that the history of slavery informed the legal proceedings. However, when slavery was invoked by the presiding judge in this case it was so that its relevance to the case could be publicly disavowed rather than recognized and examined. Johnson, a poor single biracial (black and Native American) mother of a young daughter, decided that she was unable to give up the child she was gestating to those with whom she had contracted. As in other gestational surrogacy arrangements, the fertilized embryo Johnson carried was the result of a sperm and an egg provided by the consumers of surrogacy, in this instance, Mark Calvert, a white man, and Crispina Calvert, his Filipina wife.[57] At the time the surrogacy contract between the parties was drawn up, it was agreed that Johnson would receive the final portion of a total payment of $10,000 upon delivery of the child to the Calverts. The pregnancy was difficult. During the seventh month Johnson called upon the Calverts to take her to the hospital, believing that she had gone into premature labor. She also asked the Calverts for an advance on her final payment. While the advance eventuated and the birth of a preemie did not, it was at this point in her pregnancy that Johnson realized she would be unable to relinquish the child then in utero to the Calverts. When she initiated legal proceedings to be declared the child's "natural" mother, the Calverts countersued. The court consolidated the two cases and took them up as one.[58]

In sharp contrast to the Baby M case, in which the judge ruled against the enforceability of the surrogate contract, the presiding judge in *Johnson v. Calvert* ruled in its favor. Arguing that Johnson could not be considered a "natural" mother because she was genetically unrelated to the child she gestated, Judge Richard Parslow awarded custody to the Calverts. The Calverts "owned" the genes from which the embryo that developed into a child had been formed in a petri dish and were thus, he reasoned, the child's rightful custodians.[59] In presenting this reasoning, Parslow staked out new legal ground. Building the case on ideas about the reproductive body as a passive matrix that were first expressed by ancient philosophers who gave primacy to the male seed and solely recognized male reproductive agency, Parslow cast the female reproductive laborer as less than human, as an inert substrate in which a human life that was otherwise man-made might be grown.[60] In effect he cast Johnson as a nonmother incapable of possessing a meaningful biological, psychological, or legal relationship to the child she gestated and delivered. For Parslow, genetic "parenthood" trumped all other reproductive contributions.

Although the significance of gestation and delivery had been dismissed in the Baby M case, in *Johnson v. Calvert* the surrogate's reduction to a disembodied womb and instantiation of genes as a form of private property reached new heights. As would become routine in the gestational surrogacy arrangements in the following decade, in *Johnson v. Calvert* reproductive labor was regarded as entirely fungible and its product(s) legally alienable. In short (re)productive labor was treated by the court like all other forms of contractual labor, and genetic materials were regarded as personal property and thus afforded legal protection. Moreover, as Sanders had foreseen, even though in the *Johnson* case Johnson's visible blackness might have ensured that the historical dynamics of slavery that underpinned the case would be evident for all to see, the relevance of the history of slavery was readily dismissed by a court that refused to credit the constellation of the slave past and biocapitalist present. Indeed, even as Judge Parslow selected the metaphors of "foster parent" and "wet nurse" to describe Johnson as a laborer—thus effectively describing her by comparison to two figures wrenched directly from the history of chattel slavery—Parslow disavowed the salience of these figures and thus the insights that might otherwise be gleaned from his invocation of them.[61] Consequently, even as Judge Parslow rendered Johnson's labor akin to that of a slave, the afterlife of reproductive slavery was disavowed by the court.[62]

Although the verdict left Johnson without legal recourse, the child to whom she gave birth garnered full legal protection. As in the Baby M case, this outcome involved a perverse torqueing of the logic of the doctrine of partus sequitur ventrem. Johnson's child followed the status of the surrogate (nonmother) and was thus deemed alienable; however, upon transfer to the

Calverts, this same child shed its status as human genetic property (an amalgam of genes "owned" by others) and became a rights-bearing citizen entitled to full legal protection. During slavery, no matter how "white"-looking a slave woman or her baby may have appeared, enslaved women were denied the legal right to be recognized as mothers; in all instances the children whom they gestated and to whom they gave birth could be legally stripped from them. By contrast, in the *Johnson* case, so long as the child could be stripped away from the woman who sought to mother it and transferred to the consumers who had paid to have it (re)produced, the "white"-looking child's "possession" of paternally predicated "white" genes allowed for the miraculous transformation of a reproductive commodity into a fully entitled legal subject. Tracking in similar territory, Hortense Spillers has famously observed that slave women were disinherited from inheritance by being denied the status of mother. As she elaborates in "Mama's Baby, Papa's Maybe," a watershed essay that she wrote while the Baby M case was being debated by the national media, it is for this reason that labeling slave women as matriarchs (as Senator Daniel Patrick Moynihan did in his infamous "Report") constitutes a violent misnaming, a malapropism produced by what Spillers calls "the American grammar" that systematically refused motherhood to enslaved women so as to ensure the alienation of their (re)productive labor and its products.[63] Spillers's argument underscores a specific point and a general one, each of which is relevant here. There is no precedent in the United States, de jure or de facto, that might have been called upon by Johnson or any other black-appearing woman to support her claim to be a "natural" mother. And, at the same time, Johnson need not have been recognizable to the court as a black woman for Parslow to have compared her to a "foster parent" and "wet nurse"—and thus to a female slave. It was her participation in reproductive labor, not her phenotypical blackness, that set the slave episteme (or what Spillers would call the "American grammar") into motion. Put otherwise, Parslow's ruling depended upon reproductive labor functioning as a racializing process, not upon the a priori racialization of the surrogate's person. As reproductive laborer, Johnson incarnated "the Africanist presence" of which Morrison wrote in the epigraph to this chapter. She made it possible for a white subject to fulfill his destiny, to take up his "rightful" place within the nation, in this case, as the father of genetically related progeny. Mark Calvert said as much when he characterized the custody battle in which he and Johnson were embroiled as his "blackest nightmare" and its outcome as justice served.[64]

By contrast to the court and Mark Calvert, Anna Johnson made it clear to anyone willing to listen that the history of slavery overdetermined her predicament. As she sardonically expressed it in a letter to the television host Geraldo Rivera, "I am not a slave. *Semper Fi.*"[65] Invoking the Latin motto *Semper fidelus* ("Always faithful") with which she no doubt became familiar during her service in the US Marines, Johnson asserted the precise historical referent (an insurgent slave) for her act of refusal, and simultaneously called out the stereotype about "always faithful" slaves, especially slave women laboring in the master's house and giving birth to and caring for the master's property. Indeed, Johnson's "Semper Fi" was resoundingly double-edged: "Always faithful" as an ironic account of the enslaved promoted by pro-slavery sympathizers who sought to attest to the slaves' "consent" to her foreclosed maternal desire. And, too, "Always faithful" as the motto of the formerly enslaved, who, like the committed marine, is compelled to protect rights granted by the Thirteenth, Fourteenth, and Fifteenth Amendments to the Constitution.[66] Though Johnson did not use the conceptual language that I have developed throughout this chapter, she clearly realized the insidious work of the slave episteme in her case's outcome.

Like enslaved women before her, Johnson was regarded as a breeding wench, bound to serve without complaint. Moreover, she was recognizable as a subject in the eyes of the law only when in revolt against legal injustice. As Saidiya Hartman observes in her discussion of slave women who resisted rape, forced reproduction, and other abuses by attacking and sometimes murdering their masters, it was only when found to be criminal that slave women were rendered legible as subjects in the eyes of the law.[67] Similarly Johnson became legible to the court when she was stripped of her right to be considered the "natural" mother of the child to whom she had given birth. It was only when the court intervened to bind her to her contracted role as reproductive laborer (and nonmother) that she was recognized as subject to the law and, simultaneously, dehumanized and cast as a subject lacking legal recourse. From this perspective it makes sense to consider Whitehead and Johnson as intimates, even as "sisters under the skin."[68] As we have seen, surrogacy is a form of labor that binds reproductive laborers together by racializing their labor and dehumanizing those who perform it, and this is so despite what has been called "quasi-hallucinatory racial visibility," the supposed "blackness" that would appear to decisively separate Whitehead and Johnson.[69] Implicitly expressing their mutual awareness of the (relative) irrelevance of the surrogate laborer's ascribed racial identity to the extraction of her reproductive labor and her subsequent dehumanization, Whitehead and Johnson literally stood side by side throughout the legal proceedings that stripped Johnson, as they had previously stripped Whitehead, of the right to mother the child she had brought into the world.[70]

Though the court's treatment of Johnson affirms the reproductive afterlife of slavery, in this case its treatment of the white-Filipino baby as a presumptively white subject protected by law compels additional analysis of the workings of the surrogacy/slavery nexus. As has been observed, *Johnson v. Calvert* marked the emergence of judicial attentiveness to the necessity of protecting "the cult of genetic entitlement."[71] In expanding on this observation, it can be argued that this "cult" is manifest in the ruling as affirmation of Mark Calvert's entitlement to possession of his genetic whiteness as a form of status property. In this case, Calvert's genes were treated as personal assets that ought not be transferrable across racial lines.[72] Although the legal scholar Cheryl Harris wrote her groundbreaking article on "racial status property" several years prior to the announcement of the verdict in the *Johnson* case, her argument about race as a form of status property appears, in retrospect, to have been profoundly prescient of the case's outcome.[73] The transition from the antebellum to the postbellum period, Harris observed, was marked by a radical transformation in the racial status of all forms of property in the United States. Whereas the black body was alienable and fungible throughout the antebellum period, after the Civil War whiteness was legally transformed into a form of property that lodged in the body itself. The possession of whiteness compensated those able to ascertain their possession of "white blood" and "white" genealogy for the loss of their land and former slaves. If individuals could prove themselves free of any taint of blackness, they could fully access the rights of citizenship. In the landmark Supreme Court ruling in *Plessy v. Ferguson*, Harris locates not only the codification of the "one-drop rule," the doctrine of "separate but equal," and the Jim Crow system that was built up around it but also the reification of whiteness as status property. To possess one drop of black blood was to be subject de jure to separate status, and to be subjected de facto to inferior status. This was so from the period marked by the formal end of Reconstruction through to the passage of the Civil Rights Acts and beyond, as many scholars and activists of persistent racial injustice and antiblackness attest.

In sum, to fully comprehend the afterlife of slavery as manifest in *Johnson v. Calvert* one need not hang arguments about the racialization and dehumanization of reproductive labor on Johnson's visible blackness. One need only extend Harris's genealogy of whiteness as property and update it in and for our biocapitalist times. In the past three decades the so-called genetic revolution has led to the replacement of the discourse of blood with that of genes and to recalibration of racial status property as what may most aptly be called "genetic status property." The Calverts' genes were regarded as personal property, the protection and transfer of which was affirmed in the court's verdict. This protection and transfer was in turn ensured by construction of surrogate labor as a process that is racializing and dehumanizing, and thus as a process that renders the laborer who performs it unrecognizable as a subject entitled to full legal protection. As in so many other aspects of the dominant racial formation that characterizes the so-called genomic age, in surrogacy whiteness wears genetic garb, and the blackness of the reproductive laborer emerges as a by-product of the means of (re)production. Because of the court's decision in the *Johnson* case, there now exists legal precedent— *grounded in surrogacy law*—for white paternal genes to garner legal protection in instances in which it becomes necessary to mark out personal property rights in a living product that has been reproduced by a reproductive laborer who has entered a contractual relationship that dictates that she exchange her labor power and its products for payment. Where a discourse of blood facilitated transfer of racial property across generations and the construction of racialized kinship in the slave past, today a discourse of paternally predicated genetic property ensures a similar outcome.[74]

The Surrogacy/Slavery Nexus in Biocapitalism

Thus far I have argued that it is imperative to engage the surrogacy/slavery nexus theorized by black feminist legal scholars if we wish to understand surrogacy as a racializing process that is part and parcel of a racial capitalist formation that is today often referred to as biocapitalism. In concluding this chapter, I speculate about how the insights afforded by the surrogacy/slavery nexus, brewed up in response to surrogacy as it was practiced in the US in the 1980s and 1990s, might be germane to analysis of outsourced or transnational surrogacy in the twenty-first century.[75] My hope in so doing is to address possible concerns that I have mistakenly construed racial slavery and the plantation on which slave breeding was most systematically practiced as the *nomos* of the modern, and related concerns that might result if the outsourced or transnational surrogate market were unacknowledged.[76]

As is well documented, in the 1990s surrogate arrangements shifted from the sort of "traditional surrogacy" of Mary Beth Whitehead, in which she contributed an egg and was artificially inseminated with donor sperm, to the "gestational surrogacy" of Anna Johnson, in which she gestated an embryo composed of genetic materials "belonging" to others. This shift was made possible by improvements in IVF techniques and technology that made fertilization of embryos outside the womb for subsequent transplant into the womb increasingly successful and thus practical. Gestational surrogacy is now so dominant that it is simply referred to as "surrogacy" in all contexts in which in vivo reproductive labor is sold around the globe. Social scientists offer two main reasons for consumer preference for gestational surrogacy over traditional surrogacy once the former became technologically reliable: women are more likely to sell gestational labor when their own genetic material is uninvolved, and custody disputes over the babies delivered by surrogates are far less likely when surrogates (re)produce children to whom they have no genetic relationship. Because gestational surrogacy renders the perceived racial or ethnic identity of the surrogate irrelevant to the genetic, and therefore the assumed racial or ethnic identity of the baby that will be (re)produced, poor women of color, especially in the Global South, have been recruited into the surrogate industry.[77] Predictably, distant, low-cost surrogacy arrangements are deemed preferable by consumers who find it difficult to pay for equivalent but more highly priced arrangements in the United States, for those who would be legally prevented from pursuing surrogacy in their home country, and for those who are attracted by the distance, actual and psychological, of entering into an outsourced or transnational arrangement with a reproductive laborer (or with laborers, if an oocyte vendor is also employed) who lives a world away.

While black feminists feared early on that black women and other women of color would come to constitute the primary surrogate labor force in the US, the relocation of a large portion of the surrogate market first to India and more recently to Thailand, Mexico, and elsewhere indicates a different development.[78] The move to these locations is driven by the imperatives of global outsourcing, such that today many individuals and couples seeking surrogates reside in the Global North (the United States, Canada, the United Kingdom, Europe, Australia, New Zealand, Israel, and parts of East Asia), while the surrogates whose labor is consumed reside in impoverished regions, often in the Global South. In outsourced or transnational arrangements surrogates are therefore of a different nationality, race, and ethnicity (or all of these) than the consumers of their labor and products.[79] Because until 2015 India was the second largest surrogacy market for foreigners seeking low cost and distant surrogate labor, nearly all of the existing scholarship on outsourced and transnational surrogacy treats the Indian market. It is therefore on this scholarship, largely ethnographic, that my understanding of outsourced and transnational reproduction relies.[80] From ethnographic studies we learn that consumers who are willing to travel can purchase (re)production of genetically related child/ren for tens of thousands of dollars less than they would be able to do in the United States.[81] As important, by purchasing outsourced or transnational arrangements consumers gain a range of nonmonetary benefits. The social and educational inequalities that separate surrogates from consumers ensure the outcome that consumers desire: the successful transfer of a baby from a surrogate residing in one part of the world to a consumer of surrogacy who resides in another. In the absence of robust protective legislation, surrogates laboring in the Global South are mostly without legal recourse in those instances in which medical mishaps occur or pregnancies are lost or in those in which the surrogate desires to be declared the "natural" mother of the child in utero.[82]

Until the recent imposition of restrictive legislation banning foreigners from purchasing surrogate arrangements in India, surrogacy clinics proliferated in a handful of Indian cities. Although commercial surrogacy is currently banned in many nations and subject to partial bans or regulatory regimes in others, numerous clinics now operate internationally. As already discussed, the existence of such clinics allows consumers to bypass the material and legal barriers that would otherwise prohibit their entrance into surrogacy arrangements in their home country.[83] Amrita Pande's extensive research based on interviews with surrogates reveals two situations in which Indian women enter into surrogacy: when in need of vital resources and when pressured by husbands or in-laws to do so. In other instances, documented by Daisy Deomampo, women separated from abusive or alcoholic husbands choose surrogacy in situations in which their other options include the sale of an organ or participation in a risky medical trial. Sharmila Rudrappa's research, conducted in the heart of the garment industry in Bangalore, finds that women choose surrogacy over garment work because the reproductive assembly line offers a modicum of protection from the sexual predation that is common in garment factories. Participants in surrogacy arrangements (including surrogates and their families, medical practitioners, clinic workers, surrogate recruiters, and matrons whose job it is to look after surrogates in the hostels in which they reside) testify that the money earned through surrogacy is not enough to permanently transform the lives of surrogates and their families. While a surrogate's earnings may temporarily provide for basics such as food, clothing, and shelter, and in some instances for health care for an ailing family member, education for a child, or a daughter's dowry, surrogacy is not an exit pass from the precarious circumstances that compelled entrance into surrogacy in the first place.

While some ethnographers argue that Indian surrogates, especially those who engage in surrogacy multiple times in an attempt to make a living from surrogacy, exercise what might be described as restricted or constrained agency, they simultaneously agree that surrogacy is never the win-win situation presented by pro-surrogacy media, surrogacy clinics, and other intermediaries who profit from participation in transnational surrogacy arrangements.[84] In an interview conducted by Pande, a surrogate explains her decision to become a surrogate:

> Who would choose to do this? I have had a lifetime worth of injections pumped into me. Some big ones in my hips hurt so much. In the beginning I had about twenty, twenty-five pills almost every day. I feel bloated all the time. But I know I have to do this for my children's future. This is not a choice; this is majboori [a necessity]. When we heard of surrogacy we did not have any clothes to wear after the rains. . . . What were we to do? If your family is starving what will you do with respect? Prestige won't fill an empty stomach.[85]

In an interview conducted by Sharmila Rudrappa, another surrogate attests, "I went into surrogacy so that my daughter will never have to make the kinds of choices I have made . . . [so that] she will never become a surrogate."[86] Still other surrogates suffer the loss of the baby they have gestated and birthed above all else. As one poignantly laments, "You forget the money you have earned [once it is gone]. . . . All that remains is the memory of that baby. And when you have pain like that you know you will repay the money. Really, if I could I would give back their money. . . . I want my baby back."[87]

Throughout India, surrogacy is stigmatized through its association with sex work, as it is widely believed that sex with the consumer is required for fertilization. For this reason ethnographers report that surrogates often elect to conceal pregnancy from their home communities and even from immediates. Just as a surrogate's economic need, illiteracy, and general lack of education benefit consumers of surrogacy, so too the concealment of surrogate labor that is a response to the stigma associated with it. Most surrogates are housed in hostels for the duration of their pregnancy and, if they can afford it, for postpartum recovery. Clinics and consumers also prefer this arrangement because it ensures that women's (re)productive labor can be fully surveilled and managed. Building on the work of Michel Foucault, Pande conceptualizes surrogate hostels comprising dormitories containing eight or more beds apiece as "enclosures."[88] Such enclosures allow for supervision of medical routines (for instance, injection or ingestion of drugs and hormones that maintain pregnancies), for imposition of restrictions on mobility, and for invasive hygiene regimens. When sequestered thus, surrogates are removed from contact with their existing children and other family members, from the domestic and waged work they previously performed on behalf of their families, and from sexual contact. In instances in which diversions such as computer or English lessons are provided by clinics, these are expressly engineered to produce "better" surrogates—women able to communicate with foreign consumers should communication be deemed desirable by consumers, which is not always the case.[89] Ethnographers report that interpersonal interactions between surrogates and consumers, when they occur, are conducted through translators in a language (mainly English) that surrogates do not speak. Contracts are signed by undereducated women who do not read. Birth certificates are prepared in the consumers' names alone. As has been pointed out, the Indian surrogate's erasure from the reproductive process is so complete that nowhere in the contractual paperwork does her name appear.[90]

Although Indian women constitute a distinct socioeconomic group, I am not suggesting that the surrogacy/slavery nexus ought to be engaged by scholars of outsourced or transnational surrogacy because Indian surrogates are brown and poor. Rather I suggest introduction of the surrogacy/slavery nexus into a rich and ongoing discussion of outsourced or transnational surrogacy and the larger biocapitalist economy of which it is a part because the insights of black feminists into the work of the slave episteme raise a host of fascinating and pressing questions about reproductive labor as a racializing process over biocapitalism's *longue durée*. As important, they do so in a manner that resonates with recent work that recognizes outsourcing as not only transnational but transactional—as an economic exchange that involves the crossing of reproductive cultures, and thus as an international social exchange that takes place among individuals who bring to the exchange relationship prior histories of reproduction and, in some instances, long-standing exposure to national cultures in which the slave episteme endures. Put otherwise, reproductive outsourcing involves a variety of economic and interpersonal exchanges that transpire across national borders. It involves consumers who bring to the exchange the thought systems and ideologies, both conscious and unconscious, that inform their expectations about and treatment of reproductive laborers and the living products that are consumed.[91] These thought systems and ideologies are predicated on consumers' placement within complex racial formations that may be the product of European colonialism, Euro-American imperialism, Atlantic slavery, or, most likely, a combination of all three.[92] Consequently, although the slave episteme is certainly not the only episteme that is set to work when surrogacy is outsourced, it behooves us to consider if, when, and how the slave episteme echoes in and through transnational reproductive cultures and politics alongside what might be referred to as the colonial episteme or the imperial episteme.

Returning to my earlier discussion of black Marxism, I suggest that the question that outsourced or transnational reproduction raises is twofold: How are the antinomies of accumulation that characterize transnational reproductive exchanges gendered? This is, of course, *the* question that is engaged by all feminist scholarship on surrogacy. And how does in vivo reproductive labor function as the process through which the gendered antinomies of accumulation are racialized? This is the question that this chapter has sought to address from the vantage point of the slave episteme, thus creating a bridge between the insights of black feminism and the work of scholars of outsourced surrogacy in India who have already addressed the racialization of Indian surrogacy from the vantage point of the colonial episteme.[93] Though it is clearly beyond the scope of a book focused on black feminism's philosophy of history as it has developed in the United States to offer a robust comparative study of US surrogacy and Indian surrogacy (or other forms of outsourced or transnational reproductive labor now available for purchase), it is my hope that in future others will address resonances across geographical space and conduct empirical research that examines the articulation of the history of Atlantic slavery with the histories of European colonialism and Euro-American imperialism.

I am inclined to speculate that all three modes of racial domination are entwined within the historical project of empire building and thus within contemporary processes of economic globalization.[94] In speculating thus, I follow in the footsteps of Lisa Lowe, who has observed that in order to understand the modern world system and the social inequalities that structure it, it is necessary to create what she calls an "unsettling genealogy"—an account of the past from the vantage point of the present that reveals that the property relations residing at the heart of "modern liberalism" have been and continue to be subtended by the intimacies among slavery, colonialism, and imperialism—and thus by global capitalist expansion as it has transformed over time.[95] For Lowe, "intimacy" is not a romantic, relational concept descriptive of liberal interiority or domestic relations but rather a concept metaphor that enables comprehension of connections among the global processes that benefit from ideologies (for instance, "modern liberalism") that obscure the coemergence and continued codependence of these same processes. From a perspective that highlights historical intimacies, it makes no sense to separate off the history of Atlantic slavery when seeking to understand the exchange relationships that surround us and in which we participate in contemporary biocapitalism. Rather it behooves us to examine the possibility that the afterlife of reproductive slavery is not in any simple sense restricted to those geographic locations (the Americas and the Caribbean) where Atlantic slavery originally transpired. As I have suggested, it is the stripping away from all surrogates—white, black, Indian, Thai, Mexican, et cetera—of the legal right to lay claim to the children delivered into the world that casts each surrogate as a practitioner of a form of dehumanized and racialized labor that is shaped, at least in part, by the slave episteme. This is so regardless of the "race" ascribed to each surrogate prior to her entrance into surrogate labor. Like capitalism and the global expansion of markets and the outsourcing of labor on which it relies, the slave episteme is on the move.

Chapter Two

BLACK FEMINISM *as a* PHILOSOPHY *of* HISTORY

Every image of the past that is not recognized by the present as one of its own concerns threatens to disappear irretrievably.

—WALTER BENJAMIN, "THESES ON THE PHILOSOPHY OF HISTORY" (1940)

Lessons can be gleaned from the slave era which will shed light upon Black women's and all women's current battle for emancipation.

—ANGELA Y. DAVIS, *WOMEN, RACE, AND CLASS* (1981)

Margaret Garner, a twenty-two-year-old slave mother of four young children, first came to public notice in 1856, when she went on trial. Garner had crossed the frozen Ohio River from Kentucky to Cincinnati along with seven other members of her family, braving slave catchers and a singularly frigid winter night, in a quest for freedom. Along with the other fugitives with whom she traveled, Garner was on the run for twelve tension-filled hours before apprehension by authorities. When cornered in the safe house in which the fugitives sought refuge, Garner attempted to murder her young children rather than allow them to be returned to slavery. Though she was prevented from fulfilling her plan in its entirety, she succeeded in taking the life of her two-year-old daughter. A description in one of the many newspapers that reported on the court case as it unfolded cites Garner's stated intention in a rare acknowledgment of her insurgent agency: "The Negress avowed herself the mother of the children, and said that she had killed one, and would like to kill the three others rather than see them again reduced to slavery."[1]

In the foreword to *Gendered Resistance*, the first anthology devoted to Garner's legacy, the historian Darlene Clark Hine expresses a prayer that the lives of Garner and other enslaved women will not be lost for future generations: "The commodification of vulnerable women and children is an ongoing reality. . . . There may not be as much difference between the nineteenth century and our own times as we imagine. . . . I pray that the feminist wisdom of . . . enslaved black women, and our memory of Margaret Garner, will continue to inspire and facilitate our ongoing struggles for self-ownership, empowerment, and the right to live and to achieve our full human potential."[2] Hine casts Garner as an inspirational figure through whom to access a trove of insurgent wisdom; she also observes that recollection of Garner is politically urgent in the present and vital for future survival. These sentiments are mirrored in the anthology's split foci: half the chapters treat Garner's story; half treat "global slavery, healing, and new visions in the twenty-first century." The editors explain that the volume's organization manifests their belief that Garner's story ought to be "recovered and told again and again" (xii). Like the Sankofa bird of African lore, they advise, we must return to Garner to collect "what is needed," for her story contains "the seeds" for "change, hope, and transformation" (xiii).

This simultaneously historical and presentist preoccupation with a slave woman's insurgent past is noteworthy. It encapsulates the idea that Garner's story, and stories of slave women in general, contain what Walter Benjamin would call "an image of the past" that must be recognized by the present "as one of its own concerns."[3] Put otherwise, the Garner volume expresses a unique black feminist orientation toward the history of slavery, slave women's insurgency, and the hard decisions that slave women made as they sought freedom and, in so doing, contributed to the overthrow of the system that enslaved them. This chapter explores black feminist retrospective assessments of the past in view of the present, paying special attention to black feminism's retrieval of enslaved women's insurgency. I argue that recovery and activation of what has been retrieved from the past in the present constitutes what Benjamin has called a "philosophy of history," one that I here attribute to black feminist writings produced in the 1970s, 1980s, and 1990s. In elaborating black feminism's philosophy of history, I aim to highlight its contributions to the black radical tradition, to find in these contributions a distinctively *feminist* black Marxism focused on sex and reproduction, and, finally, to suggest the importance of engaging with black feminism's philosophy of history in our biocapitalist times.

Although Margaret Garner is not a household name, because so many black feminists write about her she is today a recognizable historical figure. This is so despite the fact that Garner's story threatened disappearance for over a century. In 1856, when Garner murdered her child, was taken into custody, and put on trial for stealing her master's property (herself and her children), her case was taken up in the popular press by abolitionists and their allies.[4] Her actions and trial were poised between passage of the Fugitive Slave Act (1850), the Supreme Court's Dred Scott decision (1857), and the outbreak of the Civil War (1861). In 1856 the nation was riven by intersectional tension between pro- and antislavery forces; in such a climate abolitionists were eager to transform Garner into a cause célèbre.[5] As Mark Reinhardt demonstrates through a survey of national press coverage, the Northern abolitionist press regarded Garner with politically motivated sympathy, representing her actions as a powerful "blow for freedom" (32) and as an indictment of slavery that showed the world how a slave mother driven to the depths of despair "valued freedom above life itself" (32). In the words of the former slave and leading abolitionist Frederick Douglass, Garner was an "honored benefactress" whose actions displayed the intensity of her resistance to injustice and her love of freedom.[6] In an editorial in the *Provincial Freedman*, a black abolitionist publication, Garner was deemed "more than model of modern woman"; indeed it was predicted that Garner "would live [on] in the minds, and be cherished in the hearts of every true man and woman."[7] When Lucy Stone, the prominent suffragist and abolitionist, took the courthouse floor after closing arguments were made at Garner's trial, she protested her unjust criminalization and celebrated the righteousness embodied in her actions. Drawing upon a powerful combination of nineteenth-century Radical Republicanism and the Cult of True Womanhood, Stone observed, "The faded faces of the negro children tell too plainly to what degradation female slaves must submit. Rather than give her little daughter to that life, she killed it."[8] For Stone, Garner had fulfilled her sacred maternal charge by saving her young daughter from a life of sexual degradation, and thus had proven herself and her race worthy of freedom and the protections granted by citizenship.[9]

Despite the numerous editorials that were written and the speeches that were given on Garner's behalf, the fact remains that she was largely unremembered for over one hundred years. The presiding judge in the case upheld the Fugitive Slave Law and remanded Garner and her remaining children back to slavery.[10] Their story was all but forgotten until Toni Morrison resurrected it by including a news item about Garner's trial in a 1974 compendium of "black life" that Morrison worked on when an editor at Random House. Then, later, Morrison fictionalized Garner's story in Beloved.[11] While the story's long eclipse is not difficult to explain—the outbreak of Civil War, the failure of Reconstruction, and the subsequent demise of the abolitionist movement left Garner on the wrong side of history—dominant historiography cannot account for the profound interest in the story's resurrection, an interest first expressed by Morrison and other black feminists, and, subsequently, by millions of readers of Beloved, a Pulitzer Prize–winning novel that continues to be widely read.

While it is well known that Beloved's publication enabled Garner's story to become known for a second time in history, this chapter demonstrates how and why resurrection of Garner's act of violent insurgency ought to be understood as part and parcel of a sustained and polyvocal black feminist meditation on sex and reproduction in bondage, and thus as part of black feminism's collective meditation on slave women's insurgency and the importance of this insurgency for activism and politics across the 1970s, 1980s, and 1990s—the three decades of black feminism's most intensive and focused publication. In situating Beloved thus it is not my intent to diminish its literary greatness; it is one of the most lauded contemporary American novels and one to which I, like others, inexorably return (to wit, Beloved is the focus of my next chapter). However, before singling out Beloved, it is necessary to contextualize it within a discussion of the profuse black feminist return to and imaginative engagement with enslaved women's violent insurgency. As we shall see, the black feminist philosophy of history to which Beloved contributed in the mid-1980s began to be elaborated in the 1970s and early 1980s, as black feminists worked in multiple idioms to tell the story of sex and reproduction in bondage and to simultaneously imagine slave women's refusal of sexual and reproductive dispossession in the present moment of writing.[12] In so doing, black feminists supplemented a sparse historical archive, amended dominant historiography, and testified to the persistence of the trauma of slavery into the present. As important they imagined slave women's acts of refusal and offered them forward, believing in their relevance to struggles aimed at redressing the situation of women living and laboring in an emergent neoliberal world in which the free market was being offered as an answer to all social woes, including racism.

In reading black feminist production as the elaboration of a philosophy of history, this chapter treats black feminist accounts of women in slavery as mediating the economic conflicts and contradictions that emerged during the three decades in which black feminism was produced. Though I follow other scholars in recognizing black feminism's relationship to the long civil rights movement, dominant white iterations of the feminist movement, the dismantling of welfare, and the expansion of the carceral state, I also offer a different orientation to it. By keying black feminism not only to those political movements with which black feminists were expressly involved but also to the emergence of the new markets in reproductive labor and products discussed in chapter 1, I demonstrate its responsiveness to the ascent of biocapitalism and the neoliberal rationality that accompanied it. While it is true that only a small number of the black feminists writing in the period that interests me expressly treated the emergence of what were then referred to as the "new" reproductive technologies and surrogacy, I suggest that all black feminist writing produced in the period is both proleptic and analeptic—it reflects and refracts the commodification of human reproduction, its processes and products in slave racial capitalism, and in the present biocapitalist moment of writing.

What my approach to black feminism implies for the arguments set forth thus far is twofold. It behooves us to explore black feminist interventions into the debate about surrogacy and the emergence of biocapitalism, as I did in chapter 1. And it behooves us to examine how a robust black feminist philosophy of history emerged and came to constitute a significant contribution to the black radical tradition—a contribution that pushes us toward theorization of women's sexual and reproductive dispossession and insurgency in the slave past and in the moment in which the slave past is recollected. As I noted in my introduction, in dominant accounts of the black radical tradition it is narrated as male. In histories of the long civil rights movement a familiar cast of male activists and intellectuals is lionized, and their oratorical and scholarly contributions celebrated and parsed. In genealogies that reach back in time, including Cedric Robinson's *Black Marxism*, those positioned as the key contributors to the tradition are men. As important as is critique of the gender politics of the construction of black radicalism (as others have already pointed out),[13] in the present context I wish to take up a different aspect of the black radical tradition's masculinism: the presumptive gender neutrality of two of the central concepts around which it has been oriented, the general category of "labor" and the specific category of "slave labor."

Because Robinson's contributions have been so influential and, not least, because they underpin the idea of racial capitalism that I engage throughout this book, I begin by limning the problem of masculinist analytical categories in Robinson's work and in one of the watershed texts upon which his elaboration of black Marxism is based. As Robinson argues, Du Bois's 1935 tome, *Black Reconstruction*, is an epic treatise on the history of American slavery, the Civil War, and the failures of Reconstruction.[14] It is also the first text in which Marxism is expressly employed to situate slavery as capitalism and to cast the slave as a "worker" whose involvement in the Civil War constitutes a "strike" against the conditions of work and thus against slavery. As Robinson explains in a 1977 essay that appeared in the *Black Scholar* and presaged his more well-known reading of Du Bois, published nearly a decade later, Du Bois's recasting of the slave as "the black worker" caught up in an eruptive moment is an important materialist move and a major innovation on traditional Marxism.[15] By casting the slave as a worker Du Bois retooled the idea of the paid laborer as the model proletariat. And he rendered the unpaid, hyperexploited slave the centerpiece of a black revolution against slavery and thus against racial capitalism.[16]

Robinson's reading beautifully captures the enormity of Du Bois's shift away from traditional Marxist conceptions of historical agency and toward a more expansive understanding of the Marxist categories of work and worker. And yet, as we shall see, Robinson is not alert to an against-the-grain reading of *Black Reconstruction* that unearths questions about the black worker's gender and the gendering of slave work. Put otherwise, though Robinson treats the black worker Du Bois discusses as if this worker and the work performed were genderless, we need not reify the presumption. Instead we can ask a gender-attentive set of questions about Du Bois's treatment of the slave as a worker and of slaves' insurgency against the conditions of their work. For although it has not been done before, it is possible to read *Black Reconstruction* as a text that recognizes, if fleetingly, not only slave women's sexual and reproductive labor but also their gender-specific insurgency against the sexual and reproductive exploitation to which they were subjected. Such a reading, which I elaborate below, thickens an account of black feminism's philosophy of history by allowing us to see exactly how black feminism contributes to, while riffing off, the black radical tradition's foundational black Marxist texts and figures—Du Bois as well as Robinson.

The Gender of the General Strike

To be clear at the outset, my intent in offering the reading that follows is not to elevate Du Bois and implicitly condemn Robinson by situating Du Bois as a thinker whose feminism was overlooked by Robinson. Rather I read for gender and sexuality in Black Reconstruction to interrupt the dominant genealogy of black radicalism, to engage still contentious questions about Du Bois's relationship to feminism, and to pose the largely unasked question of black feminism's relationship to Du Bois.[17] As a range of feminist and queer scholars have demonstrated, Du Bois was a "retrograde rake" who played the role of "priapic adulterer" throughout several decades in an unhappy first marriage. He had a notoriously poor track record of publicly crediting the women antilynching crusaders, civil rights activists, and literary muses and editors by whom he was surrounded and with whom he collaborated across a long career. When he did write on gender and sexuality he was rarely self-conscious; moreover, his musings are most often contradictory or unsustained.[18] I do not turn to Black Reconstruction because it is an important black feminist text; I turn to it because it constitutes an invaluable point of entry for a wider discussion of black feminism's philosophy of history. For as we shall see, Black Reconstruction performs an explosive if fleeting opening up of the question of the sexual and reproductive politics of slavery and of slave women's insurgency against the system of slavery—a question I will henceforth refer to as the gender of the general strike.

Du Bois's opening up of the question of the gender of the general strike is most apparent when his historical narrative, which is also a historiographical corrective, is parsed for the manner in which it clears space for feminist questions about the historical processes that it describes and the methodology that it models as it tells the story of the implosion of slavery, the outbreak of the Civil War, and the foreclosed horizons that are its aftermath.[19] As he narrates this story, Du Bois notes that women engaged in acts of gender-specific refusal of their sexual and reproductive dispossession, and thus, albeit unwittingly, he clears the ground for a range of potential feminist engagements.

Given the compendious nature of Black Reconstruction's story of the transition from slavery to war and from war to the failures of Reconstruction, it is instructive that analysis of sex and reproduction is largely restricted to the book's opening chapters, those focused on the conflicts that erupted under the pressure of slavery's internal contradictions, but not in the famous chapter on the "general strike" itself. For instance, in the first chapter, "The Black

Worker," Du Bois acknowledges the importance of the self-production of "real estate" to the system of slavery and the fact that forced sex and reproduction sustained the relations of production in slavery. Making an argument that anticipates that made by feminist historians of slavery that I discussed in chapter 1, Du Bois explains that "human slavery in the South pointed and led in two singularly contradictory and paradoxical directions" (9). It led "toward the deliberate commercial breeding and sale of human labor for profit and toward the intermingling of black and white blood. The slaveholders shrank from acknowledging either set of facts but they were clear and undeniable" (11). When Du Bois proceeds on from this assertion to a discussion of the role of rape in slave breeding, he emphasizes the instrumentality of sexual violence in the discipline of female slaves. When he turns to a discussion of runaways as historical agents protesting the conditions of labor, two of the three individuals upon whom he focuses are women. His singling out of female fugitives is noteworthy. The historical consensus was and remains that men were more able and more likely to run. Women, uniquely constrained by their ties to children, considered their actions in view of their role as mothers and thus, by necessity, in view of the gendered conditions of their enslavement. However, even with this knowledge in hand, Du Bois regards slave women as insurgents, as active participants in rebellion against the system.[20]

A subsequent chapter entitled "The Planter," together with the opening chapter on the black worker, sets up the opposition of forces that animate the text's historical dialectic. Notably, in "The Planter" consideration of the gender dynamics of slavery intensifies. In a passage on the slave home, for instance, Du Bois examines the impact on slave families of women's labor in the fields and away from young children, and he imagines the destabilization of the slave family and the insecurity and vulnerability of children that this must have produced (40). He also considers the emotional toll on slave women of "raising . . . slaves . . . for systematic sale on the commercialized cotton plantations" (41), where, he points out, reproductive exploitation was especially intensive and forced separation of families routine. In such instances Du Bois is attentive to the gendered conditions of work and to the gender-specific impact of women's work on slaves' intimate, familial, and psychic lives. It is therefore somewhat ironic that it is only when Du Bois examines the toll taken by planter violence *on planter men* that he fully adumbrates the violence to which slave women were subjected.

When planters sought to increase surplus through increased exploitation of workers, Du Bois observes, they employed measures aimed at both production and reproduction. They increased crops and profits by acquiring land, and they took up the lash to force all workers to increase their productivity. Simultaneously they engineered slave women's rate of reproduction by orchestrating sexual violence and its reproductive outcome.[21] Underscoring his boldness in bringing to light what previous historians had shamefacedly left hidden, Du Bois writes that while planters "surrounded it [slave breeding] with certain secrecy, and it was exceedingly bad taste for any . . . planter to have it indicated that he was deliberately raising slaves for sale . . . that was a fact. . . . [A] laboring stock was deliberately bred for legal sale" (42–43). More to the point, Du Bois continues, because planters "could not face the fact of Negro women as brood mares and of black children as puppies," because the system they had themselves created "so affronted the moral sense of the planters, . . . they tried to hide from it" (43). They did so by treating their intensive involvement and investment in slave breeding with disavowal. This disavowal, in turn, found expression in both the quotidian and excessive forms of violence that planters directed toward enslaved women and the children these women bore for and often to them.

Somewhat predictably, in Du Bois's ensuing examination of the "sexual chaos that arose from [the] economic motives" (44) characterizing plantation life, he laments this "chaos," plainly exhibiting his abiding bourgeois concern with what he here and elsewhere refers to as the lack of a "bar to illegitimacy" (44).[22] As Du Bois's class-marked and paternalistic moral ire surfaces, it undercuts the gendered account of slavery that he has proffered in the preceding analysis. And yet, undercutting noted, what has come before—an account of sexual and reproductive extraction as foundational to slavery and to slave women's revolt against it—remains of the utmost importance. The fact remains, the main argument elaborated across two of Du Bois's pivotal opening chapters on planter-slave relations is underpinned by a story about *enslaved women* and the exploitation they endured at the hands of planters. Through an implicit teleological movement, Du Bois's narrative emphasizes even though it will ultimately foreclose the centrality of slave breeding to the profitability of slavery. In so doing the narrative tells us that planters' gendered and sexualized violence and enslaved women's revolt against this violence created the internal conflicts and contradictions that brought the slave system to its breaking point. In short, it tells us that slave women's insurgency was central to slavery's demise.

And yet, despite the recursive historical rhythm of *Black Reconstruction* (Du Bois moves from antagonism to revolt, crisis, reentrenchment, and back to antagonism, and so on), the gendered and sexualized reproductive contradictions constitutive to Du Bois's narrative of the outbreak of the Civil War go missing from the story that unfolds over the next seven hundred pages of his book. One of the significant results of this is that the famous and pivotal chapter, "The General Strike," is evacuated of the account of sexual and reproductive labor that was developed across the book's opening chapters. A second is that the black workers who strike to end slavery are no longer gender-differentiated. In fact, in the chapter on the general strike those whom Du Bois describes as "swelling," "flooding," and "swarming" Union troops (64–65), as withdrawing their labor from plantations, as sabotaging the production of surplus through labor stoppages, and as stanching the supply of food to plantations and Union troops are uniformly characterized as male.[23] A third result is that when Du Bois's narrative arrives at its apex and describes the black worker—now a full-fledged member of a black proletariat—as not merely expressing "the desire to stop work" but as participating in "a strike on a wide basis against the conditions of work" (67), these "conditions" are stripped of the gender-differentiated labor and insurgency that Du Bois had attended to until this decisive turning point.

For readers immersed in and hoping for the full development of the story of insurgent enslaved women, violent and predatory planters, and the epic antagonism between the two, Du Bois's discussion of the general strike signals an abrupt narrative break and indicates the presence of a conceptual aporia. Suddenly slaves work solely to produce agricultural commodities. And thus, readers are left to ask: What has become of those fleshy commodities posited as essential to the slave economy? And what of the black *female* workers who (re)produced them? In disappearing enslaved women and their sexual and reproductive labor and its products from the story of the Civil War, Du Bois's account of the general strike inaugurates an exquisite experience of narrative opening, possibility, and deferral. Although sexual and reproductive labor suffuses the story that precedes the account of the general strike, when Du Bois gets to the strike itself, sexual and reproductive labor is no longer part of the story. Where a black mass comprising all slaves, male and female, initially stood, a vanishing act transpires. A male labor force takes center stage for the remainder of the show, effectively disappearing the gender-differentiated labor force that had initially captured our attention.

The aporia that this disappearing act creates begets a series of questions: How might the history of slavery, the Civil War, and Reconstruction be transformed by sustained, as opposed to foreclosed, consideration of slave women as participants in the general strike against slavery? How might traditional Marxist concepts such as work, worker, and consciousness be reconceptualized by attentiveness to the gender of the general strike? Might alternative narrative idioms move us beyond the limits of the Du Boisian narrative, allowing for exploration of slave women's membership in the mass of black workers protesting the conditions of work? These questions, all raised but never answered in Black Reconstruction, are the questions that black feminism takes up forty years after its publication. As the remainder of this chapter demonstrates, black feminists not only sought to correct the historiographic tradition (as had Du Bois); they also sought to imagine new truths about slaves' gender and sexuality and about reproductive slavery's relationship to the present and the future. In short, they worked in the spirit of Black Reconstruction while simultaneously far exceeding its gender-bound project.

Black Feminism as a "Propaganda of History"

"The propaganda of history" is the only chapter in Black Reconstruction that is as oft-discussed as the chapter on the general strike. It is the last chapter of the book and is frequently excised and presented as a stand-alone treatise on historiography. In it Du Bois elaborates his ideas about historical truth and bias, offers a searing critique of how "the facts of American history have . . . been falsified because the nation was ashamed" (711), and goes on to explain how such falsified facts have been used to perpetuate white racial nationalism and colonization of people of color around the world.[24] In producing this critique, Du Bois crystallizes two of Black Reconstruction's main arguments: refutation of five decades of "scandalous white historiography" and demonstration of its role in legitimating Jim Crow and promoting a global culture of colonial and imperial domination.[25] In suggesting that all historical narratives, his own included, are implicated in contests over historical truth and therefore ought to be recognized as "propaganda," Du Bois rings changes on the term's usual meaning and anticipates the poststructuralist critique of empiricist and positivist historiography that will emerge in the second half of the twentieth century.[26] He prefigures arguments in favor of "genealogical history" advanced by Foucault a half century later.[27] And, most important for my purposes, he presages black feminism's primary methodological and political insight: historical narrative must be keyed to the moment of its production (to what Benjamin calls "the time of the now") if history is to be set to work in the service of a more liberated future. For this reason, it makes sense to suggest that black feminism proffers its own "propaganda of history," for the historical counternarrative that it elaborates across multiple idioms not only situates slave women as black workers who took part in a general strike against slavery but also it dares to *imagine* the importance of enslaved women's "freedom dreams" in the context of the 1970s, 1980s, and 1990s.[28]

Though numerous texts can be instanced in order to detail the intellectual and activist production I have thus far gestured toward with the risky catch-all *black feminism*, I turn first to several that were written in the 1970s and 1980s by activists and historians who were the first to imagine slave women's protest of their sexual and reproductive dispossession. These interventions, which are too often bypassed, set the stage for the outpouring of black feminist fictions about sex and reproduction in bondage that constitute the apogee of a sustained and collective black feminist response to the question of the gender of the general strike that is keyed both to the slave past and to the rise of biocapitalism and neoliberalism.

Angela Davis's "Reflections on the Black Woman's Role in the Community of Slaves" (1971) is, to my knowledge, the first essay to argue for the centrality of slave women's day-to-day resistance to the system of slavery. Davis posits domestic life in the slave quarters as the primary site of sustained protest. Originally written while Davis was in prison as part of an unfinished exchange with her fellow Black Panther George Jackson, her essay takes aim at the neglected history of slave women and the so-called black matriarch, a figure that at the time Davis was writing formed the basis for public debate and policy recommendations on governance of the black family, especially in the wake of Senator Moynihan's infamous report on the "tangle of pathology" supposedly passed down to modern black families through the actions of the emasculating female descendants of slave women.[29] Davis's first move is to correct the historiographic record and put Moynihan in his place.[30] Making clear that her primary concern is excavation of the past to "illuminate" the present, she begins by observing, "The matriarchal black woman has repeatedly been invoked as one of the fatal by-products of slavery. An accurate portrait of the African woman in bondage must [therefore] debunk the myth of the matriarchate. Such a portrait must simultaneously attempt to illuminate the historical matrix of her oppression and must evoke her varied, often heroic response to the slaveholder's domination" (4). In refuting "the myth of the matriarchate" "at its presumed historical inception" (3), Davis defamiliarizes the dominant historical account of slave rebellion and resistance. On the one hand, she unsettles the notion (which, she observes, is too often held by male scholars of all races) that black women "actively assented" to slavery and related to "the slaveholding class as collaborator[s]" (4).[31] On the other hand, she submits the unprecedented thesis that it was "by virtue of the brutal force of circumstances . . . [that] the black woman," as opposed to the black man, "was assigned the mission of promoting the consciousness and practice of [slave] resistance" (5).

Davis offers two interrelated arguments for "the black woman's" centrality to slave resistance. Her space, domestic space, was the site of resistance because it was at the greatest distance from slaveholders' reach: "Of necessity . . . [the slave] community would revolve around the realm which was furthermost removed from the immediate arena of domination. It could only be located in and around the living quarters, the area where the basic needs of physical life were met" (6). In ministering to the needs of men and children, Davis emphasizes, slave women performed "the only labor of the slave community which could not be directly and immediately claimed by the oppressor." She therefore concludes that it was "only in domestic life . . . away from the eyes and whip of the overseer . . . [that] slaves could . . . assert . . . freedom" (6). Whereas previous accounts of slave insurgency focused on documented rebellions and revolts, Davis (taking her cues from the "father" of social history, Herbert Gutman) highlights the quotidian. "If," she hypothesizes, "domestic labor was the only meaningful labor for the slave community as a whole" (7), then slave women's labor not only "increased the total incidence of anti-slavery assaults"; it was the "barometer indicating the overall potential for [slave] resistance" (15). Contra Du Bois, who had lamented slave women's inability to do the feminized care work involved in social and cultural reproduction, Davis insists that women's "domestic work" was a source of individual and community sustenance and of slave "resistance" tout court.[32]

Although Davis's central historical claims have been challenged,[33] in engaging the question of the gender of the general strike she took on the masculinism of the black radical tradition head on, offering forward what was up to this point missing from the discussion: a gender-specific account of slave racial capitalism's violence and of slave women's resistance to it. It thus seems not only unnecessary but also largely beside the point to adjudicate (as past scholars have) whether Davis got it right or wrong, or whether she adhered to the empirical and positivist standards and methods that were touted by more traditional historians. Rather, we must read Davis's contribution in the spirit of the project of historiographic revision that Du Bois outlines, and thus as a "propaganda of history" that counters the falsified "facts" of history. Davis's essay is an exemplary instantiation of a counterhistory that highlights the importance of slave women's gender-specific dispossession, their participation in past strikes against slavery, and too the importance of black women's participation in strikes for substantive freedom in Davis's present moment of writing. Ultimately Davis's essay contributes to black feminism's philosophy of history by retelling the story of women in slavery so that this story creates new ways of thinking about sexual and reproductive dispossession in Davis's present and for the future she sought to advance toward.

In contrast to the male historians of slavery who tended to showcase their mastery of archival evidence, Davis pushes for recognition of the necessarily *imaginative* character of the black feminist project in which she is engaged, openly acknowledging her scholarly shortcomings. In so doing she anticipates her readers' potential objections to her argument and delineates the political gains that are to be had in her present moment of writing by forging ahead with creation of a gender-focused narrative about the past regardless of potential objections and the possible pitfalls that may await her given the paucity of supporting evidence. She concedes, "No extensive and systematic study of the role of black women in resisting slavery has come to my attention," and it is no longer feasible to wait to get started on writing such a history. There is "urgency," she insists, "to undertake a thorough study of the black woman as anti-slavery rebel" (9) so that it is possible to get on with the pressing task of dismantling the hold of the past on the present.

In prison, without access to archives and the full range of academic source materials that would otherwise have been at her disposal, Davis knows that she cannot produce a complete or in-depth study of women in slavery and women's resistance to slavery. However, instead of being deterred by unjust circumstances, Davis jumps in anyway, providing her reader with "a portrait" of what she expressly labels, "the *potential and possibilities* inherent in the situation to which slave women were anchored" (14, emphasis added). In prying the story of the gender of the general strike from available materials, in working with and against the few historiographical texts available to her, Davis does not presume *to prove* that the historical portrait she paints for her readers is empirically verifiable. Rather she seeks to compel her readers to come along with her in *imagining* the truth of slave women's resistance to the forms of sexual and reproductive exploitation to which they were subjected. And, too, she urges her black female readers to come along in *imagining* how knowledge of women's myriad acts of sexual and reproductive refusal might yet impact the black liberation movement's treatment of black women's struggles for substantive sexual and reproductive freedom in the 1970s—as these were precisely the forms of freedom that were being actively proscribed by the punitive racist and sexist policies backed by the Moynihan Report.

Given the material constraints to which Davis's inquiry into slave women's insurgency was subject, it should not be surprising that she rapidly exhausts discussion of women's documented participation in slave revolts (her discussion of such participation is limited to an against-the-grain reading of Herbert Aptheker's 1943 classic, *American Negro Slave Revolts*) and moves on without apology and without the support of the usual scholarly apparatus. As she explains, to show that black women's insurgent response to "counter-insurgency [is] not as extravagant as it might seem" (8) it is necessary to build an argument for women's insurgency from a new starting place.[34] To recognize "the black woman as anti-slavery rebel" (9), she specifies, it is essential to allow oneself to *imagine* that female insurgency provoked the principal form of "counter-insurgency" to which slave women were routinely subjected by planters: rape.[35]

Davis's argument that rape is *counterinsurgency* and that women's resistance to rape is a major form of *insurgency* robustly transforms her essay into black feminist propaganda or counterhistory and paves the way for other black feminist responses to the question of the gender of the general strike. Turning attention away from "open battles," from organized acts of collective rebellion, Davis instead focuses on individual, intimate acts of refusal of sexual and reproductive dispossession that might not be evident in available archives and the scholarship based on them, but which are nonetheless entirely conceivable and credible if we accept and then reassess what we already know about slavery.

Such acts of gendered insurgency, Davis imagines, constituted the reality for most slave women, for the vast majority of women working on plantations were subjected to systematic sexual violence and reproductive exploitation. As Davis observes, "the oppression of slave women had to assume dimensions" of open insurgency. In rape and forced reproduction, the slave woman also must have "felt the edge of this counter-insurgency as a fact of her daily existence" (12). Routine acts of sexual aggression have not been but ought henceforth to be recognized as "terrorist methods designed to dissuade other black women from following the examples of their [insurgent] sisters" (12). Making recourse to the conditional tense—and thus calling attention to the politically imperative, as opposed to empirically grounded, character of the conclusions that she wishes to draw—Davis specifies, "The act of copulation, reduced by the white man to an animal-like act *would* be symbolic of the effort to conquer the resistance the black woman *could* unloose. In confronting the black woman as adversary in a sexual contest, the master *would* be subjecting her to the most elemental form of terrorism distinctively suited for the female" (13, emphasis added). Based on the idea that women's insurgency constitutes a self-evident historical "truth" (as opposed to a verifiable "fact") and based on the then, as now, controversial idea that planters routinely raped female slaves or instructed others to rape them, Davis brilliantly concludes that slave women must have routinely *provoked* and *countered* the master's counter-insurgency with more insurgency.

The power of Davis's argument resides in its ability to fold our knowledge of the truth in on itself and then to actively convert this knowledge into felt (as opposed to documented) evidence of enslaved women's resistance to slavery. From one perspective, Davis argues, women's and men's productive labor was exploited; from another perspective (one that prefigures and implicitly contests subsequent scholarship on the ungendering effects of the middle passage and the experience of plantation slavery),[36] women's resistance to exploitation must be understood as a response to gender-specific forms of sexual and reproductive dispossession. By "reestablish[ing] her femaleness by reducing her to the level of her *biological* being," Davis observes, the master directly "attack[ed] . . . the black female as a potential insurgent" (13) whose resistance to domination ought thus to be simultaneously understood as specifically female and as part and parcel of the general strike of enslaved black workers against slavery. Davis concludes, "Countless black women did not passively submit to these abuses, as the slaves in general refused to passively accept their bondage. The struggles of the slave woman . . . were a continuation of the resistance interlaced in the slaves' daily existence" (14).

Whereas Du Bois had positioned *Black Reconstruction* as a critique of white supremacist historiography dominant at the time he was writing, and as counterpropaganda possessing the power to restore agency to enslaved black workers and their descendants, Davis positions her watershed essay on black women in slavery as a critique of the prevailing masculinist historiography of slavery on which she was forced to rely, and as a propagandistic counterhistory that possesses the power to restore agency to female slaves and their descendants. Davis's slave woman is neither the emasculating matriarch of Moynihan's Report nor the shamed, tragic victim of the master's sexual predation—the figure that all too frequently appears in Du Bois's work. Rather she is a sexually and reproductively dispossessed laborer whose gendering by the master class is meted out as sexualized violence against her (re)productive body, a body that was regarded as racial property and (re)productive tool. Neither aggressor nor victim in any simple sense, Davis's slave woman is an active member of an unorganized collectivity whose amassed contributions to the slaves' struggle against slavery were, by necessity, expressed through individual, intimate acts of refusal targeted at the sexualized and reproductive conditions of women's sexual and (re)productive labor. These were the conditions responsible for reproduction of the relations of production and thus for the entire system of slavery, especially after the closure of the transatlantic slave trade in 1807. After dispensing with Moynihan's report ("a dastardly ideological weapon designed to impair our capacity for resistance by foisting upon us the ideal of male supremacy" [14]), Davis offers a final appeal to her reader (especially to "us" black women) to whom she has demonstrated that the history of slavery matters in the present and for the future.

While historians of slavery rarely cite Davis's essay, presumably regarding it as too undisciplined and far too politicized, most feminist historians have nonetheless implicitly entered into the conversation about the gender of the general strike opened by Du Bois in *Black Reconstruction* and robustly revised for the project of black feminism by Davis.[37] For instance, in 1979 Darlene Clark Hine, one of the foremothers of feminist slavery studies in the United States, questioned the then dominant focus of the field. Following in Davis's footsteps, in Hine's groundbreaking essay "Female Slave Resistance: The Economics of Sex," she called for study of the sexual economy of slavery.[38] Focusing on "black female resistance to slavery," Hine not only positioned enslaved women as insurgents (as had Davis); she provided a systematic understanding of the specific "means through which female slaves expressed their political and economic opposition to the slave system" (123). Delineating three "intimately related forms of resistance"—sexual abstinence, abortion, and infanticide—Hine argued that women's revolt against sexual and reproductive exploitation contributed to the overthrow of the slave system. When "they resisted sexual exploitation . . . [when they] reject[ed] their vital economic function as breeders," female slaves rejected their "role in the economic advancement of the slave system." In undermining the "master's effort to profit from [female slaves] . . . by exploiting [them] sexually" such resistance, though private and individualized, had "major political and economic implications" (126).[39]

Several years later, in the first historical monograph exclusively focused on the experience of female slaves in the plantation South, Deborah Gray White again picked up the thread loosened by Davis.[40] Building on Davis's understanding of the importance of the domestic realm as the site of female slave resistance, and on Hine's argument about the three forms of insurgency enslaved women practiced, White observed that "the jobs and services that slave women performed for the community were not peripheral but central to slave survival" (22), and thus to slave women's collective ability to endure sexual and reproductive dispossession. For this reason, White concluded, although "it is unfortunate" that so much "of what we would like to know about slave women can never be known," there is still much in the archive that allows us to recognize the centrality of slave women in sustaining the slave community and in reproducing fellow slaves not only for the master but also for the struggle. Like Davis, White regards the domestic realm as a crucible of slave women's resistance to slavery and thus of the slave community's resistance. Like Hine, White regards slave women's negotiation of sex and reproduction in bondage as self-defining acts that involved exchange among women, if not always conscious or organized collaboration. Although White does not extensively treat abstinence, abortion, or infanticide (as would a subsequent generation of feminist historians), she famously argues that it was through negotiation of the polarized stereotypes of the hypersexual Jezebel and the fecund Mammy—that is, through negotiation of the gendered ideology that subtended slavery and governed sex and reproduction in slavery— that slave women oriented themselves within and against the slave system.[41] White's insight that passage into motherhood was the defining event in a female slave's life is especially resonant. As she explains, it was as a mother that the female slave anchored herself to a given plantation and created ties with family and fellow slaves, and it was through motherhood that female slaves sustained their participation in the domestic space, transforming it into a space of struggle in which future insurgents in the fight against slavery could be reproduced.[42]

Suffice it to note that Davis, Hine, and White were not alone in their quest to discover and imagine black enslaved women's sexual and reproductive experiences and slave women's insurgent responses to their sexual and reproductive dispossession. By the second half of the 1980s they had been joined by numerous feminist historians who implicitly sought to respond to the question of the gender of the general strike. By the 1990s they had been joined by a new generation of scholars, many of whom were trained by the previous generation.[43] What brings all of black feminism's scholarly contributions to the study of women in slavery into common dialogue is not only a shared quest to understand the experience of slavery, its legacy in the lives of slaves, former slaves, and the descendants of slaves, but also a shared desire to innovate upon one of the most profound ideas embedded within Du Bois's account of slaves as striking "black workers." As Robinson eloquently observed, in *Black Reconstruction* Du Bois revealed that slaves and former slaves need not have been consciously or collectively organized in the traditional Marxist sense in order to become, through their struggle, agents of history.[44] As feminist historians writing about enslaved and formerly enslaved women reveal through their study of resistance to sexual and reproductive bondage, although such resistance was neither consciously nor collectively organized in the manner that was imagined by Marx and Engels (who were thinking about *organized* male industrial workers in Europe), slave women nonetheless possessed profound revolutionary force. As feminist historians reveal, in resisting sexual assault, committing infanticide, attacking and sometimes murdering their abusers, becoming fugitives, aborting or preventing unwanted pregnancies, or electing to mother their children in a manner that refused to allow mothering to be claimed as entirely labor for the master, enslaved women refused their work as sex slaves and breeding wenches. They refused to participate in the reproduction of the slave system, in the smooth reproduction of the relations of production, and in the (re)production of the human commodities that sustained it.

Overall feminist historians show us that the sexual, domestic, and maternal actions of female slaves necessarily reshape received black Marxist understandings of slave work, the black worker, and the strike against slavery. As important, they challenge us to gender as well as racialize each and every additional analytical category that can be and has been used to write the history of slavery, including consciousness and collectivity. When we view slavery from the vantage of enslaved women, we learn that the work performed by the black worker was not only agricultural and domestic but also sexual and reproductive, and that the general strike against the conditions of labor took an array of forms—not only those unanticipated by Marx or Engels but also those that were never fully acknowledged by Du Bois or the scholars of the black radical tradition that have influentially reclaimed Du Bois's work in constructing a genealogy of black Marxism. Indeed we learn that while it is exceedingly difficult to empirically verify whether or not slave women understood individual, intimate acts of refusal of sexual and reproductive dispossession as contributions to the collective overthrow of slave racial capitalism, the existence and persistence of planter counterinsurgency in the form of rape and forced breeding constitutes an excellent index of the impact that slave women's various acts of insurgency against gender-specific dispossession must have continuously exerted. It also constitutes an excellent index of the part that slave women's insurgency must have played in sustaining the slave community's strike against the economic system built upon slave women's reproductive and sexual exploitation.

The Neo-Slave Narrative as Manifesto for Sexual and Reproductive Freedom

Alongside of and then in the wake of the production of scholarship by black feminist historians, black women writers of literary fiction sought to push the limits of conventional historical narratives about slavery by writing counternarratives that corrected the record and imagined its relevance in the current moment of writing. In so doing, they used and innovated on the form of the historical novel, the bildungsroman, and the slave narrative. In her work on literature Saidiya Hartman refers to this sort of black feminist innovation as "critical fabulation" and argues for its centrality to recalibration of relationships between the slave past and the present.[45] Here I specify that such black feminist innovation is crucial to elaboration of black feminism's philosophy of history. Creating what are now commonly referred to in genre criticism as "neo-slave narratives," many black feminists used their skills as writers of fiction to imagine the experience of sexual and reproductive bondage from the vantage point of slave women and to portray the psychic struggles and complex interiority of enslaved women and their children. Utilizing the latitude offered by fiction, these writers entered the battle over the definition of historical truth. By writing novels, they effectively sidestepped the thorny empirical pressures with which their historian colleagues contended (and continue to contend), offering in place of empiricism and positivism *imagined evidence* of enslaved women's insurgency against sexual and reproductive dispossession.

Although male authors such as William Styron, Ishmael Reed, and Charles Johnson also participated in the elaboration of the genre (and in some accounts are credited with the neo-slave narrative's invention), looking back over the past four decades of black literary production, it is clear that black women's neo-slave narratives constitute the genre's dominant and most distinctive formation.[46] On the one hand, black women writers challenged attribution of formal and generic innovation to male writers; on the other hand, they contested the masculinism of the stories told about slavery by focusing on enslaved women and their kin. Materializing the power of story to inaugurate a new propaganda of history, black women writers improvised on and riffed off black feminist historical scholarship, offering to a much wider audience than might read more traditional historical monographs new stories about slavery and alternative narratives and epistemological approaches to the problem of restoring women to historical accounts of slavery. As we shall see in this chapter and the next, in contributing to black feminism's philosophy of history, these writers address themselves to the question of the gender of the general strike and imagine a response to it in and for the moment in which the writer in question, quite literally, sat down to write.

Novels focused on women in slavery, including those by Octavia Butler, Lorene Cary, Michelle Cliff, J. California Cooper, Jewelle Gomez, Nalo Hopkinson, Gayl Jones, Toni Morrison, Dolen Perkins-Valdez, Alice Randall, Alice Walker, and Sherley Anne Williams (to name only some of the most well known), thematize, *without exception*, the experience of sex and reproduction in bondage and home in on enslaved women's refusal of sexual and reproductive extraction. Daring to imagine, *again without exception*, what historical analyses of existing archives cannot readily reveal, these writers describe how individual women's acts of refusal, and the complex and often contradictory feelings that women and children had about these acts, shaped slave existence. As important, in telling stories of women who recode as they refuse sexual and reproductive dispossession, these writers collectively guide their readers toward comprehension of the relationship between the scene of writing (the 1970s, 1980s, and 1990s) and the slave past. In moving us toward new understandings of women in slavery they simultaneously move us toward *felt* awareness of the forms of sexual and reproductive dispossession that persist into the present biocapitalist and neoliberal moment in which these narratives were written and to which they always implicitly and sometimes explicitly respond.

A provisional sketch of the literary terrain reveals that in many neo-slave narratives, constellation of past and present moves in two temporal directions—both backward and forward in time. All such narratives involve more and less literal mechanisms of time travel that allow protagonists and readers alike to move between two significant periods in the solidification of the relationship between racial capitalism and biocapitalism: slavery and the neoliberal present. For instance, in the 1970s Gayl Jones and Octavia Butler presented fictional portraits of modern black women struggling to interrupt intergenerational cycles of slavery's reproduction by self-reflexively questioning their own participation in them. For Jones's and Butler's protagonists, the impulse is to realize and then alter the hold of the slave past on the supposedly emancipated present. Jones's novel *Corregidora* (1975) was published two years after the Supreme Court's passage of *Roe v. Wade* and in the context of the emergence of a women of color reproductive freedom movement spearheaded by black women health activists fighting against sterilization abuse and for expansion of what ought to count as "reproductive freedom." Jones's protagonist, Ursa, wrests control of her sexual and reproductive life from the men who attempt to possess her sexuality and her womb and, in the process, to overdetermine her relationship to her in vivo bodily processes. Specifically Ursa recodes her violently imposed infertility wrought at the hands of one of her lovers, through transformation of her "barrenness" into an embodied revision of three generations of rape, incest, and forced fecundity as experienced by her enslaved female forebears. As Jones details, Ursa's embrace of her infertility expresses itself in her refusal to "make generations." Consequently her repetition, with a difference, of a passed-on story of violent sexual and reproductive dispossession strengthens as it reworks Ursa's connection to her mother, grandmother, and great-grandmother, each of whom, unlike Ursa, has reproduced a girl-child who has been impregnated by the father/master. Straddling her ancestor's slave past and her present through song, Ursa becomes a phonic time-traveler whose chosen art form—singing—replaces childbirth with vocalization. In sum, *Corregidora* responds to the question of the gender of the general strike in the form of a manifesto for freedom from sexual and reproductive exploitation articulated by Jones and her protagonist in the textual and phonic idiom of the blues.

In Butler's celebrated and often taught novel *Kindred* (1979), the narrative is driven by another time-traveling protagonist, Dana. In the conceit of this speculative novel, this supposedly emancipated woman moves between California in the mid-1970s and a nineteenth-century Maryland slave plantation. It appears that Dana is pulled across time by a compulsion to save her white, slave-owning ancestor and, at once, by a deeply felt need to ensure that he father her enslaved female foremother so that Dana may be born several generations later. In a narrative that is focused on the complexity of obtaining freedom in either 1976 (the ironically symbolic year in which the novel opens) or the 1850s and 1860s (the decades in which the historical portions of the novel are set), it is imperative to underscore that securing her conception and birth requires Dana to manipulate the sexual and reproductive life of her enslaved ancestor, Alice. In this sense, Dana's existence and her present "freedom" are predicated on the theft of life from an enslaved woman—and, more particularly still, on Dana's orchestration of this woman's living death, in the form of the sexual and reproductive (ab)use of Alice by Dana's slave-owning great-great-grandfather, a man who regards Alice as his favorite concubine.

While available scholarship on Kindred tends to focus on Dana, Dana's distant progenitor Alice ought to be granted as much if not greater attention. As I elaborate in chapter 4, in which I treat Kindred alongside other writings by Butler, when we read Kindred as a response to the question of the gender of the general strike and thus as a contribution to black feminism's philosophy of history, we must focus on Alice's repeated, often desperate refusal of sexual and reproductive dispossession. When we do so we understand that the trauma of slavery haunts Dana and we simultaneously recognize the sexual and reproductive insurgency that Butler imagines within the claustrophobic confines of the novel. Alice battles to choose her lover and against his murder by her jealous master; she protests her sexual enslavement by her master; she fights to gain control over her children; and, she protests their being stripped from her by taking her body out of sexual and reproductive circulation, once and for all. Though we ought not sanguinely redeem Alice's suicide as an uncomplicated instance of resistance to her sexual and reproductive dispossession, we must situate her actions along a continuum that comprises the infinite forms of refusal of sexual and reproductive dispossession in which slave women were involved. Indeed Alice's insurgency against her master and against Dana's orchestration of Alice's fate are strikes for freedom against the violent exploitation to which Alice is subjected and are, therefore, part and parcel of the general strike against slavery.

Significantly, in 1978, the year prior to Kindred's publication, the successful and healthy birth of the first so-called test-tube baby, Louise Brown, through IVF was widely reported in the international press. As Butler completed her novel, debate about biotechnological engineering of human reproduction burst into popular consciousness courtesy of a combination of intensive popular coverage (Louise Brown was dubbed the "Baby of the Century") and of more focused academic scrutiny.[47] As discussed in chapter 1, it was apparent from the outset that the invention and subsequent consumption of IVF and other related reproductive technologies and services would eventually revolutionize reproductive medicine and lead to a variety of new biotechnological markets and reproductive norms. The fertilization of eggs outside the female body—the technique that enabled Louise Brown's birth—was quickly honed and developed for eager consumers. Within a few years of its introduction as an option, it became routine for women to be impregnated with genetic materials to which they were themselves unrelated, and for (other) women to labor as oocyte vendors and gestational surrogates selling reproductive products and in vivo reproductive labor to those able to purchase such commodities. Within a decade of Louise Brown's birth, a workforce of reproductive laborers had emerged in the United States. As I discussed in chapter 1, within two decades, with the aid of the World Wide Web, the reproductive market initially based in the US expanded globally. Today the full range of reproductive services has been outsourced, driving consumer costs down and enabling a rapidly growing transnational industry. As the celebrated doctors of reproductive medicine, Robert Edwards and Patrick Steptoe, raced to develop the technique that would result in Louise Brown's birth, Butler, along with other black women writers, catalyzed the outpouring of fictions about sex and reproduction in bondage that was, I argue, uniquely positioned to keep pace with these changes in the cultures and politics of human reproduction and thus with changes in racial capitalism precisely because it was complexly keyed to a range of biotechnological and thus biocapitalist developments, as well as to the concurrent neoliberal conflicts and contradictions made visible through the consumption of reproductive products and in vivo labor.

When black women's publication of neo-slave narratives reached its apex in the late 1980s, popular and scholarly outcry over various forms of reproductive exploitation and the emergence of ever-expanding forms of commodification of human reproduction had become loud and insistent. As discussed in chapter 1, when the surrogate mother Mary Beth Whitehead publicly breached contract and refused to turn her baby over to the couple who had paid her to reproduce a child for them, "Baby M" became a household name. As black feminist legal scholars sought to understand the emergence of an in vivo reproductive industry enabled by the advent of reproductive technologies and powered by poor women's reproductive labor and products, they launched a series of sustained arguments against baby selling, against the commodification of human reproductive labor power, and against creation of a class of hyperexploited breeder women, whom, they presciently forecast, would be transformed into a living natural resource by those wealthy enough to pay "other" women to reproduce their children for them.[48]

In an essay on reproductive cultures and politics in the 1990s, written nearly two decades after the initial treatise on enslaved women's insurgency discussed earlier in this chapter, Angela Davis offered an analysis of the current scene that expressly constellated reproduction in the slave past and Davis's present, thus advancing an understanding of the role of surrogacy in establishing a relationship of historical reciprocity between slave racial capitalism and contemporary biocapitalism. Arguing that the historical parallels between motherhood in what Davis referred to as "late capitalism" (and what I specify as biocapitalism) and motherhood in slavery run in two temporal directions simultaneously, Davis suggested that the past of slavery impacts the present, just as current market practices reshape—or at least ought to reshape—our understanding of the past. Davis elaborated, "The reproductive role imposed upon African slave women bore no relationship to the subjective project of motherhood. . . . Slave women were *birth mothers* or *genetic mothers*—to employ terms rendered possible by the new reproductive technologies—but they possessed no legal rights as mothers of any kind. Considering the commodification of their children—indeed, of their own persons—their status was similar to that of the contemporary surrogate mother."[49] In this passage Davis echoes arguments put forward by black feminist legal scholars whose work on the surrogacy/slavery nexus I examined in chapter 1. She also pushes these arguments in an expressly dialectical direction. As Davis explains, surrogacy and the conceptual terminology that it ushered in as it became widespread *necessarily alter understanding of slavery and vice versa.* "The term surrogate mother," Davis observes, "might be invoked as a retroactive description of . . . [slave women's] status because the economic appropriation of their reproductive capacity reflected the ability of the slave economy to produce and reproduce its own laborers" (212). Conversely, although "new technological developments have rendered the fragmentation of maternity more obvious [than it was in the past], the economic system of slavery fundamentally relied upon alienated and fragmented maternities, as women were forced to bear children, whom masters claimed as potentially profitable machines" (213).

Davis's point about the language of surrogacy beautifully encapsulates the black feminist philosophy of history that it has been this chapter's goal to limn. Surrogacy and the rise of the reproductive economy that it signals are connected to slavery not because contemporary surrogacy is performed solely by black women or by the descendants of slaves, or because it is increasingly performed by women living in those regions in the Global South where reproductive labor is today outsourced.[50] Rather surrogacy recalls the long history of slavery because it is in and through the slave episteme that subtended slavery and today subtends biocapitalism that surrogacy became *conceivable* in both senses of this heavily laden term. To cite Dorothy Roberts's concise observation once again, "It is the enslavement of Blacks that enables us to imagine the commodification of human beings, and that makes the vision of fungible breeder women so real."[51] From the perspective of the black feminist philosophy of history to which Davis and all the other thinkers discussed in this chapter contributed, surrogacy and slavery ought not to be analytically separated. They are necessarily bound historically and conceptually. Slavery constitutes surrogacy's irrepressible historical antecedent and its epistemic condition of possibility. To discuss surrogacy without discussing slavery is to disavow the significance of the history of slavery to the analysis of biocapitalism and to potentially lose sight of a history, knowledge of which is essential to creating a more liberated future.

IN THIS CHAPTER I HAVE argued that black feminism's philosophy of history retrieves images of the slave past and recognizes them as present concerns. However, this is not only, as Benjamin would have it, so that these images may be prevented from "disappear[ing] irretrievably" but also so that such images may be set to work in the present and for the future. As if in implicit acknowledgment of the obstacles to creating a philosophy of history that constellates slavery and biocapitalism using social scientific tools alone, at the end of her essay on reproductive cultures and politics in the 1990s Davis invokes Morrison's *Beloved* while discussing slave breeding and its relationship to surrogacy. She indicates that the plight of that novel's protagonist, Sethe, and that of contemporary surrogates ought to be recognized as connected despite the historical distance that would appear to separate them. And, too, she implicitly notices what scores of literary scholars who have treated Morrison's novel have been seemingly unable to fathom. Morrison was not simply telling a story about one woman's experience of motherhood in slavery; she was contributing to the elaboration of black feminism's philosophy of history, arguing for the importance of its methodology in her moment of writing, and at the same time recognizing that this philosophy of history could not be adequately elaborated in any one discursive idiom. As Morrison's contribution made manifest, fiction is a constitutive part of black feminism's polyvocal project.[52]

In the next chapter, I elaborate on this last observation, offering a reading of Morrison's fictionalization of Margaret Garner's escape with her children from slavery (the historical story of insurgency with which the present chapter began) that treats the murder of a "crawling already" baby girl as a story about the slave past that resonates in and through Morrison's present. As we shall see, this was a present in which violent insurgency against sexual and reproductive dispossession animated a wider politics of black feminist refusal and ongoing protest. In elaborating its contribution to black feminism's philosophy of history, I argue that Morrison's novel meditates on the possibilities and pitfalls of laying claim to past acts of violent insurgency in the present and for the future. In this way, it also provides another vantage point from which to see that the slave episteme affords contemporary sex and reproduction both their violence and their grammar.

Chapter Three

VIOLENT INSURGENCY,
or "POWER to the ICE PICK"

The challenge is to transform reproductive work from work
that reproduces people for the market to work that reproduces them for the struggle.

—SILVIA FEDERICI, "THE EXPLOITATION OF WOMEN" (2014)

Although it would be a misreading of Toni Morrison's Pulitzer Prize–winning
novel to argue that it is manifestly preoccupied with reproductive technologies, the emergence of a market in commercial surrogacy, and therefore biocapitalism, this chapter interprets *Beloved* as a meditation on and a mediation
of its moment of production and publication in the 1970s and 1980s. I argue
that *Beloved* necessarily, if implicitly, engages the material transformations in
the meaning and practice of reproduction that the rise of contemporary biocapitalism in these decades augurs. As Morrison explains in her retrospective
2004 foreword, her goal was to write a novel historically truthful and simultaneously keyed to her present. The invention of Sethe, her protagonist, allowed her to plumb Margaret Garner's story for what "was historically true
in essence, but not strictly factual" so as to better relate Garner's story "to
contemporary issues about freedom, responsibility and women's 'place.'"[1]
For Morrison resurrection of the fugitive slave woman who murdered her
daughter to save her from enslavement was a vehicle for interrogation of
the meaning of freedom in the context of slavery and its immediate aftermath and, she expressly tells us, in the 1970s and 1980s. In these decades
women's freedom was being hotly debated by black feminists, especially by
members of the black women's health movement and by those involved in the
movement to end the criminalization of women who defended themselves,

through use of lethal force, from their attackers. The former group had begun to mobilize against the mainstream feminist movement's too narrow focus on abortion by attending to a range of crises, including sterilization abuse, the war on poor black mothers ("crack moms" and "welfare cheats"), and the routine sexual violence to which black women and girls were disproportionately subjected.[2] The latter group, as I discuss in the chapter's final section, had begun to mobilize in support of a number of women of color who were serving prison sentences for acts of violence that were taken in self-defense and against racial disparities in capital punishment and sentencing.

Beloved has principally been read as an account of one enslaved woman's struggle to free her children and herself from slavery. By contrast, I read it as a materially and psychologically attuned account of women's refusal of sexual and reproductive dispossession not only in slavery but also in Morrison's present. In reading Beloved thus, I shift from the dominant scholarly approach, which has centered the representation of motherhood in slavery and its aftermath, to a critical and speculative approach that tracks women's refusal of sexual and reproductive dispossession across time. I read Sethe as a violent insurgent who strikes a substantive blow against slave racial capitalism and biocapitalism, and thus as a freedom fighter, a participant in what I described in chapter 2 as a gendered general strike against slavery. As important, I read Sethe's insurgency and Morrison's representation of it as a contribution to black feminism's philosophy of history, a contribution that Morrison elaborates in and for her present alongside the other black feminist thinkers discussed in chapter 2.

In underscoring Beloved's political function, I hew close to Morrison's stated understanding of the work that literary fiction ideally ought to do. As she explains in "The Site of Memory," her novels are "a kind of literary archeology."[3] Her aim in writing them is to journey back to the past in order "to see what remains were left behind and to reconstruct the world that these remains imply" (302). At the same time, she regards writing as an "imaginative act" (as opposed to an empirical science) in that it relies on "the image" rather than "the fact" when it mobilizes "the world that . . . [the] remains imply" in the interest of social justice. Just as Walter Benjamin urges us to retrieve "images" of the past so that we may create a more liberated future, Morrison urges retrieval of such images because they impart "a kind of truth," not otherwise available. Although fiction is most often understood to be distinct from fact, Morrison finds the opposition disabling. The "real tension," she advises, lies between "fact" and "truth," because "fact can exist without human intelligence, but truth cannot" (303). To get at truth we need fiction, and thus Morrison imaginatively travels from the historical image to the fictional text. In accessing the image of the past she brings to the surface the "route to . . . reconstruction of a world" and to revelation of a "kind of truth" about this world that is relevant in and for the present in which the fiction in question animates the image that has been received (304).

While in "The Site of Memory" Morrison only touches upon Beloved (she obliquely refers to it as "the novel that I'm writing now" [304]), her ideas about the tension between fact and truth shed light on the image of Garner that she retrieves and reworks in Beloved. Based on the extensive historical research on Garner that has been done in the wake of Beloved's publication, it has become clear that far from being fact-based, the novel imaginatively spins the image of Garner into something new. Put otherwise, Morrison's interest is less in historical accuracy (read: fact) than in portrayal of the truth about women's refusal of sexual and reproductive dispossession in the past and in Morrison's moment of writing.[4] As Morrison repeatedly observes, she did little historical research on Garner beyond her initial retrieval of the news article reporting the case, the one that she had previously included in The Black Book (1974), the compendium of black life that she co-edited. As important, throughout Beloved she bends the facts of history to historical truth. Whereas Garner and her children were remanded back to slavery once apprehended by slave catchers, Sethe (although tried and imprisoned prior to the start of Morrison's narrative) ultimately goes free, along with her remaining children. Barbara Christian argues that this fictional revision is significant because it allows Sethe to confront her own actions. I argue that it is also important because it allows otherwise unavailable truths about women's violent insurgency to be surfaced and contemplated by Sethe and the reader alike.[5] Three of these truths animate my discussion: first, the successful nature of Sethe's violent insurgency against slavery; second, Sethe's materialization of an alternative rationality that exposes the irrationality of slave racial capitalism and, by extension, its relationship to biocapitalism; and third, Sethe's painfully earned sense of the collective (or, to put it in Du Boisian terms, "the general") nature of the strike against slavery to which she contributes.

In his influential book The Black Atlantic, Paul Gilroy argues that Garner ought to be placed alongside male slaves such as Frederick Douglass because she used physical violence to contest dehumanization in a similar manner.

Like Douglass, Garner recognized that the master's authority could not be undone without recourse to violence toward his person or property, and thus she too realized the "necessity of violence in the cause of black emancipation." At the same time, Gilroy argues, Garner's story offers a paradigm for theorizing a specifically gendered form of violent insurgency. Her "emancipatory assault on her children" indicates the existence of insurgency expressly grounded in motherhood.[6] Sara Clarke Kaplan extends Gilroy's claim, arguing that Beloved's overlooked contribution is its unflinching reworking of the conventional understanding within slavery studies of the relationships among race, gender, violence, and political subjectivity.[7] Morrison uses the idiom of fiction to represent what, in other contexts, has been rendered unspeakable—namely, the violent acts to which women made recourse as they fought the system of slavery. Building off prior work by Hortense Spillers and Gayatri Chakravorty Spivak, Clarke Kaplan concludes that dominant historiography has depended on erasure of enslaved and subaltern women's violent agency, or what Spillers calls their "monstrosity."[8] Gilroy's call for attention to the gendered paradigm embedded in Garner's actions and Clarke Kaplan's critique of the erasure of female violence in dominant historiography resonate here. And yet my argument is distinct. While Gilroy turns to Garner's story and Clarke Kaplan to Morrison's revision of it in order to challenge historical knowledge production about the nature of slave women's insurgency, I turn to Morrison's novel to explore how Morrison's representation of violent insurgency challenges not only dominant conceptions of the slave past but also our imagination of the role of women's violent insurgency in the present—the biocapitalist, neoliberal present in which Morrison felt it imperative to transform Garner's story into Sethe's. For as already pointed out, in Morrison's hands, Garner's story morphs into one in which violent actions move a woman and her children toward freedom (rather than back into slavery), however psychologically complex this freedom may be for the insurgent and her kin.

In advancing this reading I do not mean to diminish the grief or trauma that critics routinely attribute to Sethe and treat as aftereffects of slavery as experienced by a putatively free woman who, in so many ways, is still bound. Relatedly, I do not wish to sidestep the lasting psychological wound inflicted on Sethe by her murder of her daughter and her attempted murder of her two sons. The novel demands to be read as an exploration of the enduring impact of past actions on the agents of such actions and as a critique of platitudes about the availability of freedom from violence and dehumaniza-tion for those who escaped from slavery or were manumitted. As all analy-ses correctly observe, the novel reveals the persistent impact of slavery on individual, familial, and collective consciousness and extends discussion of this impact to the psychological, often unconscious ravages experienced by slaves and their descendants in the wake of the failure of Reconstruction. Yet I am also inclined to follow those few scholars who have insisted that *Beloved* comments on Morrison's present by commenting on the slave past, and that the novel in this way begs a series of questions about the meaning of Morrison's return to Garner in the 1970s and 1980s.[9] In so doing, I focus this chapter closely on what *Beloved* discloses about the psychological cost of violence on insurgents and their children, and on what it tells us about the importance of recalling women's violent insurgency in and for the pres-ent. Although one of *Beloved*'s important contributions is clearly its reprisal of Garner's story, what has far less often been acknowledged is the novel's sympathetic representation of a violent agent of change—an insurgent slave woman through whom readers may entertain questions about the role of violence in the struggle for substantive freedom in Morrison's present and, too, in their own.

Whereas abolitionists jumped to celebrate Garner as an iconic freedom fighter, in transforming Garner into Sethe, Morrison moves contemporary readers beyond iconicity and political symbolism and toward critical en-gagement with insurgent violence. She does so by imbuing readers with the capacity to sit with Sethe's actions without condemning them and by plac-ing readers face to face with Sethe's humanity, as opposed to her supposed animal instincts, the "characteristics" that are attributed to her by School Teacher and his nephews. She emboldens us to hold two competing but never mutually exclusive ideas: Sethe's violent insurgency constitutes a ra-tional response in a situation of crisis, and this is so even though the cost in human life of Sethe's actions and the psychological wounds that are their remainder are profound. In a watershed essay written shortly after *Beloved*'s publication, Mae Henderson offers a related observation: Morrison "nei-ther condemns nor condones, but rather 'delivers' her protagonist" to her readers.[10] Building on this insight I observe that Morrison presents the hy-pocrisy of the legal questions that would have been adjudicated by the court in which Garner was tried had she been tried for murder (as opposed to theft of self and progeny) precisely by refusing inclusion of Sethe's trial in her nar-rative. In refusing to depict the fact of Garner's trial, Morrison focuses the reader on the historical truth: insurgent rationality can successfully alter the course of history—in this case, by moving a fugitive slave mother and her children closer to freedom.

Sethe's insurgent rationality is nowhere more starkly represented than in the passage in which Morrison describes her internal response to her lover Paul D's question about her murder of her "crawling already" baby girl. As Sethe spins and wheels "round and round the room" while narrating her story, it is what she does not say as much as what she does say to Paul D that informs Morrison's portrait of the woman and her deed. On the outer edge of the circle that Sethe creates are assertions of proud motherhood. She tells Paul D of her numerous quotidian efforts, while enslaved, to keep her toddling children out of trouble on the Sweet Home plantation where she and Paul D were captive. And, too, she tells him that by running away she freed herself to successfully bring her milk to her children and in so doing to put a stop to School Teacher's and his nephews' theft of her life-giving fluid through what can be regarded as a nursing rape. As Sethe moves toward her circle's center—the place we expect to be occupied by an answer to Paul D's question—she asserts her sense of triumph in having engineered her own and her children's escape: "I did it. I got us all out" (190).[11] In so saying, Sethe attributes agency to herself and expressly links her capacity to act to her possession of an alternative rationality that has allowed her to recognize her "claim" to self and kin as legitimate. As Sethe boasts, all "got . . . out" on account of "me using my own head" (190). Use of her "own head" is also connected by Sethe to acquisition of new feelings—feelings she was unable to fathom when enslaved. Upon arrival and reunion with her children at Baby Suggs's house at 124 Bluestone Road, Sethe recalls that she "felt good. Good and right" but also expansive: "when I stretched out my arms all my children could get in between. I was that wide. Look like I loved them more after I got there. Or maybe I couldn't love 'em proper in Kentucky because they wasn't mine to love. But when I got there . . . there wasn't nobody in the world I couldn't love if I wanted to" (191). Though Paul D does not respond directly, he clearly understands Sethe's meaning. Recalling revelations he had had while incarcerated on a Georgia chain gang, he observes, "You protected yourself and loved small"; when free, when no longer in need of "permission for desire," you had "big love," love that amounted to "freedom" (191).

As Sethe continues to circle Paul D and his question, she too has a revelation. She suddenly "knows" that she will "never close in, pin it down for anybody who had to ask. . . . Because the truth was simple" (192). Her conviction about "the truth" is so strong that it resists capture in discourse. It requires neither ratification through verbalization nor reception by another person because the truth resides in the flesh. Indeed, it is predicated on possession of a rationality so deeply seated in Sethe's maternal body that it manifests itself directly in the movements this body makes as it launches into action in time and space. Capturing the irrelevance of metacognition (and thus discourse) to production of the insurgent rationality that compelled Sethe's act of infanticide, Morrison writes, "if she thought anything" as School Teacher and his nephews entered her yard to claim her children and take them back to Sweet Home, "it was No. No. Nonono. Simple. She just flew. Collected every bit of life she had made, all the parts of her that were precious and fine and beautiful, and carried, pushed, dragged them through the veil, out, away, over there where no one could hurt them" (192).

In this oft-cited passage, "every bit of life" is equated with "all the parts of her that were precious," such that Sethe's children become indistinguishable from herself. This act of reclamation of her right to motherhood and to her children is of course an express refusal of the doctrine of *partus sequitur ventrem*, the predication of a mother's dispossession and a child's enslavement on the fact of birth from an enslaved womb, and thus the doctrine around which, I argued in chapter 2, slavery necessarily turned. The act of bringing her "parts" into safe harbor is a movement from one space to another, a movement "through the veil" and thus from a space of enslavement to a space of freedom that is also, by necessity, a space of death in a context in which slavery remained the law of the land. Signifying on one of Du Bois's most famous metaphors, Morrison casts "the veil" through which she drags her children as double-edged: it produces the death-dealing divide between black and white worlds, the worlds of the enslaved and the free, and it is also a source of revelation. In Du Bois's account of the death of his infant son in Georgia in *The Souls of Black Folk* (1903) he describes Burghardt as residing, in death, "above the Veil," in a zone mercifully free of racism. Morrison's invocation of the veil suggests that Sethe's dead child also resides above it. Beloved's death is in Sethe's mind nothing short of "a mercy" precisely because the insurgent rationality upon which Sethe's murderous action is based effectively liberates Beloved from enslavement.[12]

There is an instructive break in Sethe's circling at the point in her narration when she tells Paul D that she has taken her children "through the veil," and thus too there are ellipses in Morrison's representation of Sethe's words and actions. Consequently—and as Sethe had predicted in the internal monologue to which readers are privy—she never right out tells Paul D that she murdered her child in order to grant her freedom above the veil; rather she indicates this by reiterating that she successfully prevented School Teacher and his nephews from remanding her children back to slavery. "I stopped him," she concludes by way of non sequitur. "I took my babies where they'd be safe" (193). As Saidiya Hartman has argued in the context of a discussion of slave narratives, "The dashes, the ellipses, and circumlocutions hint at the excluded term by way of the bodies of slave women." In Beloved, as in the historical archives that Hartman mines, Sethe's maternal body constitutes a textual enigma "pregnant with the secrets of slavery."[13] While Paul D refuses to read the maternal body's secreted truths and instead offers a judgment of Sethe that is immediate and dehumanizing ("What you did was wrong. . . . You got two feet, Sethe, not four" [194]), Morrison positions readers to respond to Sethe differently. We are horrified that in Sethe's world—that of the Fugitive Slave Act—killing one's child could be merciful, and thus we find that we can neither animalize nor criminalize Sethe. Instead we are left to search within her actions for other meanings. As we do so, we perceive the insurgent rationality that subtends navigation of an irrational system, and we begin to understand that Sethe has not only imagined but also actualized a challenge to this system by responding to systemic irrationality with an alternative rationality finely calibrated to her moment of crisis. We come to see that the act of infanticide is keyed to the specific violence that slavery exacted upon those whom it sought to strip of humanity. And we come to see that Sethe's actions must therefore tangle with the definition of human life as property in order to subvert the system that commodifies life itself.[14] We see, as Spillers has observed, that slave women asserted the contrapuntal "law of the mother" in claiming ownership over their children and thus refusing a system of human commodification powered by the forced reproduction of slave women's kinlessness.[15]

In representing Sethe's alternative rationality thus, Morrison posits it as both situational and insurgent. It is grounded in a sensibility that is uncomfortable, almost intolerable to contemplate but nonetheless reasonable when contextualized within the irrational circumstances to which it opposes itself. In this sense, Morrison compels us to consider what many still do not want to admit: the widespread perception that an economic and social system predicated on transforming women into breeders and children into chattel was deemed entirely rational, not to mention legal. This is the brutal common sense of slavery that is extoled by School Teacher, expressed in his lessons to his nephews, and starkly revealed when he arrives at 124 Bluestone Road to find Sethe in the woodshed with her murdered child in her arms living amid people whom School Teacher can only conceive of as "crazy nigger[s]" (175–76). As Morrison expresses it, in language that acknowledges the common sense on which School Teacher's rationality is based, "It was clear [to him], there was nothing there to claim. The three . . . pickaninnies they had hoped were alive and well enough to take back to Kentucky . . . to do the work Sweet Home desperately needed, were not [alive and well enough to take back]. [And] . . . the woman . . . having ten breeding years left . . . she'd gone wild" (175–76).[16] Expressly aligning Sethe with a domesticated animal "gone wild" and casting her "pickaninnies" as property ruined beyond reclamation, School Teacher concludes that Sethe has become so feral she is capable of biting "your hand clean off" (176). As in response to Paul D's judgment, in response to the scene of infanticide we find ourselves allied with Baby Suggs: we cannot "approve or condemn Sethe's rough choice" (212).[17] However, in contrast to Baby Suggs, whose "marrow weariness" (212) sets in after the trial that ensues and who elects to "up and quit" (208), to stop preaching self-possession and self-love to the former slaves who had once eagerly gathered in the Clearing to hear her speak "the Word," readers are called upon to respond otherwise. After all, we have the luxury of retrospection that allows for a modicum of distance from the immediate crisis produced by Sethe's actions, at least to the extent that we find ourselves able to eschew false oppositions (right and wrong, good and evil) and to avoid some of the "marrow weariness" that prevented Baby Suggs from fully acknowledging Sethe's complex success.[18]

Significantly Marx understood the power of insurgency in the face of crisis in a way that resonates with Sethe's understanding. He recognized that crises are always viewed as irrational by those set on maintaining the hegemony. And, too, he understood that violent insurgency against the prevailing mode of production is invariably perceived as irrational by those who benefit from the system—those involved in the preservation of its appearance of rationality and thus its hegemony. By contrast, for those fighting for freedom from the system, "the crisis" constitutes an opportunity for radical change. It represents the surfacing of the system's internal contradictions and thus it opens the possibility for robust transformation, perhaps even defeat of the system and its replacement by something new. As Stuart Hall has argued, building off Marx's insights in the black Marxist fashion celebrated by Cedric Robinson and discussed in chapter 2, crisis represents a historical opportunity for a new form of reason to prevail and thus for what first appears as an alternative rationality (and therefore an apparent irrationality) to take its place as a new rationality and, ideally, as a new iteration of hegemony.[19] In the same way that society gains wide access to the striking workers' common sense once the strike is over and the eight-hour day established as the new norm, our understanding of Sethe's rationality is cultivated across the arc of a narrative that functions pedagogically to incrementally immerse us in an understanding of the irrationality of Sethe's world and the rationality of her violent refusal of it. Indeed it is accurate to suggest that most readers come to recognize her insurgency as an expression of what Robin Kelley would call a "freedom dream."

The majority of scholars writing on Beloved in the decades since its publication have emphasized the end of the novel, and here I follow suit. Whereas the overwhelming critical tendency has been to read the events that conclude the narrative—Beloved's exorcism, Denver's move out into the community, and the reunion of Sethe and Paul D—as evidence of "psychological healing," of a laying to rest of the brutalities of the past, my approach is somewhat different.[20] I do not dispute that key characters emerge at the novel's end from the depths of their pain through the process by which each has differently engaged Beloved (as longed-for sister, predatory lover, and lost daughter); however, I urge close attention to the fact that Sethe's violent insurgency and associated pain are not so much put behind her as left in medias res. Sethe is represented neither as psychologically whole (whatever this would mean) nor as repentant for her actions. She never stands down from her assertion of their necessity and thus their reasonableness. Rather Morrison allows Sethe's actions to persistently if perversely loom over the text as a utopian wish, as an insistence on the existence of a freedom more substantive than that which is currently on offer. As Sethe reflects to herself (employing language that reprises her earlier dialogue with Paul D), "No no, nobody on this earth, would list her daughter's characteristics on the animal side of the paper. No. Oh no. . . . Sethe had refused—and refused still" (296, emphasis added).

Morrison's verb choice (refuse) is instructive and allusive. The political theorist Kathi Weeks points out that Marxist autonomists recognize and theorize insurgency beyond organized (union) action, and therefore focus on the refusal of work rather than on its reform. In refusing the rationality of the capitalist system that presents work as the only way to make meaning in life, autonomists create a new understanding of the role that work plays in defining the subject and in freeing the subject.[21] For autonomists, freedom is a practice and a process, not a possession or a goal. It is never reducible to the freedom to elect to work for a wage or to be free of some measure of the exploitation that labor (whether paid or unpaid) entails. Rather freedom is a line of flight, a practice of world building that requires recasting the role of labor in life, including the role of reproductive labor and motherhood (at least for autonomist *feminists* the latter is true). From the autonomist perspective the end to slavery (autonomists are thinking exclusively about wage slavery; here I substitute chattel slavery) is realized only through full-scale reconceptualization of social reproduction, through dismantling of the system that organizes the distribution of life itself. Throughout this chapter and elsewhere in this book I use the term *refusal* to describe slave women's insurgent actions and Garner's and Sethe's acts of infanticide. In so doing I follow Morrison in casting violent insurgency as refusal of sexual and reproductive dispossession, and thus as refusal of the relations of (re)production on which slavery is predicated. Refusal uniquely captures the insurgent rationality that challenges the (ir)rationality that undergirds slave racial capitalism and the central role that the extraction of women's reproductive labor played in subtending it. As Weeks expresses it, "The refusal of work is a model of resistance, both to the modes of work that are currently imposed . . . and to their ethical defense, and [refusal is] a struggle for a different relationship to work . . . born from collective autonomy."[22]

Just as important as Morrison's representation of refusal is her keying of Sethe's psychological journey to an emergent sense of the existence of a larger collectivity, a group of insurgent women who have, like Sethe, refused slave racial capitalism and the sexual and reproductive dispossession that subtends it. Sethe accesses these women through "rememory," specifically through rememory of the part taken by each in the general strike against slavery. Notably this group of enslaved women does *not* coincide with "the community of women" about which other literary critics have written. To be clear, I am not referring to the women who move down Bluestone Road en masse to exorcise Beloved from 124. Rather the group of women that interests me comprises violent insurgents who have each engaged in infanticide and thus, like Sethe, have risked everything in refusing sexual and reproductive dispossession. As Christian, reminds us, *Beloved* is "replete with examples of slave women who killed children" (42). What must be added to this reminder is twofold: Sethe's journey entails gaining a *sense* (as opposed to consciousness) of her solidarity with other "slave women who killed children," and Sethe's sense of solidarity with these women can and ought to be read—like the black feminist philosophy of history expressed throughout the novel that manifests this sensibility—as analeptic and proleptic. It is analeptic in that it is a function of Sethe's ability to move back into slavery from the 1870s and to connect, through rememory, with other women who have committed infanticide. It is about an(other) insurgent woman's ability to express a feeling of solidarity with Sethe. And it is proleptic in that it is about the readers' emergent understanding of the rationality of Sethe's actions in Morrison's present and, too, the moment of reading.

The first time it becomes clear that Sethe senses she is not alone but part of a collectivity is when Beloved draws her into a rememory of Nan, a woman who knew Sethe's mother during the middle passage and later helped to care for Sethe. What Sethe rememories is Nan telling her of Sethe's mother's multiple acts of infanticide.[23] Significantly this rememory of Nan and thus of Sethe's mother is elicited by Beloved's incessant questioning, by her demand that Sethe tell her story to Beloved so that Beloved may greedily immerse herself in Sethe's words. Nan recalls that as she and Sethe's mother were hauled across the Atlantic they were "taken up many times by the crew" (74) and raped. What Nan wants Sethe to know is that her mother (and Nan too?) "threw them all away but you. The one from the crew she threw away on the island. The others from more whites she also threw away. Without names, she threw them. You she gave the name of the black man. She put her arms around him. The others she did not put her arms around. Never. Never. Telling you. I am telling you, small girl Sethe" (74). While Sethe recalls that as a "small girl" she was "unimpressed" by Nan's disclosure, in Sethe's rememory of their exchange she finds herself newly and deeply impacted. She is "angry" and she is also overcome by a desire for connection with a (m)other woman that is expressed as a "mighty wish for Baby Suggs" (74). When Sethe reflects on these paired feelings she is uncertain about their source, and therefore as readers we are left with questions: Is Sethe angry with Nan for burdening her with a traumatic image that can be so readily "bumped" into? Is she angry with her mother for her murderous or life-giving actions? Or, alternatively, is Sethe angered by the injustice of her mother's situation, a situation that resonates with her own?

The use of the word *angry* and Morrison's description of Sethe's desire for connection with a (m)other woman together compel consideration of the possibility that Sethe's feelings are called forth by identification with her mother (and with Nan?), and thus that these feelings constitute an inchoate response to a sense of connection that has been heretofore unobserved. Although we can presume, as Christian does, that there is a distinction to be made between Sethe's murder of Beloved and her mother's acts of infanticide—only Sethe kills for "the sake of a child she knows and loves rather than . . . against the rapist slaveowner"—the idea that mother-love and violent insurgency are somehow distinct, antagonistic, or mutually exclusive does not hold up.[24] Sethe's actions cannot be reduced to mother-love; they also express insurgent rationality that undoes the system itself. Likewise Sethe's mother's actions cannot be reduced to resistance; they also express mother-love. Put otherwise, all acts of infanticide are complexly targeted at the contradictions that subtend reproduction in bondage regardless of whether reproduction results from rape or, as in Seth's case, is the result of a sexual relationship with a chosen lover.[25] And thus we are left to conclude that Sethe's feelings— her anger and her "mighty wish" for connection to a (m)other woman—are sparked by a shared gender-specific injustice and by an emergent structure of feeling among those who have also experienced this injustice *despite the differences* that might superficially separate insurgents from one and other, Sethe's mother and Nan included.

As will be noted by some, I borrow a term developed by Marxist literary scholar Raymond Williams in suggesting that Sethe's anger and her "mighty wish" for connection constitute a "structure of feeling." As Williams explains, the term connotes an inchoate affective formation that, while experienced as individual and private, is nonetheless linked to pervasive material conditions and, thus, by necessity, may be on the verge of expressing a shared set of social relations. This is so, Williams explains, even though the individual experiencing and expressing the feeling in question may not (yet) be conscious (or perhaps may never become conscious) of the sociality therein embedded.[26] Though Sethe's affective response is neither consciously understood by Sethe nor in any way the product of consciously articulated collectivity, I am suggesting that it necessarily indexes deeply felt opposition to the hegemony and her sense of and longing for affinity with other enslaved and formerly enslaved women who have created life and refused its commodification through acts of infanticide.[27]

If Sethe moves toward the (m)other women through rememory, Ella (a woman who is initially the most vociferous in her rejection of Sethe) moves toward Sethe in the process of coming to terms with her own violent insurgent past. Ella's movement toward Sethe is precipitated by contemplation of Sethe's situation and her own growing sense of the similitude between her own and Sethe's actions. Although readers do not immediately comprehend why Ella's judgment of Sethe is so harsh ("I ain't got no friends that take a handsaw to their own children" [221]) or why she appears to suddenly change her mind about Sethe, we eventually come to understand that Ella's antipathy toward Sethe represents a displacement of feelings about her own past onto Sethe. And, too, we come to understand that Ella's change of heart represents her recognition that Sethe is as psychologically haunted by her past actions as is Ella.

Ella's story begins to unfold in a chapter in which Sethe queries Beloved about her origins—her mother, her people, and "what kind of whites" she has fled (140). Before Sethe identifies Beloved as her murdered daughter returned, she imagines that this beautiful, amnesic young woman has escaped from a situation similar to Ella's, a situation so traumatic that it has precipitated Beloved's "disremembering," her inability to recall anything specific about her past, and thus her inability to remember any detail that might allow Sethe to help Beloved reconnect with her people.[28] As Sethe explains to Denver, "Beloved has been locked up by some whiteman for his own purposes, and never let out the door." Sethe continues in the form of an internal monologue that pulls her into recollection of other, similar stories: "Something like that had happened to Ella except it was two men—a father and son—and Ella remembered every bit of it. For more than a year, they kept her locked in a room for themselves" (141). In the last section of the novel readers discover that Ella has orchestrated the death of the child born of rape, for though she delivered "a hairy white thing, fathered by the 'lowest yet,'" she refused to nurse it (305). While on the surface Ella's actions are akin to Sethe's mother's (both women murder infants that are products of rape), Ella and Sethe are also affiliated through this recollection despite the initial hesitance to compass their connection. Indeed, when we reread the novel with the story of Ella's past in mind, it becomes retrospectively evident that Ella senses (though she does not cognate) her connection to Sethe from the moment she first encounters her.[29] In this way, Ella's evolving feelings about Sethe mirror as they resonate with Sethe's affective response to her rememory of Nan and the story that Nan tells to Sethe about her mother. And thus it becomes less surprising when Ella's vitriol toward Sethe transforms into empathy, and then mutates further into an expression of solidarity that materializes in her acting on Sethe's behalf.

As is invariably discussed by critics, at the end of the novel it is Ella who decides, upon learning that Beloved has come back "in the flesh" to haunt Sethe, that she cannot abide the past "taking possession of the present" (302).

And it is Ella who moves into action to protect Sethe, gathering together and then leading a group of thirty women down Bluestone Road to 124, where they commence the ululations that allow them to "take a step back to the beginning" (305) and together perform a powerful, wordless exorcism ("the sound that broke the back of words" [308]) that functions to release Sethe from the murderous grip of Beloved and the past. In most readings of the novel, this narrative resolution is read as transformative or "healing," and this makes some sense. The exorcism releases Sethe from continued starvation and, presumably, from some of the mental anguish accompanying her cohabitation with Beloved, and thus with her past incarnate. It also profoundly impacts Sethe's teenage daughter, Denver, who is henceforth released from her heretofore isolated life in a house with her ostracized mother and liberated to venture forth and engage with the wider world by becoming a known and cared for member of the community of women gathered on Bluestone Road.

And yet, to reduce interpretation of the complex material and metaphysical events that close the book to personal transformation or psychic healing (Sethe's or Denver's) erases the robust political content of the violent insurgency by which Sethe and Ella are bound in and through these events. It also erases a shared (re)assertion of the rationality of commitment to violent insurgency as, in certain circumstances, both necessary and effective. This shared sensibility is most poignantly expressed in the elaborate dance that ensues between the two women in the scene that transpires when Bodwin arrives at 124 to inform Sethe that she must move from the house that she and Denver have taken on from Baby Suggs years earlier. In these closing pages Morrison describes Sethe's attack on Bodwin, the abolitionist who, eighteen years earlier, had argued before the court for Sethe's freedom.[30] Crucially, she also describes with instructive precision Ella's intervention into this attack—she "clipped [Sethe] . . . put her fist in her jaw" [312]—noting that Ella's decisive action prevents Sethe from stabbing Bodwin with a hand that has been transformed into an "ice pick." Indeed, this blow is *the decisive action* that prevents Sethe from being brought before a court for a second time in her relatively short life.

Critics have neglected the violent insurgent solidarities forged among women at the novel's end, preferring instead to focus on the community that emerges among the women who have gathered on Bluestone Road. Consequently almost all critical focus has been on the collective catharsis rather than on the radical connection that is forged between Ella and Sethe as they contend with Bodwin and all he represents. This has had the unfortunate effect of obscuring recognition of the shared structure of feeling that is compelled by (and perhaps compels) acts of violent insurgency. It has also had the unfortunate effect of foreclosing recognition of the radical political content of what, I have just argued, is too often elevated as narrative resolution or "healing" at novel's end.[31] While I do not dispute that Morrison paints a portrait of female community among the women on Bluestone Road, in concluding this chapter I attend to the uncomfortable but, in my view, more significant structure of feeling that Morrison depicts, and to the seemingly small action—Ella's refusal of Sethe's attack on Bodwin when Ella puts "her fist in her jaw"—through which a quite different, albeit more inchoate solidarity is expressed. For as we shall see, the nuanced dance, the back-and-forth between Ella and Sethe (and Sethe and Nan, and through Nan, Sethe and Sethe's mother), not only brings Ella and Sethe face to face with each other and with the past, it also materializes black feminism's philosophy of history.

In some of the most interesting criticism, Sethe's attack on Bodwin is thought to cite and revise her earlier attack on her children in the woodshed, the attack that results in Beloved's death and in Sethe's and her children's eventual manumission. This criticism is premised on the idea that when Sethe gets it "wrong" by mistaking Bodwin for School Teacher (both men wear hats and enter her yard uninvited), she effectively gets it absolutely right.[32] In attacking Bodwin, whose prior work on her behalf has done little to provide Sethe or her children with substantive freedom, she realizes the hidden connection between the slave owner and the abolitionist, affirming through her mistake of one for the other that Bodwin is, in the words of James Berger, "a vain and self-absorbed man whose chief interest in abolitionism may have been the feelings of moral elevation and political excitement he derived from the movement personally."[33] As some critics further argue, in rechanneling rage against the white master toward the white abolitionist, Sethe reveals the inner complicity between slavery and liberalism.[34] Building on this reading, it is also possible to argue that Sethe's attack on Bodwin constitutes an affirmation of the politically salient results of insurgent rationality expressed as violent insurgency, while Ella's "fist in her jaw" constitutes an affirmation of insurgency's effectivity in creating solidarities among women.

When Sethe's attack on Bodwin and Ella's refusal of it are read thus, we can see that what has not been adequately addressed elsewhere is how the nuanced dance between these women resonates in Morrison's moment of writing. In addition to citing and revising the episode in the woodshed, Ella's infanticide, and Sethe's mother's (and Nan's?) many acts of refusal, this nuanced dance also cites and revises a far more recent act of refusal of sexual and reproductive dispossession and the collective feminist response to it. I refer to a murder committed by Joan (aka Joann or Joanne) Little, a twenty-year-old black prisoner, incarcerated in Washington, North Carolina, who, in 1974, stabbed the sixty-two-year-old white male jailer, Clarence Alligood, who entered her cell to rape her; the feminist campaign that rose up in support of Little; and the ensuing feminist movement that sought to expose the routine violence to which black women, especially prisoners such as Little, were subjected, and to secure the right of all women to act in self-defense against attackers attempting to dispossess them of their sexual and reproductive autonomy.

Although it may be argued that it is merely coincidental that Morrison places Joan Little's weapon of choice into Sethe's hands—it was with an *ice pick* that Little defended herself against Alligood, just as it is with her hand turned into an *ice pick* that Sethe attacks Bodwin—the shared weapon and shared sentiment of the two women establishes a historical web of intertextual and radical political connections that stretch across time and reveal continuities that otherwise would be unavailable.[35] These include connections between the 1870s and the 1970s, especially those between the insurgent women represented in *Beloved* and the real-life black feminist supporters of Little among whom Morrison can be situated. Put otherwise, when Sethe attacks Bodwin her actions enliven epistemological relationships between black women's response to sexual and reproductive exploitation in the past and their response to sexual and reproductive dispossession in the decades during which black feminist cultural production was most robust. These are also the three decades during which racial liberalism and postracial neoliberalism prevailed and in turn came to buttress the recalibration and refinement of the relationship of historical reciprocity between slave racial capitalism and biocapitalism.

The historians Danielle McGuire, Emily Thuma, and Christina Greene, among others, have demonstrated that Joan Little was one of four related legal cases around which antiracist feminist activists gathered as they sought to redefine rape as a crime of violence, aggression, humiliation, and power, to develop arguments for women's right to self-defense against sexual assault, including use of lethal violence, and to call for an end to the discriminatory treatment of people of color in the criminal justice system.[36] The Little case in particular drew national attention when Angela Davis joined the campaign to free Little, giving speeches, helping Little prepare for trial, and publishing an article on the case in Ms. Magazine that circulated widely.[37] In this rhetorical tour de force (one that Davis argues she was compelled to write on "personal grounds" after having been supported by so many in her own struggle against unjust incarceration) she invokes the long history, dating back to slavery, of black women's criminalization and subjection to sexual and reproductive dispossession at the hands of white men.[38] She calls out, as had Ida B. Wells-Barnett before her, the manner in which the scapegoating of black men as rapists constitutes a hypocritical response to (and disavowal of) the history of white men's routine sexual and reproductive abuse of black women. She thus places Little's insurgency within a longer history of black women's refusal of sexual and reproductive dispossession, effectively creating a genealogy that stretches back to slavery and forward to Davis's moment of writing, in which, she notes, insurgency "crystallized into a militant campaign" against white men's rape of black women and other women of color (154).

Davis's analysis of the Little case resonates with her previous and subsequent writings on rape. It stresses the impossibility of understanding rape without recognizing that the "one feature" of all rape that remains constant over time is "the overt and flagrant treatment of women . . . as property" (154). Though Davis concedes that particular cases "express different modes in which women are handled as property," she also avers that without an understanding of sexual aggression's persistent linkage to the property system imposed by capitalism, rape "cannot be successfully challenged." In cases in which a white man rapes a black woman, Davis specifies, rape must be regarded as a "weapon in the arsenal of racism," a tool used to impress authority over another human being that reduces the other to property and thus recalls the slave master's "tyrannical possession of slave women as chattel" (154). As in Davis's historical writings on the rape of slave women that I treated in chapter 2, in the Ms. Magazine article Davis's analysis of historical continuity in the dialectic of insurgency against sexual and reproductive dispossession and white male counterinsurgency is instructive. It allows us to recognize that when Morrison places into Sethe's hands the same weapon that Little used to kill her white male attacker, she implicitly links Sethe's attack on Bodwin and School Teacher (attacks on the property system and the commodified notion of freedom on which liberalism depends) to Little's attack on her jailer. In so doing Morrison shows us that there is no rational distinction that can be made among Bodwin, School Teacher, and Alligood.

In attacking such men Sethe and Little implicate liberalism, (slave) racial capitalism, and biocapitalism as together complicit in the perpetuation of the sexual and reproductive dispossession that began in slavery and continues to inform the present—a doubled or constellated present that belongs to Sethe and to Little, to Angela Davis and to Toni Morrison, and to the millions of readers of Morrison's epic novel about sex, reproduction, and motherhood. Put otherwise, it is with a hand turned ice pick and an ice pick turned weapon of liberation that Morrison constellates slave women's violent insurgency and Little's violent insurgency. Just as it is with the image of a hand turned ice pick and an ice pick turned weapon of liberation that she materializes black feminism's philosophy of history and in so doing constellates the slave past with the present moment of writing, effectively connecting both to subsequent moments in which readers of Beloved receive the image of insurgent refusal that they pull from the pages of Beloved in their present.

In concluding this chapter I offer the speculative provocation that the slogan "Power to the Ice Pick," emblazoned on the T-shirts worn by Little's supporters in 1975, might well have been scrawled across a makeshift banner held high in the air by Ella as she rallied the forces and marched down Bluestone Road to 124. For Ella not only calls upon the women she amasses to surround and then pile upon Sethe so that she is unable to reach Bodwin and sink her weapon into his flesh; Ella flies into action beside Sethe, expressing her sense of solidarity with Sethe's insurgency by "clipping her" with a "fist in her jaw" so that she can prevent Sethe from being subjected, once again, to criminalization for an entirely rational response to sexual and reproductive dispossession. In this reading we must recognize that although Sethe may not entirely understand what transpires as it transpires (addled as she is by starvation and by Beloved's hold upon her body and mind), Ella understands it well. As Morrison observes, Ella had "thought it through" (301). She rallies the forces because she has already come to a conclusion: like herself, Sethe is capable of violent insurgency when confronted by the dehumanizing injustice of a system that turns women into sexual objects and breeders and transforms their children into property. Indeed Ella's actions express an emergent awareness that in the past she and Sethe participated in gendering the general strike against slavery and that they remain ready to strike against sexual and reproductive dispossession or, more globally, against the reproductive afterlife of slavery as it expresses itself in the compact between liberalism and private property, slave racial capitalism and biocapitalism. Unlike Baby

Figure 3.1 T-shirt owned by Marjory Nelson. Creator unknown. Image courtesy of the Sophia Smith Collection, Smith College, Northampton, Massachusetts.

Suggs, whose marrow weariness takes over, Ella still has the fight in her. As Morrison explains, Ella is moved to action by the feeling that no woman deserves to be haunted by her insurgent past, nor, for that matter, to be victimized or criminalized for refusing sexual and reproductive dispossession. Ella, Morrison concludes, had "been beaten every way but down" (305).

When we read the feeling that compels Ella, we find it is proleptically (and uncannily) scripted by the lyrics to a song written by the legendary singer-activist Bernice Johnson Reagon, a Little supporter and member of the Free Joan Little campaign. In 1975 (the year after Morrison published the article on Garner in *The Black Book*) Reagon crooned the following chorus to the crowds that gathered to rally in Little's defense:

Joanne Little, she's my sister
Joanne Little, she's our mama . . .
Joanne's the woman
Who's gonna carry your child . . .
Joanne is you and
Joanne is me
Our prison is
This whole society.[39]

In focusing in on the ice pick that makes an appearance at novel's end, on Sethe's refusal to lay it down, and, as important, on Ella's expression of solidarity with Sethe, I have shuttled between the slave past and Morrison's moment of textual production, in effect enabling the connection of Garner, Sethe, Ella, and Joan Little—to name only four of the violent insurgent women whose stories Morrison's novel and its black feminist philosophy of history "pass on" to future generations.[40] Just as Sethe's actions and those of her supporters resulted in manumission of Sethe and her remaining children, Little's actions and those of her supporters were impactful. Little was acquitted of murder on August 15, 1975, in a watershed ruling that set the stage for subsequent rulings in support of women's right to self-defense against sexual and reproductive dispossession.[41]

IN CHAPTERS 1 AND 2 I have suggested that it is imperative to situate black feminism in its biocapitalist context of production, publication, and reception and to recontextualize and recalibrate a range of black feminist publications as together constituting a philosophy of history that is responsive to the slave past, the present moment of writing, and the future yet to come. I have also placed black feminism squarely within a long black radical tradition that has too often been cast as male, and have demonstrated how it picks up and expands upon questions posed but never answered by Du Bois in *Black Reconstruction*—questions about the gender of the general strike against slavery and about the importance of women's refusal of sexual and reproductive dispossession to the wider struggle for human liberation. In so doing I have argued that black feminist engagement with slavery ought not to be narrowly construed as a historical corrective. Although black feminism persistently returns to the slave past to revise and refine our understanding of it, it also animates enslaved women's freedom dreams so that such dreams might yet enable our imagination of refusal of the afterlife of slavery—not least, by inspiring us to consider the role that insurgent rationality, and, when necessary, violent insurgency, can play in liberating women from sexual and reproductive dispossession not only in the past but also in the present. As Morrison explained in an interview that she gave in the year *Beloved* was published, "The past, until you confront it, until you live through it, keeps coming back in other forms. The shapes redesign themselves in other constellations, until you get a chance to play it over again."[42] Notably, Morrison mobilizes Benjamin's term, *constellation*. *Beloved* and the black feminism of which it is a constitutive part ought to be recognized as a *constellated* replay—as a confrontation with the past so that it can be lived through and redeemed.

The sheer outpouring of black feminist meditations on what it has meant and what it yet might mean for women to reproduce substantive freedom suggests that there was in the 1970s and 1980s a collective sense of urgency among black feminists that those committed to the present fight for substantive sexual and reproductive freedom today need to reawaken. Although each black feminist contribution that I have discussed differently and uniquely explores the pitfalls and possibilities that inhere in the idea of freedom, hinged and unhinged from racialized and commodified sex and reproduction, each also contributes to a larger cultural and political formation, the existence of which clears new epistemological ground and points the way toward new idioms of political expression. In reading black feminism as what Du Bois called a "propaganda of history"—in particular, by situating *Beloved* as part and parcel of a philosophy of history—I suggest that black feminism possesses the power to reveal the political significance of stories of sexual and reproductive dispossession set in the slave past, so that women might yet, in some future moment, reproduce freedom instead of commodities.

And yet it would be foolhardy to conclude the preceding discussion on a naively triumphalist note. Black feminism's philosophy of history offers a memory of insurgency, but it also rings out a warning about the ease with which black women's freedom dreams can be and have been dashed. Even as those black feminist texts that I have discussed present utopian ideas about women's contributions to a gendered general strike against sexual and reproductive dispossession, there are other black feminist contributions that caution against an overzealous embrace of the female reproductive body as a site from which to launch a struggle for substantive freedom and against creation of heroines instead of fully realized, and necessarily flawed, human beings. Several of these dystopian texts are cautionary speculative fictions written by Octavia Butler, whose novels and short stories, all written across the same three decades that have been the focus of chapters 1 and 2, articulate a prescient analysis of the rise of neoliberalism and its incorporation and effective disarming of many of the radical black feminist impulses examined thus far. Although Butler's work contributes to black feminism's philosophy of history by constellating past and present and revealing the need to redeem the past in the present and for the future, she couples her examination of black feminist freedom dreams with a meditation on the self-governance and self-enslavement that too often characterized quests for genealogy and kinship in the contemporary world—a world poisoned by neoliberal individualism, by reproductive consumerism as an expression of individual freedom, and, not least, by naturalization of the intrusion of (bio)capitalist rationality into the most intimate aspects of our sexual and reproductive lives and the choices we supposedly freely make when we reproduce biological kinship and personal genealogy in lieu of participation in transformative forms of collectivity and kinship.

Chapter Four

The PROBLEM *of* REPRODUCTIVE FREEDOM *in* NEOLIBERALISM

Choice is the essence of freedom. . . . This freedom—to choose and to exercise our choices—is what we've fought and died for. Brought here in chains, worked like mules, bred like beasts, whipped one day, sold the next—for . . . years we were held in bondage. Somebody said that we were like children and could not be trusted to think for ourselves. . . . Somebody said that Black women could be raped, held in concubinage, forced to bear children year in and year out, but often not raise them. Oh yes, we have known how painful it is to be without choice in this land.

—AFRICAN AMERICAN WOMEN ARE FOR REPRODUCTIVE FREEDOM, "WE REMEMBER" MISSION STATEMENT (1984)

In an essay published in 2009, Dorothy Roberts examines the impact on race, gender, and class formation of what she synthetically labels "reprogenetic technologies" and diagnoses the emergence of what she refers to as a "new reproductive dystopia." She characterizes this new dystopia as a form of stratified reproduction that limits access to reproductive health care (and thus the possibility of genealogical futurity) to those who can pay and renders all women self-governing subjects who willingly submit to technological interventions into their reproductive bodies that amount to population control. Roberts, one of the most outspoken black feminist legal scholars focused on linkages between contemporary cultures and politics of reproduction and those of slavery, sharply contrasts this "new reproductive dystopia" with the "old reproductive dystopia" that had been her prior focus, especially in her watershed book, *Killing the Black Body: Race, Reproduction and the Meaning of Liberty* (1997; see discussion in chapter 1). Roberts thus distinguishes the old dystopia, which was subtended by predictable racial hierarchies, from the new dystopia, which is marked by neoliberal forms of self-governance that render all women, regardless of race, self-exploiting subjects who enter the market as consumers and freely choose to participate in the economic exchanges that dominate them. In the old dystopia "a reproductive caste system contrasted policies that penalize poor black women's childbearing with the high-tech fertility industry that promotes childbearing by more affluent white women."[1] As a consequence, the old dystopia produced a eugenic social order in which white women were granted resources that allowed them to reproduce white progeny, while black women's reproduction was pathologized and devalued and their access to childbearing and child-rearing resources denied. Whereas in the old dystopia black and white women were pitted against each other as laborers and consumers, respectively, in the new dystopia all women function as consumers of reprogenetic technologies and are thus bound in common plight by the "neo-liberal trend toward privatization and self-governance."[2]

In building her argument Roberts insightfully singles out Margaret Atwood's *The Handmaid's Tale* and Gena Corea's *The Mother Machine* as two well-known dystopias that in the early 1980s helped readers comprehend contemporaneous reproductive cultures and politics. Atwood's novel depicts the exploitation of surrogate laborers in its portrait of the so-called handmaids of Gilead, who are forced to reproduce white babies for the white Christian theocracy. Corea's nonfiction polemic warns of a future in which poor women are compelled to provide reproductive services to women able to pay for the use of wombs and fertile eggs, and thus for genetically engineered children. Roberts's point in invoking Atwood's and Corea's contributions is twofold: to observe that literature has usefully been used to critique reproductive cultures and politics in the past and, as important, to alert readers that we currently lack the elucidating cultural forms that accompanied the old reproductive dystopia. According to Roberts, in the twenty-first century we are in dire need of a literature that is keyed to the dystopian politics of human reproduction in neoliberalism and, it is implied, to the postracial reproductive landscape that neoliberalism supposedly augurs.[3]

This chapter treats fiction written in the 1970s and 1980s by the award-winning black feminist author Octavia E. Butler and demonstrates that a

already exists

speculative dystopian literature that deeply and critically engages reproductive cultures and politics in neoliberalism *already* exists and has been in existence for some time. In highlighting the fact that Butler produced her fictions during the decades of neoliberalism's ascent, I take issue with the assertion that we require invention of new dystopian visions or predictive warnings. Rather I demonstrate that the critical power of Butler's literary production of the 1970s and 1980s lies in its *conjunctural* intervention—its timely and time-sensitive refusal of clear-cut divisions between old and new dystopias, and thus its capacity to constellate past and present realities in the interest of imagining the future that lies in the balance. In exposing the relationship between the old dystopia that Roberts regards as rooted in slavery and the new dystopia characterized by self-governance through consumer choice and the ideology of postracialism, Butler's fictions eloquently speak to the sublation of slavery in contemporary biocapitalism—an iteration of capitalism, as explored in chapter 1, that emerged and was solidified over the decades during which she wrote.

In reading Butler's dystopian writings as a conjunctural intervention I nuance the discussion of black feminism's philosophy of history as I elaborated it in chapters 2 and 3. Here, rather than explore how black feminism locates and reclaims slave women's insurgency and freedom dreams (as I did in the previous two chapters), I examine the manner in which black feminism cautions against overly simplified or romanticized ideas about the possibility of revolt in a neoliberal context in which disavowal of reproductive slavery was and remains palpable. In reading Butler's fictions thus, I situate them as uniquely important contributions to the black feminist philosophy of history that this book treats and to which it contributes. These fictions about reproduction in bondage—both those that Butler sets in the distant past and those she sets in the far future—not only constellate slave racial capitalism and contemporary biocapitalism; they also meditate on the problem of pursuing substantive reproductive freedom in circumstances characterized by the narrowing of the potentially powerful concept of "choice" that is captured in my epigraph to the selection of one form of unfreedom over and above another form of unfreedom that is distinguishable from the former only in degree and modality.

In presenting Butler as a contributor to black feminism's philosophy of history I place her into dialogue not only with other black feminists but also with Walter Benjamin, the Marxist philosopher whose ideas about historical materialism are one of my touchstones. In "Theses on the Philosophy of History," an essay Benjamin wrote as fascist totalitarian leaders and movements rose to power throughout Europe in the 1930s, he insightfully observes that history appears to move elliptically rather than teleologically. He therefore admonishes his readers not to apprehend history as a series of causal events that proceed logically, one from the other, but rather as a *constellation in which past and present are enmeshed and the future necessarily ensnared*.[4] When seen with a historical eye (that of a "historical materialist," as opposed to that of a traditional historian or historicist, whom, Benjamin claims, is naively invested in a form of historical narration wed to linear progress), the possibility of glimpsing failed futures, recognizing unredeemable pasts, and apprehending retrograde outcomes "in the time of the now" opens wide. These bleak pasts, presents, and futures are unrelated to what might otherwise be called "development," "civilization," "recovery," or "advance."[5] Benjamin explains, "Historicism contents itself with establishing a causal connection between various moments in history. But no fact that is a cause is for that very reason historical. It becomes historical posthumously. . . . A historian who takes this [insight] as his point of departure stops telling the sequence of events like the beads of a rosary. Instead, he grasps *the constellation which his own era has formed with a definite earlier one* . . . [and] establishes a conception of the present as '*the time of the now*'" (263, my emphasis). Like Benjamin's philosophy of history, Butler's consists in constellating the present with the past and in recognizing the importance of constellation for the project of redeeming the past in present, for a future yet to come.

The resonance between Benjamin's and Butler's ideas becomes apparent when we trace Butler's engagement with the long-standing reliance of slave racial capitalism and biocapitalism on various forms of biopower, and biopower's related reliance on the rise of neoliberalism and the disavowal of the violent history of slavery that produces the supposed postracialism that neoliberalism augurs. The concept of biopower, most often attributed to Foucault, denotes power over life itself—individual lives and the life of populations—that became especially visible at the end of the nineteenth century, though it had been several centuries in the making.[6] According to Foucault, biopower is keyed to the demise of overt forms of sovereign power, the upsurge in scientific calculation and the scientific management of populations, the pursuit of regulations and norms as standards against which individual deviance is measured and managed, and the implementation of racialized governance of entire populations, be they nations or racialized subgroups within nations. Whereas sovereign power was exercised over individual lives through the ability to *make die*, biopower is exercised by dividing populations into those who are made to live and those who are left to die. For this reason, Foucault observes, biopower represents the entrance of life into the realm of politics. This entrance signals the emergence of the modern episteme with which, I have argued, the slave episteme ought to be regarded as concomitant and co-constitutive.[7]

When we read across Butler's writings, we invariably find that slavery is constelled with contemporary cultures and politics of reproduction, in and through what Benjamin calls "the time of the now," even though the familiar form of racial slavery that divided the free from the enslaved, and therefore the human from the less-than-human along strictly drawn black and white lines, is rarely present on either the manifest level of Butler's fictions or on the visible surfaces of the bodies that are exploited within her fictional worlds.[8] In these worlds reproductive bodies are neither necessarily black or female, nor are they necessarily members of the human species. Indeed when we read across Butler's fictions we see that racial slavery is subject to a variety of transformations that render the work of the slave episteme possible but at once challenging to apprehend. In Butler's fictions the same self-governing subjects whom Roberts associated with the new reproductive dystopia that emerges in neoliberalism—that in which individuals choose to self-govern and thus self-exploit—exists both in the present, in which consumers of reproductive labor and products select the genetic materials, technological processes, and individual laborers who will gestate children for them (see chapter 1), and in the past in which reproductive laborers were forcibly enslaved and their reproductive labor rendered alienable, fungible, and disposable. In other words, in Butler's fictions there are no postracial reproductive worlds populated by free subjects, and, it is implied, there never have been. Instead past and present formations are together organized by continuously recalibrated *racialisms* that rationalize the forms of racial capitalist dehumanization that are necessary to reproductive extraction (and thus reproduction of the relations of [re]production), even though it appears that the social formations that are described are no longer structured around familiar black and white racial ascriptions and identities.[9]

In reading Butler's fictions as contributing to and nuancing a black feminist philosophy of history keyed to the rise of neoliberalism, I treat it as a meditation on evolving forms of racialized and gendered dispossession as these are recalibrated to changes in the mode of (re)production catalyzed by

the rise of contemporary biocapitalism and consolidated by a postracial ideology that disavows the salience of processes of reproductive racialization to the extraction of life itself on which biocapitalism depends.

To further develop this reading of Butler's literary fictions, throughout this chapter I draw on Raymond Williams's ideas about "dominant," "residual," and "emergent" cultural formations.[10] Though Williams did not consider racial or gendered power when he developed these analytical concepts in the 1970s, his ideas about how cultural formations mediate historical and thus material processes resonates with Butler's ideas about mediation as expressed in her novels about enslavement. As Williams's conceptual trilogy suggests, literature not only allows for apprehension of dominant cultural formations; it also allows us to access "residual" (formed in the past but still "active" in the present) and "emergent" ("alternative" and yet often inchoate) cultural formations that continuously exert pressure on, compete with, and reshape dominant ones. Whereas residual formations are routinely incorporated into dominant ones through processes of reinterpretation, dilution, projection, inclusion, and exclusion, emergent cultural formations reveal "new meanings and values, new practices, new relationships and kinds of relationship" (123). Emergent formations come in two varieties: those that are elements of some new phase of the dominant culture, and those that are "substantially alternative or oppositional to it" and thus connected directly, if unevenly, to the emergence of new social classes (123).

When we take up Williams's conceptual terminology, we see more clearly how Butler's fictions render visible the incorporation and reinterpretation of racial slavery as a residual formation within the dominant biocapitalist processes that are depicted. Put in the language used elsewhere in this book, Butler's fictions render visible the sublation (read the negation and the preservation) of slavery in biocapitalism. In giving expression to more than one cultural formation and representing more than one economic formation (or, perhaps more aptly, in representing what Stuart Hall would describe as complexly articulated economic formations, including slavery and biocapitalism), Butler's fictions reveal the contestation that goes on among the array of reproductive cultural projects that are currently in existence. In so doing they make visible the afterlife of reproductive slavery in the form of a cultural residue that is alive and well in contemporary biocapitalism. And they reveal the possibility of opposition to biocapitalism and neoliberalism in the form of emergent cultural processes. These emergent cultural processes might ideally challenge the hegemony, by rejecting the ideologies that secure the smooth functioning of racial capitalism and biocapitalism through elevation of neoliberal market values in all social interactions and celebration of the obsolescence of race.

By refusing to represent clean breaks and discrete historical epochs, by insisting on complex economic structuration, Butler's fictions reveal multiple modes of production vying for hegemony. And they reveal that an active and ongoing contest for reproductive hegemony is always already under way. Recognizing (albeit without citing) the Benjaminian maxim "Only that historian will have the gift of fanning the spark of hope in the past who is firmly convinced that *even the dead* will not be safe from the enemy if he wins," Butler uses fiction as a weapon in a war against "the enemy" (read: historicism), refusing, through creation of her various dystopian worlds, to allow the enemy "to be victorious."[14] She does not pander to myths of progressive departure, or to the inevitability of defeat. Instead she offers us an array of representations and a philosophy of history in view of which she invites readers to grasp the material complexity in which we have been and continue to be immersed. In so doing she urges her readers to stop wasting time—to jump into what amounts to an ideological fray. After all, the outcome will determine our collective future.

Slavery as Biopolitics

For the most part, readers and scholars interested in Butler's ideas about slavery have focused on her first major novel, *Kindred* (1979), the time-travel narrative, discussed in chapter 2, in which Dana, a black woman from 1976, finds herself transported to the 1850s, to a Maryland plantation on which her ancestors, black and white, live. There Dana witnesses and to some degree experiences slavery firsthand and simultaneously feels compelled to engineer the birth of the enslaved ancestor who, she believes, will become her great-grandmother. But there is a hitch. To ensure her future existence, Dana feels she must abet the violent, predatory sexual desires of her great-great-grandmother's master, a man she believes to be her great-great-grandfather. In genre terms, *Kindred* has variously been read as a time-travel narrative, as a neo-slave narrative, and sometimes, if less often, as black feminist theory. It is generally cast as a commentary on the enduring violence and trauma of slavery in the lives and psyches of the descendants of slaves and on the nation as a whole; as a reflection on the ruse of freedom in the lives of modern black women, like Dana, who remain chained to the slave past; and as a meditation on the difficulties of writing the history of women in slavery from the vantage point of the enslaved given the paucity of the archive.[13] In short, *Kindred*'s focus on plantation slavery and its engagement with epistemological questions that have traditionally been posed by historians of slavery has led critics to read the novel as Butler's principal discussion of racial slavery and to consider it somewhat anomalous when contextualized among her other writings, most often classified as speculative or science fictional because they depict future worlds that are either at a distance from the slave past or because they refuse the realism that characterizes the detailed portrait of plantation slavery that is presented in *Kindred*.[14]

I join a few other scholars who argue that it is an interpretive mistake and missed opportunity to separate *Kindred* from the rest of Butler's corpus or to regard it as her main commentary on slavery.[15] Such a move obscures existing linkages among racial slavery, neoslavery, and neoliberal dystopia that can emerge when we read across texts. Moreover, as this chapter demonstrates, separating *Kindred* out obscures rather than highlights the historical and materialist complexity that characterizes Butler's corpus, its persistent constellation of past and present, and thus its participation in the elaboration of black feminism's philosophy of history. Here, in order to underscore Butler's contributions to a black feminist philosophy of history, I read not only across Butler's fictions but also across the temporal and geographical landscapes that each represents. As we shall see, such a reading practice reveals the racialized and gendered power dynamics of slavery at work in each of the worlds that Butler crafts. And, as important, it shows us how neoliberal self-governance obstructs substantive reproductive freedom in the present, "in the time of the now," and too in *the slave past*—that is, in a historical context in which both neoliberalism and self-governance would appear, at least initially, to be wild anachronisms.

For present purposes, it is instructive to bracket *Kindred* on one side by *Wild Seed* (1980), a speculative novel about reproductive bondage and the pursuit of kinship, and on the other side by "Bloodchild" (1986), a short story about gestational surrogacy across species. Both were written during the period that witnessed the rise of the surrogate industry, the larger biocapitalist economy of which it is a part, as well as the aggressive implantation of neoliberalism.[16] As I read across this triplet of texts, the myriad ways in which Butler constellates past and present—slave racial capitalism, biocapitalism, and neoliberalism—come to the fore. And thus Butler's refusal to tell the sequence of historical events "like the beads of a rosary" (as Benjamin put it) becomes palpable. In each of these fictions reproductive hegemony is under siege and thus vulnerable to insurgency, even as insurgency against sexual and reproductive dispossession is continually compromised and substantive forms of sexual and reproductive freedom pushed out of reach.

I begin with *Wild Seed*, a novel published just one year after *Kindred*, because it powerfully evinces Butler's understanding of the centrality of power over sex and reproduction to the maintenance of hegemony across time. As in the other black feminist fictions discussed in the previous two chapters, *Wild Seed* constellates slave racial capitalism and biocapitalism and examines the relationship between the two as it evolves in the modern period. Within Butler's larger corpus, *Wild Seed* functions as the backstory that illuminates the narrative arc of a four-book series that examines the creation of genetically engineered populations and their capacity to alter what it means to be human.[17] *Wild Seed* depicts an epic battle between two immortal beings that inaugurates the time-straddling, multicentury conflict over genealogy, kinship, and the genetic composition of individuals and populations that is also the focus of the other novels in the series. As is true of all of Butler's fictions, *Wild Seed* is also an examination of the power play that evolves between individuals who have (and allegorically represent) overlapping and yet incompatible life projects and visions for the future of the human species, or, more aptly, for the future of the beings (no longer entirely human) who have descended from those who were at one time recognizable to readers as beings more like ourselves.

Doro, the antagonist, has already been alive for three thousand years at the novel's start, the end of the seventeenth century. Doro's life project is propagation of an empire populated by individuals who possess unique psychic and physical abilities that allow for mind and body control, and thus for control over the creation of life itself and the reproduction of immortality at the level of the gene. Doro's explicitly eugenic breeding program, which defies all known prohibitions against incest and endogamy, is deeply enmeshed in the transatlantic slave trade. The trade that commences in Africa is a primary source of the fecund bodies that Doro ships to the breeding "settlements" that he has strategically located throughout the New World. Although Doro's métier is creation of new life, what is unique about him is that he must kill to create, as his immortality is predicated on the transfer of his essence or spirit from one body to another, each of which is destroyed in the process of being inhabited, used, and finally discarded by him. To borrow the terminology developed by theorists of biopower who were Butler's contemporaries, Doro instantiates sovereign power and biopower. He puts individual subjects to death with impunity, as would a sovereign whose power was, as Doro's often is, threatened. And he simultaneously makes live, creating populations of genetically engineered individuals, each of whom is reproduced to his exacting (though never entirely achievable) specifications so that each may become future breeding stock.

As already noted, theories of biopower, especially those that have emerged from black studies, have called out the neglect of the colony and the slave plantation by the concept's two most well-known European theorists, Foucault and Agamben. In an influential meditation on what he labels "necropolitics," the philosopher Achille Mbembe instances South Africa and Palestine and argues that the colony ought to be recognized as a biopolitical space in which life is rendered disposable and the population managed through a politics of extermination and genocidal control.[18] Jared Sexton, a US-based black studies scholar, has criticized Mbembe for exceptionalizing the colony and sidelining the slave plantation. As Sexton argues, the plantation ought to be understood as what Agamben names "the nomos" of the modern; thus Sexton advances what amounts to a counterexceptionalism that replaces the concentration camp as well as the colony with the plantation. Sexton's argument for the slave plantation as the exemplary instantiation of modern power is based on his understanding of antiblack racism as central to the theorization and practice of biopolitics (Foucault) and necropolitics (Mbembe), and his belief that the plantation best captures the racialized structure of modern power.[19] In her portrait of Doro, Butler would seem to have arrived at related conclusions several decades prior to either Mbembe or Sexton. In casting Doro as a colonist and a slave master, as invested in taking life and making life, Butler refuses the dichotomy between colony and plantation, effectively revealing not only the intimacy but also the impossibility of separating colonialism from Atlantic slavery when theorizing power over life itself in the time of the now.

Like Doro, Anyanwu, the novel's protagonist, is an engineer of life itself. However, in contrast to Doro, who creates life in order to destroy it, Anyanwu creates life to nurture and augment it. Already alive for three hundred years at the narrative's outset, Anyanwu works as a healer and spirit woman in what appears to be eastern Nigeria, where she resides among a tribe that critics have identified as the Onitsha Igbo.[20] Like Doro, Anyanwu possesses the capacity to be immortal; unlike Doro, her immortality never necessitates murder. Anyanwu's métier is intensive study of the constituent components of raw, biological life, mimicry and manipulation of the cellular structures that build and rebuild life, or, in Agamben's terminology, deconstructive engagement with zoē, life before it enters political calculation. Anyanwu regenerates herself and others by healing wounds and curing disease and by guiding the transformation of bodies on the genetic level. She possesses what today would be called an epigenetic understanding of life and the power to transform it, an understanding of the interaction between DNA and the material forces of history that Doro can do no more than guess at as he fumbles through an array of misguided and violent breeding experiments in his quest to create a species that can companion him into eternity.

While Doro's biopolitical project is selfishly destructive and, as a result, unselfconsciously narrow, Anyanwu's is expansive and self-consciously life-affirming. Through her ability to manipulate the reproductive process, especially through selection and directed fertilization of sperm and egg in her own body, she seeks to celebrate diverse life forms, to cross existing divisions among sexes and species, and to in all ways embrace the differences that she reproduces. Like the Oankali in Butler's 1987 novel, *Dawn*, Anyanwu believes that human futurity paradoxically resides in becoming less recognizably human, in promoting all forms of hybridity, and in embracing all forms of life, regardless of whether they violate species boundaries or adhere to existing norms. This is a future-orientated politics of radical difference, an "impossible politics" of difference that some have attributed to black feminism more generally.[21] For Anyanwu the making and remaking of all forms of biological life is a life-affirming project. And thus the reproductive power Anyanwu deploys is the inverse of that wielded by Doro. These competing embodiments of power are subtended by diametrically opposed concepts of futurity, such that the question of the future that lies in the balance necessarily emerges as the axis that bisects the competing approaches to life and the reproduction of life that are depicted within the novel. Whereas Doro's people are forced to breed under penalty of death and are compelled to proffer themselves and their children for sexual and reproductive service, the diverse beings whom Anyanwu gathers around her or creates mate only if, and when, they choose. Together with Anyanwu, they are involved in a collective project of speciation.

Even though the ship that transports Doro's human breeding stock from coastal African slave pens to the New World provides a middle passage experience that is devoid of otherwise familiar forms of violence (there are no

shackles, overcrowded hulls, rapes, beatings, murders, or scarcities of food and water), those aboard Doro's vessels experience "natal alienation," the condition of profound dislocation and unmooring from the human community of which the sociologist Orlando Patterson wrote. They are severed from place and kin and swathed in a building terror about their immersion in dehumanizing forms of bodily and psychic subjection.[22] When Anyanwu, whom Doro discovers on one of his African sojourns, is initially coerced into joining him on his travels to the slave coast and from there to the New World, she does so in exchange for a promise (which Doro breaks) not to enslave her children, and an offer of marriage (which he later rescinds) that she at first mistakes for an invitation into a shared realm of power. During her middle passage, when the reality of her enslavement imposes itself on her mind and body, Anyanwu, like other African captives before and after her, contemplates suicide: "She would leap into the sea. . . . Its waters would take her home, or they would swallow her. Either way, she would find peace. Her loneliness hurt her like some sickness of the body, some pain that her special ability could not find and heal" (66). When Anyanwu is prevented from leaping into the waves of the Atlantic by one of Doro's men, it is only so that she may be transformed into a breeder whom Doro can use to reproduce healing and regenerative abilities in her offspring.

Though Anyanwu's enslavement violently constrains her choices, effectively rendering the use of the term to describe her situation oxymoronic, it does not foreclose her sexual and reproductive insurgency against Doro's various acts of terror and counterterror. Anyanwu has not been transported by Doro to perform productive labor, as have other slaves brought to the New World. Rather her slavery is entirely reduced to its sexual and reproductive core, a reduction that renders it continuously open to her various insurgent acts of sexual and reproductive refusal. Anyanwu has been enslaved to function as a sexual partner to Doro and thus as a breeder able to transfer to future generations the biological capital that both of their genes hold. But breeding and genetic manipulation are not only Anyanwu's vulnerability; they are her forte. Her ability to control in vivo reproductive processes provides her a unique venue through which to challenge biopower by taking herself, her reproductive labor, and its potential products in and out of circulation. Whereas, as I argued in previous chapters, sex and reproduction are the site and stake in slave women's insurgency, in Anyanwu's case sex and reproduction are the fulcrum on which an epic battle for the future of the human race pivots.

While many histories of slavery suggest that the economic motivations of the enslaver reside in the capture and exploitation of slaves' labor power, *Wild Seed*, like the histories of female enslavement that I examined in chapter 1, suggests that the motivation for female enslavement is always also sexual and reproductive. Instructively, Doro takes no interest in extracting agricultural surplus from his various settlements; he invests solely in reproductive futures—in biological processes and genetic materials, and, of course, in fertile progeny and populations. Doro is thus a slave master and a biocapitalist in the weak sense of the former term and the strong sense of the latter; all exchanges in which he is involved and that involve his people are in the flesh, as the most precious commodity that Doro possesses is the reproductive body and the genetic potentiality that in vivo processes foretell, Anyanwu's above all others. Because Anyanwu is invaluable, Doro is eventually flummoxed by his dependence on her. To realize his eugenic goal of creating an immortal race, Anyanwu's genes must be passed on as often as possible. And yet each time Doro forces Anyanwu to breed he not only creates a being who may be his undoing; he angers the only being whom he must control. Consequently the ongoing war between Doro and Anyanwu evolves in fits and starts: Doro attempts to extract all he can from Anyanwu's reproductive body; Anyanwu counters Doro's reign of terror by claiming control over her in vivo processes and, at least temporarily, moving both herself and her children beyond Doro's reach.

In staging historical dialectics as a conflict between competing biopolitical projects that center on the reproduction of life itself, Butler revises the history of capitalism. She also reprises the masculinism of black Marxism in the same manner as do other black feminists who contribute to black feminism's philosophy of history: She places in vivo labor at the center of biocapitalism in general, and slave racial capitalism in particular, by recognizing that the extraction on which each is predicated is reproductive. Butler's expressly feminist take on historical materialism is manifest in her detailed exploration of the manifold ways in which Anyanwu's insurgency produces the text's structuring conflicts and contradictions and thus its dialectical movement. Indeed attack and counterattack produce the narrative's momentum (which is not necessarily forward) and a detailed portrait of modern power as a complex and constantly shifting constellation of slave racial capitalism and biocapitalism. On one occasion, after an attempt to make life has been defeated by Doro, Anyanwu places herself out of Doro's reach by transforming herself into a dolphin.[23] (When she takes nonhuman form she is inured to

Doro's power.) Yet Butler does not regard Anyanwu's retreat from humanity and thus from the dialectic of history as an adequate response. So she compels the narrative to unfold by returning Anyanwu to human form and in so doing forcing her struggle with Doro to continue. As one critic observes, in representing Anyanwu's battle with Doro as ceaseless, Butler theorizes the complexities of power, the forced acceptance of power, the hard reality that there is no outside to power, "no escape from power," but also that "attempts to reclaim and/or redirect power" never end.[24]

As in Angela Davis's account of enslaved women's sexual and reproductive insurgency and my account of black feminist neo-slave narratives that fill in the historical record by imagining enslaved women's refusal of sexual and reproductive dispossession, in *Wild Seed* Butler imagines Anyanwu's insurgency by representing in great detail her various efforts to transform the hegemony that Doro struggles to maintain through his persistent acts of what Davis would call "counterinsurgency" against her insurgency. In contrast, however, to other black feminist theories and literary representations of sexual and reproductive insurgency treated in previous chapters, in which insurgency is part and parcel of a general strike against slavery and thus transformative of history, Butler is preoccupied with the foreclosure of transformation, with the compromises women make, with the partiality of "success," and, above all else, with the problems that emerge when participation in revolt is construed to be a matter of choice.

In the worlds that Butler creates—worlds characterized by desperation and relentless subjection to dehumanizing forms of unfreedom—the insurgent reproductive laborer is not only under siege, but she repeatedly runs the risk of complete evisceration. With her portrait of Anyanwu, Butler insistently raises the possibility of agentile action and simultaneously explores the problem of presuming that the slave woman can in any simple sense choose resistance. Indeed in placing her protagonist in contexts in which there is little space to maneuver and scant ability to act collectively to transform the relations of power that demand continuous sexual and reproductive extraction, Butler shows us where insurgency might take hold and why it so often fails to take hold. Her portrait of Doro and Anyanwu's battle therefore refuses the triumphalism of the black feminist texts discussed in previous chapters, as it is punctuated by a thick and unrelenting portrait of Doro's imposition of myriad constraints, by Anyanwu's necessary negotiation of sexual and reproductive unfreedom, and, by necessity, by an account not of a general strike—nay, a revolution that ends in emancipation of the enslaved—but rather by a detailed account of compromise and accommodation *on both sides.*

As the novel unfolds we witness Anyanwu's difficulties as she struggles to appropriate her reproductive body and her in vivo processes and Doro's continual effort to track her down, check her, and extract her reproductive resources. Indeed it is possible to turn to almost any page of the novel to examine the microdynamics of this struggle. For instance, in a passage situated at the apex of the narrative's arc, the question of Anyanwu's perpetual enslavement appears to be momentarily up for grabs. Doro has taken her deep into the woods to force her to "mate" with a fellow "wild seed," a man who possesses vast psychic powers that Doro wishes to transfer to his progeny.[25] When Anyanwu first encounters Thomas he is covered in vermin and open sores; he has stopped eating and is soaked in alcohol; and his mind is quite literally out of his control as it leaps in and out of her own in an attempt to take possession of it. Thomas's initial response to Anyanwu exposes his sense of futility in the face of his excessive (and to him unbearable) ability, his self-hatred, his vicious racism and sexism, and not least his subjection to Doro. He first rejects sex with Anyanwu unless she transforms herself into a white woman. And when she refuses to do so, he attempts to rape her. To Doro, Thomas's desperate response is inconsequential; his seed is valuable and will be transferred by any means necessary. By contrast, even though he has attempted to rape her, Anyanwu regards Thomas as someone who can be healed on the cellular level—and thus as someone she can transform into kin. Because of her perception of this potentiality, Thomas's body becomes the newest site and stake in Doro and Anyanwu's war. As Anyanwu explains to Thomas, she "would rather lie with [him] . . . than" with Doro (179); moreover she would rather die on the spot than allow Doro to dispose of Thomas's body after she has begun to heal it. In response to Doro's plan to take Thomas's life after he extracts his seed (and thus his DNA), Anyanwu's insurgency reaches new heights. She not only stands by Thomas; she and Thomas momentarily join forces, each opening themselves to Doro's deadly attack, effectively placing their combined genetic bounty out of his reach. Although their unified front is swiftly defeated, the significance of this emergent formation cannot be overlooked. Anyanwu has in this moment demonstrated her ability to bring one of Doro's people into an oppositional formation, revealing how a truly alternative biopolitical hegemony might yet take root. At the same time, the passage exposes the price of insurgency against Doro: life itself, in this instance Thomas's.

In a part of the novel entitled "Canaan," the constrained choice available to Anyanwu and thus the difficulty of refusal is revisited. We learn that over the course of nearly a century Anyanwu has succeeded in creating a group of kith and kin that she has sequestered on a Louisiana plantation for safekeeping. Masquerading, when necessary, as the master by transforming herself into a prosperous-looking white planter, Anyanwu effectively creates a slave utopia in the heart of the Cotton Kingdom. In the process she queers patriarchy (she marries and impregnates a white woman), destabilizes heterosexuality, and contests white supremacy. Indeed in her guise as master she manages to not only gather and protect but also grow and nurture a community of nonnormative beings who together possess imposing psychic and physiological powers that would otherwise render them "witches," "misfits, malcontents, [and] troublemakers" (235).[26] Unsurprisingly, when Doro discovers Anyanwu's Canaan he immediately recognizes it as "competition" (231).[27] Wearied of endless war and saturated with feelings of loss, when Doro once again encroaches, Anyanwu again elects suicide. And yet, in contrast to her prior suicide attempts, on this third occasion she ultimately allows Doro to save her from putting herself to death—that is, she lets him make her live. This biopolitical act is double edged. Although Anyanwu realizes that her concession to Doro entails further subjection to him, she also realizes that it ensures that Doro's power will remain perpetually in check. As Doro concedes, only Anyanwu can effectively contest his "centuries old habit" of killing all those who disobey him. Only Anyanwu can lay siege to the biopolitical hegemony by engaging others in an alternative biopolitical project. As the omniscient narrator confirms, "There had to be changes. . . . Anyanwu could not have all she wanted . . . [and] Doro could no longer have all that he had once considered his by right" (297).[28] As a meditation on the reproductive afterlife of slavery, *Wild Seed* reveals the persistence of residual formations across time, the presence of emergent formations that queer slavery and (ab)use sexual and reproductive power, and the fact that biocapitalism's sublation of slavery—its negation and preservation of slavery—necessarily creates a world in which past and present are constellated.

In their theorization of the genre, scholars of science fiction argue that one of its central functions is the creation of critical distance. In creating alternative worlds, Darko Suvin famously observes, science fiction enables estrangement from the present inhabited by the reader and thus the reader's critical cognition of the problems with their present—just enough critical cognition to allow for apprehension of how and why the reader's world differs from the fictional world, and thus just enough to enable the reader to imagine how she might work to change her present in order to change the future.[29] In the work of Marxist theorists who treat science fiction (Fredric Jameson, Carl Freedman, and Tom Moylan, for example), representations of alternative worlds, utopian and dystopian alike, function as radical political resources that potentially raise consciousness and herald the possibility of revolutionary transformation.[30] In presenting a world that reflects and refracts the present, such fictions enable imagination of the forms of political agency—including violent insurgency—that might be required to create substantive change. Returning to this chapter's opening, it is apparent that in calling for dystopian fiction that meditates on current reprogenetic technologies and practices, Roberts implicitly assumes these Marxist understandings of the critical work that sf (especially dystopia) can perform. However, as Butler's fictions reveal, the insights gained may as often be about the difficulties, dangers, and constraints that contour the supposed choices that are made as we engage in the struggle for substantive freedom, as about the possibilities that are associated with creation of a new future. To express this somewhat differently, Wild Seed's critical edge lies in its ability to reveal complex constellations in which insurgent responses to slave racial capitalism and biocapitalism are articulated, even if they are not, as Benjamin cautions, productive of linear progress or positive forms of historical transformation. In refusing to resolve historical conflicts and contradictions, in presenting an ongoing biopolitical battle over reproduction and its extraction, Butler provides an account of historical processes in which one form of power is unable to handily conquer and proceed from that which came before. And thus we learn as we read Wild Seed that dominant, residual, and emergent cultural formations coexist because sexual and reproductive enslavement is always coupled to sexual and reproductive insurgency and vice versa.

Kinship as Killing

If Wild Seed imagines the reproductive power struggle at the heart of biopower, Kindred, published just one year prior, imagines biopower's connection to neoliberalism and the terrifyingly complete foreclosure of the forms of insurgency that Anyanwu orchestrates throughout Wild Seed. In this sense, the former ought to be read as a prescient commentary on the latter, a refinement on its portrait of power that recalibrates it to the rise and entrenchment of new forms of power. Whereas *Wild Seed* imagines an endless struggle for hegemony, *Kindred* imagines successful neoliberal incorporation, co-optation, and diffusion of insurgency. In *Kindred* slavery is accessed by readers through the novel's protagonist, Dana, who time-travels, through a plot device and narrative structure that shuttles the present into the past as Dana shuttles back and forth across time. Traveling between 1976 and the 1850s, Dana reflects on what she has imagined slavery to be from the vantage point of her present, on how her lived experience of slavery compares to what she has imagined slavery to have been, on how to represent her present to those whom she meets in the past, and, reciprocally, on how to represent slavery for posterity. The last is expressly a question about how to write history and in which idiom. Like Butler, Dana is an author whose writings necessarily reflect and refract her experience and, we can speculate, treat the relationship between the history of slavery and its imaginative representation. However, while readers of *Kindred* take as given Butler's ability to narrate the story we are reading, Dana's narrative abilities are thrown into question, effectively placing the issue of historical truth at the center of *Kindred* and, too, at the center of Butler's philosophy of history. Indeed Butler portrays Dana as an unreliable narrator who appears, in stark contrast to Anyanwu (and to Butler herself), to be almost entirely blind to her complicity in the violence by which she is surrounded. Put otherwise, Dana is compromised in her capacity to constellate and thus take stock of the relationship between her present and the slave past. As a result, the supposed freedom being celebrated by the nation and its citizens in 1976 gains an increasingly sinister aspect as it is revealed to readers that Dana's present, unbeknownst to her, is not as distinct from the slave past as it initially appears to be.

The ongoing work of the slave episteme and the constellation of present and past that Dana comprehends least is biopolitical—the condition that Foucault associates with the ascent of neoliberalism in his 1978–79 lectures, "The Birth of Biopolitics."[31] Specifically Dana fails to see that the struggle in which she is involved in the past (which is rendered as her present when she time-travels to the plantation) is not only a struggle to ensure physical existence but also a struggle over kinship, genealogy, and human futurity. Unlike Anyanwu, Dana does not comprehend the political and economic dimensions of sexual and reproductive power and the relationship of slave breeding to the question of human freedom. Rather she regards her present struggle as personal, as first and foremost pertinent to *her future* as opposed to *the future*. Because of her failure to recognize the implications of her quest for self-creation, Dana is blind to the fact that sexual and reproductive insurgency and counterinsurgency function as the motor of history—the point above all others that *Wild Seed* drives home to readers. Whereas Butler represents reproduction of kinship and genealogy as power's source and stake—and therefore as its vulnerability—Dana appears to draw a blank in the face of the violence that is a by-product of her quest to self-preserve and thus self-create. Consequently the mechanism by which neoliberal hegemony is maintained is put on display, even as the novel's protagonist fails to perceive her involvement in the work of maintenance.

On the level of plot, as is typical of time-travel narratives, Dana is convinced that her existence depends upon her ability to go back in time to engineer her own birth. Thus, while she might have returned to the 1850s to manumit her relative through either purchase or theft, effectively helping to ensure her enslaved ancestor's sexual and reproductive sovereignty, she never appears to consider this option. Instead she acts as if the only choice that she can reasonably make is to orchestrate her ancestors' sexual and reproductive dispossession—a choice that perpetuates the other woman's bondage and shores up the system of slavery. On a practical level, because Dana fails to question her quest to reproduce herself, her freedom becomes dependent on another woman's enslavement and eventual death. In sum, in *Kindred* Dana's pursuit of kinship is killing. It results in the soul murder of another woman, in this woman's subjection to living death, and eventually in her demise.[32]

Significantly, assessment of Dana's complicity is often neglected in the existing criticism on the novel, in which Dana is cast as a sympathetic victim of slavery who is caught up in circumstances that are far beyond her control. In fact, save for a few notable exceptions, critics take Dana at her word and therefore interpret her story as if her reasoning is sound and her narration of events reliable. Dana believes that she has been called back in time to ensure her futurity, that time travel ought to be oriented around the individual quest for survival, and most critics do not question this.[33] As is frequently observed, when Rufus, the slave master whom Dana believes to be her progenitor, is in mortal danger, Dana is wrenched from her present and returned to the plantation on which Rufus resides. Once there, she leaps to Rufus's aid, saving his life, restoring his power over his slaves, and thus ensuring his future capacity to impregnate her great-great-grandmother and bring Dana into existence. Because she needs him to live, Dana protects Rufus even when this entails incurring serious injury. Although Dana's condition is not identical to that of other female slaves (she maintains a privileged relationship to Rufus throughout the novel), she too is vulnerable to the master's whims, the overseer's lash, and, in the end, to sexual violation by Rufus and loss of her reproductive sovereignty.

Alternatively, when we read *Kindred* as a novel about Dana's pursuit of kinship as killing, she cannot be regarded as a hapless victim of time travel, slavery, and Rufus's will. She must instead be recognized as Rufus's accomplice, a historical actor whose unquestioning acceptance of the logic of genealogy and acquiescence to the legitimacy of her personal genealogical project, amounts to a choice she makes again and again despite the profound violence that this choice entails for others. Put otherwise, it is alongside many of *Kindred*'s critics that Dana fails to consider the possibility that she is pulled back in time not by Rufus and his needs (which she mistakenly construes as coincident with her own) but rather by Alice, the woman whom Dana identifies as her black female progenitor. By contrast to Rufus, Alice's summons of Dana into slavery might be so that Dana will join forces and fight alongside her, assisting her not in the reproduction of Dana's future but in the refusal of the sexual and reproductive bondage in which Alice is ensnared. In stark opposition to Anyanwu, who intuitively and correctly perceives what is at stake in the biopolitical battle in which she and Doro are involved and who battles on by engaging in self-sacrifice on behalf of self and others, Dana conceives of her time travel in narrowly individualistic terms, effectively foreclosing the possibility of participation in a collective fight for substantive sexual and reproductive freedom.

These contradictions reach a crisis point in a disturbing passage in which Dana feels compelled to pimp Alice to Rufus. Again, this is a passage that has gone largely untreated by critics who focus on Dana as a victim rather than a co-conspirator with Rufus. Such critics prioritize analysis of the master and slave dynamic over treatment of the relationships that exist among women who are differently situated in relationship to the dominant structures of power that shape life on the Weylin plantation.[34] The upshot is that Rufus and Dana's shared biopolitical agenda—their shared need to make Alice live so that she may be available for sex with Rufus and for reproductive labor—is neglected.[35] By contrast, if we explore the complexities that arise when complicities are acknowledged and antagonisms among women exfoliated rather than pushed aside, we see that Dana and Alice are not only antagonists but that Dana and Rufus are allied despite the superficial assumption that a black woman and a white slave master ought to be construed as unequivocally adversarial.

At various points in the novel Dana and Alice are expressly compared to each other. On several occasions Butler describes them as being so similar in physical appearance that one can be readily mistaken for the other. Moreover their life trajectories, although separated by over a century, overlap. Each is born free, and each finds herself subjected to Rufus. For his part, Rufus fantastically and perversely connects the two women. Alice and Dana are two halves of a single person, he quips. Together they satisfy all his needs and desires, emotional and sexual: Dana is his savior and thus his partner in crime; Alice is his enslaved concubine and breeder. And yet, even if Rufus fails to fully recognize what truly differentiates the two women whom he subjects, Butler clearly represents Dana and Alice as antagonists necessarily distanced by the power differential that exists between them and that overrides their apparent likeness and supposedly biological kinship. As Butler makes plain, Alice is a sexual and reproductive laborer whose refusal of her sexual and reproductive dispossession is continuously elicited and checked by Rufus's violence against her person and her children. Dana is a putatively free woman who shares Rufus's investment in Alice's sexual and reproductive dispossession, even though Dana soothes her conscience by befriending Alice and, more disturbingly, by telling herself that her reasons for helping to subject Alice to Rufus, and thus to slavery, are ultimately sound.

Dana's failure to recognize that her genealogical quest is killing Alice eventually renders her a prisoner and victim of the biopolitical order that she aids and abets. She must dutifully perform the role of slave when on Rufus's plantation to save her own skin, yet fulfillment of her genealogical plan directly implicates her in the violence perpetuated against Alice by Rufus. Through her collaboration with Rufus, Dana renders Alice's body and life disposable, exerting a degree of sovereign power over Alice that does not differ entirely from that exerted by Rufus over Alice and his other slaves, save that Rufus violates Alice's body directly while Dana violates it by proxy.[36] There are two scenes that reveal the complex power dynamics in which Alice and Dana are involved and the toll, in human life, of Dana's quest to ensure her own birth. In the first, Dana brings Alice back to life (and, for the first time, into slavery) after Alice has been severely beaten. In the second, Dana accedes to Rufus's request that she persuade Alice to comply with his sexual demands. Together these scenes reveal Dana's complicity with biopower by showing her part in the perpetuation of another woman's sexual and reproductive en-slavement. Simultaneously these scenes reveal Dana's self-subjection through self-governance. For ultimately Dana's commitment to genealogical futurity requires her subjection of Alice and, as important, Dana's self-subjection to the neoliberal systems of valuation that lead her to mistake her capacity to ex-ercise individual choice for her possession of substantive freedom and to con-fuse the pursuit of self-interest for a genuine commitment to human futurity.

In the first of the two scenes, Rufus attempts to rape Alice and winds up in a life-and-death battle with Alice's enslaved husband, Isaac. As is her wont, Dana arrives just in time to save Rufus from Isaac. Some readers believe that Dana pursues Alice's well-being when she bargains with Rufus to give Alice and Isaac time to run; however, Dana's intervention serves only to delay Isaac's apprehension by a posse, his sale, and Alice's near-death beating and subsequent enslavement for aiding the escape of her husband, a fugitive. In other words, through Dana's actions and the social and legal relations that flow from them, both Rufus and Dana get what each seeks: Alice's sexual and reproductive subjection. It is Dana, moreover, who heals Alice's wounded body so that she may become sexually serviceable. The dialogue that ensues when Alice regains consciousness and realizes her newly enslaved condition makes apparent that even though Alice states her preference for death over slavery and the sexual and reproductive dispossession that it entails, Dana is inured to Alice's insurgent reasoning.

> ALICE: If you'd had any sense, you would have let him [Rufus] die!
> DANA: If I had, it wouldn't have kept you and Isaac from being caught. . . . It might have gotten you both killed. . . .
> ALICE: Doctor-Nigger . . . Think you know so much. Reading-nigger. White-nigger! Why didn't you know enough to let me die? (160)

Perhaps unsurprisingly, Dana is naively unprepared to play the role of pimp. She concedes, "I had thought that [Rufus] would just rape her [Alice] again—and again. . . . I didn't realize that he was planning to involve me in that rape. He was, and he did." When Rufus charges Dana with her task ("You talk to [Alice]—talk some sense into her—or you're going to watch while Jake Edwards [the driver] beats some sense into her!"), Dana is still unable to imagine that Alice's stated preference for actual death over living death is expressive of her true feelings. Dana therefore proceeds to further rational-ize her own actions: "No, I couldn't refuse to help the girl—help her avoid at least some of her pain." Even as Dana notes that she "didn't think much of herself" for "helping her [Alice] in this way," she believes she has weighed the options wisely (162–63) and that refusal of Rufus is out of the question. After all, Rufus's plan for Alice's sexual rehabilitation neatly coincides with Dana's own biopolitical agenda.

While numerous interpretations of Dana's decision to abet Rufus are possible (the majority sympathetically situate Dana between a rock and a hard place), as in my analysis of *Wild Seed*, in my analysis of *Kindred* I find it is useful to home in on Butler's meditation on choice in the contexts of both slavery and Dana's present, 1976. When Dana complies with power, when she self-governs, she does so by refusing to reframe her choices as such, by refusing to recalibrate her sense of her own agency, and therefore by refusing to explore the insurgent alternatives open to her.[37] In short, Dana behaves according to the neoliberal rationality that Roberts attributes to women in our supposedly "new reproductive dystopia" not only in her present but also when she enters the slave past. She consumes life itself by choosing to, as she puts it, "help the girl" submit to power, and by herself submitting to power. And this is so even though Alice informs Dana of one of the many other options open to her: killing Rufus by cutting "his damn throat" and putting an end to the struggle in which they are all involved (167). When we understand that Dana is inured to Alice's insurgent sensibility, we also recognize that Dana unwittingly imposes her neoliberal and thus enslaving rationality on her enslaved ancestor. By traveling back to the slave past (Alice's present) with her neoliberal rationality in tow, Dana imposes her enslaved thinking on Alice, forcing Alice to acquiesce to a neoliberal mind-set that is in fact antithetical to Alice's insurgent mind-set.

Although Dana successfully maintains Alice in bondage for years, and significantly just long enough for Alice to give birth to Dana's supposed ancestor, Alice eventually succeeds in taking her sexual and reproductive labor out of circulation through an act of suicide. (This act of *refusal* directly inverts, as it reprises, Anyanwu's final decision to live on and continue her struggle against Doro.) On her last journey into slavery, Dana returns to find Alice's lifeless body hanging from a beam in a barn on Rufus's plantation. It is the pairing of the life that Alice makes and her choice of death that should give readers pause, for it alerts us to the fact that this novel meditates not only on the violence of slavery but also—when read as a philosophy of history that constellates present and past—on neoliberal violence, particularly neoliberalism's implantation of the compulsion to self-govern through exercise of supposedly free choice. Although Dana repeatedly states that Rufus has killed

Alice by driving her to despair, when we read against the grain we can see that Dana too is responsible. Dana has blindly persisted in the belief that her personal genealogy must be secured at all costs. Alice's disposability, although tragic, is a price that Dana is willing to pay for a life of supposed freedom.

Critics generally concur that Dana's return to Los Angeles and her white husband, Kevin, with an arm that is so maimed in transit through time that it must be amputated, is one of the novel's most intriguing symbols of the afterlife of slavery. Dana's injury, seemingly caused by Rufus's grip on her arm as she time-travels, is read as a materialization of, or better yet as an enfleshment of, the long reach of past trauma, of the past's capacity to grab hold of the living and wreak not only mental but also physical havoc.[38] While this is a powerful reading, it can be deepened. From the vantage point enabled by Butler's constellating of present and past—from the vantage point of Butler's black feminist philosophy of history—Dana is maimed not only by slavery but also by her recursive ensnarement in neoliberalism in the present in which she lives and in the past to which she returns armed with an abiding if unconscious need to adhere to neoliberalism's imperatives, which, it turns out, are also those that abet slave racial capitalism. For Dana, it matters little where she is located in time or space. Whether in modern Los Angeles or on the antebellum plantation, Dana is unable to conceive of freedom as a collective practice and line of flight. For her it is instead a personal possession to which she feels entitled.[39] Thus readers are left to conclude that it is from within neoliberalism that Dana emerges blinded to the fact that her mind and body have been violently marked by slavery and by her choice to self-govern through assent to a neoliberal rationality that amounts to a politics of self-enslavement.

Surrogacy, Slavery, and Neoliberalism

In questioning the meaning of substantive sexual and reproductive freedom *Kindred* enters the debate about contemporary reproductive cultures and politics in a manner that has been entirely neglected in existing criticism on the novel. This is especially striking when we realize that Alice's story is about insurgency against sexual and reproductive dispossession, and thus about what I have been referring to as the surrogacy/slavery nexus. Lest this seem an analytical stretch, we need only recall that Butler names Alice's baby (Dana's ancestor) after the Old Testament figure Hagar, a slave belonging to Sarah, the barren wife of Abraham, who is often regarded as the first surrogate mother. As the story goes, Hagar bore Abraham a son, Ishmael, when Abraham ordered Hagar, at his wife's request, to do so. In later years, when Sarah gave birth to her own biological child, Isaac, Ishmael became an obstacle to Isaac's inheritance. To ensure that Isaac would assume the covenant, Ishmael and Hagar are exiled into the wilderness. While Isaac prevails in inheriting from his father, exile has unexpected consequences for Hagar, who finds a way where there is no way, effectively transforming a death sentence into freedom from bondage. According to both the Old Testament and the Quran, Hagar survives her ordeal and Ishmael grows to become a progenitor of the Arab people, a patriarch of Islam, and a prophet. In Christian theological discussions of Hagar (discussions that are implicitly narrated from Sarah's perspective), Hagar is cast as an unruly, insubordinate slave. By contrast, from the vantage point of black feminist theology, which gained a footing in the late 1970s and 1980s, the years during which Butler wrote the fiction under consideration in this chapter, Hagar is cast as a black Egyptian who endures the trials of slavery, poverty, racial ostracism, sexual exploitation, forced surrogacy, rape, domestic violence, homelessness, motherhood in bondage, and single parenthood. And she not only survives, she bucks Semitic authority and crafts an alternative relationship to God and the future.[40]

In her theological treatise *Sisters in the Wilderness*, Delores Williams, the best-known proponent of what is sometimes referred to as the "Hagar-centered tradition," reinterprets the portions of Genesis in which Hagar appears. Williams "lifts up" Hagar by imagining what her story meant to her, effectively reclaiming Hagar's protest against sexual and reproductive dispossession as an "analogue" for black women's protest against sexual and reproductive exploitation across time. Williams explains that through Hagar "black women's history . . . [becomes visible] as reproduction history . . . as history that uses *labor* as a hermeneutic to interpret black women's biological and social experience of reproducing and nurturing the species and *labor* as an interpretive tool for analyzing and assessing black women's creative productions as well as their relation to power" (10). Through Williams's lens, Alice's naming her daughter Hagar expresses a black feminist philosophy of history that coincides with Butler's own. It advances ideas about slave women's insurgency as worthy of reclamation in the present and for the future.[41] Moreover, the naming of Alice's daughter Hagar allows for both Alice and Butler to critique Dana's complicity with the biopolitical order, her compulsion to self-govern, and thus to comply with neoliberal imperatives. The name Hagar broadcasts Alice's and Butler's hope that freedom will be achieved through refusal of the afterlife of reproductive slavery, through refusal to perpetuate the surrogacy/slavery nexus—and, ultimately, through refusal of the imposition of one woman's biopolitical agenda on the body and life of another woman.

Williams's rendering of Hagar as an insurgent slave is a major theological and historiographical innovation that sits easily alongside other contributions to black feminism's philosophy of history, and the surrogacy/slavery nexus that brings this philosophy of history into focus. Williams's interpretation of Hagar constitutes "a route to black women's issues," to black women's "social-role exploitation" across the ante- and postbellum periods (60). The biblical slave Hagar had no control over her body or her labor, her sexual or reproductive processes, just as women enslaved in the Americas and the Caribbean were stripped of such control. Forced to breed property, to serve as wet nurses, to nurture other people's children, to function as white men's concubines, slave women labored as surrogates for over four centuries. When the Civil War ended, black women's installation, via wage labor, as domestics in white people's homes placed them in updated surrogate roles that were not entirely distinct from the roles they had been forced to play when enslaved. While in the contemporary period the "social role surrogacy" (care work, domestic work, intimate labor, and sex work) on which Williams focuses has often been analytically separated from what she labels "biological surrogacy," Williams is quick to point out (as did the black feminist legal scholars discussed in chapter 1) that in the 1980s "the growing surrogacy industry in North America and the escalating poverty among black people can pressure poor black women to become heavily involved in this industry at the level of reproduction," effectively returning black women to the forms of in vivo labor they performed as slaves (62). Extending her analogical analysis of surrogate and slave labor to the etymological relationship between contemporary surrogacy and slave breeding, Williams poignantly concludes, "What black women know is that . . . the language associated with commercial surrogacy today is a throw-back to American slavery, when certain slave women were set apart to function as 'breeder women.' . . . The question for black women today is whether forced surrogacy can happen again in their history" (82). For Williams, Hagar's story—and black women's surrogacy more generally—ought to be recognized as an invaluable heuristic device that is germane to analysis of slave racial capitalism and contemporary biocapitalism alike.

In "Bloodchild," the last fictional work I treat in this chapter, Butler builds on the reading of enslaved sexuality and reproduction developed in *Wild Seed* and *Kindred*, expressly treating the linkages between slavery and contemporary surrogacy by representing gestational surrogacy as an uncanny and horrifying practice in which all of those who are enslaved are involved. In the dystopian world depicted in "Bloodchild," an alien species, the centipede-like Tlic, are the master class whose breeding and routine use of human beings as sexual and gestational surrogates is essential to its futurity. Tlic must implant larval eggs in warm-blooded bodies where they can grow to maturity, at which point they are forcibly removed from their "hosts," or, alternatively, left to kill them as they eat their way through vital organs and flesh. Not only have human beings become the preferred surrogate labor force, but they are compelled by Tlic to reproduce themselves as a surrogate/slave class. In short, on the Tlic planet humans are required to reproduce Tlic and themselves, for, as Marx observes, all labor forces must reproduce the relations of production that subtend the dominant organization of power. As in plantation slavery and contemporary biocapitalism, the biopolitical organization of power and population on the Tlic planet is predicated on sexual and reproductive extraction, and on the (re)production of human life itself as a form of biological capital.

The story's protagonist, a teenage boy named Gan, explains that when human beings first arrived on the Tlic planet as refugees from Earth and the wars that left it uninhabitable, they were caged, drugged, and mated like the other animals that Tlic had already domesticated and used to gestate their young. By contrast to this early period, in a later period (that in which the story is set) a supposedly more civilized system for managing the human refugees has become normative. Instead of being caged, humans are corralled within "Preserves" where human families are "cared for" by individual Tlic who adopt and protect them from predation by other Tlic in "exchange" for access to humans' sexual and gestational labor. In these interspecies reproductive units, female Tlic couple with humans (usually but not necessarily male), in whom they deposit larvae and from whom they harvest the grubs that will grow into adult Tlic—imposing insects with immense physical power and many legs. Within this system, euphemistically dubbed by Tlic the "joining of families," affective attachments emerge (12). The narrative that unfolds revolves around the complexities of Gan's relationship with T'Gatoi, a Tlic dignitary who raises him from infancy to be her sexual partner and the surrogate for her young.

Despite the evident inequalities among species on the Tlic planet, some critics have been inclined to interpret Tlic-human relations as symbiotic. Humans fleeing a postapocalyptic planet have been integrated into an alien world in exchange for their reproductive labor.[42] At least superficially, such a reading of interspecies collaboration appears to be buttressed by Butler's oft-invoked statement about her intent in writing this story. In her retrospectively written afterword, she admits that it "amazes [her] that some people have seen 'Bloodchild' as a story of slavery," and she admonishes readers that "it isn't." Instead she labels it a "love story between two very different beings," further implying that the Tlic-human relationship involves mutuality (30). I suggest that what Benjamin would call historicist interpretations (on the part of Butler and her critics) ought to be challenged, as such readings shore up the biopolitical dynamics and neoliberal rationality that the story can otherwise be read to expose to view. Indeed when authorial protestations and available critical (mis)readings are pushed to the side, Tlic methods of reproduction can be seen for what they are: breeding practices that are subtended by residual formations (slavery) and by emergent formations (biocapitalism) that have been disavowed (slave breeding) and incorporated (gestational surrogacy) by those who benefit from the smooth functioning of the biopolitical system—that is, the Tlic who populate Butler's imagined world, and contemporary consumers of reproductive labor and products who populate the actual world in which Butler wrote. Put otherwise, it is precisely because the surrogacy/slavery nexus subtends Tlic hegemony that "Bloodchild" ought to be read as a meditation on the afterlife of reproductive slavery, and thus as a contribution to a black feminist philosophy of history that constellates the biocapitalist present and the slave past and in so doing reveals the ongoing work of the slave episteme.

If slavery is what Raymond Williams would treat as a residual formation that is incorporated and made integral to the dominant formation represented in "Bloodchild," it is nonetheless important to observe that Atlantic slavery and the practice of slave breeding, as it is imagined by most readers, has been significantly distorted through the processes by which it has been incorporated into Tlic hegemony. Indeed slave breeding in "Bloodchild" is uncanny in that it is at once familiar and unfamiliar, recognizable and chill-inducing in its (un)familiarity. While gestational surrogacy is part of the story's manifest thematic content, slave breeding is more difficult to discern because it is unmoored from recognizable racial and gender conventions. Put as plainly as possible, in "Bloodchild" slavery and the laboring bodies that reproduce Tlic hegemony have undergone transformation. They are no longer necessarily black or female. Rather all Terrans have become reproductive laborers, as surrogacy is the universal condition of human being. Consequently, as reproduction bursts out of the heterosexual matrix, reproductive heterosexuality is revealed as a possible but not inevitable by-product of reproductive extraction. In "Bloodchild" all reproductive laborers—regardless of race, gender, or sexuality—together make up an enslaved class.[43] From the vantage point of the Tlic, all humans are reproductive resources available for direct exploitation, investment, and speculative development. To the extent that Butler consciously recognizes that production has been subsumed by reproduction in the world she has depicted, she notes in her afterword that "Bloodchild" is a "pregnant man story" and "a coming-of-age story" in which the protagonist's maturity is signaled by his acquiescence to (or, perhaps more aptly, by his interpellation into) Tlic ideology and the roles within the labor force into which it interpellates humans as subjects subjected to Tlic ideology (30). Gan eventually elects to self-govern, *choosing* as his lot in life gestational surrogacy—the adult choice that he is expected to make by T'Gatoi and everyone else.

In a world in which racial difference is transvalued as species difference, in which the species divide becomes the caesura separating those who are made to live from those who are left to die, surrogacy/slavery becomes a specifically and at once universally human activity. As the differences among human beings are flattened and homogenized, all of humanity is feminized by the historical paleonomy entailed by its universal reproductive ontology and function. In turn, all of humanity is racialized by association with slave breeding as it was practiced in the Americas and the Caribbean for four hundred years. The upshot: even though Tlic ideology prevents human beings from consciously recognizing themselves as racialized and feminized slaves engaged in reproductive labor, it ought to be all but impossible for readers to miss the real relationship to the imaginary conditions under which the enslaved human beings who reside on the Tlic planet labor (to borrow, and tweak, Louis Althusser's famous formulation) to reproduce the relations of reproduction on which human subjection to the Tlic is predicated.[44]

The feminization and racialization of human reproductive labor and laborers is dramatized in a violent birth scene that provides the story's central spectacle. Bram Lomas, who is described as having "brown flesh," has the misfortune of going into labor while away from his Tlic, the only living being that is biochemically conditioned to aid him in birthing the larvae with which she has impregnated him. Because Lomas is struck down by pain near Gan's home, and because T'Gatoi is on this day visiting Gan's family, Gan and T'Gatoi together midwife Lomas's ill-timed birth. Though T'Gatoi is unable to ease Lomas's suffering, when she cuts Lomas open and removes larvae from inside him and places them in a large farm animal that Gan has slaughtered, she successfully saves Lomas's all-too-human flesh from being devoured by the wriggling young creatures that have begun to emerge from it. For his part, Gan assists in the unanesthetized operation on his fellow human that he concedes amounts to "torture" (15):

> Lomas's entire body stiffened under T'Gatoi's claw, though she merely rested it against him as she wound the rear section of her body around his legs. He might break my grip, but he would not break hers. He wept helplessly as she used his pants to tie his hands, then pushed his hands above his head so that I could kneel on the cloth between them and pin them in place. She rolled up his shirt and gave it to him to bite down on.
>
> And she opened him.
>
> His body convulsed with the first cut. He almost tore himself away from me. The sound he made . . . I had never heard such sounds come from anything human. T'Gatoi seemed to pay no attention as she lengthened and deepened the cut, now and then pausing to lick away blood. . . .
>
> She found the first grub. It was fat and deep red with his blood. . . . It had already eaten its own egg case but apparently had not yet begun to eat its host. . . . T'Gatoi picked up the writhing grub carefully and looked at it, somehow ignoring the terrible groans of the man.
>
> Abruptly, the man lost consciousness. (15–16)

In a passage that echoes scenes of gang rape and those of torture described in nineteenth-century slave narratives, a human body is mastered and subjected and in the process feminized, racialized, and dehumanized. As Lomas's body becomes surrogate it is forced to surrender human life for Tlic life (uttering "sounds that could not come from anything [any longer] human"), effectively becoming the animalized, disposable fount of the master's futurity. Lomas's value resides in his flesh, specifically in its in vivo surrogate function. Like the slavers and planters of the Old South, Tlic are biocapitalists invested in use and propagation of life itself. As Gan observes, not only did it seem that he was abetting T'Gatoi's "torture" of Lomas; he was also helping her to "consume" him (16). As in slavery, in Tlic surrogacy the master consumes the surrogate/slave, who, in being consumed, reproduces the conditions of enslavement such that surrogacy becomes sign and function of gendered, racialized, and animalized disposability. Important ★

For Gan, Lomas's ordeal is a turning point, a partial awakening to the relations of (re)production and the exploitative conditions in which humans are forced to labor. Significantly, however, Gan's awakening does not catalyze insurgency any more readily or obviously than did Dana's realization that she was killing Alice by helping to subject her to Rufus. Rather Gan's awakening appears to compel his self-governance and in so doing facilitates his interpellation into the same neoliberal rationality that guided Dana's actions in relation to Alice. Put otherwise, "Bloodchild," like Kindred, reveals the biopolitical dimensions of slave racial capitalism, biocapitalism, and neoliberalism. As important, it exposes how substantive reproductive freedom is foreclosed in contexts in which it is imagined that freedom is an individual possession that can be chosen by beings who are not regarded as fully human and have been stripped of their capacity to perceive and act on the alternatives. After Lomas's birthing of larval Tlic, Gan struggles to reconcile the violence he has witnessed and facilitated with his professed love for T'Gatoi and his desire to gestate her offspring. It is only by squelching his recently gained awareness of his condition (or perhaps more aptly by subordinating his emergent consciousness of his painful reality to the prevailing neoliberal rationality) that Gan chooses to become a surrogate.

As in Wild Seed and Kindred, in "Bloodchild" it is once again useful to scrutinize the idea of choice and the protagonists' capacity for insurgency within the conditions of unfreedom that are depicted. Although Gan "had been told all [his] life that this [human gestational surrogacy] was a good and necessary thing Tlic and Terran did together," and had, until now, believed this to be true, after Lomas's experience Gan confesses that he has come to recognize that human gestation of Tlic young is "something else, something worse . . . [a reality he] wasn't ready to see," yet one he "couldn't not see" (16–17) once it played out before his eyes. In other words, Gan admits he was previously blind to the relations of (re)production in which he and all his kin and kind are involved. As the story intimates, blindness of this sort results from consuming the narcotic eggs with which Tlic drug humans, supposedly to extend human longevity but more pragmatically to extend human (re)productivity. But it is also clearly a response to the feelings of familialism and the attendant ideology of interspecies mutuality and symbiosis that are perpetuated by Tlic (and, as I have indicated, by some of the story's critics). For this reason, although Butler never intimates whether Gan recognizes in Lomas's torturous ordeal the residual formation (slave breeding) that was practiced on his old planet, the internal conflict in which Gan becomes ensnared signals his vexed apprehension of the options that lie before him: Acceptance or rejection of his assigned role? Consent to or dissent from the hegemonic (Tlic) view of human surrogacy as mutually beneficial? Disavowal or recognition of the connection between surrogacy in his world and the history of slave breeding—the history that might transform his understanding of Terran-Tlic reproduction? Participation in the human community as currently constituted by Tlic hegemony, or refusal of the current reduction of human being to surrogate/slave?

At the story's outset Gan observes that Tlic power is enforced throughout the Preserve by the imposition of prohibitions, reminiscent of nineteenth-century Black Codes, on human possession of guns. Gan also unwittingly indicates that insurgency is most effectively countered not by a repressive state apparatus or by sovereign power but by an ideological apparatus that normalizes human submission to Tlic and upholds the biopolitical status quo that the Tlic require for survival. From Gan's perspective, it is the thick affective ties that the Tlic actively promote that bind humans to familial structures in which subjection to the reproductive needs of Tlic are rescripted as the desire for intimacy, love, and kinship. For this reason, above all others, it makes sense when Butler insists in her afterword that she intended "Bloodchild" to be read as a "love story," as it is through the filter of love and kinship that Gan considers his options and through this same filter that Tlic control the human beings upon whose surrogate/slave labor they rely.[45] Unwittingly evincing the complexity of the affective world in which he lives, Gan observes, without remarking upon the contradiction, that T'Gatoi "parceled us out to the desperate and sold us to the rich and powerful for their political support," and, too, she considered us "an independent people." Gan's reified mind does not recognize that caged humans are necessities and status symbols that are owned by Tlic, and that this is so despite Gan's notable use of each of these terms when describing himself and his fellow human beings as "an independent people" (5).

It is uncertain whether Gan fully apprehends the extent of his unfreedom and whether he can act upon his understanding of his situation at the story's conclusion, which follows the scene in which Lomas gives birth to the larvae. Afterward Gan engages in a prolonged process of probing his desire for T'Gatoi and questioning how it binds him to her. And although initially it seems as if he is about to reconsider his options, actual transformation is tricky business. The tensions that arise as Gan mulls over what has happened are distinctly uncomfortable. For this reason, "Bloodchild" can be read as a sadomasochist narrative in which Gan submits to *and* takes pleasure in his submission to T'Gatoi. (This is of course a redemptive reading that, it must be cautioned, is *not* antagonistic to the symbiotic reading that I have critiqued.) However, I argue that once the links between slavery and surrogacy are established, it is necessary to read "Bloodchild" as a story not about sadomasochism in an abstract sense but about sadomasochism in slavery, and thus about a slave who opts to act as surrogate for his master rather than rise in revolt against her. In the end Gan gives in to and actively nurtures his desire for unfreedom, electing to participate in the reproduction of the status quo.

The dystopian world depicted in "Bloodchild" enables readers to experience both estrangement and cognition because the text creates a world in which freedom and surrogacy/slavery are never entirely distinct, and thus a world in which the disavowal of slavery (and thus of this lack of distinction) subtend the biopolitical hegemony in which surrogates such as Gan labor. Through estrangement and cognition, readers come to see that Butler has not positioned freedom and unfreedom in an oppositional relationship but rather on a continuum. We come to see that the rationality of this situation in which freedom and enslavement are, as it were, bound is acceded to by self-governing subjects who actively desire continued and always deepening subjection. When Gan agrees to sex with and impregnation by T'Gatoi, and therefore to gestation and birth of her young, readers realize the disabling repercussions of his expression of and submission to his felt desire for T'Gatoi, as well as the personal gain that Gan perceives to be the payoff of his participation in the reproductive relations that subtend the Tlic world. ALSO L.B.?

Evidence of Gan's decision to accommodate the hegemony emerges most forcefully in two interconnected passages that simultaneously (and thus paradoxically) reveal his emergent consciousness, his awareness of his belonging within an oppressed group of fellow human beings, and his willingness to acquiesce to the biopolitical and neoliberal formation that obstructs consideration of the alternatives that might otherwise be available to him and the oppressed group to which he belongs. The first passage, in which Gan rejects the rebellious route taken by his older brother Qui, is presaged by Gan's midwifing of Lomas's birth, an activity for which Qui berates him. Having long ago recognized that he might be called on by T'Gatoi to function as her surrogate if anything were to happen to Gan, Qui has devoted himself to the twofold task of Gan's physical preservation and of running as far away from T'Gatoi as he can within the confines of the Preserve. Replaying a power dynamic that recalls that between Dana and Alice in *Kindred*, Qui frees himself by sacrificing his kin, or, more aptly, by pimping Gan to T'Gatoi. In the second passage, Gan rejects Qui's individualistic, self-serving response to the human condition by choosing to serve T'Gatoi as surrogate, an act that saves Gan's other siblings (specifically his sister, Hoa, who appears to be next in the gestational line-up) from laboring thus. However, in the scene in which Gan demands that T'Gatoi impregnate him, he forecloses any simple interpretation of this demand as an act of solidarity with his sister. For in this scene Gan earnestly expresses his deeply felt desire to play the role of surrogate and thus his desire to replace his sister and accede to his own feminization, racialization, and dehumanization. Put otherwise, in this scene Gan succumbs to Tlic rationality and thus to the feeling that familial love and desire for T'Gatoi require him to choose to be her surrogate/slave.

Perhaps predictably, in an epic confrontation that rescripts (as it recalls) other such confrontations between slave and master, Gan at one point confronts T'Gatoi by pointing an illegally stashed rifle at himself. However, Gan elects neither to kill himself nor to turn the gun on T'Gatoi and demand his freedom from her. Instead, in this moment of truth, a moment that perversely reprises what Frederick Douglass described as the "turning point in his career as a slave," Gan requests that T'Gatoi acknowledge her dependence on him, his special place in her heart, before impregnating him.[46] This request for affective acknowledgment from the master—which is also a move away from Gan's emergent consciousness of his sexual and (re)productive dispossession—should give readers pause. From one vantage point, Gan's choice to engage in a sexual encounter with T'Gatoi that culminates in her impregnation of him and Gan's becoming a surrogate can be interpreted as acts of accommodation under duress—acts that resonate with Anyanwu's departure to the New World with Doro. And yet to interpret Gan's choice thus is to misunderstand the neoliberal rationality that shapes it and at once separates Gan's actions from Anyanwu's. Although in choosing to become a surrogate Gan refuses complicity in T'Gatoi's subjection of his siblings, he also chooses self-governance, a choice that both Anyanwu and Alice are unwilling to make. More important still, Gan experiences the choice to self-govern and thus comply as a good choice because it fulfills his strongly felt desire for T'Gatoi.

In lowering his gun Gan removes not only T'Gatoi but also Tlic hegemony  (read: biocapitalism and neoliberalism) from his sights. In contrast to An-yanwu, who elects to live on so that she can continue to resist Doro and keep the hegemony that he represents in check, the disturbing transcript of Gan and T'Gatoi's postcoital pillow talk reveals that Gan desires subjection (both sexual and reproductive), and his continued enslavement. To Gan's expression of the last glimmer of agency—his suggestion that humans should at the very least be shown by Tlic what they are in for when they choose to become surrogates—T'Gatoi responds by silencing him. Significantly Gan's riposte is to go silent. Humans must be "protected from seeing," T'Gatoi advises; birth has always been and will remain "a private thing." Installing reproduction of the species within familial networks of privacy, affect, tradition (and, in this case, heterosexuality, albeit between species), T'Gatoi asserts and Gan accepts the Tlic worldview and her (sic) paternalism: "I'll take care of you," she chillingly reassures him in the story's last line (29).

Although I have argued that Gan chooses to self-govern, it would be wrong to conclude that "Bloodchild" somehow endorses the inevitability of accommodation to Tlic power, and thus to biocapitalism and neoliberalism. The awakening of Gan's consciousness when he witnesses Lomas's ordeal, an awakening evinced in his most intimate and exploitative moment with T'Gatoi, marks the site of an emergent formation in which readers might potentially partake even though Gan does not. After all, the surrogate condition described in "Bloodchild" is represented as the universal human condition, our condition. This story about the surrogacy/slavery nexus is not only about a far-off planet. As I have argued, surrogacy in "Bloodchild" is not represented as black women's plight and thus a thing of the distant past. It is represented as an enduring and universal condition that touches the entire human race insofar as we are all written by the history of slavery, whether we elect to acknowledge or to disavow the presence of slavery's reproductive afterlife in our biocapitalist and neoliberal times. In this sense, "Bloodchild" proffers what might most usefully be construed as a *dystopian gift:* the critical distance that allows readers to estrange our world, and thus to generate the critical distance that allows us to cognize the residual and emergent formations that surround the human refugees who live among the Tlic and those that surround us in the biocapitalist and neoliberal world in which we live.

In conclusion, it appears that Butler's meditations on the afterlife of reproductive slavery constitute precisely the sort of dystopian representation of the cultures and politics of reproduction that Roberts called for in the essay I discussed at this chapter's outset. As I hope to have demonstrated, dystopias such as *Wild Seed*, *Kindred*, and "Bloodchild" together offer readers a black feminist philosophy of history that shuttles us backward and forward in time—into a past in which we might learn about slavery and the centrality of sexual and reproductive extraction to the continuous expansion of (slave) racial capitalism and biocapitalism, and into a neoliberal world, cast as hegemonic, in which the slave episteme lives on even as individuals appear to disavow its persistence. Expressed in Benjaminian terms, I have argued that Butler's philosophy of history allows us to "seize hold of a memory," in this case a memory of reproductive slavery "as it flashes up at a moment of danger"[47]—a moment such as our own. In our time of the now, in which freedom amounts to the choice to self-govern, it behooves us to carefully consider the modalities (material, ideological, and affective) through which we collectively reproduce futurity, our own and that of others.

Chapter Five

A SLAVE NARRATIVE
for POSTRACIAL TIMES

The contemporary moment is so replete with assumptions
that freedom is made universal through liberal political en-
franchisement and the globalization of capitalism that it has
become difficult to write or imagine alternative knowledges, or
to act on behalf of alternative projects or ways of being.

—LISA LOWE, *THE INTIMACIES OF FOUR CONTINENTS* (2015)

In 2005 two texts with tightly linked thematic foci emerged nearly simultaneously, each garnering popular attention, albeit of different kinds: director
Michael Bay's thriller *The Island*, and Kazuo Ishiguro's award-winning novel
Never Let Me Go.[1] These two dystopian texts were created in the wake of several
widely reported events: the birth in 1997 of Dolly the sheep (the first complex
mammal to be successfully cloned from adult tissue cells), the completion
in 2000 of the sequencing of the human genome, and the announcement
by a South Korean researcher in the prominent journal *Science* in 2004 of the
supposed cloning of thirty human embryos.[2] Film and novel treat these intertwined real-life events through depiction of fictional worlds in which the
cloning of human beings has become a quotidian way to sustain population
and status quo. Clones, distinguished from human beings (known as "originals," "normals," or "sponsors"), constitute a life-support system, providing
bodily organs, tissues, and reproductive processes required by an aged and
diseased population apparently ignorant of or inured to the fact that (re)pro-
duction of disposable (cloned) bodies subtends (uncloned) human life.[3] Indeed
the conceptual conceits of film and novel are nearly identical: cloning allows for
efficiency in the reproduction of bodies; cloned bodies are profitably construed

as less than human; as a consequence, in the face of perceived scarcity of organs, harvesting of organs derived from clones has become a common, even banal practice.[4] This chapter explores the representation of the banalization of this reproductive violence. I treat cloning as a thick metaphor for the range of biotechnological practices that have enabled biocapitalist extraction over the past four decades and the recalibration of the slave episteme in and for neoliberal and supposedly postracial times.

In both film and novel cloned populations are scientifically and expertly managed by varied combinations of technological know-how, ideological indoctrination, and outright repression. A repressive apparatus in the form of a clone prison-factory dominates in *The Island*; an ideological apparatus, in the form of a boarding school, interpellates clones as "carers" (of fellow clones) and "donors" (of organs) in *Never Let Me Go*. In both texts, clones, like those who receive their organs, appear to acquiesce to the system—or at least initially. In the film they do so because they are kept in the dark and thus prevented from learning that they are spare-part warehouses. In the novel they accede to the upward distribution of the biological resources extracted from their bodies even though they are aware that repeated organ harvesting entails death. Although these narratives share much, they diverge dramatically in their treatment of the long history of human reproductive dispossession and thus the connections among human cloning, the contemporary organ trade, and the practice of slave breeding in the Americas and the Caribbean. While this chapter's main focus is Ishiguro's novel, I begin by juxtaposing it with Bay's film to highlight the stakes in popular depictions of cloning.[5] Cloning and the organ trade are rarely considered in discussions of the long history of slave racial capitalism, but I argue that dystopian sf's depictions of cloning and the organ trade ought to be read as meditations on the relationship between slave racial capitalism and biocapitalism within the context of neoliberalism.

The difference between the film's and the novel's treatments of slavery is filtered through distinct portraits of insurgency against dispossession, or, as the case may be, the absence thereof. Whereas in the film belated awareness of their disposability eventually leads to a clone/slave revolt that catalyzes the demise of the corporation that operates the facility where clones are reproduced and stored, in the novel clones are never sparked to action, and this remains the case even after they become fully conscious of their plight. In contrast to the perplexing message embedded in the novel, the film's message is direct and abundantly clear: contemporary biotechnological practices are not coincident with slavery. As viewers can see, if slavery were to surface within biocapitalism, it would be duly banished by fundamentally moral individuals eager to concede the evil of their ways. Performing the historical condensation (the merging of a residual slave past with the biocapitalist present of the film) and the subsequent banishment of the slave past necessary to production of the film's narrative closure, the clone/slave revolt that is depicted in The Island is led not only by two white clone fugitives (played by Scarlett Johansson and Ewan McGregor) but also by an African clone hunter/slave catcher who has switched sides and become a stalwart abolitionist. Significantly this character is played by Djimon Hounsou, an actor who first garnered attention for his portrayal of Cinque, the African leader of the shipboard slave revolt that was fictionalized in Steven Spielberg's Amistad (1997). In The Island an expressly multiracial abolitionist mod squad shepherd the cloned and enslaved multitudes into a brave new world in which, it is implied, clones/slaves will henceforth be regarded as the equals of other human beings. The closing sequence is not subtle. As clones bust out of their postmodern barração into the fresh air of an empty, biblical desert landscape, the sound track swells, arms are raised in jubilee, and clones/slaves (symbolically clad in white) are transvalued. They are a chosen people, a wrongly persecuted people who have now assumed their rightful destiny: life in the promised land. As the screen fades to black viewers can rest easy. Corporate excess and immoral regimes of biocapitalist accumulation are outrageous dystopian projections that will be kept at bay by moral agents operating within a self-cleansing free-market system constitutively unable to tolerate the violence it generates. The friendly face of biocapitalism will smile down upon us if we continue to function as the humanists we already are by recognizing that clones are people too.[6]

In comparison to this technophilic and postracial vision of bioengineered human futurity and biocapitalist free-market benevolence, the vision of cloning in Never Let Me Go is unrelentingly dystopian. There is no happy ending, just acquiescence to disposability. Clones produced and educated to function as donors of vital organs and carers for those who donate do not imagine insurgency; they never attempt to refuse the roles they have been created to occupy. Moreover, to the reader's initial surprise, subsequent consternation, and increasing discomfort, Ishiguro's clones appear to participate in naturalizing their condition and its supposed inevitability. Awareness of unfreedom coexists with commitment to the system that creates and (ab)uses them. Unlike the revolutionary, freedom-loving clones/slaves depicted in The Island,

Figure 5.1 (ABOVE) Newly freed clones flood out of their prison. Film still from Michael Bay, director, *The Island*. DreamWorks Pictures, Warner Bros. © 2005.

Figure 5.2 (OPPOSITE) Leading the clones to freedom. Djimon Hounsou as Albert Laurent. Film still from Michael Bay, director, *The Island*. DreamWorks Pictures, Warner Bros. © 2005.

Ishiguro's clones self-govern. Like Gan, the protagonist in Octavia Butler's "Bloodchild," Ishiguro's clones dutifully play out the suicidal part collectively assigned them in the bifurcated world (human being versus disposable, less-than-human being) in which they reside. This world, like those depicted by Butler, is hyperbolically biopolitical. It is also necropolitical. It functions by instantiating norms for individuals and populations that make some live and let others die, and it emphasizes the death function within processes of massification.[7] In the world of the novel, survival for human "originals" requires the active (if torturously slow) putting to death of their less-than-human duplicates, as sequential donation ends in extermination. In contrast to *The Island*, which places necropower in a future that viewers are ultimately assured will be fended off, *Never Let Me Go* depicts necropower as saturating the present that is occupied by the novel's narrator and the implied reader. As the reader is alerted on the novel's first page, the events described constitute our immediate past—"England, late 1990s"—a decidedly familiar place. In other words, through inversion of the sf genre's anticipated temporal schema, the world of the novel is transformed into the past out of which our present has emerged.[8]

Throughout Ishiguro's novel, extraction is never operated through clone racialization as black or African or through the sort of association of clones and black Africans that is a blatant part of the casting in *The Island*.[9] And yet, as we shall see, the slave episteme nonetheless powers the (re)production of life itself in the biopolitical and necropolitical world that is depicted. As we learn through the novel's glacially paced reveal, like clones, readers inhabit a biocapitalist society with slavery, to which we, like the organ recipients depicted, are unresponsive, and thus with which we are complicit.[10] Although neither the white female narrator nor her fellow white clones perceive it thus, their world is predicated not only on cloning but also on racialized dehumanization of their disposability.[11] As a consequence, rather than glibly reassuring us that biocapitalism and slavery are antithetical (as does *The Island*), *Never Let Me Go* constellates slave racial capitalism and biocapitalism, effectively revealing to readers that the narrator's and our own neoliberal, supposedly postracial society is predicated on the death function (necropolitics) and on the complex, albeit disavowed and invisible racialization of the population that has been (re)produced for disposability.[12]

As in chapter 4, in which I read across Butler's fictions to reveal their sustained meditation on the surrogacy/slavery nexus in the slave past and the neoliberal present, in this chapter I read Ishiguro's novel as a related, if distinct meditation on the afterlife of reproductive slavery in the supposedly postracial times that neoliberalism claims to augur. As in the chapter on Butler, in the present chapter I demonstrate that dystopian fiction has a unique capacity to constellate past and present. In contrast to Butler's fiction, however, Ishiguro's performs, on the surface of the text, the disavowal of the slave past within contemporary representations of human cloning and the related trade in human organs. In reading Ishiguro's novel with a focus on this disavowal, I treat it as a symptomatic and simultaneously self-reflexive account of the workings of the slave episteme in a world—our own—that fails to recognize the constellation of past and present in what Benjamin would call "the time of the now," and thus perpetuates a historicist conceptualization of decisive historical ruptures and smooth linear progress. In short, I treat Ishiguro's text as a contribution to a philosophy of history vital to survival, but not to the same philosophy of history elaborated by black feminists who expressly worked to make visible not only the afterlife of reproductive slavery but too the insurgency of slave women.

Over the course of this chapter I take up three distinct dimensions of the philosophy of history elaborated in *Never Let Me Go*: (1) the novel's form and the manner in which Ishiguro's formal choices construct slavery as a blind spot for the narrator and reader—a discussion that takes a necessary detour through Marx's account of the value form and of Aristotle's ideas about exchange; (2) the novel's representation of the Holocaust of World War II as the overdetermined relay point through which racial slavery passes as it is recalibrated for neoliberal and supposedly postracial purposes; and (3) the novel's reworking of the nineteenth-century slave narrative, a form, I argue, that is whitewashed in order to update it for neoliberalism and postracialism.

Kathy, Aristotle, and the Blind Spot of Slavery

The novel's form stands out and has been routinely remarked upon by critics. The first-person narration addresses the reader as if she occupies a position that is structurally similar to the narrator's own (thus Kathy's repeated refrain: "I don't know how it was where you were but at Hailsham we . . ." [13]). Over the course of the novel Kathy recollects her life, recalling days spent at Hailsham, the pastoral boarding school where she and other clones were raised by "Guardians"; months spent at "the Cottages," the substandard rural housing where clones come of age and prepare themselves for organ harvesting; and years spent as a "carer" working to ensure the smooth "completion" of fellow clones. When we meet Kathy she is thirty-one. We leave her with a few months left before she quits her job as a carer to begin to donate her own organs. While at the novel's outset Kathy boasts that she has "done her work well" for eleven years (3), readers do not accumulate enough information to comprehend the nature of this "work" until a third of the way through the novel. It is thus belatedly that we recognize that so-called caring is a form of killing, and so-called donation a euphemism for murder. And it is only as we move through the novel's denouement that we grasp the violence that Kathy's narration banalizes, as it is only alongside Kathy that we learn that the rumored "deferral" of donations is impossible and the murderous encroachment of necropower inevitable. The consequence for readers of this belated reveal of the clone's subjection to premature death is that even though Kathy addresses us as if we immediately relate to her story, we realize that it is only in retrospect that we have assimilated enough information to recognize her story as our own, and thus only belatedly that we have become aware of our complicity in assent to the banalization of the necropolitical violence that appears to be continuous across time and social formations, fictional and actual.[13]

Another way to express the discomfiting experience of reading *Never Let Me Go* is to acknowledge that as an unreliable narrator, Kathy's blindness to her situation necessarily shapes the reader's understanding of her narrative. As Tommy, Kathy's school friend and eventual lover, explains (unaware of the uncanny accuracy of his characterization), clones are "told and not told"; they know and don't know what's going on. They sense, but are never certain, that "donor" is not a badge of distinction but rather an executioner's mark designating them victims of genocide. Knowing and not knowing implicates Kathy in caring as killing; it also shapes her narrative, forcing readers to reduplicate her complicity, albeit with a difference. For the narrator's knowing/not knowing ultimately redounds for us as a series of self-reflexive questions: By what means have we moved from the past that is depicted as our own in this novel into the present moment of reading? Have we assented to the banalization of dehumanizing violence already? Do we today participate in disavowal of the slave episteme, and thus the extractive reproductive processes that fuel biocapitalism?

Never Let Me Go is a profoundly compelling and at once uncomfortable novel to read—no doubt why it has been variously described as "most unsettling," "shadowy," evocative of "disquietude," and rife with "roiling emotions."[14] Critics suggest that the feelings it readily generates are "uncanny."

I extend the suggestion: it is not only the affect produced by reading that unsettles; the representation is itself uncanny in a Freudian sense. It shuttles between the familiar and the unfamiliar (*heimlich* and *unheimlich*), producing disavowal and the simultaneous horror of recognition. When I teach the novel students routinely express frustration with and outrage at Kathy's failure to recognize her complicity. They are especially galled that she neither runs nor rages upon learning that there are no deferrals.[15] Students point out that neither chains nor shackles bind Kathy, and there are no whipping posts.[16] Despite her apparent ability to exit the system (after all, she has a car and can drive it anywhere she likes), Kathy and the other clones dutifully show up for donations as each, in turn, endures the harvest of their vital organs and, finally, the harvest of life itself. For most students, unanswered questions proliferate: Why do the clones self-govern? Why do they abet each other's murder? Most pressing, how can we make sense of Ishiguro's choice to represent them thus?[17]

Never Let Me Go has become a mainstay in the Marxist literary theory course I routinely teach, and it was in the context of teaching *Capital* that I recognized what has become for me a fascinating resonance. In the famous first chapter of volume 1, in the process of analyzing the commodity's value form, Marx positions his reader in relationship to Aristotle's struggle to understand exchange and value in Ancient Greece in a manner that is analogous to that in which Ishiguro positions his reader in relationship to Kathy's struggle to understand exchange and value in her world. Like Kathy, Aristotle knows and does not know how value is created. He knows and does not know how to make sense of the exchanges he witnesses, and thus he experiences a cognitive struggle akin to Kathy's. More important, like Marx, Ishiguro asks readers to dwell on rather than skip over this struggle and the epistemological failure it precipitates, effectively demanding that readers not only confront but also comprehend the reasons for the narrator's confusion. However, unlike Ishiguro, who allows Kathy to meander and lead readers astray before letting us know what is happening, Marx deftly leads us into and through Aristotle's perplexity. He begins by posing the question of the substance of value and concludes by answering it.[18] What is it that makes a commodity such as twenty yards of linen, a coat, or a wooden table valuable? In contrast to the classical political economists whom he critiques, Marx argues that the commodity is neither unitary nor stable. It possesses a "two-fold character," utility and exchangeability (or use-value and exchange value), and these are mutually contingent. However, while the former can be understood as simply the commodity's ability to satisfy human needs, the latter is harder to grasp. As Marx explains, exchange value does not inhere in the commodity; rather quantities of it are "congealed" in and through the process by which one commodity is exchanged for another. As the plot thickens, Marx concedes that exchange value is best understood as a metaphor (what Jacques Derrida will later call a "concept metaphor"), an appearance of something that makes visible a concept—in this case, the concept of abstract social labor power. In short, exchange value is the form of appearance of something else. It is the form that social labor power takes when congealed in a commodity that is equated with and then exchanged with another commodity in which an equal quantity of abstract social labor power is objectified. "We have seen," Marx elaborates, "that when commodities are in the relation of exchange, their exchange value manifests itself as something totally independent of their use-value. . . . The progress of the investigation [thus leads] . . . us back to exchange value as the necessary mode of expression, or form of appearance of value" (128).

In so saying Marx acknowledges Aristotle as his intellectual predecessor, "the great investigator who was the first to analyze the value-form" (151) and, too, the first investigator whom it eluded. As Marx elaborates, Aristotle understood operations of equivalence. He understood that it is only through the activity of exchange that the "equality" of different durable things, and thus their value-form, is established. Yet beyond this initial insight Aristotle could not go. Underscoring the impasse, Marx notes that Aristotle "clearly" understood

> that the money-form of the commodity is only a more developed aspect of the simple form of value, i.e., of the expression of the value of a commodity in some other commodity chosen at random, for he says:
>
> 5 beds = 1 house
> is indistinguishable from
> 5 beds = a certain amount of money
>
> He further sees that the value-relation which provides the framework for this expression of value itself requires that the house should be qualitatively equated with the bed, and that these things, being distinct to the senses, could not be compared with each other as commensurable magnitudes if they lacked this essential identity. (151)

And yet, Marx concludes, Aristotle "falters and abandons further analysis of the form of value" at this point.[19] Indeed Aristotle "falters" because although he recognizes that "'there can be no exchange . . . without equality, and no equality without commensurability'" (151), he cannot discern the basis on which commensurability is established.

Slowly but surely it becomes apparent that Marx has drawn our attention to Aristotle's faltering because it is as important as what Aristotle readily comprehends. As Marx observes, anyone lacking the concept of "the homogeneous element, i.e. the common substance, which the house represents from the point of view of the bed" (151), would be unable to formulate the "concept of value," and anyone of Aristotle's intellectual stature unable to formulate this concept could be forced to abandon his quest only by material circumstances. Having cleared the way for the revelation Marx has been pushing us toward all along, he finally comes out with it: Aristotle could not conceive of the concept of *abstract human labor power* because such an "identical social substance" exists only in a capitalist society, and Ancient Greece was a society with slavery.[20] In Aristotle's world, labor power was of unequal value, because a portion of all human labor was performed without compensation by slaves. "Because Greek society was founded on the labour of slaves . . . [and] hence had as its natural basis the inequality of men and of their labour powers" (152), Marx concludes, Aristotle could not recognize that "commodities possess an objective character as values only in so far as they are all expressions of an identical social substance, human labor" (138). Apparently Aristotle was written by his times and therefore epistemologically undone by slavery.

Ultimately it is Aristotle's faltering that allows Marx to set forth the materialist premise central to his own thought. This is expressed nowhere more succinctly than in the preface to *A Contribution to a Critique of Political Economy*, in which Marx asserts that what we know is always conditioned by the mode of production and the relations of production and thus that our social existence conditions our consciousness rather than the other way around.[21] I have taken the preceding detour to underscore the profound importance of this insight on its own terms, and also because Marx's meditations on Aristotle are key to understanding Ishiguro's portrait of Kathy. As we shall see, Marx's meditations on Aristotle explain how and why Kathy falters when she attempts to comprehend the exchange relationship in which she and other clones are involved and, too, how and why readers of Kathy's narrative become uncomfortably conscious of our seduction by the postracial pieties that lead us to abandon our quest to make sense of the exchanges in which we are involved—exchanges that are predicated on the afterlife of reproductive slavery in our time.

The Art of Exchange in a Biocapitalist Society with Slavery

As attested to by scholars of the contemporary trade in commodities derived from the human body, tens of thousands of vital organs, tissues, bones, units of blood, gametes, and stem cells are exchanged each year around the world. These exchanges often result in the maiming or death of those whom recipients are led by the obfuscating language of the market to believe have freely chosen to donate their body parts. Thus scholars of the trade urge us to become attuned to the reality that donors are quite often "harvestees" whose bodies and lives are wantonly used and discarded. In such exchanges huge profits are generated (by one admittedly loose estimate, "several billion dollars' worth of humanity changes hands" annually), and the flow of human biological materials is decidedly upward: from the Global South to the Global North, from the poor to the wealthy, from women to men, and from children to adults.[22] Although body parts are not (yet) harvested from clones, current harvesting from the most vulnerable populations constitutes an ample basis on which to draw an analogy between the fictional world in which Ishiguro immerses us and our own. And yet it is not only this brutal reality that interests me here. As in previous chapters, my present focus is on constellation of past and present, on the recalibration of past ideas for contemporary circumstances, and on how endurance of the slave episteme renders extraction of reproductive labor and its products thinkable in the first place.

Insofar as Kathy falters when she seeks to comprehend the exchanges in which she is involved, the portrait of her faltering allows readers to imagine that we too might be blind to slavery and its shaping of our world. Put otherwise, Kathy's failure to apprehend that she lives in a biocapitalist society with slavery allows readers to reflect on what we may have failed and may continue to fail to understand about the production of value in our world. Our exposure to Kathy's blind spot opens onto an awareness of our own potential blindness to the constellation of past and present in the contemporary organ trade, and thus of the persistence of the slave episteme in biocapitalism. Several passages in the novel are my focus in the remainder of this chapter. Each offers a window through which we may view the epistemological complexities that are today involved in apprehending reproductive extraction in biocapitalism as a process enabled by the slave episteme, a thought system that shapes racialized dehumanization in neoliberalism despite the pervasiveness of postracial ideology.

The first passage concerns the "tokens controversy" (39) that emerges when Kathy and fellow Hailsham students come together to question why they must give their best artwork to Madame, an associate of Miss Emily (Hailsham's headmistress), for "the Gallery" that Madame displays beyond Hailsham's walls. As Kathy explains, the emergent sense of unfairness peaked among the students "by the time we were ten . . . [when] this whole notion that it was a great honour to have something taken by Madame collided with a feeling that we were losing our most marketable stuff" (39). After all, student success at seasonal "Exchanges," the social and economic events through-out the year at which clones receive "tokens" for the art that they produce, is foreclosed by Madame's requisition of their art. Without tokens, students are unable to purchase artwork created by their peers and the secondhand goods made available to them at the "Sales"—and these are the only two opportuni-ties afforded them for participation in commerce. After discussion among themselves, students agree to agitate for compensation. Although the protest is quickly quieted by school Guardians who concede that students may re-ceive tokens for art that is taken away (if "not many" [40], as Kathy flatly observes), the momentary agitation nonetheless reveals the students' intuition of an injustice, as well as their inability to fully countenance the nature of their actual dispossession. Indeed compensation in tokens emerges as a symbolic amelioration that inures students to the fact that payment for their art is not only trivial but a ruse in comparison to the fact that they await a killing theft for which there is and can be no recompense. Like all human chattel, clones lack property in the self. In such a situation receipt of tokens for art amounts to a pedagogical exercise that adjusts clones to exchange of something for nothing and, more important, to (mis)perception of a surface injustice (theft of their art) for the deep injustice: theft of life itself through a process by which human biological life is abstracted and integrated into the exchange relationship. Finally, because the real theft evades them, clones miss the profound coexistence and collision of distinct modes of valuation in their world—a biocapitalist society with slavery in which some lives are deemed valuable and others are disposable, some subject to legal protection and others entirely alienable and fungible. In the clones' world, human equal-ity vies with inequality because their society lacks, as societies with slavery do, "the equality of men and of their labor power."[23]

At the end of his chapter on the commodity, Marx tells readers that the injustice of capitalist exchange is obscured by the fetishism of the commod-ity. *Fetishism*, Marx's term for the "mysterious" or "hieroglyphic" process by which abstract human labor is "congealed" in the commodity, leaves the consumer with the impression that she has exchanged money for a desired good rather than for a quantity of social labor power. For Marx, when workers collectively cut through fetishism and recognize the social nature of abstract human labor power, human liberation becomes possible. In contrast to Marx's workers, Ishiguro's clones appear to be constitutively unable to cut through fetishism, not simply because, like most, they are captivated by it, but also because they do not recognize that they are enslaved—that they are living beings whose humanity has been stripped from them in a world from which slavery has supposedly been banished but in fact lives on. Ultimately it is by treating the issue of the commodification of human beings (and their constitutive parts) as a buried truth that Ishiguro finally parts ways with Marx, who, as we have seen in previous chapters, mistakenly regards slavery as a precapitalist formation and human labor (rather than human beings) as the primary commodity that is for sale in capitalism. It is also by treating the enslavement of the clones in biocapitalism that Ishiguro joins the black Marxists discussed in previous chapters not only in positing slavery and capitalism as articulated economic formations, but also in recognizing that social domination operates through the continuous recalibration of hegemonic modes of racialized dehumanization.[24]

Instructively, despite the rich scholarship on slave racial capitalism (see chapter 1), the racialization of biocapitalism has not been engaged by scholars of so-called neoslavery—the forms of slavery typically associated with the organ trade and other markets in human biological commodities.[25] In his field-shaping book, *Disposable People: New Slavery in the Global Economy*, to take one prominent instance, Kevin Bales schematizes the distinctions between what he calls "the old slavery" and "the new slavery," taking plantation slavery in the Americas as representative of the old, and bonded labor, sexual servitude, and child labor as typical of the new.[26] Bales, a sociologist and director of the global NGO Free the Slaves, bases his analysis of the deracination of contemporary slavery on research conducted in South and Southeast Asia, northern and western Africa, parts of South America, as well as the United States, Japan, and a number of European countries. His findings indicate that there are more slaves today (27 million by his admittedly conservative count) than at the height of the Atlantic slave trade. However, rather than treat neoslavery as resonant with Atlantic slavery, Bales foregrounds differences and ultimately disavows the centrality of processes of racialization to neoslavery (and therefore to contemporary capitalism). As he observes, today slavery "is a shadowy, illegal enterprise" (8) that depends on short- rather than long-term relationships that fulfill the demands and pace of the global economy and its need for flexible labor and continuous accumulation. Slaves are no longer regarded as valuable property, purchased at high cost. Instead legal ownership is avoided, purchase deemed unnecessary, and slaves disposed of when worn out.[27] In a section of his introduction entitled "What Does Race Have to Do with It?" Bales blankly asserts that in the new slavery, "race . . . means little" (10). In his view, modern slaveholders, freed of ideas of "racial inferiority" that previously restricted "the status of slaves to *others*," have no need "to explain or defend their . . . methods of labor recruitment and management" (10). Instead they enslave any individual sufficiently weak, gullible, or "vulnerable enough to be enslaved" (11).

It is temptingly easy to use Bales's deracinated ideas about neoslavery to interpret Ishiguro's white British clones as postmodern slaves. The clones are weak, gullible, deprived, and thus enslave-able. Like other trafficked persons recognized as slaves by the UN Protocol to Prevent and Suppress and Punish Trafficking in Persons, the clones are not only (ab)used; they are completely disposable and replaceable.[28] And yet, despite the ease with which Ishiguro's clones might be slotted into Bales's liberal humanist framework, if we hope to understand the relevance of the history of slave racial capitalism to Ishiguro's novel—a move that necessarily demands consideration of slavery as a race-making process—we must push aside the easy analogy and dive beneath the novel's whitewashed surface.[29] As we shall see, the slave episteme subtends extraction of life itself in *Never Let Me Go*, which, therefore, should not be read as an account of neoslavery as somehow postracial but rather as a meditation on the afterlife of reproductive slavery and the persistence of the slave episteme in biocapitalism. As we shall see, despite its whitewashed surface, the novel constellates the slave past and biocapitalist present, and in so doing *exposes* rather than consolidates neoliberal pieties about the irrelevance of racial slavery (or, for that matter, racism) to present circumstances.

Surfacing Racial Slavery

To advance the claim that *Never Let Me Go* provides insight into the constellation of past and present, slave racial capitalism and biocapitalism, I suggest that we read the novel's portrait of its present (our recent past) not as the final moment in a process of progressive historical development inexorably moving away from racial slavery and toward postracial "freedom," but rather as "the time of the now"—a time that is shot through with "shards" from the past, with bits and pieces of the past that may be constellated with the present in order to envision a more liberated future.[30] For ultimately Ishiguro's novel reveals that cloning and the organ trade are necessarily if invisibly linked to the slave past and that the liberal humanism that powers institutions such as Hailsham is actually keyed to a form of racial capitalism that subtends reproductive extraction. And yet, because Ishiguro's clones are never directly referred to as slaves in the novel and never perceive themselves to be slaves, surfacing racial slavery is methodologically difficult. In short, we cannot simply interpret manifest figuration. Instead it is necessary to treat slavery as a ghostly presence that haunts the narrative and provides the center around which it coheres. I therefore proceed to locate the paradoxically tangible occlusion of slavery—by treating slavery as an absent presence—so that I can approach the workings of the slave episteme in the neoliberal world that Ishiguro depicts as well as in our own.

In discussions about the politics of reading, a critique of "depth reading" has gained a degree of currency within literary studies. This critique, which has variously been labeled "postsymptomatic reading," "reparative reading," and "descriptive reading," has been elaborated by scholars such as Eve Kosofsky Sedgwick, Sharon Marcus, and Stephen Best, among others.[31] Although approaches differ, these scholars are united in their elevation of textual surfaces and manifest description over textual depth. Together they express suspicion of dominant methods of interpretation that find hidden or repressed meaning beneath textual surfaces. Rather than reading for historical conflicts and contradictions that require excavation, surface readers attend to what is manifest. In discussing the "alternatives to symptomatic reading," Best and Marcus recommend taking "surface to mean what is evident, perceptible, apprehensible in texts; what is neither hidden nor hiding; what, in the geometrical sense, has length and breadth but no thickness, and therefore covers no depth. A surface is what insists on being looked *at* rather than what we must train ourselves to see *through*."[32]

Since I suggest that racial slavery never appears on the surface of the text in *Never Let Me Go*, surface readers would presumably argue that the suggestion that it haunts the text is misguided. As Best and Marcus put it, "Just reading sees ghosts as presences, not absences, and lets ghosts be ghosts, instead of saying what they are ghosts *of*" (13).[33] Yet, from another vantage point, one that illuminates the neoliberal context of textual production under discussion in this chapter, a superficial or descriptive reading of slavery as an absent presence is exactly what Ishiguro's text demands of its readers *on the surface*. It is, as we have seen, precisely on the surface that Kathy's narrative falters. And it is in faltering that her narrative demands we pay attention to what we and our narrator alike know and do not know and therefore can and cannot articulate about the forms of extraction that subtend the exchanges that are depicted and those in which we are involved. Put otherwise, Kathy's narrative demands consideration of the problem initially posed by Kathy's schoolmate Tommy as the predicament of all Hailsham students: how to make meaning of their lives when they are told and not told, when they know and do not know what is going on. Like other Hailsham students, Kathy is forced by circumstance and convention to engage with the hegemonic representation of the exchanges in which she is involved. For her, the problem of superficiality exists on the surface, and it is therefore only by posing the problem of superficiality that readers are able to see that the probing of depth is necessary.[34] Put otherwise, the narrator's superficial and affectively flat descriptions of the problems she confronts paradoxically force readers to go deeper than Kathy can or will, to probe beneath the surface, to dive deep so that we might yet understand her insistent superficiality.

The relationship between narrative surface and interpretive depth that characterizes Ishiguro's novel acquires additional meaning when we read the portrait of the clones through Orlando Patterson's groundbreaking work on the institution of slavery across time and cultures. In *Slavery and Social Death* Patterson analyzes numerous slave societies and concludes that racialization, dehumanization, and commodification have been but are not always part of enslavement. As his meticulous comparisons reveal, the connection between blackness and slavery in the Americas and the Caribbean is an exception rather than a rule. Universal processes of slave making, including those Patterson famously labels "natal alienation" and "social death," exist across slave societies, but racialized dehumanization is not one of these. Slavery is produced by the master's severing of the slave's ties to community and kin and by the social isolation of the slave. It has also been produced by the imposition of the impossible bind in which the slave is held, the "choice" between bondage and death that amounts to "living death."[35] A surface or descriptive reading of the clones reveals natal alienation and social death per Patterson's description. As disposable beings, as industrially (re)produced orphans stripped of kith and kin, whose only choice appears to be donation and thus death, clones are classifiable as slaves. Yet, just as it was tempting but inadequate to use Bales's deracinated conception of the new slavery to describe

Ishiguro's clones, so, too, Patterson's conception of slavery. For one of Patterson's central claims is that individuals become slaves precisely because they are forced to *feel* natal alienation and *experience* social death—forms of psychological subjection that the clones never consciously experience. Indeed Ishiguro's clones know and don't know that they are slaves and it is this uncertainty that animates their struggle on the surface of the text.[36]

It is in the face of such struggles that arguments in favor of surface reading break down and demand supplementation by materialist interpretive methods able to contend with the problem of superficiality that has been generated on the surface. The urgency of this demand is palpable. Kathy's superficial reading practice, her abundant failure to read deeply, is, quite literally, killing her. As important, insofar as readers witness and identify with her struggle, we perceive that our failure to read deeply might well redouble the violence.[37] As Benjamin admonishes, in "the state of emergency" (257) in which we live, we must bring past phenomena to the surface, for it is only by constellating the past and present that we can redeem the past for the present and lay claim to a different future.

In their collaborative work on filmic and literary "genres of neoliberalism," Jane Elliott and Gillian Harkins provocatively suggest that there is a relationship between surface reading and neoliberal hegemony.[38] Following Foucault, they explain that neoliberalism refuses a depth model of the economic individual. It presumes that individuals choose to pursue economic self-interest without internal molding by ideology, and thus presumably without interpellation by what Althusser would call an ideological state apparatus. Neoliberalism "diagrams a form of rule that expressly leaves untouched the 'free' interior core in which the individual's own judgments lie" (10). In this way, neoliberalism rules by allowing individuals to imagine themselves capable of acting in their own self-interest when they select among the options available to them—those proscribed by neoliberal economic imperatives that do not announce themselves as such. Consequently individuals in neoliberalism feel as if they have actively chosen (un)freedom. Elliott and Harkins do not argue for a connection between the form of neoliberal economics that relies on a surface model (the ability to rule without penetrating the subject's interiority) and the methodology of surface reading ("the attempt to read without implying depth" [10]) to suggest that surface reading is in any simple sense a neoliberal practice. Rather their point is that the structural synergy between the two compels "diagnosis and critique." This realization returns them to Marxism and the materialist probing of depth that surface reading eschews. And it brings me to a pressing question: How is the problem of surface reading that Ishiguro's text poses on the surface keyed to the biocapitalist society with slavery that the text's narrator, Kathy, so eloquently describes but fails to understand? Relatedly, how might attention to the novel's insistent superficiality allow for the reader to make a connection between the apparent disavowal of slavery on the surface of the text, and the smooth functioning of the neoliberal hegemony and biocapitalist extraction that it depicts?

Elliott's study of neoliberalism extends to a survey of contemporary North American and British fiction that imagines neoliberal personhood. Across such fictions she finds that agency is experienced as emotional affliction, or what she labels "suffering agency."[39] In a reading of *Never Let Me Go* she focuses on Kathy's experience of her agency "as a curse" that somehow never becomes "a farce" (84). Kathy suffers because she senses that she has a choice and yet she nonetheless elects to live in a manner that produces the death of others as well as her own death through self-governance. Any interest in life that Kathy expresses therefore becomes a burden she bares but not one she can desire. Although Elliot does not do so, for present purposes it is instructive to situate Kathy's suffering agency in the contexts of biocapitalism and slave racial capitalism. The suffering she endures is directly keyed to the persistence of the slave episteme in her world and to her refusal of this realization through her self-governance. Put otherwise, Kathy's suffering agency is directly keyed to her knowing and not knowing, to what Benjamin would call her "historicism," her failure to constellate past and present, and thus her failure to realize the connection between the history of slave racial capitalism and the forms of extraction that shape her world. As Benjamin explains, in the "outlook of historicism . . . every image of the past that is not recognized by the present as one of its own concerns threatens to disappear irretrievably" (255). Such disappearances foreclose redemption because they arrest the setting to work of the past in the present on behalf of a more liberated future.

Surfacing the Slave Ship to Freedom

Although clones do not comprehend slavery as their plight, the novel makes clear, on the surface, that Kathy recognizes World War II, the Holocaust, and the concentration camp as the historical past that is most relevant to her situation. Throughout her narrative the concentration camp surfaces alongside a variety of familiar eugenic practices: The clones share a collective fantasy about an electric fence surrounding Hailsham that prevents escape and in so doing recalls for them that electric fences were once used to enclose prisoners during the war. They appear to be aware of a prior history of experimentation on living subjects and circulate rumors about clones who are kept alive beyond the fourth donation that officially terminates conscious existence. And, toward the novel's end, Kathy and Tommy share the revelation that the world in which they live was unleashed during "the war" and consolidated in its aftermath. Miss Emily relates their history to them:

> After the war, in the early [nineteen] fifties, when the great break-throughs in science followed one after the other so rapidly, there wasn't time to take stock, to ask the sensible questions. Suddenly there were all these new possibilities laid before us, all these ways to cure so many previously incurable conditions. This was what the world noticed most, wanted the most. And for a long time, people preferred to believe these organs appeared from nowhere, or at most that they grew in a kind of vacuum. . . . By the time people became concerned . . . about students, by the time they came to consider just how you were reared, whether you should have been brought into existence at all, well by then it was too late. There was no way to reverse the process. How can you ask a world that has come to regard cancer as curable . . . to put away that cure, to go back to the dark days? (262–63)

In describing the provenance of "the cloning programme" Miss Emily indicates that the upward distribution of life itself that was enabled by cloning quickly became unstoppable. Despite the existence of the "little movement" to which she and Madame once belonged, reformers' efforts "to square the circle" failed. In retrospect Miss Emily concludes that the postwar consensus—organs/life for some and donations/death for others—was too firmly set in place to be budged. Clones were cast as "shadowy objects in test tubes," beings bred to "supply medical science" (261) and nothing more.

Ironically and tellingly, Kathy and Tommy also learn from Miss Emily that the tide-turning event that led to banalization and thus widespread acceptance of cloning, the so-called Morningdale scandal, involved the revelation that "superior" children were being reproduced using the same technologies used to reproduce clones for medical science. As Miss Emily explains, the eponymous Scottish scientist devoted his life to engineering "superior intelligence, superior athleticism, that sort of thing" (264). When his work, "far beyond legal boundaries," was discovered, "they put an end to it." However, this same work ushered in a "certain atmosphere" that was, post facto, unalterable (264). Morningdale's creation of superior children, Miss Emily clarifies, "reminded people . . . of a fear they'd always had. . . . It's one thing to create students . . . for the donation programme. But a generation of created children who'd take their [normal people's] place in society? Children demonstrably *superior* to the rest of us? Oh no. That frightened people. They recoiled from that" (264). In this topsy-turvy postwar world one side of the Nazi project is minimized and the other fervently embraced: people "recoil[ed] from . . . [creation of] demonstrably *superior*" human beings but rejoiced in the eugenic ordering of society when it involved industrial (re)production of disposable, inferior, less-than-human beings. In this biopolitical declension, an entire racialized population is expressly bred for use and destruction. And, ultimately, it is this uncanny portrait of the past on the surface of the text that ushers in the specter of racial slavery. Although the clones do not appear to have knowledge of the history of slavery in the same way they have knowledge of World War II, readers know that it was in the context of four hundred years of racial slavery in the Americas and the Caribbean that an inferior class of beings was expressly bred to enable the livelihood of a superior class of people made up of those exclusively granted the designation "human being."

In addition to revealing slavery and the practice of slave breeding as an absent presence, Miss Emily's historical narrative points toward a broader cluster of historical truths. The 1950s and 1960s are routinely if too glibly understood as marked by a growing unease with racial stratification, the rise of the civil rights movement, objection to overt forms of eugenic governance, and embrace of invigorated ideas about the unity of "the family of man" and the related production of UN conventions protecting universal human rights. However, these decades are less often recognized as marked by eugenic violence sanctioned in the name of the state—biopolitical control over populations ethnic cleansing, and incarceration of racialized populations—as marked by actual historical events that reveal the inner solidarity of fascist totalitarianism and modern, postwar democracy.[40] Thus the conceit of postwar humanism that is conventionally upheld in dominant historicist narratives focused on "progress" morphs and topples in this novel. "Postwar humanism" instead comes to describe a world divided between those in possession of a legally protected right to life and those lacking not only rights but recognition as human beings. In revealing to readers a retrograde postwar world whose specific forms of violence are embedded in histories (including slavery) that are disavowed, Miss Emily's historical narrative resonates with previously discussed scholarship on biopower that has failed to focus on and thus implicitly disavows the racist underpinnings of the reproductive extraction upon which biopower relies.[41] Alexander Weheliye succinctly expresses the problem with much existing scholarship when he observes that dominant theories of biopower miss the fact that "The concentration camp, the colonial outpost, and slave plantation suggest three of many relay points in the weave of modern politics, which are neither exceptional nor comparable, but simply relational."[42] Telling the story of biopower as a story of racism is not a matter of elevating one "relay point" above the others so as to render a particular racial order the nomos of the modern (as Agamben does when he renders Auschwitz the biopolitical paradigm for the modern world). Rather telling the story of biopower is a matter of situating various forms of racism *relationally* through examination of epistemic connections that reveal the integral components of the violent modernity that we have inherited.

Whereas Nazis invoked racial inferiority (especially but not exclusively Jewishness) to rationalize the distinction between the human and the less-than-human, and racial slavery used blackness to instantiate the division between those subjected to premature death and those able to profit from it, in *Never Let Me Go* the clone—the being that is racialized as a less-than-human *replicant*—subtends the distinction between those regarded as human and those regarded as disposable. The upshot is the creation of a fascinating historical palimpsest: the Holocaust and the period in which the novel is set (between the mid-1970s and 1990s) are superimposed, while the relationship between the Holocaust and racial slavery and, by extension, racial slavery and the present are constellated beneath the textual surface. However, because the common denominator in this complex textual sedimentation is "the war," the Holocaust emerges as an overdetermined, superficially visible historical relay point that stands in for a historical constellation comprising all the relay points that have existed across racial capitalism's longue durée.

By placing the concentration camp on the surface of the text, *Never Let Me Go* positions it as the space and "the war" as the event that transacts among disparate biopolitical regimes, rendering it the visible—nay, *superficial*—figuration through which racial slavery necessarily, albeit inconspicuously, passes on its way to assuming its postracial afterlife in and for the postwar period and the neoliberal present that is occupied by the novel's readers. On the surface of the novel this representational logic appears as Holocaust exceptionalism. And yet my point is that this apparent exceptionalism not only performs the ideological consolidation of neoliberalism but simultaneously exposes neoliberalism's and biocapitalism's reliance upon the disavowal of the history of racial slavery and all other forms of racialized dehumanization that can and ought to be constellated together with the Holocaust but are not.

In its portrait of clones reproduced by the imposition of a biological caesura that is ultimately racial in character, *Never Let Me Go* challenges and supplements existing theories of biopower.[43] On the one hand, it allows readers to recognize the biopolitical governance of enslaved populations that is at work in biocapitalism. On the other hand, it reveals that the racial differences that organized four hundred years of slavery are necessarily recalibrated to suit neoliberalism's postracial imperatives. Consequently blackness appears to flicker off in this novel, allowing for the Holocaust to emerge as the dominant sign of dehumanization. In arguing thus I should be clear that I am neither proposing that the Holocaust and Atlantic slavery are analogous nor obscuring the fact that poor people of color are the primary source of organs in the global organ trade. Rather I am suggesting that Ishiguro's novel about the reproduction of disposable beings draws our attention to the *transvaluation over time* of forms of racialized dehumanization that were originally brewed up in the context of Atlantic slavery, specifically within its culture of slave breeding.[44] As important, this novel allows us to recognize how the Holocaust of the Jews functions as an overdetermined relay point through which previous forms of racialized dehumanization—including Atlantic slavery—pass in neoliberalism. Put otherwise, in this novel one historical memory never simply replaces another, although it may initially appear to have pushed it beneath the surface of the text. To see the process of transvaluation and submersion at work I began by examining the whitewashed surface of the text; to take the analysis further I peer beneath the whitewashed surface. For what is required—if we wish to surface slavery—is attunement to the absent presence that has been incorporated both into the biocapitalist hegemony represented and into the weave of modern politics that characterizes the world beyond the text.

Two scenes near the end of the novel illuminate what is to be gained by attunement to slavery as an absent presence. In the first, Kathy and Tommy (now Kathy's lover) seek out Madame years after the closure of Hailsham. Kathy now works as Tommy's carer as he awaits a fourth and final donation. Even though the lovers are that much nearer death (or perhaps because they are) they are inspired to locate Madame and present their case for "deferral," having been led by long-standing rumor to believe that Madame has the power to grant them time together should they be able to present her with proof of their love and thus their humanity.[45] Such proof, they believe, lies in their artwork, especially the "really good stuff" previously selected for display in Madame's Gallery.[46] When Tommy and Kathy eventually locate Madame, they discover that she lives with Hailsham's wheelchair-bound, "frail and contorted" (255) former headmistress, Miss Emily. As the dialogue between the two older women and the lovers evolves, the hopes of the latter are dashed. In answer to questions about her Gallery, Madame replies that she herself is no longer clear on its purpose, disillusioned as she has become with the "little project" of which it was a part. When the lovers proceed to inquire about deferral, Miss Emily concedes that "even when Hailsham was considered a shining beacon, an example of how we might move to a more humane and better way of doing things," delay of donations was impossible (258). These disclosures rock to the core Kathy's long-held beliefs about Hailsham as a special place for special students: "Why train us, encourage us, make us produce all of that [art]?" she exclaims. "[What was the purpose] if we're just going to give donations . . . [and] die, why all those lessons? Why all those books and discussions?" (259). In answer to Kathy's challenge—her belated calling out of the "sham" that was Hail/sham—Miss Emily responds by returning to the tokens controversy, at which point she finally reveals to Kathy and Tommy what they (and we) have until now been told and not told: "We took away your art," she concedes, "because we thought it would reveal your souls. Or to put it more finely, we did it to *prove you had souls at all*" (260).

When Kathy counters with befuddlement—"Why did you have to prove a thing like that? . . . Did someone think we didn't have souls?" (260)—she reveals her interpellation by the ideological state apparatus that was the school/ family dyad of Hailsham in its heyday. And she pinpoints the contradictions that beset the old abolitionist discourse upon which depends Miss Emily and Madame's "little movement" to reform the treatment of clones, effectively revealing that these twentieth-century reformers are *too* cleanly cut from nineteenth-century cloth. These "new women" après la lettre seek humane treatment for those regarded as disposable, but wish to take no part in the quest for substantive freedom. Rather than advocating for the abolition of the system that relies on the reproduction of a less-than-human class of beings, they have promoted Hailsham as a *substitute* for "deplorable institutions" that have elsewhere been used to reproduce clones. As Miss Emily hypocritically protests in paternalistically laden prose, "Whatever else, we at least saw to it that all of you [clones] in our care, you grew up in wonderful surroundings. And we saw to it too, after you left us, you were kept away from the worst of [the] horrors. . . . But this dream of yours, this dream of being able to *defer*. Such a thing would always have been beyond us to grant, even at the height of our influence" (261). Revealing the reformer's hypocritical hand, Miss Emily indignantly adds, "I hope you can appreciate how much we *were* able to secure for you. Look at you both now! You've had good lives, you're educated and cultured" (261).

Overlooking Tommy's immanent death and Kathy's facilitation of it, Miss Emily insists that she and Madame have done all they could have done in language uncannily reminiscent of the passage in *Capital* in which Marx discusses Aristotle. As Miss Emily explains, no other outcome was possible in a situation—a biocapitalist society with slavery—in which clone humanity was "not a notion [that was] universally held" (260). Stephanie Smallwood, the historian of slavery, has developed the concept of "commodified freedom" to capture the corrupted notion passed down to the present out of Atlantic slavery. Her concept, which I borrow here, succinctly describes the "little project" at which Madame and Miss Emily have labored.[47] Although the Thirteenth Amendment emancipated slaves, the freedom gained rested upon the same fundaments that upheld the slave system. These were inherited from Enlightenment discourse and grounded in Lockean notions of property that constricted the potentially expansive notion of freedom to the freedom to own and protect property.[48] Even as emancipation ushered slaves into paid labor, it held in place the property system that rendered commodification of life itself possible in the first place. As a consequence freedom in the wake of slavery remained keyed to individual rights to possession of private property, including property in the self. Recasting Smallwood's insights in language used elsewhere in this book, the slave episteme lives on in and through the system of private property, which is protected by law, in capitalism. This salient fact leaves the doors wide open to further commodification of human beings, albeit under new guises, including the organ trade, surrogacy, and all the other markets in life itself treated by scholars of neoslavery.

In its subterranean engagement with the slave episteme, *Never Let Me Go* recognizes that the problem of commodified freedom is a result not only of neoliberalism's triumphant commodification of all social interactions but also of its continuous transvaluation of race, and thus of the meaning of "human being" that accompanies the saturation of life itself by market forces and values. One of Madame's passing remarks to Kathy subtly and hauntingly indicates that she anticipates Miss Emily's immanent liberation from her wheelchair. Like others who are able to claim the status of human being in the biocapitalist society with slavery in which she lives, Miss Emily awaits the donation of a vital organ extracted from a clone (perhaps a former Hailsham student), whose premature death will ensure the reproduction of her all too human futurity. Despite having tried their hands at reform, Madame and Miss Emily evidently intend to be beneficiaries of the biopolitical hierarchy. Despite their discomfort with certain *superficial* aspects of the system they euphemistically refer to as "the donations programme," they never intended to radically challenge the relations of reproduction that subtend the biocapitalist society with slavery in which they live.

Whereas the history of racial slavery in the Americas and Caribbean was punctuated by rebellion and revolt and, as argued in chapter 3, by myriad forms of insurgency that together contributed to the general strike against slavery that resulted in the Civil War, in the world depicted in *Never Let Me Go* enslavement and acquiescence to the system of enslavement go hand in hand. As Kathy forthrightly explains, she and her fellow clones comply with a set of rules that they "imposed on ourselves" (32). This is nowhere more apparent than in the second passage to which I turn to examine the novel's meditation on the transvaluation of race over time. In this passage, which occurs prior to that in which Kathy and Tommy seek out Madame for a deferral, Kathy, Tommy, and Ruth (a former Hailsham student who was once Kathy's best friend and Tommy's childhood girlfriend), take a road trip to see a boat that lies grounded in a marshy, barren landscape a distance from the "donation centre" at which Tommy resides. The trip is physically difficult. Tommy and Ruth have been severely weakened by recent organ harvestings. And, too, it is emotionally fraught. During the journey Ruth reveals to Tommy and Kathy that she had intentionally kept them apart when the three were at Hailsham and the Cottages. Before Ruth "completes" she hopes to make amends by helping the lovers procure a deferral (it is Ruth who provides them with Madame's address). Though the trip is overshadowed by physical and emotional pain, for a brief moment, after the three friends make it beyond a barbed-wire fence (a symbol of the Holocaust as relay point?) through which they must pass to view the boat, their bodily discomforts and frayed emotions appear to evaporate. With the boat in view, they share a moment of calm that appears to be catalyzed by their collective association of the boat, the bleak landscape that surrounds it, and their old school. Tommy is the first to blurt out the feeling that builds among them: "I always see Hailsham being like this now. No logic to it. In fact, this is pretty close to the picture in my head. . . . It wouldn't be so bad, if it's like this now" (225). Ruth picks up on the conversational thread, adding that in a recent dream she envisioned Hailsham similarly. Recalling the feelings that her dream of Hailsham as a decimated shell on a flood plain evoked, Ruth echoes Tommy's sense of relief: "There wasn't any sense of panic or anything like that. . . . It was nice and tranquil, just like it is here" (225). Although Kathy does not chime in, association of the boat, the barren landscape, and their former school seems to resonate for all three. And thus the question arises: Why might such depressing scenes strike the clones as "beautiful" and "tranquil"? More particularly, why might a grounded boat evoke a nostalgic reverie for the only home the clones have ever known?

Presumably most individuals awaiting subjection to a final donation and thus to death would regard a stranded boat as providential—if not exactly a golden ticket, at least a potential escape vehicle in need of repair. Yet the clones do not apprehend the boat thus. Rather, in its stationary, broken-down, and abandoned state, they conclude that it reminds them of Hailsham, a place more akin to a concentration camp or slave plantation—a bleak place, now shuttered, from which all life has been extinguished. The clones' perplexing reaction to the boat is not, however, at odds with but rather in keeping with their prior responses to their predicament, or, perhaps more aptly, their nonresponse to their subjection to premature death. And thus their reaction to the boat is not the enigma it first appears. Rather it reveals that their freedom dreams have been negated by assent to dispossession in a neoliberal world in which the clones imagine that the extraction of life itself, body part by body part, is an existence that they have chosen for themselves.[49] At the close of the scene, as the three friends turn back toward their parked car, Tommy remarks, "At least we've seen it." This statement concisely expresses the clones' affective experience (what Elliot calls their suffering agency) and thus their elective if paradoxically inexorable movement toward premature death. Underscoring the point, Ruth pauses to ask her fellow clones a question that disturbingly demands no answer: "I was like you Tommy, I was pretty much ready when I became a donor. It felt right. After all, it's what we're supposed to be doing, isn't it?" (227).

A Slave Narrative for Postracial Times

Because clones choose enslavement and in so doing disavow any relationship between the slave past and their present, it is worth considering whether it makes sense to regard Kathy's narrative as a slave narrative for postracial times—a slave narrative paradoxically characterized by the slave's refusal to imagine enslavement and, therefore, insurgency against it.[50] Such a narrative completely inverts the generic conventions ascribed to nineteenth-century slave narratives and unwittingly alerts us to one possible response to slavery's afterlife. Whereas the historical slave narrative moves from bondage to freedom, from imposed inhumanity to acquisition of full humanity, Kathy's narrative is resolutely characterized by stasis. Whereas the nineteenth-century slave narrative is authenticated by white abolitionists and/or an amanuensis, Kathy's narrative self-authenticates through production of her condition as the universal condition—one that is readily recognizable by the reader, who, it is implied, shares Kathy's world.[51] Finally, whereas the nineteenth-century narrative constitutes an eloquent call for the abolition of slavery (as opposed to its reform), Kathy's narrative calls on her fellow clones to do nothing at all. After all, from Kathy's vantage point there is nothing to be done because there is nothing that ought to be done in present circumstances.

Returning to Marx and the chapter on the commodity with which he begins *Capital*, we can say that Kathy's narrative is one in which the living commodity speaks and represents itself as satisfied to speak as a commodity. In fact the language of the commodity is the only language in which Kathy feels truly at home. Her narrative neither protests her wrongful enslavement nor attests to her true humanity. Instead she devotes herself to describing in meticulous detail a life that is lived in accord with the (ir)rationality of the system and the role within it that Kathy has been reproduced to fill. In this way Kathy's narrative returns us directly to Marx's discussion of commodity fetishism, for it is while discussing fetishism that Marx asks his readers to consider what commodities would say if they could speak and then supplies an answer: "If the commodities could speak, they would say this: our use-value may interest men, but it does not belong to us as objects. What does belong to us as objects . . . is our value. Our own intercourse as commodities proves it. We relate to each other merely as exchange values" (177). In ventriloquizing the commodity, Marx explores what Georg Lukács decades later will describe as the "reified mind," the psychic saturation by the logic of commodification that is experienced by workers in capitalism. This reification results in workers' perception of their world as created in the image of the commodity, and in workers' belief that the world in which they labor is the only world that can rationally exist.[52] In such a world human beings appear to be objectified values whose exchange as such secures the self-legitimating premise of the system; as Marx's speaking commodity puts it, "Our own intercourse as commodities proves it."

Marx created the speaking commodity to reveal to his readers, the classical political economists, and nineteenth-century workers alike, their inability to hear and thus comprehend how we are all collectively "misled by the fetishism attached to the world of commodities" (176), by the chatter of objects that can, at least metaphorically, be overheard by us as our social labor is objectified and stolen from us. When we operate from within the system (or from within the reified mind of the commodity, as Lukács would have it), we come to regard the relationships among human beings and thus our relationships with each other as relationships among things. And it is here that the necessary and final questions present themselves: If Kathy speaks as a commodity, in this case a slave who does not comprehend her bondage and thus assents to it, what is it that her commodity talk, her narrative, says to readers about the exchange relationship in which she is involved? Relatedly, what is it that it says about the reader's apperception in a biocapitalist age in which biotechnological (re)production has made it possible to commodify life itself?[53]

Answers to these last questions can be approached by analyzing the novel's titular phrase, which is repeated so many times that it resonates multiply. This phrase is first introduced as a refrain from a song by a fictional 1950s torch singer, Judy Bridgewater, that is permanently cued up on Kathy's cassette tape player.[54] Though she is aware that she has probably misinterpreted the song's lyrics, when she sneaks off to listen, hugging her pillow to her chest as she dances alone in her dormitory at Hailsham, Kathy imagines the song as a warning sung by a mother to the child whom she was told she would not be able to conceive. This mother is so afraid of losing her longed-for child that she croons to it to hold fast, "to never let me go" (271). Kathy's attachment to Bridgewater's song is poignant for several reasons. As we learn as the narrative unfolds, Kathy and her fellow clones have been genetically modified to be sterile and thus are radically dispossessed of their own reproductive futurity, though their bodies are used to guarantee futurity for others. For this reason, the lyric expresses longing for a foreclosed future involving progeny. Because all clones hope to be granted a deferral, the lyric also expresses desire for enduring connection, a hope that clones might, by some miraculous dispensation, be held tightly, if only for a few moments longer. While these interpretations resonate, there is another, far more cynical interpretation to which I gravitate, one that renders the lyric not only poignant but also profoundly disturbing. If we take the lyric at face value (precisely as surface readers suggest we should) and read it as an expression of sincere and strongly felt desire, it neatly describes the clones' ascent to their enslavement and to the system of reproductive extraction in which they play the starring role: "'Oh, baby, baby, never let me go,' don't let me exit the neoliberal, postracial world. I require no release from my bondage because I have chosen it."

This last interpretation finds support in the novel's closing scene, which amply evinces Kathy's acquiescence to her plight and simultaneously elicits a now familiar if highly complex affective response from the reader. Just weeks after Kathy has learned of Tommy's completion, she drives to Norfolk, the happy "corner" where Tommy had once, long ago, discovered and purchased a used copy of the Bridgewater cassette tape for Kathy (as a replacement for her lost or stolen "original"). By the side of the road she pulls her car over and stops to gaze out over a fallow field, a bleak and barren landscape reminiscent of the one that she, Tommy, and Ruth had gazed out upon on their visit to the grounded boat. As on that prior occasion, on this one Kathy is confronted by a barbed-wire fence that separates her from the landscape across which she gazes. This time, rather than choosing to move beyond the fence (as she had when she and her friends went to see the boat), she allows the barbed wire to arrest her progress. As she stops before it, she gazes upon all the "rubbish [that] had caught and tangled" in it (287) and offers readers an account of her ruminations during a quiet moment of solitude that provides perfectly fitting closure to her narrative in that it brings the play between knowing and not knowing to its final standstill.

The bits of rubbish caught by the fence lead Kathy into a reverie in which she fantasizes that she has finally found the spot where everything she has lost since childhood has "washed up," Tommy included. She explains, "If I waited [at this spot] long enough, a tiny figure would appear on the horizon across the field, and gradually get larger until I'd see it was Tommy" (287–88). If Kathy fleetingly perceives that she might have refused to self-govern, that she might have refused to let Tommy go, she immediately dismisses this inchoate freedom dream. Instead, like Benjamin's "angel of history," whose wings are caught in a storm that is "blowing out of paradise," Kathy watches as the wreckage of the past piles up before her. (In this instance, the wreckage literally materializes before her as "torn pieces of plastic sheeting" and "old carrier bags.") Although Kathy is arrested by the barbed-wire fence, she can neither grasp it as a historical memory of enslavement that "flashes up in a moment of danger," nor can she recognize the rubbish caught in the fence as "messianic shards" of a slave past that might yet be constellated with her biocapitalist present.[55] Instead, with her face turned toward the past, Kathy reassures us—readers of her narrative whom she has persisted in addressing over hundreds of pages as fellow clones—that although an emotional storm built inside her, she was inured to its force: "The fantasy [of being united with Tommy] never got beyond that—I didn't let it—and though the tears rolled down my face, I wasn't sobbing or out of control. I just waited a bit, then turned back to the car, to drive off to wherever it was I was supposed to be" (288). In these, the novel's final sentences, Kathy behaves as any self-respecting self-governing subject would, like the angel of history, with her back turned, she propels forward into the future.

Kathy's narrative assumes the readers' interpellation and thus our complicity in the banalization of the violence that structures her world. However, her superficial narrative also exposes us to the violence of the erasure from the surface of the historical past that lurks beneath it. As a result, unlike Kathy and because of Kathy, our interpellation into neoliberalism is never complete. The blind spot of slavery, the absent presence that haunts Kathy, is visible to us beneath the text's whitewashed surface, and thus we are forced to consider whether the dehumanizing reproductive and racial violence that structures Kathy's world also structures our own. We feel that the clones' predicament is terribly sad, and we perceive that it is atrociously unjust. But perhaps most important, we understand that countering injustice requires rejection of our supposed position alongside the clones who inhabit the placid surface of Kathy's narrative. For it is only when we push beneath to the textual depths that we can grasp the powerful incongruity between Kathy's choice to hold back her tears and turn back to her car to drive off to wherever it was she was supposed to be and our own sense of rage that she elects to do so. And too, it is only when we push beneath the surface that we realize, in a flash, that our rage ought not to be directed at Kathy and the other clones whose lives we have entered as we have read her narrative, but that it should instead be directed at ourselves.

Epilogue

The **END** *of* **MEN** *and the*
BLACK WOMB *of the* **WORLD**

Mankind, which in Homer's time was an object of contemplation for the Olympian gods, now is one for itself. Its self-alienation has reached such a degree that it can experience its own destruction as an aesthetic pleasure of the first order. This is the situation of politics which Fascism is rendering aesthetic. Communism responds by politicizing art.

—WALTER BENJAMIN, "THE WORK OF ART IN THE AGE OF MECHANICAL REPRODUCTION" (1936)

For the enslaved, reproduction does not ensure any future other than that of dispossession nor guarantee anything other than the replication of racialized disposable persons.

—SAIDIYA HARTMAN, "THE BELLY OF THE WORLD" (2016)

I conclude this book by circling back from my discussion of cloning and the organ trade in chapter 5 to the discussion of the surrogacy/slavery nexus with which I began in chapter 1. The circle is required. After all, the persistent lacunae in cultural texts that treat cloning is the female reproductive body—its parts, processes, and products—and the necessary dispossession of this body in the cloning process. In such texts clones are brewed up in high-tech birth tanks or test tubes and are supplied with nutrients and conditioning that allow maturation without experience of gestation in and passage out of the female body. This masculinist fantasy is evident in the earliest portraits of cloning and remains part and parcel of the neoliberal and supposedly postracial depictions of cloning that mistakenly imagine that clone reproduction can be severed from the long history of reproductive extraction and thus from slave breeding. In Aldous Huxley's *Brave New World* (1932), for instance, clones produced through "the Bokanovsky Process" are gestated in and birthed from glass bottles that chug along conveyor belts kept at an ideal temperature and supplied, in vitro, with sustenance and subliminal indoctrination.[1] In more recent depictions, including *The Island* and *Never Let Me Go*, the female womb as first home is likewise entirely absent. In fact *The Island* does little more than update Huxley's earlier vision of biotechnological prowess sans women. In the cloning process the film depicts, full-grown beings emerge from giant synthetic sacs from which they are released by the surgical knife of the technician attending the sanitized and denaturalized "birth." In *Never Let Me Go*, although clones contemplate their genetic "originals" (mainly in their effort to imagine what their lives would have been like if they were not replicated beings subjected to premature death), they never wonder about the bodies mined for the eggs that must be enucleated and filled with new DNA to bring forth clones, nor do they wonder about, let alone yearn for, the wombs from which they have presumably emerged. In sum, imagined worlds that rely upon cloning represent cloning as entirely independent of the female body and in vivo reproductive labor. Significantly, this is the case despite the material reality that constitutes *the limit* of all currently known cloning techniques—that such techniques necessitate both egg harvesting and gestational labor at a bare minimum.[2] Thus, in their omission of the maternal body and its reproductive products, texts on cloning require us to ponder the reproductive body in absentia and the surrogacy/slavery nexus in which, as we have seen, the reproductive body in biocapitalism is bound.

To return to the discussion of *Never Let Me Go* with this material limit in mind, we are compelled to ask several questions: Where have the oocyte vendors and gestational surrogates gone in "England late 1990s"? Do they live out their lives offshore on vendor farms? Are they corralled in surrogate colonies? Or do they labor alongside the clones whose lives they enable? Why does Ishiguro's novel focus exclusively on the dispossession of the clones when other dispossessed bodies are necessarily involved in the reproduction of the so-called organ donation program that is depicted? Rather than provide answers, the novel bypasses these questions, effectively circumventing direct treatment, on the surface of the text, of the surrogacy/slavery nexus that operates in and through all the other texts (legal, historical, fictional, and philosophical) that I have examined throughout this book.[3] In closing, rather than allow the empty space where the body of the surrogate/slave resides in contemporary speculative texts about the reproduction of human life on earth to remain unoccupied, I clear space for engagement with the surrogate/slave as fount of human futurity in a context of the destruction of the human race that dystopian sf imagines and that I call "the end of men."

I do so by taking up a final dystopian portrait of reproduction, that found in *The Children of Men*. Alfonso Cuarón's 2006 film (based on P. D. James's 1992 novel) simultaneously depicts human self-destruction through evisceration of human fertility and dreams of human salvation through instantiation of a less-than-human black African surrogate as the source of *all* future human life on earth. Indeed, in *Children of Men* cloning meets its limit and its fantastical other: mass-scale human infertility is coupled with what might most aptly be described as "the black womb of the world." Where infertility reigns, the black womb emerges as savior—not an agent of history but a less-than-human tool of human futurity. As should by now be clear, the black womb of the world is a hyperbolic instantiation of the reproductive afterlife of slavery that I have sought to limn and refuse; thus, it is useful to meditate on this figure in closing.

The near future of 2027 that is lavishly depicted in *Children of Men* is beset by continuous warfare, unceasing anti-immigrant and antirefugee violence, Islamic fundamentalism, terrorism, end-of-days frenzy, national insularity, and extreme nativism. It is also shaped by myriad forms of environmental destruction that have, it is implied, destroyed the human capacity to populate the globe, as well as much of the natural world that depends upon the planet's health. As the film opens, viewers learn that the final child born, a celebrity affectionately named Baby Diego, has just died in Brazil at the tender age of eighteen. When his death is announced, the remaining population is reminded that it is destined to inexorably move toward complete oblivion unless new life can be reproduced and enabled to henceforth reproduce itself. In this sense, the film engages in what the queer studies scholar Lee Edelman has called "reproductive futurism." It presupposes human reproduction of "the Child" (Edelman capitalizes the term to underscore the figure's symbolic function) as a universal good and mistakenly suggests that reproduction of the Child is the only meaningful way in which to imagine human futurity—in short, the Child is the only response to universal infertility and thus the end of men.[4]

Like Ishiguro's novel, Cuarón's film is set in Britain, a place that feels uncanny in its simultaneous familiarity and foreignness. While the gray London streets and looming Parliament building are readily recognizable, from the film's opening sequence to its long closing chase scene, viewers are placed in a destabilized state, one catalyzed by the visual chaos of the mise-en-scène—a chaos that creates in the viewer a potent combination of estrangement and cognition, all at an alarmingly rapid pace. To give some sense of the film's jarring feel, I turn to the opening montage, inside a coffee shop where the protagonist, Theo (Clive Owen), has stopped on his way to a dreary day at the office. Before Theo exits the shop with caffeinated beverage in hand, we see and hear above the shop counter a TV news broadcast that covers, among updates on the continued closure of Britain's borders to all immigrants and refugees, the day's top story: the death of Baby Diego. As the cynical Theo flees the gathering crowd of fellow customers (who, in contrast to Theo, are held rapt by the news), a bomb blast reverberates, body parts and glass fly, and we realize that Theo has escaped death by a mere breath. In this montage, as throughout the film, viewer focus is drawn to the chaos unfolding in the background (in this case the TV news and the mayhem of the bombed street), such that the background of the film becomes what several critics argue is the real or dominant spectacle and story.[5]

Unlike the novel on which the film is based, which focuses on the existential suffering of a middle-aged, widowed Oxford historian who seeks to make meaning of his ravaged world, Cuarón's film provides an opulent view of this world's crumbling and decay and of the quotidian violence and dispossession that are represented as the pervasive crisis with which everyone must, by necessity, contend according to their means (or, as the case may be, their connections to those in power), nationality, or citizenship. This is a biopolitical world in which the remaining population has been divided into those deserving of old age and the basic resources to support death through aging, and those who have been reduced to less-than-human or "fugee" status and thus slated for premature death.

The world that the film depicts as our near future comes to us in visual fragments, what Benjamin would call "messianic shards." We are thus compelled to grab hold of bits and pieces as they flash up in the background and move across our visual field in what Benjamin refers to as "a moment of danger." Our fleeting engagements with the history of the present (we are confronted by images of Auschwitz, the Warsaw Ghetto, mad cow disease, political prisons such as Abu Ghraib and Guantanamo Bay, the protest against the World Trade Organization in Seattle ["the battle in Seattle"], the 2005 London bombings, and the bombings of World War II) last just long enough for us to apprehend the fact that the dystopia depicted exhibits a powerful combination of our past's (more distant and most recent) pressing social, political, economic, and environmental problems raised to an exponential power. As in Ishiguro's novel, in Cuarón's film we recognize our world, reflected and refracted for our inspection.

Some critics of *Children of Men* have treated it as a post-9/11 commentary on the rise of terrorism and the state of emergency that has become normative in its wake; others have treated it as an extended meditation on women's reproductive dispossession in the context of the conservative assault on reproductive rights and the rise of reproductive technology; in a few essays still others have interpreted it as an examination of the black and fecund woman who stands at the center of the reproductive drama that unfolds. What critics have not focused on is the surrogacy/slavery nexus and thus the philosophy of history examined by the film, especially through its portrait of a black and fecund woman as what Hartman calls "the belly of the world."[6] In my remaining pages, I focus on the aptly named Kee (Clare-Hope Ashitey), an African refugee who, I argue, constitutes yet another *key* to understanding the afterlife of reproductive slavery in biocapitalism. As we shall see, Kee is a figure that materially and epistemically subtends the biocapitalist world with slavery that the film depicts. This is a world in which the reproductive body is used to generate human life not for herself but for others. In sharp contrast to the novel on which the film is based, in which the crisis in human fertility is precipitated by male impotence, in the film the infertility crisis is placed squarely on women's inability to successfully gestate human life. In the film, women shoulder the blame for the end of men. And it is not just any woman who emerges to repopulate the globe, but a black African refugee. In short, Kee ultimately bears the responsibility for serving all of humanity as surrogate/slave.[7]

The film's plot is simple and at once epic. Theo, a one-time lefty activist who has lost his only son to a global flu pandemic (and who has subsequently lost his marriage), has been tasked by the "Fishes," the antigovernment, pro-refugee group to whom his ex-wife belongs, with transporting Kee out of Britain and into the hands of "the Human Project," a covert humanitarian organization about which we learn almost nothing save that members travel the seas in search of a solution to the immanent end of human life on earth. A cure to infertility, it is implied, is not being adequately sought by those who occupy the seats of power, because they (including Theo's powerful cousin) are more concerned with orchestrating mass suicide, or "Quietus," as they hoard classical works of art presumably plundered from nations that have gone under while Britain soldiers on. Theo's journey with Kee involves him in a series of complex, life-threatening negotiations with the various political factions that hope to abduct Kee to make her baby a "flag" for their various, though not dissimilar causes. As the narrative unfolds, it becomes evident that despite differences, the factions share a desire to instrumentalize Kee and her living product. In fact no one save for Theo, his ex-wife, and a midwife (the latter two of whom are killed early on) seek substantive freedom for Kee and her baby. When the plan for the Fishes' transport of Kee to the Human Project is thrown off course by interference from warring factions, Theo and Kee become fugitives running from their former allies and the British government. As they move through the Surrey countryside and then the Bexhill refugee camp that they have broken into to gain access to the coastline and thus to the ship sent to intercept Kee, Kee gives birth with Theo's assistance. Consequently Theo becomes not only Kee's protector but also the surrogate father to her newborn girl. In the final scene, after Theo has been severely wounded by gunfire, we see Theo and Kee slowly making their way in a small unstable boat, as Theo rows Kee, with babe in arms, to the buoy at which she is scheduled to meet her saviors. A ship with the name *Tomorrow* emblazoned across its prow emerges from the thick gray mist, and Theo takes his last breath, leaving Kee and her daughter to await an unknown future alone in the boat.

While some critics and scholars have interpreted Cuarón's representation of Kee as utopian, even revolutionary—as an image of a black Madonna who gives birth to a black female Messiah—such celebratory readings are not only misguided, they perpetuate rather than refuse the uncertainty that pervades the film's last scene and the film's apparent endorsement of the slave episteme.[8] This is because such readings are predicated on several uninterrogated assumptions that implicitly lead to disavowal of the afterlife of slavery: first, that the *Tomorrow*'s crew will treat Kee as a full human being rather than as a less-than-human refugee, an experimental animal from whom they may extract eggs and other biological products; second, that Kee's infant will likewise be treated as a full human being rather than as a black womb in the making, a natural resource whose fertile eggs are waiting to be mined; and third, that the Human Project is radically distinct from the other political groups depicted in the film, each of which has been revealed to be self-interested and thus politically ineffective.

By contrast with salvific interpretations, I suggest interpreting the film as a cautionary allegory for biocapitalist times. When read thus, the film leaves us deeply wary, anxious rather than hopeful. Moreover, it begs rather than answers a series of questions whose irresolution ought to give us pause: Might the *Tomorrow* be a slave ship storing within its submerged hull the racialized reproductive bodies it has collected as it has made its way around the world's depleted oceans? Might the tomorrow that lies in store for Kee and her daughter represent a continuation rather than cessation of a world predicated on the material and epistemic endurance of slave breeding? Given the possibility that such questions may reasonably be answered in the affirmative, rather than regarding Kee as the black mother of a black female Jesus it makes more sense to regard her as related to the biblical handmaid Hagar, the enslaved Egyptian woman who was forced to act as surrogate mother for those who eventually sentenced her to death in the wilderness.

No scene in the film more robustly supports this reading than that in which Kee reveals her pregnancy to Theo in a barn, filled with dairy cows and hay, to which she has summoned him on a dark and cold winter night. While some have suggested the scene recalls the biblical manger in which Jesus was born (a reading no doubt provoked by the fact that the film opened in the United States on Christmas Day 2006), it is notable that while Kee wryly jokes with Theo about being a virgin, she is also robustly associated with prostitution (it was one of her Johns who impregnated her; she doesn't know which) and with the biological utility of the dairy cows among which she stands. These creatures, Kee points out in the monologue she delivers to Theo, have been brutally maimed so that they may serve the needs of the human beings who own and extract value from them. Kee explains that a pair of each cow's "titties" has been "cut off" so the remaining teats may be connected to milking machines having only four receptacles. While amputation is certainly not the high-tech solution to efficiency that one might expect in biocapitalist times (Kee reasonably ponders aloud why they do not modify the machines to suit the cows), the maiming of the cows and Kee's expression of empathy for them speaks to their mutual dispossession as natural resources whose reproductive processes and products may be extracted. Once Kee has captured Theo's attention, rather than attempt to explain her unfathomable (as opposed to "miraculous") condition, she sheds her dress to show him her swollen belly. Theo initially assumes that Kee is disrobing to offer him sex, but when the camera follows Theo's point of view as it pans over Kee's naked torso it becomes clear that she is proffering something else entirely: knowledge of her fertility and thus consciousness of her profound vulnerability to exploitation and violence. As Kee states and Theo realizes once the momentary shock of

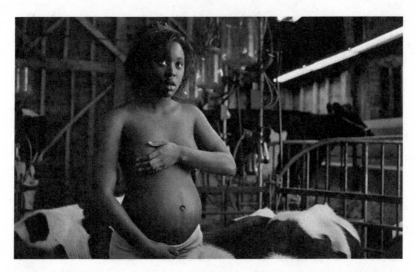

Figure E.1 Disclosure of pregnancy in a milking barn. Clare-Hope Ashitey as Kee. Film still from Alfonso Cuarón, director, *Children of Men*. Universal Studios © 2006.

the revelation has worn off, he must save her from the vying political factions, the Fishes included, that wish to use her or kill her to possess her child and thus, they hope, the key to the future.

While in the novel there is also an unfathomable pregnancy, the pregnant woman depicted is a white British citizen rather than a black African refugee. In other words, through transformation of the book's prior racialization of its central reproductive conceit, the film represents the reproductive body capable of saving the world as blackened and animalized—as a less-than-human being whose life is deemed valuable because it is available for plunder. To put it as plainly as possible, in the film Kee is a surrogate/slave who reproduces property that may be stolen by others. As Toni Morrison explains in the discussion of surrogacy with which I began chapter 1, in the United States blackness has been used to cast black people as objectified surrogates who bring into being white subjects and, in so doing, secure the equation of whiteness with citizenship and national futurity.[9] In Cuarón's film, the figure of the black surrogate that Morrison regarded as a literary trope is literalized and globalized. Kee is materialized as a black womb capable of gestating the world. Her function as savior is clearly at the cost of her agency and her humanity.

In her historical study of reproduction in slavery (see chapter 1), Jennifer Morgan argues that one of the central ideas about black reproduction that subtended the ideology and material practice of slavery was that enslaved women experienced little or no pain in childbirth—that somehow their biological otherness afforded them the natural ability to bring forth and nurture life without sacrifice.[10] The film associates Kee with slave women by giving her a short and easy labor. This is done by deploying *ThereCam*, the cinematic code for the roller-coaster ride of megarealism that often incorporates computer-generated images.[11] In what appears to be a single unbroken real-time tracking shot (but is, in fact, a composite shot), Kee lies down on Theo's coat and in a matter of minutes gives birth to a healthy baby. Though she briefly strains and curses (this is megarealism, after all), there is nothing in the scene to suggest that childbirth is unduly difficult or draining; rather it is represented as instinctual and thus animal, if a bit daunting for Theo, who is unprepared to act as midwife. Adding to the sense that Kee's ability to labor with ease is a function of her blackness (rather than the other way around), the living product of her reproductive labor can be read as belonging to others. Kee names her infant girl after Theo's dead son (Dylan), indicating that Theo is the spiritual if not the actual father of the child and that the child's intended parents are the white heterosexual couple (Theo and his ex-wife) for whom Kee has labored as a surrogate/slave tasked with replacing the dead white male heir with new female life and thus futurity.[12]

To read Cuarón's film as allegory (as I have) is to read it as the type of narrative that most interested Benjamin, the theorist who has been one of my imagined companions in thinking about black feminism's philosophy of history throughout this book. When read thus the key/Kee moments in this film can be treated as dialectical images. The naked and pregnant Kee amid the cows, Kee giving birth, the baby named Dylan—these images flash before our eyes in what Benjamin would call "a moment of danger," effectively clearing space for realization that the afterlife of reproductive slavery is perpetuated through collective imagination of human futurity as reproduced by a blackened surrogate/slave. As importantly, to read this film allegorically is to read it from the vantage point of the specifically black feminist philosophy of history that this book has sought to examine and to which it contributes. From this vantage point, representation of Kee constellates the slave past and the present. To recall the arguments of chapters 4 and 5, we live in a historical conjuncture in which cultural texts either work to assuage fears about the afterlife of slavery in biocapitalism (as does *The Island*) or, alternatively, to expose the sublation and disavowal of the slave episteme in biocapitalism, neoliberalism, and postracialism (*Wild Seed*, "Bloodchild," and *Never Let Me*

Go, respectively). In such a conjuncture, what Benjamin would call "the time of the now," *Children of Men* does something related and at once distinct. It represents the afterlife of reproductive slavery in biocapitalism by casting the less-than-human womb as the blackened fount of human futurity—and thus as a racialized reproductive spectacle that we ignore at our peril. For Kee's black body, animalized and fecund, may either be aestheticized (as it is when critics read it as an instantiation of a black Madonna) such that it inures us to the surrogacy/slavery nexus and the afterlife of reproductive slavery, or it may be politicized (as I have sought to do through my reading of it) such that it alerts us to the necessity of grappling with the endurance of the slave episteme as we create a world in which substantive reproductive freedom is unbound from neoliberal and postracial understandings of that unnecessarily vexed category *human being*.

NOTES

Introduction

1 Saidiya Hartman, *Lose Your Mother: A Journey along the Atlantic Slave Route* (New York: Farrar, Straus and Giroux, 2007), 6. Hartman concludes, "I, too, am the afterlife of slavery." Hartman's formulation resonates throughout other texts on the afterlife of slavery that have informed my thinking. See Christina Sharpe, *In the Wake: On Blackness and Being* (Durham: Duke University Press, 2016); Salamishah Tillet, *Sites of Slavery: Citizenship and Racial Democracy in the Post–Civil Rights Imagination* (Durham: Duke University Press, 2012); Kimberly Juanita Brown, *The Repeating Body: Slavery's Visual Resonance in the Contemporary* (Durham: Duke University Press, 2015); Dennis Childs, *Slaves of the State: Black Incarceration from the Chain Gang to the Penitentiary* (Minneapolis: University of Minnesota Press, 2015); Alexander Weheliye, *Habeas Viscus: Racializing Assemblages, Biopolitics, and Black Feminist Theories of the Human* (Durham: Duke University Press, 2014); Simone Browne, *Dark Matters: On the Surveillance of Blackness* (Durham: Duke University Press, 2015); Jared Sexton, "People-of-Color-Blindness: Notes on the Afterlife of Slavery," *Social Text* 28.2 (2010): 31–56.

2 I return to a discussion of neoslavery in chapter 5.

3 Walter Benjamin, "Theses on the Philosophy of History" (1940), in *Illuminations*, trans. Harry Zohn, ed. Hannah Arendt (New York: Schocken Books, 1968), 253–64, quote 263.

4 Raymond Williams, *Keywords: A Vocabulary of Culture and Society* (Oxford: Oxford University Press, 1976), 24.

5 Cedric J. Robinson, *Black Marxism: The Making of the Black Radical Tradition* (Chapel Hill: University of North Carolina Press, 1983), 1–28.

6 Barbara Christian, *Black Women Novelists: The Development of a Tradition, 1892–1976* (Westport, CT: Greenwood, 1980), *Black Feminist Criticism: Perspectives on Black Women Writers* (New York: Pergamon, 1985), and "The Race for Theory," *Cultural Critique* 6 (1987): 51–63; Hortense J. Spillers, "Mama's Baby, Papa's Maybe: An American Grammar Book," *Diacritics* 17.2 (1987): 65–81, and *Black, White, and in Color: Essays on American Literature and Culture* (Chicago: University of Chicago Press, 2003); Hazel V. Carby, *Reconstructing Womanhood: The Emergence of the Afro-American Woman Novelist* (New York: Oxford University Press, 1987); Valerie Smith, *Self-Discovery and Authority in Afro-American Narrative* (Cambridge, MA: Harvard University Press, 1987).

7   While adoption might appear to fit within the scope of the present argument, it doesn't. Babies put up for adoption are infrequently (re)produced through the express engineering of reproductive labor that interests me here. See Laura Briggs, *Somebody's Children: The Politics of Transracial and Transnational Adoption* (Durham: Duke University Press, 2012).

8   See Catherine Waldby and Robert Mitchell, *Tissue Economies: Blood, Organs, and Cell Lines in Late Capitalism* (Durham: Duke University Press, 2006); Melinda Cooper, *Life as Surplus: Biotechnology and Capitalism in the Neoliberal Era* (Seattle: University of Washington Press, 2008); Melinda Cooper and Catherine Waldby, *Clinical Labor: Tissue Donors and Research Subjects in the Global Bioeconomy* (Durham: Duke University Press, 2014); Kaushik Sunder Rajan, *Biocapital: The Constitution of Postgenomic Life* (Durham: Duke University Press, 2006); Kaushik Sunder Rajan, ed., *Lively Capital: Biotechnologies, Ethics, and Governance in Global Markets* (Durham: Duke University Press, 2012).

9   I use *neoliberalism* to refer to processes by which unfettered markets, brought forth and sustained by deregulation of corporations and financial institutions, privatization, proliferation of free trade policies, and decline of the social welfare state, determine economic and social relations. In neoliberalism, labor unions, social programs, and democratic processes are dismantled and individuals burdened with survival, self-care, and self-governance. For present purposes, the most salient features of neoliberalism are the burdening of women with excessive responsibility (but less and less compensation) and the hyper-exploitation of people of color—processes that coincide with neoliberalism's promotion of an ideology of official race neutrality, color-blindness, and thus what I call throughout this book postracialism. See David Harvey, *A Brief History of Neoliberalism* (New York: Oxford University Press, 2005); Wendy Brown, "American Nightmare: Neoliberalism, Neoconservatism, and De-Democratization," *Political Theory* 34.6 (2006): 690–714, and "Neo-liberalism and the End of Liberal Democracy," *Theory & Event* 7.1 (2003), https://muse.jhu.edu/article/48659; Jodi Melamed, *Represent and Destroy: Rationalizing Violence in the New Racial Capitalism* (Minneapolis: University of Minnesota Press, 2011); Immanuel Wallerstein, *After Liberalism* (New York: New Press, 1995).

10 Elsewhere I argue that race and reproduction are bound together when the maternal body is conceptualized as the source of racial identities and racial formations, including modern nations. I have called the conceptual edifice that racializes reproduction the "race/reproduction bind." See Alys Eve Weinbaum, *Wayward Reproductions: Genealogies of Race and Nation in Transatlantic Modern Thought* (Durham: Duke University Press, 2004).

11 *Spartaco: Schiavi e Padroni a Roma*, Museo dell'Ara Pacis, March 31–September 17, 2017. This is a multimedia exhibit on Roman slavery since Spartacus.

12 See Jennifer L. Morgan, "*Partus Sequitur Ventrem*: Law, Race, and Reproduction in Colonial Slavery," *Small Axe* 55 22.1 (March 2018): 1–17. Also see Joseph Dorsey, "Women without History: Slavery and the International Politics of *Partus Sequitur*

Ventrem in the Spanish Caribbean," *Journal of Caribbean History* 28.2 (1994): 167–69. For discussion of practices prior to the official implementation of the doctrine, see Kathleen M. Brown, *Good Wives, Nasty Wenches, and Anxious Patriarchs: Gender, Race, and Power in Colonial Virginia* (Chapel Hill: University of North Carolina Press, 1996), especially 128–35.

13 See Silvia Federici, *Caliban and the Witch: Women, the Body, and Primitive Accumulation* (New York: Autonomedia, 2004), and *Revolution at Point Zero: Housework, Reproduction, and Feminist Struggle* (New York: Autonomedia, 2012); Leopoldina Fortunati, *The Arcane of Reproduction: Housework, Prostitution, Labor and Capital* (1981), trans. Hilary Creek (New York: Autonomedia, 1995); Mariarosa Dalla Costa, "Capitalism and Reproduction," *Capitalism, Nature, Socialism* 7.4 (1996): 111–21. Also see Kathi Weeks, *The Problem with Work: Feminism, Marxism, Antiwork Politics, and Postwork Imaginaries* (Durham: Duke University Press, 2001), especially 92–96. Autonomist feminists first launched the critique of housework as reproductive labor and developed the "wages for housework" platform. See Mariarosa Dalla Costa and Selma Jones, *The Power of Women and the Subversion of Community* (Bristol, UK: Falling Wall, 1973); Wendy Edmond and Suzie Fleming, eds., *All Work and No Pay: Women, Housework, and the Wages Due* (Bristol, UK: Falling Wall, 1975); Harriet Fraad, Stephen Resnick, and Richard Wolff, *Bringing It All Back Home: Class, Gender, and Power in the Modern Household* (London: Pluto, 1994).

14 See Evelyn Nakano Glenn, "From Servitude to Service Work: Historical Continuities in the Racial Division of Paid Reproductive Labor," *Signs* 18.1 (1992): 1–43, and *Forced to Care: Coercion and Caregiving in America* (Cambridge, MA: Harvard University Press, 2010); Eileen Boris, *Home to Work: Motherhood and the Politics of Industrial Homework in the United States* (New York: Cambridge University Press, 1994); Eileen Boris and Jennifer Klein, *Caring for America: Home Health Workers in the Shadow of the Welfare State* (New York: Oxford University Press, 2012).

15 On racialization of care work, domestic work, and sex work see Grace Chang, *Disposable Domestics: Immigrant Women Workers in the Global Economy* (Cambridge, MA: South End Press, 2000); Rhacel Salazar Parreñas, *Servants of Globalization: Women, Migration, and Domestic Work* (Stanford: Stanford University Press, 2001); Arlie Russell Hochschild, *The Outsourced Self: Intimate Life in Market Times* (New York: Metropolitan Books, 2012); Eileen Boris and Elisabeth Prügl, eds. *Homeworkers in Global Perspective: Invisible No More* (New York: Routledge, 1996); Eileen Boris and Rhacel Salazar Parreñas, eds., *Intimate Labors: Cultures, Technologies, and the Politics of Care* (Stanford: Stanford University Press, 2010).

16 See Parreñas, *Servants of Globalization*.

17 I am indebted to Marxist and socialist feminists who parsed and critiqued Marx and Engels's writings on reproductive labor and their subsuming of reproduction within the supposedly broader category of production. See Zillah R. Eisenstein, ed., *Capitalist Patriarchy and the Case for Socialist Feminism* (New York: Monthly Review Press, 1978); Heidi Hartmann and Lydia Sargent, eds., *The Unhappy Marriage of Marxism and Feminism: A Debate on Class and Patriarchy* (London:

Pluto Press, 1981); Lydia Sargent, ed., *Women and Revolution: A Discussion of the Un-happy Marriage of Marxism and Feminism* (Boston: South End Press, 1981); Shulamith Firestone, *The Dialectic of Sex: The Case for Feminist Revolution* (New York: Farrar, Straus and Giroux, 1970); Michèle Barrett, *Women's Oppression Today: Problems in Marxist Feminist Analysis* (London: Verso, 1980); Rosalind Coward, *Patriarchal Prece-dents: Sexuality and Social Relations* (Boston: Routledge Kegan & Paul, 1983). Build-ing on world systems theory, Maria Mies, *Patriarchy and Accumulation on a World Scale: Women in the International Division of Labour* (London: Zed Books, 1986) and Swasti Mitter, *Common Fate, Common Bond: Women in the Global Economy* (London: Pluto Press, 1986) developed the account of the international division of repro-ductive labor upon which so much current feminist work on the global economy is based.

18 Heather Jacobson, *Labor of Love: Gestational Surrogacy and the Work of Making Babies* (New Brunswick, NJ: Rutgers University Press, 2016), 16, 177. Also see Debora L. Spar, *The Baby Business: How Money, Science, and Politics Drive the Commerce of Concep-tion* (Boston: Harvard Business School Press, 2006).

19 See, for instance, Jenny Reardon, *Race to the Finish: Identity and Governance in an Age of Genomics* (Princeton: Princeton University Press, 2005); Dorothy Roberts, *Fatal Invention: How Science, Politics and Big Business Re-create Race in the Twenty-First Century* (New York: New Press, 2011); Catherine Bliss, *Race Decoded: The Genomic Fight for Social Justice* (Stanford: Stanford University Press, 2012).

20 Daisy Deomampo, *Transnational Reproduction: Race, Kinship and Commercial Surrogacy in India* (New York: New York University Press, 2016); Laura Harrison, *Brown Bod-ies, White Babies: The Politics of Cross-Racial Surrogacy* (New York: New York University Press, 2016); France Winddance Twine, *Outsourcing the Womb: Race, Class, and Gesta-tional Surrogacy in a Global Market* (New York: Routledge, 2011).

21 I have chosen the word *flicker* because it is a visually laden term that alludes to the historical association of blackness with racial visibility. The term suggests the episodic waning of the old racial imaginary that sought to consolidate this as-sociation in a context in which race retreats from view through its attribution to "invisible" sources of genetic determination. *Flicker* tells us that "blackness" is not visible and never has been, though it was construed as visible when visibility could be used to objectify and dehumanize. In this sense this formulation refuses the overdetermination of visible blackness in contemporary biocapitalism. Thanks to Sonnet Retman and Chandan Reddy for the lengthy engagements that resulted in this precise formulation and to Sue Shon for her work on the historical con-solidation of blackness and visuality. See Shon, "Making Sense: Race and Modern Vision," PhD diss., University of Washington, 2016. As I have argued elsewhere, despite the fact that there is no single gene that determines the visibility of race, genetic ideas about racial visibility inform the practice of biotechnology, espe-cially when eggs and sperm are selected for use. See Alys Eve Weinbaum, "Racial Aura: Walter Benjamin and the Work of Art in a Biotechnological Age," *Litera-ture and Medicine* 26.1 (2007): 207–39. Finally, *flicker* is meant to resonate with and

depart from Benjamin's *flash*, the concept he uses to describe how the historical past makes itself evident in a present moment of danger in which the forgetting of the past appears likely. In our present biocapitalist moment, slave breeding is the past that threatens to disappear irretrievably. This noted, it should be clear that the "flickering off and on of blackness" I describe happens *inside* capitalist abstraction. By contrast, when slavery "flashes up," this represents a rupture with capitalist abstraction and the forms of historicism to which, Benjamin argues, it is wed. See Benjamin, "Theses."

22 Entry for "sublate," *Oxford English Dictionary*, 3rd ed., accessed online August 20, 2017, University of Washington. In Marx's writings *aufhaben* is the German verb that is often, though not exclusively translated as *to sublate*. Though it is beyond the scope of the present discussion, Marxist scholars continue to debate how best to translate the term in Marx's writings and how best to conceptualize the historical and dialectical process it describes.

23 My ideas about reproductive exploitation remain grounded in conversations years ago with Gayatri Chakravorty Spivak and, in particular, in formative readings of "French Feminism Revisited," in *Outside in the Teaching Machine* (New York: Routledge, 1993), 158–92, and "Diasporas Old and New: Women in the Transnational World," *Textual Practice* 10.2 (1996): 245–69.

24 As Lisa Lowe explains, recognition of the imbrication of colonialism, empire, slavery, and global capitalism ought to move us beyond platitudes about the global division of labor (that it is feminized and racialized) and toward an understanding of labor as a process that produces gendered and racialized identities mobilized by capitalism(s). See Lowe, *Intimacies of Four Continents* (Durham: Duke University Press, 2015), 1–41. Gayatri Chakravorty Spivak makes a similar observation in "In a Word: An Interview," interview by Ellen Rooney, *Differences* 1.2 (1989): 124–56.

25 Weheliye, *Habeas Viscus*; Achille Mbembe, "Necropolitics," trans. Libby Meintjes, *Public Culture* 15.1 (2003): 11–40. I return to a discussion of scholarship on biopower in chapters 4 and 5.

26 Weheliye, *Habeas Viscus*, 3.

27 See David Roediger, *The Wages of Whiteness: Race and the Making of the American Working Class* (London: Verso, 1991); Theodore W. Allen, *The Invention of the White Race*, vol. 1: *Racial Oppression and Social Control* (London: Verso, 1994); Moon-Ho Jung, *Coolies and Cane: Race, Labor, and Sugar in the Age of Emancipation* (Baltimore: Johns Hopkins University Press, 2006).

28 Dorothy Roberts, *Killing the Black Body: Race, Reproduction and the Meaning of Liberty* (New York: Pantheon, 1997).

29 Though they do not treat biocapitalism, scholars who read black feminism of the 1970s, 1980s, and 1990s as a response to late capitalism and neoliberalism are fellow travelers. See Grace Kyungwon Hong, *The Ruptures of American Capital: Women of Color Feminism and the Culture of Immigrant Labor* (Minneapolis: University of Minnesota Press, 2006) and *Death beyond Disavowal: The Impossible Politics of*

Difference (Minneapolis: University of Minnesota Press, 2015); Roderick A. Ferguson, *Aberrations in Black: Toward a Queer of Color Critique* (Minneapolis: University of Minnesota Press, 2004); Katherine McKittrick, *Demonic Grounds: Black Women and the Cartographies of Struggle* (Minneapolis: University of Minnesota Press, 2006); Weheliye, *Habeas Viscus.*

30 I am indebted to an anonymous reader for offering this description of my method.

31 W. E. B. Du Bois, *Black Reconstruction in America, 1860–1880* (1935; New York: Free Press, 1998).

32 On *disavowal* and its function in neoliberalism, see Hong, *Death beyond Disavowal.*

33 Benjamin, "Theses," 257.

34 Jacques Derrida, *The Post Card: From Socrates to Freud and Beyond,* trans. Alan Bass (Chicago: University of Chicago Press, 1987), 292–337. I return to the question of "surface reading" in chapter 4.

35 Jennifer L. Morgan, "Archives and Histories of Racial Capitalism: An Afterword," *Social Text* 33.4 (2015), 156.

36 Saidiya Hartman, "Venus in Two Acts," *Small Axe* 12.2 (2008), 7, and *Scenes of Subjection: Terror, Slavery, and Self-Making in Nineteenth-Century America* (New York: Oxford University Press, 1997), 79–112.

37 I return to the distinction between traditional and gestational surrogacy in chapter 1.

38 Carla Spivack, "The Law of Surrogate Motherhood in the United States," *American Journal of Comparative Law* 58 (2010): 97–114, quote 97.

39 Orlando Patterson, *Slavery and Social Death: A Comparative Study* (Cambridge, MA: Harvard University Press, 1982), 5–10; Spillers, "Mama's Baby," 73–74.

40 Karl Marx and Friedrich Engels, *The Communist Manifesto* (1848), trans. Samuel Moore (New York: Oxford University Press, 1992); Smallwood, "Commodified Freedom: Interrogating the Limits of Anti-Slavery Ideology in the Early Republic," *Journal of the Early Republic* 24.2 (2004): 289–98.

41 Carole Pateman, *The Sexual Contract* (Stanford: Stanford University Press, 1988), 149; Weeks, *The Problem with Work,* 23.

42 Lowe, *Intimacies,* 16. Also see Uday Singh Mehta, *Liberalism and Empire: A Study in Nineteenth-Century British Liberal Thought* (Chicago: University of Chicago Press, 1999); Dipesh Chakrabarty, *Provincializing Europe: Postcolonial Thought and Historical Difference* (Princeton: Princeton University Press, 2000).

43 Lowe, *Intimacies,* 24.

44 Amy Dru Stanley, *From Bondage to Contract: Wage Labor, Marriage, and the Market in the Age of Slave Emancipation* (New York: Cambridge University Press, 1998); Sarah Haley, *No Mercy Here: Gender, Punishment, and the Making of Jim Crow Modernity* (Chapel Hill: University of North Carolina Press, 2016); Tillet, *Sites of Slavery;* Childs, *Slaves of the State;* Loïc Wacquant, "Deadly Symbiosis: When Ghetto and Prison Meet and Mesh," *Punishment and Society* 3.1 (2001): 95–134; Naomi Murakawa, *First Civil Right: How Liberals Built Prison America* (New York: Oxford University Press, 2014).

45 This account of outsourced and transnational surrogacy in India is indebted to ethnographic scholarship by Amrita Pande, *Wombs in Labor: Transnational Commercial Surrogacy in India* (New York: Columbia University Press, 2014); Kalindi Vora, *Life Support: Biocapital and the New History of Outsourced Labor* (Minneapolis: University of Minnesota Press, 2015); Sharmila Rudrappa, *Discounted Life: The Price of Global Surrogacy in India* (New York: New York University Press, 2015); Deomampo, *Transnational Reproduction*; Sayantani DasGupta and Shamita Das Dasgupta, eds., *Globalization and Transnational Surrogacy in India: Outsourcing Life* (Lanham, MD: Lexington Books, 2014). Also see Harrison, *Brown Bodies*. I return to a discussion of outsourced and transnational surrogacy in the last section of chapter 1.

46 Jacobson, *Labor of Love* is the only book-length ethnography of gestational surrogates in the United States. Jacobson demonstrates that surrogates and consumers of surrogacy alike hold fast to the idea that neither children nor labor are being sold. In her earlier study of traditional surrogates, Heléna Ragoné found that most describe their labor as altruistic. See *Surrogate Motherhood: Conception in the Heart* (Boulder, CO: Westview, 1994). Such obfuscations are part and parcel of the disavowal of the history of slavery and thus the persistence of the slave episteme.

47 See Natalie Fixmer-Oraiz, "Speaking of Solidarity: Transnational Gestational Surrogacy and the Rhetorics of Reproductive (In)Justice," *Frontiers* 34.3 (2013): 126–63.

48 Spillers, "Mama's Baby"; Hartman, *Scenes of Subjection*, especially 85; Roberts, *Killing*; Angela Davis, "The Legacy of Slavery: Standards for a New Womanhood," in *Women, Race, and Class* (New York: Vintage, 1981), 3–89.

49 Robin D. G. Kelley, *Freedom Dreams: The Black Radical Imagination* (Boston: Beacon, 2002), xii.

50 Kimberly Springer, *Living for the Revolution: Black Feminist Organizations 1968–1980* (Durham: Duke University Press, 2005); Bettye Collier-Thomas and V. P. Franklin, eds., *Sisters in Struggle: African American Women in the Civil Rights–Black Power Movement* (New York: New York University Press, 2001); Kimberly Springer, ed., *Still Climbing, Still Lifting: African American Women's Contemporary Activism* (New York: New York University Press, 1999); Deborah Gray White, *Too Heavy a Load: Black Women in Defense of Themselves, 1894–1994* (New York: Norton, 1999); Paula Giddings, *When and Where I Enter: The Impact of Black Women on Race and Sex in America* (New York: William Morrow, 1984).

51 Jennifer Nelson, *Women of Color and the Reproductive Rights Movement* (New York: New York University Press, 2003); Jael Silliman et al., eds., *Undivided Rights: Women of Color Organize for Reproductive Justice* (Cambridge, MA: South End Press, 2004); Kimala Price, "What Is Reproductive Justice? How Women of Color Activists Are Redefining the Pro-Choice Paradigm," *Meridians* 10.2 (2010): 42–65.

52 Walter Johnson, "On Agency," *Journal of Social History* 37.1 (2003): 113–24; Hartman, "Venus in Two Acts"; Sharpe, *In the Wake*.

53 Hong argues that black feminism has had difficulty surviving, not least because so many black feminist academics have passed away prematurely (*Death*, 125–49). Also see Ferguson, *Aberrations*.

54 Hartman, "Venus in Two Acts," 7.

1. The Surrogacy/Slavery Nexus

1 Karl Marx, *Capital: A Critique of Political Economy*, vol. 1 (1867), trans. Ben Fowkes (New York: Vintage, 1977), 926.

2 As discussed below, the latter term is Walter Johnson's.

3 Toni Morrison, *Playing in the Dark: Whiteness and the Literary Imagination* (New York: Vintage Books, 1992), 51–52.

4 Amy Dru Stanley, *From Bondage to Contract: Wage Labor, Marriage and the Market in the Age of Slave Emancipation* (New York: Cambridge University Press, 1998), xi.

5 Saidiya Hartman, *Scenes of Subjection: Terror, Slavery, and Self-Making in Nineteenth-Century America* (New York: Oxford University Press, 1997).

6 Stanley limns the relationship between labor and marriage contracts and argues that the latter was enslaving for black women, predicated as it was on men's "domestic rule" over all dependents (*From Bondage to Contract*, especially chapters 1 and 4).

7 The term had previously been used to discuss the South African economy under apartheid. Robinson's innovation was to expand the concept as it was used previously to encompass the racial character of capitalism in all its iterations.

8 Cedric J. Robinson, *Black Marxism: The Making of the Black Radical Tradition* (1983; Chapel Hill: University of North Carolina Press, 2000), xxix; hereafter cited parenthetically.

9 Robinson notes that even though Marx and Engels did not recognize racism as a globe-shaping force, they understood its import in the intra-European context (*Black Marxism*, 79–80, 339–40).

10 Jodi Melamed, "Racial Capitalism," *Critical Ethnic Studies* 1.1 (2015): 77.

11 Melamed, "Racial Capitalism," 77.

12 Jodi Melamed, *Represent and Destroy: Rationalizing Violence in the New Racial Capitalism* (Minneapolis: University of Minnesota Press, 2011), 1–90.

13 See Edward Baptist, *The Half Has Never Been Told: Slavery and the Making of American Capitalism* (New York: Basic Books, 2014); Walter Johnson, *Soul by Soul: Life inside the Antebellum Slave Market* (Cambridge, MA: Harvard University Press, 1999), and *River of Dark Dreams: Slavery and Empire in the Cotton Kingdom* (Cambridge, MA: Harvard University Press, 2013); Stephanie Smallwood, *Saltwater Slavery: A Middle Passage from Africa to American Diaspora* (Cambridge, MA: Harvard University Press, 2007); Moon-Ho Jung, *Coolies and Cane: Race, Labor, and Sugar in the Age of Emancipation* (Baltimore: Johns Hopkins University Press, 2006).

14 Johnson, *River of Dark Dreams*, 14.

15 Although I considered coining and using the concept "racial biocapitalism" throughout, I eventually elected to stick with the already existent "biocapitalism." The latter holds the potential prefacing term ("racial") under erasure, effectively marking the neoliberal disavowal of racial violence that interests me.

16 See Deborah Gray White, *Ar'n't I a Woman? Female Slaves in the Plantation South* (New York: Norton, 1985); Darlene Clark Hine, *Hine Sight: Black Women and the Reconstruction of American History* (Bloomington: Indiana University Press, 1994); Marietta Morrissey, *Slave Women in the New World: Gender Stratification in the Caribbean* (Lawrence: University of Kansas Press, 1989); Barbara Bush, *Slave Women in Caribbean Society, 1650–1838* (Bloomington: Indiana University Press, 1990); Stephanie M. H. Camp, *Closer to Freedom: Enslaved Women and Everyday Resistance in the Plantation South* (Chapel Hill: University of North Carolina Press, 2004); Sharla M. Fett, *Working Cures: Healing, Health, and Power on Southern Slave Plantations* (Chapel Hill: University of North Carolina Press, 2002); Thavolia Glymph, *Out of the House of Bondage: The Transformation of the Plantation Household* (New York: Cambridge University Press, 2003). This scholarship was presaged by the emergence of social historical scholarship on the slave family and quotidian forms of resistance. See Herbert Gutman, *The Black Family in Slavery and Freedom, 1750–1925* (New York: Pantheon, 1976); John W. Blassingame, *The Slave Community: Plantation Life in the Antebellum South* (New York: Oxford University Press, 1972); Eugene D. Genovese, *Roll, Jordan, Roll: The World the Slaves Made* (New York: Vintage, 1972).

17 See Hilary McD. Beckles, *Natural Rebels: A Social History of Enslaved Women in Barbados* (New Brunswick, NJ: Rutgers University Press, 1989); Jennifer L. Morgan, *Laboring Women: Reproduction and Gender in New World Slavery* (Philadelphia: University of Pennsylvania Press, 2004). Both are hereafter cited parenthetically. Sasha Turner's *Contested Bodies: Pregnancy, Childrearing, and Slavery in Jamaica* (Philadelphia: University of Pennsylvania Press, 2017) was published after completion of this book. Had I had it in hand, I would have included discussion of it here. Turner explores not only how reproduction functioned as the motor of slavery but also the complicity of those abolitionists who imagined that slave women might reproduce a free population of laborers capable of performing the work previously done by slaves.

18 Although men proved stronger physically, women demonstrated greater stamina, a requirement in harsh tropical conditions. Beckles observes that management's initial refusal to shelter women from arduous tasks indicates that "productivity differentials were not expected to exist between the sexes" (*Natural Rebels*, 31). First gang women hoed soil, dug drains, and cut, bundled, and planted canes (33–34).

19 Beckles notes that urban slave owners also "encouraged" slave women to reproduce as a means of future securitization (*Natural Rebels*, 92). In instances in which slaves were leased for sexual use they generated three income flows: from labor, from sex work, and from reproduction (144).

20 Thus Morgan's focus on representations of black women's breasts, supposedly slung over shoulders so that children might suckle while perched on laboring backs (*Laboring Women*, 12–49).

21 Descendants of Eve, unlike African women, were thought to be cursed with pain in childbirth. Such ideas paved the way for polygenesis and related discourses about European racial superiority in the eighteenth and nineteenth centuries. Morgan, *Laboring Women*, 40–47. Heather Jacobson's ethnography of gestational surrogacy in the US, *Labor of Love: Gestational Surrogacy and the Work of Making Babies* (New Brunswick, NJ: Rutgers University Press, 2016), reveals that contemporary surrogates are generally women thought to be "good" at pregnancy because pregnancy and birth are "easy" for them. She shows that this discourse (which, notably, she does not historicize) covers over the arduousness of surrogate labor (56).

22 With her astute analysis of wills that instructed planters' heirs on how to distribute property, Morgan renders reproductive speculation tangible. Wills reveal that planters created notions about transfer of wealth through speculative transfer to future generations of enslaved women's reproductive capacity. When little was left behind, the bequest of a female slave allowed the slave owner to produce the semblance of munificence in the face of actual scarcity (*Laboring Women*, 92).

23 The formulation is Morgan's, *Laboring Women*, 167.

24 Kaushik Sunder Rajan, *Biocapital: The Constitution of Postgenomic Life* (Durham: Duke University Press, 2006); hereafter cited parenthetically.

25 On the genealogy of the concept see Stefan Helmreich, "Species of Biocapital," *Science as Culture* 17.4 (2008): 463–78. Helmreich's critique of Sunder Rajan resonates with my sense that Sunder Rajan misses "the bio side of things" due to exclusive focus on the "capital side" (465). Helmreich's genealogy stretches back to the 1980s, and includes contributions by Hortense Spillers and Donna Haraway. Other overviews trivialize feminist contributions. See, for instance, Kean Birch and David Tyfield, "Theorizing the Bioeconomy: Biovalue, Biocapital, Bioeconomics or . . . What?" *Science, Technology, & Human Values* 38.3 (2012): 299–327.

26 Melinda Cooper elaborates similar arguments in *Life as Surplus: Biotechnology and Capitalism in the Neoliberal Era* (Seattle: University of Washington Press, 2008), 20.

27 See Sarah Franklin, *Biological Relatives: IVF, Stem Cells, and the Future of Kinship* (Durham: Duke University Press, 2013).

28 Sarah Franklin and Margaret Lock, "Animation and Cessation: The Remaking of Life and Death," in *Remaking Life and Death: Toward an Anthropology of Biosciences*, ed. Sarah Franklin and Margaret Lock (Santa Fe, NM: School of American Research Press, 2003), 7. Franklin and Locke attribute their ideas about reproduction's importance to their exchanges with Charis Thompson and Hannah Landecker. At the symposium upon which their anthology is based Landecker argued that biocapital is not simply dependent on reproduction but is constituted by it (7, 10).

29 Maria Mies argues similarly in *Patriarchy and Accumulation on a World Scale: Women in the International Division of Labour* (London: Zed Books, 1986). As she explains,

global capitalism relies upon the exploitation of the female body and labor and simultaneously disavows the female body's productivity.

30 Catherine Waldby and Robert Mitchell, *Tissue Economies: Blood, Organs, and Cell Lines in Late Capitalism* (Durham: Duke University Press, 2006); Debora Spar, *The Baby Business: How Money, Science, and Politics Drive the Commerce of Conception* (Boston: Harvard Business School, 2006); Sarah Franklin, *Dolly Mixtures: The Remaking of Genealogy* (Durham: Duke University Press, 2007), and *Biological Relatives*; Cooper, *Life as Surplus*; Donna Dickenson, *Body Shopping: The Economy Fueled by Flesh and Blood* (Oxford: Oneworld, 2008); Melinda Cooper and Catherine Waldby, *Clinical Labor: Tissue Donors and Research Subjects in the Global Bioeconomy* (Durham: Duke University Press, 2014); Kalindi Vora, *Life Support: Biocapital and the New History of Outsourced Labor* (Minneapolis: University of Minnesota Press, 2015); Arlie Russell Hochschild, *The Outsourced Self: Intimate Life in Market Times* (New York: Metropolitan Books, 2012).

31 In a much earlier engagement with surrogacy I explored it through the lens of Marx's labor theory of value and argued that in surrogacy (re)productive labor power as a commodity and the (re)productive product are exchanged. The surrogate supplies a measurable quantity of social labor power that is "congealed" (to borrow Marx's uncannily biological terminology) in the object consumed. In this exchange (re)productive labor in its "fluid state" is transformed into a commodity that is quite literally delivered to the consumer in its "solid state," in "object form." As in other exchanges, the relationships between people are transformed into relationships among things and the social nature of labor power is obfuscated by the fetishism that attaches itself to the baby commodity. In surrogacy the fetish character of the commodity is its babyness. See Weinbaum, "Marx, Irigaray, and the Politics of Reproduction," *Differences* 6.1 (1994): 98–128.

32 Cooper and Waldby write of hearing Sunder Rajan speak, "We both realized that we, and the rest of the field, had neglected the question of labor. While there was an extensive body of work on the expert cognitive labor of the scientist and its centrality to the knowledge economy, the labor of those who provide the *in vivo* platforms for clinical experimentation and tissue provision did not figure in any account as labor" (*Clinical Labor*, vii).

33 Catherine Waldby and Melinda Cooper, "The Biopolitics of Reproduction: Post-Fordist Biotechnology and Women's Clinical Labor," *Australian Feminist Studies* 23.55 (2008): 58.

34 Waldby and Cooper, "The Biopolitics of Reproduction," 60; Cooper and Waldby, *Clinical Labor*, 34.

35 The baby was named Sara Elizabeth by Whitehead and Melissa Elizabeth by the Sterns. Although the media's references to "the Baby M case" suggest bias in favor of the Sterns, I follow popular usage to underscore the hegemonic construction.

36 My account is based on feminist scholarship and reportage in the *New York Times* from 1986 to 1988. See Katha Pollitt, "The Strange Case of Baby M," *The Nation*,

May 23, 1987, 688; Lorraine Stone, "Neoslavery—'Surrogate' Motherhood Contracts v. the Thirteenth Amendment," *Law & Equality: A Journal of Theory and Practice* 6.2–3 (1988): 63–73; Judith T. Younger, "What the Baby M Case Is Really All About," *Law & Equality: A Journal of Theory and Practice* 6.2–3 (1988): 75–82; Valerie Hartouni, "Reproductive Technologies and the Negotiation of Public Meanings: The Case of Baby M," in *Provoking Agents: Gender and Agency in Theory and Practice*, ed. Judith Kegan Gardiner (Chicago: University of Illinois Press, 1995), 115–32; Carol Sanger, "(Baby) M Is for the Many Things: Why I Start with Baby M," *Saint Louis University Law Journal* 44.4 (2000): 1443–63 and "Developing Markets in Baby-Making: In the Matter of Baby M," *Harvard Journal of Law and Gender* 30.1 (2007): 67–97; Ellen Faulkner, "The Case of 'Baby M,'" *Canadian Journal of Women and the Law* 3.1 (1989): 239–45; Sonia Jaffe Robbins, "When Is a Mother Not a Mother? The Baby M Case," *Women and Language* 13.1 (1990): 41–46. The following articles from the *New York Times* were consulted: Elizabeth Kolbert, "A Dispute on Baby M," October 6, 1986; Robert Hanley, "Wife in Baby M Dispute Recalls Tearful Appeal," January 7, 1987; "Reporter's Notebook: Grief over Baby M," January 12, 1987; "Father of Baby M Thought Mother Had Been Screened," January 14, 1987; "Bonding Is Described at Baby M Hearing," February 28, 1987; "Testimony Ends at Baby M Hearing," March 10, 1987; "Father of Baby M Granted Custody; Contract Upheld; "Surrogacy Is Legal," April 1, 1987; "Court Restores Baby M Visits by Whitehead," April 11, 1987; "Baby M's Mother Wins Broad Visiting Rights," April 7, 1988; Iver Peterson, "Baby M, Ethics and the Law," January 18, 1987, "Baby M and Controversy over Fertility," January 31, 1987, and "Baby M Trial Splits Ranks of Feminists," February 24, 1987; James Barron, "Views on Surrogacy Harden after Baby M Ruling," April 2, 1987; "Baby M: Groping for Right and Law," April 2, 1987; E. R. Shipp, "Parental Rights Law: New Jersey Supreme Court Will Examine If Standard Rules Affect Baby M Case," April 8, 1987.

37 Whitehead nursed the baby until the Sterns took custody. Whitehead appealed the court's ruling in 1988, suing baby broker Noel Keane for failure to properly screen her. She won an out-of-court settlement and gained limited visitation rights as the baby's "natural" mother. As I discuss later, when surrogacy becomes predominantly gestational, the surrogate's "natural" motherhood is taken off the table. See "Noel Keane, 58, Lawyer in Surrogate Mother Cases, Is Dead," *New York Times*, January 28, 1997.

38 As expressed in the language of the court: "We invalidate the surrogacy contract because it conflicts with the law and public policy of this state. While we recognize the depth of yearning of infertile couples to have their own children, we find payment of money to a 'surrogate' mother illegal, perhaps criminal, and potentially degrading to women." See C. J. Wilentz, "The Matter of Baby 'M,'" New Jersey Supreme Court, N.J., 537, *Atlantic Reporter*, 1234 (1988), quoted in Kelly Oliver, "Marxism and Surrogacy," *Hypatia* 4.3 (1989): 95.

39 The terminology used to refer to participants in surrogacy is diverse and contested. As Daisy Deomampo, *Transnational Reproduction: Race, Kinship and Commercial*

Surrogacy in India (New York: New York University Press, 2016) explains, choice of terminology "reflects a particular stance on assisted reproduction. The terms are value laden and vary in accordance with one's social position, culture and discipline. Many . . . indicate bias either in favor of or opposed to commercial surrogacy" (14–15). Here I elect terminology that highlights rather than disavows the exchange relationship at the heart of surrogacy and the surrogate's relegation to the status of nonmother. For similar reasons, though *birth mother* and *gestational mother* are often used in discussions of surrogacy, I use *surrogate, surrogate laborer,* or *reproductive laborer,* save when I wish to express a surrogate's express desire to be recognized as a mother.

40 Pollitt, "The Strange Case of Baby M," 682.

41 Pollitt, "The Strange Case of Baby M," 682.

42 Pollitt reports that Whitehead was condemned thus by Sorkow. As Sorkow additionally noted, Whitehead was a high school dropout, her husband a garbage collector. He sought the "best interests" of the child and this required placement of Baby M with the educated and resource-rich biochemist William Stern and his wife.

43 Stone, "Neoslavery," 67; hereafter cited parenthetically.

44 Pollitt, "The Strange Case of Baby M," 684. Pollitt's piece, published prior to the verdict, set the terms of debate for many feminist commentators.

45 Genea Corea, *The Mother Machine: Reproductive Technologies from Artificial Insemination to Artificial Wombs* (New York: Harper and Row, 1979), 276. Although Corea discusses "breeder women" as a class, she never discusses slavery.

46 Noel Keane, who brokered the contract, received $15,000 for his services. This was a fraction of the $300,000 he earned in surrogate contract fees the year Baby M was born. Keane would go on to negotiate six hundred surrogacy contracts worldwide before his death in 1997. His firm, the Infertility Center of America, was taken over by his son, also a lawyer specializing in surrogacy. See "Noel Keane, 58, Lawyer in Surrogate Mother Case Is Dead."

47 For instance, Kelly Oliver asserts that "most people do not perform their services 24 hours a day *unless they are slaves.* And most people only sell their labor, labor performed by the body, but perhaps distinguishable from it. 'Surrogates' on the other hand, perform their services 24 hours a day and sell the body itself" ("Marxism and Surrogacy," 97–98). For Oliver, surrogates and slaves are "estranged laborers" (as opposed to "alienated laborers"). Their social being is denied through visceral exploitation that transforms the body into "the machinery of production over which the contractor has ultimate control" (106). As a beast of burden, the surrogate's putative freedom becomes "an illusion" (108). Also see Mariarosa Dalla Costa, "Capitalism and Reproduction," *Capitalism, Nature, Socialism* 7.4 (1996): 111–20, especially 111–12. Like other Marxist feminists, Oliver and Dalla Costa treat slavery as an analogue rather than as a historical instantiation of racial capitalism.

48 France Winddance Twine observes, "With few notable exceptions US public policy debates about the ethics of commercial surrogacy have been framed in

ways that avoid the obvious histories of commodification of slave children and the contemporary commodification of white children." She notes that only black feminist legal scholars have taken up slavery as precedent for surrogacy. See Twine, *Outsourcing the Womb: Race, Class, and Gestational Surrogacy in a Global Market* (New York: Routledge, 2011), 8, 16. Patricia J. Williams was among the first to treat the Baby M case in relationship to slavery, in "On Being the Object of Property," *Signs* 14.1 (1988): 5–24, reprinted in *The Alchemy of Race and Rights: Diary of a Law Professor* (Cambridge, MA: Harvard University Press, 1991), 216–38, and the title essay in *The Rooster's Egg: On the Persistence of Prejudice* (Cambridge, MA: Harvard University Press, 1995).

49 See Anita Allen, "Surrogacy, Slavery, and the Ownership of Life," *Harvard Journal of Law & Public Policy*, 13.1 (1990): 140n9; hereafter cited parenthetically.

50 Angela Davis excoriates Stowe's sentimental figuration of Eliza, pointing out that Eliza's flight was portrayed as a maternal act of courage but never as an attack on slavery. In contrast to Eliza, Davis argues, slave women "were driven to defend their children by their passionate abhorrence of slavery. The source of their strength was not some mystical power attached to motherhood, but rather their concrete experiences as slaves." See *Women, Race, and Class* (New York: Vintage, 1981), 29. I return to a discussion of Davis and slave women's insurgency in chapter 2.

51 See Allen, "Surrogacy, Slavery, and the Ownership of Life," and "The Black Surrogate Mother," *Harvard Blackletter Journal* 8 (1991): 17–31. Allen discusses Polly in both articles.

52 Allen does not use the Latin term but is clearly discussing *partus sequitur ventrem*, the doctrine codified in Virginia Law in 1662. See Jennifer Morgan, "*Partus Sequitur Ventrem*: Law, Race and Reproduction in Colonial Slavery," *Small Axe* 55 22.1 (March 2018): 1–17, and "'The Breedings Shall Goe with Their Mothers': Gender and Evolving Practices of Slaveownership in the English American Colonies," in *Laboring Women*, 69–106.

53 Dorothy Roberts, "Reproduction in Bondage" and "Race and the New Reproduction," in *Killing the Black Body: Race, Reproduction, and the Meaning of Liberty* (New York: Pantheon, 1997), 22–55, 246–93; hereafter cited parenthetically. Charlotte Rutherford, "Reproductive Freedoms and African American Women," *Yale Journal of Law and Feminism* 4 (1992): 255–90; Deborah R. Grayson, "Mediating Intimacy: Black Surrogate Mothers and the Law," *Critical Inquiry* 24.2 (1998): 525–46; April L. Cherry, "Nurturing in the Service of White Culture: Racial Subordination, Gestational Surrogacy, and the Ideology of Motherhood," *Texas Journal of Women and the Law* 10.2 (2001): 83–128.

54 Patricia J. Williams presaged Roberts's arguments when she linked her great grandmother's treatment as a breeder to that of a contemporary surrogate: "On Being the Object of Property," 15.

55 The practice was previously documented by Angela Davis in "Reflections on the Black Woman's Role in the Community of Slaves," *Black Scholar* 3.4 (1971): 2–15, and *Women, Race, and Class*, 9.

56 As Cheryl J. Sanders puts it in "Surrogate Motherhood and Reproductive Technologies: An African American Perspective," *Creighton Law Review* 25.5 (1992): 1709, in the "current discussion of surrogate motherhood" there is little or no acknowledgment of "the *actual* abuses and exploitation that took place in this country when slave mothers and children alike were regarded as someone else's property." The suggestion "is made that the modern surrogate arrangement is a 'rented womb,'" but this glosses over "the fact that as recently as four generations ago, white Americans 'owned' the entire bodies of African American women of childbearing age, and routinely exploited them for sexual pleasure, physical labor, procreative productivity, and profit."

57 Crispina Calvert's prior hysterectomy left her unable to gestate a child but able to produce fertile eggs.

58 See Grayson, "Mediating Intimacy"; Robyn Wiegman, "Intimate Publics: Race, Property, and Personhood," *American Literature* 74.4 (2002): 859–85; Valerie Hartouni, "Breached Birth: Reflections on Race, Gender, and Reproductive Discourse in the 1980s," *Configurations* 2.1 (1994): 73–88; Mark Rose, "Mothers and Authors: *Johnson v. Calvert* and the New Children of Our Imaginations," *Critical Inquiry* 22.4 (1996): 613–33; Ruth McElroy, "Whose Body, Whose Nation? Surrogate Motherhood and Its Representation," *European Journal of Cultural Studies* 5.3 (2002): 325–42; Heather Dillaway, "Mothers for Others: A Race, Class, and Gender Analysis of Surrogacy," *International Journal of Sociology of the Family* 34.2 (2008): 301–26; Lisa C. Ikemoto, "Destabilizing Thoughts on Surrogacy Legislation," *University of San Francisco Law Review* 28.3 (1994): 633–645; Rutherford, "Reproductive Freedom and African American Women"; Cherry, "Nurturing in the Service of White Culture"; Allen, "The Black Surrogate Mother." In the popular press see Seth Mydans, "Science and the Courts Take a New Look at Motherhood," *New York Times*, November 4, 1990; "Surrogate Denied Custody of Child: Judge in California Rules for Genetic Parents and Bars Two-Mother Situation," *New York Times*, October 23, 1990; "Parental Rights Denied to a Surrogate Mother," *New York Times*, May 22, 1993; "Psychiatrist Testifies in Surrogate Birth Case," *New York Times*, October 11, 1990; "Surrogate Is Denied Custody," *New York Times*, September 22, 1990; "Surrogate Mother Sues for Baby's Custody," *New York Times*, August 15, 1990; Bruce L. Wilder, "Surrogate Exploitation," *New York Times*, November 22, 1990; Katha Pollitt, "When Is a Mother Not a Mother?," *The Nation*, December 31, 1990, 1, 840, 842–5, 846; Martin Kasindorf, "And Baby Makes Four: *Johnson vs. Calvert* Illustrates Just About Everything That Can Go Wrong in Surrogate Births," *Los Angeles Times Magazine*, January 20, 1991, 10–34; Scott Armstrong, "California Surrogacy Case Raises New Questions about Parenthood: Mother Seeks Custody, but She Has No Genetic Link to Child," *Christian Science Monitor*, September 25, 1990; Dan Chu, "A Judge Ends a Wrenching Surrogacy Dispute, Ruling That Three Parents for One Baby Is One Mom Too Many," *People*, November 5, 1990; Susan Tifft, "It's All in the (Parental) Genes," *Time*, November 5, 1990, 77; Jeremy Rifkin and Andrew Kimbrell, "Put a Stop to Surrogate Parenting Now," *USA Today*, August 20, 1990.

59 Although I regard genetic reasoning and protection of racial status property by the lower court as decisive, it should be noted that some argue the final ruling was also based on the intent of the parties involved.

60 On Aristotelian ideas about the female body and their misapprehension by those inattentive to the aleatory force of becoming, see Emanuela Bianchi, *The Feminist Symptom: Aleatory Matter in the Aristotelian Cosmos* (New York: Fordham University Press, 2014); Irina Aristarkhova, *Hospitality of the Matrix: Philosophy, Biomedicine, and Culture* (New York: Columbia University Press, 2012). On the biological contributions made by Johnson's maternal body see Laura Harrison, *Brown Bodies, White Babies: The Politics of Cross-Racial Surrogacy* (New York: New York University Press, 2016), 104–28.

61 Slave women nursed and raised slave children for masters and fostered black and white children on plantations and in the master's home. On the historical continuation of the racial division of reproductive labor see Evelyn Nakano Glenn, "From Servitude to Service Work: Historical Continuities in the Racial Division of Paid Reproductive Labor," *Signs* 18.1 (1992): 1–43. On racially "stratified reproduction" in the context of care work, domestic labor, and affective labor see Shellee Colen, "'Like a Mother to Them': Stratified Reproduction and West Indian Childcare Workers and Employers in New York," in *Conceiving the New World Order: The Global Politics of Reproduction*, ed. Faye Ginsburg and Rayna Rapp (Berkeley: University of California Press, 1995), 78–102; Rhacel Salazar Parreñas, *Servants of Globalization: Women, Migration, and Domestic Work* (Stanford: Stanford University Press, 2001); Eileen Boris and Elisabeth Prügl, eds., *Homeworkers in Global Perspective: Invisible No More* (New York: Routledge, 1996); Eileen Boris and Rhacel Salazar Parreñas, eds., *Intimate Labors: Cultures, Technologies, and the Politics of Care* (Stanford: Stanford University Press, 2010); Neferti X. M. Tadiar, *Things Fall Away: Philippine Historical Experience and the Makings of Globalization* (Durham: Duke University Press, 2009). Today, as in the nineteenth century, impoverished women produce breast milk for sale rather than for consumption by their own children. See Carolina Buia, "The Booming Market for Breast Milk," *Newsweek*, May 23, 2015. Buia depicts milk vendors as black women.

62 The dissenting judge in the case pointed out the problem: "This case is what critics who oppose surrogacy have been warning legislators [about]. . . . What we are going to see is a wealthy couple like the Calverts preying on the poor, which generally translates into preying on blacks. I hope this is recognized as a civil rights issue and a classic case of exploitation and a slave contract." Justice Kennard quoted in Rutherford, "Reproductive Freedoms," 272.

63 Hortense J. Spillers, "Mama's Baby, Papa's Maybe: An American Grammar Book," *Diacritics* 17.2 (1987): 68. On "disinheritance" as an apt description of intergenerational transmission in slavery, see Williams, *The Alchemy of Race and Rights*, 216–17. Notably scholars have focused on the stereotypes of black motherhood on which Parslow's ruling draws, arguing that Johnson's maternity was perceived through the lens of discourses consolidated in the prior decade and composed

of several intertwined strands: ideas about so-called black welfare queens; ideas about supposedly pathological black families; and related ideas about supposedly emasculating mothers abandoned by black men. As Grayson argues in "Mediating Intimacy," 530, Johnson's black body signified on preexisting meanings and ideas of black mothers as breeders whose (re)productive role in augmenting the master's property was necessarily severed from the cultural and social functions of motherhood. Also see Hartouni, "Breached Birth" and "Containing Women: Reproductive Discourse in the 1980s," in *Technoculture*, ed. Constance Penley and Andrew Ross (Minneapolis: University of Minnesota Press, 1991), 27–58; Ikemoto, "Destabilizing Thoughts on Surrogacy Legislation"; Harrison, *Brown Bodies, White Babies*, 106–18. Though most critics note that Johnson's visible blackness informed the case's outcome, they argue that it was determined by the court's insistence on maintenance of the heteronormative family and thus its refusal of a two-mother legal solution. On the discourses in question, see Ana Teresa Ortiz and Laura Briggs, "The Culture of Poverty, Crack Babies, and Welfare Cheats: The Making of the 'Healthy White Baby Crisis,'" *Social Text* 21.3 (2003): 39–57; Wahneema Lubiano, "Black Ladies, Welfare Queens, and State Minstrels: Ideological War by Narrative Means," in *Race-ing Justice, En-Gendering Power: Essays on Anita Hill, Clarence Thomas, and the Construction of Social Reality*, ed. Toni Morrison (New York: Pantheon, 1992), 323–63.

64 Hartouni, "Breached Birth," 83.

65 The letter is cited in Kasindorf, "And Baby Makes Four" and Grayson, "Mediating Intimacy."

66 Johnson's letter to Geraldo recalls Frederick Douglass's "What to the Slave Is the Fourth of July?," in *The Oxford Frederick Douglass Reader*, ed. William A. Andrews (New York: Oxford University Press, 1996), 108–30. Like Douglass, Johnson questioned rather than affirmed the promise of freedom by revealing enshrined legal hypocrisy.

67 Hartman, *Scenes of Subjection*.

68 Here I retool a phrase coined by Carey McWilliams in his influential 1943 treatise, *Brothers under the Skin: African Americans and Other Minorities* (Boston: Little, Brown, 1943).

69 This is Balibar's term for the ethnicization of difference that takes place in racial nationalist contexts in which nationalism is predicated on racial exclusion or inclusion. See Étienne Balibar and Immanuel Wallerstein, *Race, Nation, Class: Ambiguous Identities* (New York: Verso, 1999), 60.

70 See Kasindorf, "And Baby Makes Four."

71 Twine, *Outsourcing the Womb*, 10. The cult of "desperateness" is an adjunct of "the cult of genetic entitlement," in that the infertile imagine that the "need" for a genetically related child justifies recourse to ARTs. See Sarah Franklin, "Deconstructing 'Desperateness': The Social Construction of Infertility in Popular Representations of New Reproductive Technologies," in *The New Reproductive Technologies*, ed. Maureen McNeil, Ian Varcoe, and Steven Yearley (London: Macmillan, 1990), 220–29.

72 Here I suggest that Crispina Calvert's genetic contribution was "whitened" and subsumed by her husband's such that her "Filipina genes" became part of a patriarchal property claim made by the Calverts as a legally recognized marital unit. Though it is beyond the scope of my argument to expand the idea fully, such paternally predicated whiteness renders inaccessible the long history of Filipina domestic labor and care work that might otherwise connect Crispina Calvert and Anna Johnson. See Rhacel Salazar Parreñas, *The Force of Domesticity: Filipina Migrants and Globalization* (New York: New York University Press, 2008), and *Servants of Globalization*. For an alternate reading that stresses the importance of the Calverts as a biracial couple creating mixed-race progeny see Wiegman, "Intimate Publics."

73 Cheryl I. Harris, "Whiteness as Property," *Harvard Law Review* 106.8 (1994): 1709–91. Also see Lisa Cacho, *Social Death: Racialized Rightlessness and the Criminalization of the Unprotected* (New York: New York University Press, 2012).

74 Elsewhere I argue that although there is scientific consensus that race is a statistically insignificant genetic variation, race persists as the lens and logic through which meaning is made in a genomic age in which use of reproductive technology is informed by mistaken ideas about the visibility of "genetic" blackness. See Weinbaum, "Racial Aura: Walter Benjamin and the Work of Art in a Biotechnological Age," *Literature and Medicine* 26.1 (2007): 207–39. Also see Michael Omi, "'Slippin' into Darkness': The (Re)Biologization of Race," *Journal of Asian American Studies* 13.3 (2010): 343–58; Howard Winant, "Race and Racism: Towards a Global Future," *Ethnic and Racial Studies* 29.5 (2006): 986–1003; Dorothy Roberts, *Fatal Invention: How Science, Politics, and Big Business Re-create Race in the Twenty-First Century* (New York: New Press, 2011); Alondra Nelson, *The Social Life of DNA: Race, Reparations, and Reconciliation after the Genome* (Boston: Beacon, 2016). In a fascinating twist, Johnson's attorney sought to use the Indian Child Welfare Law to prevent the Calverts from gaining custody, arguing that the baby could not be adopted by them because it was born to an Indian woman. Tribal officials who were brought in as experts undercut this argument, arguing that the logic of blood quantum translates into the language of genetics and trumps maternal connection to the child. Like the court, these experts did not view gestation or parturition as formative. See Harrison, *Brown Bodies, White Babies*, 125.

75 Throughout this section I have elected to use the compound terminology *outsourced or transnational surrogacy* to indicate that when reproductive labor is outsourced, transnational reproduction is taking place. In general, when ethnographers discuss outsourcing, they are referring to use of surrogates in geographic locations at a distance from the consumers of surrogacy, although the term is on some level redundant when we recall that all surrogacy technically involves the outsourcing of reproductive labor. When ethnographers discuss transnational reproduction, they are referring to arrangements in which multiple parties are involved, as for instance when an egg is supplied by a white woman in Johannesburg and gestated by an Indian woman in Anand for a gay couple in California. In almost all outsourced surrogacy arrangements in which the consumer is unable to supply

an oocyte, eggs from vendors are used. These vendors may be flown to the gestational surrogate for egg retrieval, fertilization, and implantation since unfertilized eggs cannot be frozen and transported. Alternatively vendor eggs may be fertilized for subsequent transport to a second, distant location where the surrogate resides. Though discussion of the reproductive labor involved in oocyte vending is beyond the scope of this book, it is worth noting that the most lucrative markets involve eggs collected from college-educated white women in the US, white women from Eastern and Southern Europe, white South African women, and Asian women. Prices are driven upward by the vendor's "possession" of supposedly heritable cultural capital, including educational achievement, musical talent, athleticism, and so forth. Prices are crudely determined by "possession" of light skin, blond hair, and blue eyes—that is, by supposedly heritable qualities that consumers caught up in the ideology of genetic infallibility and the desirability of lightness (mistakenly) imagine will find phenotypic expression in the child that is (re)produced from "light" or "white" eggs. Ironically consumers who prefer "black" eggs find them difficult to procure and especially costly. See Cooper and Waldby, *Clinical Labor*, 62–83; Donna Dickenson, *Body Shopping*, 63–89; Twine, *Outsourcing the Womb*, 30–36; Sven Bergmann, "Fertility Tourism: Circumventive Routes That Enable Access to Reproductive Technologies and Substances," *Signs* 36.2 (2011): 280–89; Lisa C. Ikemoto, "Eggs as Capital: Human Egg Procurement in the Fertility Industry and the Stem Cell Research Enterprise," *Signs* 34.4 (2009): 763–81; Rene Almeling, *Sex Cells: The Medical Market for Eggs and Sperm* (Berkeley: University of California Press, 2011); Deomampo, *Transnational Reproduction*, 95–122; Harrison, *Brown Bodies, White Babies*, 129–164.

76 Several scholars have challenged the Eurocentrism of Foucault's and Agamben's accounts. Achille Mbembe and Jared Sexton call for reconsideration of the concentration camp as what Agamben refers to as "the *nomos* of the modern." Alexander Weheliye critiques Foucault's Eurocentric conceptualization of racism (influentially developed in *Society Must Be Defended*). I am sympathetic to these interventions and inspired by Weheliye's suggestion that we need not replace the camp with the colony or plantation but ought to instead focus on the relationships among the various forms of dehumanization that together shape the category of "the human." See Foucault, *The History of Sexuality, Volume 1: An Introduction* (1978), trans. Robert Hurley (New York: Vintage, 1990), and *Society Must Be Defended: Lectures at the Collège de France, 1975–76*, trans. David Macey, ed. Mauro Bertani and Alessandro Fontana (New York: Picador, 2003); Agamben, *Homo Sacer: Sovereign Power and Bare Life*, trans. Daniel Heller-Roazen (Stanford: Stanford University Press, 1998); Mbembe, "Necropolitics," trans. Libby Meintjes, *Public Culture* 15.1 (2003): 11–40; Sexton, "People-of-Color-Blindness: Notes on the Afterlife of Slavery," *Social Text* 28.2 (2010): 31–56; Weheliye, *Habeas Viscus: Racializing Assemblages, Biopolitics, and Black Feminist Theories of the Human* (Durham: Duke University Press, 2014).

For-profit clinics exist in the United States, India, Thailand, Malaysia, South Africa, Mexico, Guatemala, Russia, and Belarus. Surrogacy is widely practiced and subsidized by the state in Israel. However, single Israeli men and male couples must seek surrogacy arrangements abroad because the state bans all male participation in surrogacy. See Elly Teman, *Birthing a Mother: The Surrogate Body and the Pregnant Self* (Berkeley: University of California Press, 2010); Susan Martha Kahn, *Reproducing Jews: A Cultural Account of Assisted Conception in Israel* (Durham: Duke University Press, 2000).

77 Heléna Ragoné first observed the racial dynamics heralded by the shift to gestational surrogacy in the US. She explained, "Racial difference is [now viewed as] . . . a positive factor, one that actually facilitates the process of separation between surrogate and child." "Of Likeness and Difference: How Race Is Being Transfigured by Gestational Surrogacy," in *Ideologies and Technologies of Motherhood: Race, Class, Sexuality, and Nationalism*, ed. Heléna Ragoné and France Winddance Twine (New York: Routledge, 2000), 66. Subsequent scholarship confirms these trends globally. See Deomampo, *Transnational Reproduction*; Harrison, *Brown Bodies, White Babies*.

78 Grayson expressed a shared worry: "Gestational surrogacy invites the singling out of black women for exploitation not only because a disproportionate number of black women are poor and might possibly turn to leasing their wombs as a means of income, but also because it is incorrectly assumed that black women's skin color can be read as a visual sign of their lack of genetic relation to the children they would bear for the white couples who seek to hire them" ("Mediating Intimacy," 540). Grayson's concerns were presaged by Gena Corea, who speculated about "reproductive brothels" selling wombs alongside vaginas, mouths, and anuses (*The Mother Machine*, 275–76), and Barbara Katz Rothman, who speculated about "baby farms" full of young "Third World women" in *Recreating Motherhood: Ideology and Technology in Patriarchal Society* (New York: Norton, 1989), 237, and "Reproductive Technology and the Commodification of Life," in *Embryos, Ethics and Women's Rights: Exploring the New Reproductive Technologies*, ed. Elaine Hoffman Baruch, Amadeo F. D'Adamo, and Joni Seager (New York: Harrington Park, 1988), 95–100.

79 It is telling that poor women in the Global South and women of color in the US have the highest rates of infertility and are the least likely to access reproductive technology and assistance. In general, infertility is a function of exposure to environmental pollutants, malnutrition, and lack of access to adequate health care, including prenatal and obstetrical care. In the United States (which has one of the highest maternal mortality rates in the developed world) and in India (where one quarter of all annual maternal deaths occur worldwide) women are exposed to risk simply by engaging in gestation and childbirth without access to health care and other necessities such as clean water. Whereas two thirds of Indian women receive little or no prenatal or postnatal care and deliver their babies at home, Indian surrogates receive medical care, nutrition, and rest throughout the pregnancies that they undertake on behalf of consumers. See "Pregnancy Mortality Surveillance System," Centers for Disease Control and Prevention, https://www

.cdc.gov/reproductivehealth/maternalinfanthealth/pmss.html; "Trends in Maternal Mortality: 1990 to 2015: Estimates by WHO, UNICEF, UNFPA, World Bank Group and the United Nations Population Division" (Geneva: WHO Document Production, 2015); Alison Bailey, "Reconceiving Surrogacy: Toward a Reproductive Justice Account of Indian Surrogacy," *Hypatia* 26.4 (2011): 715–41.

80 See Amrita Pande, "'It May Be Her Eggs but It's My Blood': Surrogates and Everyday Forms of Kinship in India," *Qualitative Sociology* 32.4 (2009): 379–97; "Not an 'Angel,' Not a 'Whore': Surrogates as 'Dirty' Workers in India," *Indian Journal of Gender Studies* 16.2 (2009): 141–73; "Commercial Surrogacy in India: Manufacturing a Perfect Mother Worker," *Signs* 35.4 (2010): 969–92; "'At Least I Am Not Sleeping with Anyone': Resisting the Stigma of Commercial Surrogacy in India," *Feminist Studies* 36.2 (2010): 292–312; and *Wombs in Labor: Transnational Commercial Surrogacy in India* (New York: Columbia University Press, 2014); Kalindi Vora, "Indian Transnational Surrogacy and the Commodification of Vital Energy," *Subjectivity* 28.1 (2009): 266–78, and *Life Support*; Daisy Deomampo, "Transnational Surrogacy in India: Interrogating Power and Women's Agency," *Frontiers* 34.3 (2013): 167–88, and *Transnational Reproduction*; Jyotsna Agnihotri Gupta, "Parenthood in the Era of Reproductive Outsourcing and Global Assemblages," *AJWS* 18.1 (2012): 7–29; Natalie Fixmer-Oraiz, "Speaking of Solidarity: Transnational Gestation Surrogacy and the Rhetorics of Reproductive (In)Justice," *Frontiers* 34.3 (2013): 126–63; Sharmila Rudrappa, *Discounted Life: The Price of Global Surrogacy in India* (New York: New York University Press, 2015); Sayantani DasGupta and Shamita Das Dasgupta, eds., *Globalization and Transnational Surrogacy in India: Outsourcing Life* (Lanham, MD: Lexington Books, 2014). Also see Amana Fontanella-Khan, "India, the Rent-a-Womb Capital of the World," *Slate*, August 23, 2010; Abigail Haworth, "Surrogate Mothers: Womb for Rent," *Marie Claire*, July 29, 2007; Tamara Audi and Arlene Chang, "Assembling the Global Baby," *Wall Street Journal*, December 10, 2010; Judith Warner, "Outsourced Wombs," *New York Times*, January 3, 2008.

81 Though costs of surrogacy in India fluctuate based on a clinic's reputation and a surrogate's prior success rate, an arrangement with an Indian surrogate costs roughly one-third of a comparable arrangement with an American surrogate residing in the US. Pande, *Wombs in Labor*, 12; Rudrappa, *Discounted Life*, 5.

82 Rudrappa, *Discounted Life*, 124–125; Vora, *Life Support*, 118; Fixmer-Oraiz, "Speaking of Solidarity," 131; Bailey, "Reconceiving Surrogacy," 718. When a surrogate is left with postpartum complications, she is often responsible for her own medical care. If she miscarries, she must forego the bulk of her payment, which is predicated on successful delivery.

83 Surrogacy is banned in Australia, China, the Czech Republic, Denmark, France, Germany, Italy, Spain, Switzerland, Taiwan, Turkey, and in some US states. There are partial bans in Brazil, Israel, and the UK. There exists regulation in India, Belgium, Finland, and Greece. See Twine, *Outsourcing the Womb*, chapter 1. Indian commercial surrogacy was legalized in 2002. Government guidelines meant to streamline business practices were announced in 2008 and updated in 2010 and

2013, at which time surrogacy arrangements involving gay couples and single men were banned. Rudrappa estimates that in 2012, approximately one third of the ten thousand clients who visited India were single or gay. See Rudrappa, *Discounted Life*, 39–40; Pande, *Wombs in Labor*, 13–14. On November 4, 2015, India imposed a ban on US citizenship for children born to Indian surrogates, effectively shutting down a large part of the market: see "Surrogacy, ART, and IVF," U.S. Embassy and Consulates in India, accessed January 30, 2017, https://in.usembassy.gov/u -s-citizen-services/birth/surrogacy-art-and-ivf/?_ga=1.252220873.1173353544 .1482467571. The Israeli state subsidizes surrogacy for heterosexual couples and all women (Teman, *Birthing a Mother*). Since 2013 gay couples and individuals from Europe, the UK, and North America have circumvented Indian regulations by paying Indian surrogates to migrate to neighboring countries such as Nepal for the duration of their pregnancies. See Jey Saung, "Reproducing the Nation-State: Surrogate 'Gaybies,' Queer Family, and Biopolitics of Colonialism," presented at the Biopower and Biopolitics Graduate Seminar, Seattle, Washington, March 3, 2016. On factors that lead consumers to travel abroad see Gupta, "Parenthood in the Era of Reproductive Outsourcing"; Bergmann, "Fertility Tourism." Surrogacy is unevenly regulated in the United States. Most states have no restrictions; some ban commercial surrogacy; others ban all forms of payment but not the practice of surrogacy. The state of California is entirely unregulated. Many predict that outsourcing or transnational surrogacy is fast becoming dominant. See Hochschild, *The Outsourced Self*, 101.

84 Pande treats surrogates as "agents" who make "constrained choices" to lessen hardships. She rejects Eurocentric portrayals that do not incorporate discussion of surrogacy as a chosen survival strategy. Similarly, though she describes surrogacy as "undoubtedly exploitative," Rudrappa casts surrogates as "active participants in emergent intimate industries, shaping a new ethics of caring and giving a whole new meaning to the social and economic value of babies and motherhood" (*Discounted Life*, 8, 56, 65, 86–98). Fixmer-Oraiz examines obfuscating media rhetoric in "Speaking of Solidarity." Deomampo analyzes how foreign consumers of surrogacy buy into the "rescue narrative" by believing that they are saving poor women from dire circumstances by employing them (*Transnational Reproduction*, 59–94). Vora finds that clinics overplay the benefit to surrogates of payment and advance a discourse of "rehabilitation through surrogacy" that relieves consumers of anxiety about the stark economic inequalities at the heart of the exchange (*Life Support*, 117–19, 121).

85 Pande, "'At Least I'm Not Sleeping with Anyone,'" 302.

86 Rudrappa, *Discounted Life*, 72.

87 Rudrappa, *Discounted Life*, 60.

88 Pande, "Commercial Surrogacy in India," 12.

89 Surrogacy clinics generally prohibit unmediated interactions between surrogates and consumers; many refuse to facilitate contact after delivery. See Rudrappa, *Discounted Life*, 135, 137.

90 Rudrappa, *Discounted Life*, 5.

91 When Indians living abroad or wealthy Indian citizens consume surrogacy in India, the exchange is shaped by religion, caste, and race. As Vora argues, the "vital energy" that is transferred from surrogate to consumer follows circuits of exchange set in place by colonialism, by India's history of bonded labor, and by culturally specific reproductive practices that have for centuries compelled household servants and extended family to reproduce children who will be parented by those able and willing to provide for them (personal communication and *Life Support*, 25–42, 103–40). Vora stands strongly on one side of the ongoing debate about the relevance of the history of slavery and bonded labor in South Asia to the practice of surrogacy. Also see Indrani Chatterjee, *Gender, Slavery, and Law in Colonial India* (London: Oxford University Press, 1999); Indrani Chatterjee and Richard M. Eaton, eds., *Slavery and South Asian History* (Bloomington: Indiana University Press, 2006).

92 Deomampo's discussion of the "racial reproductive imaginaries" that inform the interactions between consumers of outsourced surrogacy in India and the surrogates whose labor they consume moved me to speculate thus. She discusses consumers' production of the surrogate as a "racialized Other"—a term that, she argues, encompasses the consumer's Orientalization of the Asian surrogate. Here I suggest it might also include the consumer's imposition of ideas about women of color as "natural" breeders, ideas that emerge from Atlantic slavery. See Deomampo, *Transnational Reproduction*, especially chapter 2. Relatedly Kalindi Vora observes that foreign consumers of surrogacy bring with them to India ideologies and expectations about reproduction that are often foreign to Indian women. See "Re-imagining Reproduction: Unsettling Metaphors in the History of Imperial Science and Commercial Surrogacy in India," *Somatechnics* 5.1 (2015): 88–103, especially 90.

93 Deomampo, *Transnational Reproduction*, and Vora, *Life Support*, most robustly take up the racializing work of the colonial episteme, though neither uses this terminology.

94 Laura Harrison's *Brown Bodies, White Babies* is the first study to bring together discussions of the racial politics of outsourced surrogacy in India and cross-racial surrogacy in the US. Harrison focuses on the perceptible (ascribed and self-identified) racial differences among the individuals involved in surrogacy arrangements and explores how these shape surrogacy arrangements. She convincingly demonstrates that cross-racial surrogacy arrangements shore up the interests of the dominant racial group as they are predominantly used to create wealthy, white, heterosexual families that reside in the Global North.

95 See Lisa Lowe, *The Intimacies of Four Continents* (Durham: Duke University Press, 2015), 3.

2. Black Feminism as a Philosophy of History

1 Mark Reinhardt, "Introduction: An Extraordinary Case?," in *Who Speaks for Margaret Garner? The True Story That Inspired Toni Morrison's Beloved* (Minneapolis: University of Minnesota Press, 2010), 5; hereafter cited parenthetically. Garner was given voice only through this oft-repeated account of her intent. As Reinhardt notes, because slaves could not provide testimony Garner never took the stand.

2 Darlene Clark Hine, "Foreword: Gendered Resistance Now," in *Gendered Resistance: Women, Slavery, and the Legacy of Margaret Garner*, ed. Mary E. Frederickson and Delores M. Walters (Urbana: University of Illinois Press, 2013), x; hereafter cited parenthetically.

3 Walter Benjamin, "Theses on the Philosophy of History" (1940), in *Illuminations*, trans. Harry Zohn, ed. Hannah Arendt (New York: Schocken Books, 1968), 255; hereafter cited parenthetically.

4 Though two charges were brought, one for destruction of property and one for violation of the Fugitive Slave Act, Garner was tried only in relation to the latter despite abolitionists' attempts to expose the Slave Act's hypocrisy by having her instead tried for murder. As Stephen Best observes, supporters of slavery regarded fugitives as criminals involved in theft of self. *The Fugitive's Properties: Law and the Poetics of Possession* (Chicago: University of Chicago Press, 2004), 81–82.

5 The Southern press paid Garner scant attention; Reinhardt interprets this as political censorship (*Who Speaks for Margaret Garner?*, 30–31).

6 Douglass cited in Reinhardt, *Who Speaks for Margaret Garner?*, 32.

7 Douglass cited in Reinhardt, *Who Speaks for Margaret Garner?*, 41.

8 Stone cited in Reinhardt, *Who Speaks for Margaret Garner?*, 40–41. Recent scholars who follow Stone's lead observe that Garner's daughter was light skinned and thus especially vulnerable to sexual abuse. Others claim Garner's actions were compelled by the fact that her children were fathered by her master. See Delores M. Walters, "Introduction: Re(dis)covering and Recreating the Cultural Milieu of Margaret Garner," in Frederickson and Walters, *Gendered Resistance*, 8–13; Steven Weisenburger, *Modern Medea: A Family Story of Slavery and Child-Murder from the Old South* (New York: Hill and Wang, 1998), 47, 75–76.

9 In a survey of literary representations of the 1850s Sarah N. Roth argues that slave infanticide was treated as suicide, as violence against the mother rather than infant. Slave mothers who committed infanticide were thus viewed as self-sacrificing heroines. Roth places Garner's story alongside novels by Stowe, Jollife (Garner's lawyer), and M'Keehan. "'The Blade Was in My Own Breast': Slave Infanticide in 1850s Fiction," *American Nineteenth Century History* 8.2 (2007): 169–85.

10 Garner's second daughter, Cilla, was drowned when the steamboat on which the Garners were traveling to Mississippi capsized. The possibility that Cilla's drowning was also an act of infanticide lends credence to Garner's assertion that she was committed to execution of her initial plan even after her capture. Walters, "Introduction," 5.

11 M. A. Harris, Bill Cosby, and Toni Morrison, eds., *The Black Book* (New York: Random House, 1974), a compilation of news clippings and archival materials that Morrison shepherded through publication. Morrison claims that the account of Garner included therein inspired *Beloved*. See Cheryl A. Wall, "Toni Morrison, Editor and Teacher," in *The Cambridge Companion to Toni Morrison*, ed. Justine Tally (New York: Cambridge University Press, 2007), 143–46.

12 *Beloved* is routinely assigned in high school and college; there is a popular cinematic adaptation starring Oprah Winfrey, an opera based on Garner's life that features a libretto by Morrison, and a daunting amount of scholarship on the novel, including nearly nine hundred entries in the International Modern Language Association database.

13 See Joy James, "Profeminism and Gender Elites: W. E. B. Du Bois, Anna Julia Cooper, and Ida B. Wells-Barnett," 69–95, and Hazel Carby, "The Souls of Black Men," 234–68, collected in *Next to the Color Line: Gender, Sexuality, and W. E. B. Du Bois*, ed. Susan Gillman and Alys Eve Weinbaum (Minneapolis: University of Minnesota Press, 2007).

14 Cedric Robinson, *Black Marxism: The Making of the Black Radical Tradition* (Chapel Hill: University of North Carolina Press, 1983), 185–240; W. E. B. Du Bois, *Black Reconstruction in America, 1860–1880* (1935; New York: Free Press, 1998); hereafter both cited parenthetically.

15 See Cedric Robinson, "A Critique of W. E. B. Du Bois' *Black Reconstruction*," *Black Scholar* 8.7 (1977): 44–50, and *Black Marxism*, 199–203.

16 In this way, Robinson continues, Du Bois positions slavery as a subsystem of world capitalism, and the Civil War (and the crushing of the revolutionary impulses that animated it) as world historical events that set the stage for the violent modernity we have inherited—a modernity grounded in a racialized global division of labor. Also see Moon-Ho Jung, "*Black Reconstruction* and Empire," *South Atlantic Quarterly* 112.3 (2013): 465–71.

17 Susan Gillman and Alys Eve Weinbaum, "Introduction: W. E. B. Du Bois and the Politics of Juxtaposition," in Gillman and Weinbaum, *Next to the Color Line*, 1–34; Alys Eve Weinbaum, "The Sexual Politics of Black Internationalism: W. E. B. Du Bois and the Reproduction of Racial Globality" in *Wayward Reproductions: Genealogies of Race and Nation in Transatlantic Modern Thought* (Durham: Duke University Press, 2004), 187–226.

18 See chapters by Joy James, Hazel Carby, and Michele Elam and Paul C. Taylor, all collected in Gillman and Weinbaum, *Next to the Color Line*, quote 209. Also see David Levering Lewis, *W. E. B. Du Bois: The Fight for Equality and the American Century, 1919–1963* (New York: Henry Holt, 2000), 267.

19 *Black Reconstruction* exhibits a textual form that I elsewhere describe as Du Bois's "politics of juxtaposition." In placing unremarked discussions of gender and sexual exploitation and violence "right next to" discussion of racist and imperialist exploitation and violence, Du Bois demonstrates the need for (but does not offer) an intersectional analysis of racism, sexism, and capitalism. See Gillman

and Weinbaum, "Introduction: W. E. B. Du Bois and the Politics of Juxtaposition," and Weinbaum, "Interracial Romance and Black Internationalism," in Gillman and Weinbaum, *Next to the Color Line*, 1–34 and 96–123.

20 Deborah Gray White explains, "For those fugitive women who left children in slavery, the physical relief which freedom brought was limited compensation for the anguish they suffered." *Ar'n't I A Woman: Female Slaves in the Plantation South* (New York: W. W. Norton & Co., 1985), 71; hereafter cited parenthetically. John Hope Franklin and Loren Schweninger estimate that roughly 20 percent of run-aways were women: *Runaway Slaves: Rebels on the Plantation* (New York: Oxford University Press, 1999), 210. As Cheryl Janifer LaRoche observes in "Coerced but Not Subdued: The Gendered Resistance of Women Escaping Slavery," in Franklin and Walters, *Gendered Resistance*, 49–76, feminist historians question reliance on advertisements for fugitives as the basis for such statistics as advertisements were less frequently posted for missing women than missing men. Women's absences were often regarded as temporary "lying out" and thus of less concern. La Roche adds that the tendency to define temporary or unrealized escape attempts as statistically insignificant also diminishes the agency of slave women and their complex negotiations of familial ties.

21 Du Bois observes that the planter's "only effective economic movement . . . could take place against the slave. He was forced, unless willing to take lower profits, continually to beat down the cost of slave labor. . . . One method called for more land and the other for more slaves" (*Black Reconstruction in America*, 41).

22 Du Bois writes, "Child-bearing was a profitable occupation that received every possible encouragement, and there was not only no bar to illegitimacy, but an actual premium put upon it. Indeed, the word was impossible of meaning under the slave system" (*Black Reconstruction in America*, 44).

23 When Du Bois mentions women in the war he undercuts their role by noting that they "accompanied" husbands. Thavolia Glymph clarifies that from the beginning of the conflict black women with children fled to Union lines without men and that enlistment of black men as soldiers in the Union Army left wives especially vulnerable, a situation that led to "swelling" numbers of black women among those Du Bois describes as "swarming." Personal communication. As Stephanie Camp argues, it was the absence of men on plantations that led slave women to rely mainly upon each other when organizing escape. *Closer to Freedom: Enslaved Women and Everyday Resistance in the Plantation South* (Chapel Hill: University of North Carolina Press, 2004), 123–27.

24 On the distinction between "fact" and "truth" see Toni Morrison, "The Site of Memory" in *Out There: Marginalization and Contemporary Cultures*, ed. Russell Ferguson (Cambridge, MA: Massachusetts Institute of Technology Press, 1990), 299–305, and chapter 3 below. Also see Robinson, *Black Marxism*, 44.

25 This global culture has led to a global racial division of labor predicated on exploitation of those whom Du Bois described as "the darker peoples of the world." On the reproductive politics of Du Bois's black internationalist vision see Alys Eve

Weinbaum, "The Sexual Politics of Black Internationalism," in *Wayward Reproductions*, 187–226.

26 In his introduction to *Black Reconstruction in America, 1860–1880*, by W. E. B. Du Bois (New York: Free Press, 1998), xiii, David Levering Lewis designates *Black Reconstruction* "propaganda for his people," observing that Du Bois's book instantiates slaves and former slaves as historical agents. Also see Charles Lemert, "The Race of Time: Du Bois and Reconstruction," *Boundary 2* 27.3 (2000): 215–48.

27 Michel Foucault, "Nietzsche, Genealogy, History" (1977), in *The Foucault Reader*, ed. Paul Rabinow (New York: Pantheon, 1984), 76–100.

28 The term is Robin Kelley's. See the discussion in my introduction.

29 Angela Y. Davis, "Reflections on the Black Woman's Role in the Community of Slaves," *Black Scholar* 3.4 (1971): 2–15; hereafter cited parenthetically. This essay was reprinted in *The Black Scholar* in 1981 as part of the special issue "The Black Woman"; parts of it subsequently appeared as "The Legacy of Slavery: Standards for a New Womanhood," chapter 1 in *Women, Race, and Class* (New York: Vintage, 1983), 3–29; hereafter cited parenthetically. Also see Daniel Patrick Moynihan, *The Negro Family: The Case for National Action* (1965), in *The Moynihan Report and the Politics of Controversy*, ed. Lee Rainwater and William L. Yancey (Cambridge, MA: MIT Press, 1967), 47–94.

30 Davis cites *Black Reconstruction* and *Darkwater*. While she does not use the term *strike*, she picks up Du Bois's terminology when she refers to slaves as "workers."

31 Here and elsewhere Davis singles out E. Franklin Frazier's *The Negro Family in the United States* (Chicago: University of Chicago Press, 1939) as the account of the slave family upon which Moynihan based his "tangle of pathology" argument. Davis, "Reflections," 4.

32 I draw on contemporary social scientific scholarship on care work in crafting my understanding of its devaluation, feminization, and racialization. Some social scientists implicitly link women's slave labor and care work. As Rhacel Salazar Parreñas notes, one of the contradictions of the outsourced care work that Filipina migrants perform is that they care for the children of their employers rather than their own. See Eileen Boris and Rhacel Salazar Parreñas, eds., *Intimate Labors: Cultures, Technologies, and the Politics of Care* (Stanford: Stanford University Press, 2010); Rhacel Salazar Parreñas, *Servants of Globalization: Women, Migration, and Domestic Work* (Stanford: Stanford University Press, 2001), and *The Force of Domesticity: Filipina Migrants and Globalization* (New York: New York University Press, 2008). Elsewhere Parreñas critiques the conceptual efficacy of "care work," arguing for the term's replacement by "reproductive labor": "The Reproductive Labour of Migrant Workers," *Global Networks* 12.2 (2012): 269–75.

33 Some query Davis's ideas about domestic life in slavery and her emphasis on women's domestic role. Others take issue with attribution of agency to slaves in general. In *Killing the Black Body: Race, Reproduction, and the Meaning of Liberty* (New York: Pantheon, 1997), 55, Dorothy Roberts cautions that slave women's work was easily co-opted, as masters "ultimately profited from their care of other slaves."

Walter Johnson cautions against the presumption of slave agency in social historical scholarship produced in the 1970s, noting the need, at that time, to romantically redeem the past: "On Agency," *Journal of Social History* 37.1 (2003): 113–24. Notably, Davis reworks this part of her argument a decade later. In "The Legacy of Slavery" she argues that because women's field labor was the same as that performed by men, slave women were ungendered. Paradoxically gender irreducibly conditioned slave women's subjection to counterinsurgency in the form of rape and "other barbarous mistreatment that could only be inflicted on women" (6). "Expediency governed the slave holders' posture toward female slaves," she further clarifies. "When it was profitable to exploit them as if they were men, they were regarded, in effect, as genderless, but when they could be exploited, punished and repressed in ways suited only for women, they were locked into their exclusively female roles" (6). In this expanded argument, Davis notes her reservations about imagining the domestic space as female, observing that slave men engaged in domestic labor and men and women—working side by side in the field and home—possessed "positive equality" (18). See Davis, "The Legacy of Slavery," 6–8. Such corrective arguments have also provoked criticism.

34 In an against-the-grain reading of Aptheker, Davis locates evidence of black women as members of fugitive and maroon communities, as insurgents within plantation households, and as participants in organized rebellions. As she laments, if reigning (male) historians would only interpret their own evidence "correctly" they would discover that women were "the most daring and committed combatants" and thus "the custodian[s] of a house of resistance" ("Reflections," 8–9).

35 When Davis updates these arguments in 1981 she does so by comparing the rape of slave women to the rape of Vietnamese women by American troops. In both instances rape is a "weapon of domination . . . designed to intimidate and terrorize" ("The Legacy of Slavery," 23–24). Davis has elsewhere written about how personal sexual violation fuels her imagination of slave insurgency against rape and her focus on the gendered linkages between plantations and prisons. See "Rape, Racism, and the Capitalist Setting" (1978), "JoAnne Little: The Dialects of Rape" (1975), "Violence against Women and the Ongoing Challenge to Racism" (1985), all in *The Angela Y. Davis Reader*, ed. Joy James (Malden, MA: Blackwell, 1998), 129–60, and "How Gender Structures the Prison System," in *Are Prisons Obsolete?* (New York: Seven Stories, 2003), 60–83.

36 See Hortense J. Spillers, "Mama's Baby, Papa's Maybe: An American Grammar Book," *Diacritics* 17.2 (1987): 65–81.

37 In the first major black feminist anthology, Erlene Stetson details a course taught on the history of slavery that focused on female slaves prior to the emergence of black feminist histories of slavery. Instructively Stetson begins her course by juxtaposing Davis's essay and Du Bois's *Black Reconstruction*. See Stetson, "Studying Slavery: Some Literary and Pedagogical Considerations on the Black Female Slave," in *All the Women Are White, All the Blacks Are Men, but Some of Us Are Brave: Black*

Women's Studies, ed. Gloria T. Hull, Patricia Bell Scott, and Barbara Smith (Old Westbury, CT: Feminist Press, 1982), 62–84.

38 Hine cites scholarship by field-shapers such as Herbert Aptheker, Eugene Genovese, and Winthrop Jordan. Though she does not cite Davis, the solidarity of their projects is evident. See Darlene C. Hine, "Female Slave Resistance: The Economics of Sex," *Western Journal of Black Studies* 3.2 (1979): 123–27; hereafter cited parenthetically.

39 In the 1990s black feminist scholars began to examine how nineteenth-century slaves and midwives used herbs (tansy, rue, cotton root and seed, pennyroyal, cedar gum) and other techniques to prevent or destroy pregnancy. See Roberts, *Killing the Black Body,* 47; Sharla M. Fett, *Working Cures: Healing, Health, and Power on Southern Slave Plantations* (Chapel Hill: University of North Carolina Press, 2002); Marie Jenkins Schwartz, *Birthing a Slave: Motherhood and Medicine in the Antebellum South* (Cambridge, MA: Harvard University Press, 2006); Liese M. Perrin, "Resisting Reproduction: Reconsidering Slave Contraception in the Old South," *Journal of American Studies* 35.2 (2001): 255–74. Hine argues that some acts of reproductive resistance (including abortion) ought to be recognized as collaborative, if not collectively organized ("Female Slave Resistance," 125).

40 See White, *Ar'n't I a Woman?*

41 White begins her book with a discussion of the figures of Jezebel and Mammy. Here I suggest that in so doing she reveals not only the stereotypes that informed the master's treatment of slave women but also the gendered ideology to which slave women had to actively respond. See White, "Jezebel and Mammy: The Mythology of Female Slavery" in *Ar'n't I a Woman?,* 27–61.

42 White argues that although "few sources illuminate the interaction of slave women in their private world," they shared knowledge about sex and motherhood cross-generationally, especially when working on "trash gangs" composed of children too young, women too pregnant, and elders too weak to endure the heaviest aspects of field work. White further imagines that because they were forced to rely on each other, slave women would have been closer to each other than to their children or their men—both of whom were likely transient (*Ar'n't I a Woman?,* 23, 119–41).

43 See Mia Bay, *The White Image in the Black Mind: African American Ideas about White People, 1830–1925* (New York: Oxford University Press, 2000); Barbara Bush, *Slave Women in Caribbean Society, 1650–1838* (Bloomington: Indiana University Press, 1990); Camp, *Closer to Freedom;* Fett, *Working Cures;* Mary Farmer-Kaiser, *Freedwomen and the Freedmen's Bureau: Race, Gender, and Public Policy in the Age of Emancipation* (New York: Fordham University Press, 2010); Thavolia Glymph, *Out of the House of Bondage: The Transformation of the Plantation Household* (New York: Cambridge University Press, 2003); Tera W. Hunter, *To 'Joy My Freedom: Southern Black Women's Lives and Labors after the Civil War* (Cambridge, MA: Harvard University Press, 1997); Jacqueline Jones, *American Work: Four Centuries of Black and White Labor* (New York: Norton, 1998), *The Dispossessed: America's Underclasses from the Civil War to the Present* (New

York: Basic Books, 1992), *Labor of Love, Labor of Sorrow: Black Women, Work, and the Family from Slavery to the Present* (New York: Basic Books, 1985), and *A Social History of the Laboring Classes from Colonial Times to the Present* (Malden, MA: Blackwell, 1999); Jennifer L. Morgan, *Laboring Women: Reproduction and Gender in New World Slavery* (Philadelphia: University of Pennsylvania Press, 2004); Marietta Morrissey, *Slave Women in the New World: Gender Stratification in the Caribbean* (Lawrence: University of Kansas Press, 1989); Nell Irvin Painter, *Sojourner Truth: A Life, a Symbol* (New York: Norton, 1996), and *Southern History across the Color Line* (Chapel Hill: University of North Carolina Press, 2002); Amy Dru Stanley, *From Bondage to Contract: Wage Labor, Marriage, and the Market in the Age of Slave Emancipation* (New York: Cambridge University Press, 1998).

44 Here I follow Robinson's observation that "the general strike had not been planned or centrally organized. Instead, Du Bois termed as a general strike the total impact on the secessionist South of a series of actions circumstantially related to each other. . . . These events were a consequence of contradictions within Southern society rather than a revolutionary vanguard that knit these phenomena into a historical force." Robinson continues, "With respect to class consciousness, Du Bois perceived that official Marxism had reduced this complex phenomenon to a thin political shell consisting of formulae for the dominance of state and/or part of workers' movements. In resisting this tendency, Du Bois sought to reintroduce the dialectic in its Hegelian form as the cunning of reason. No party could substitute itself for the revolutionary instrument of history: a people moved to action by the social and material conditions of its existence" ("A Critique," 48, 50).

45 Saidiya Hartman, "Venus in Two Acts," *Small Axe* 12.2 (2008): 11.

46 Rushdy and Bell invented the generic label. Ashraf H. A. Rushdy, *Neo-Slave Narratives: Studies in the Social Logic of a Literary Form* (New York: Oxford University Press, 1999); Bernard W. Bell, *The Afro-American Novel and Its Tradition* (Amherst: University of Massachusetts Press, 1987). Subsequent feminist critics expanded the criterion for generic inclusion. See, for example, Angelyn Mitchell, *The Freedom to Remember: Narrative, Slavery, and Gender in Contemporary Black Women's Fiction* (New Brunswick, NJ: Rutgers University Press, 2002); and Jenny Sharpe, *Ghosts of Slavery: A Literary Archeology of Black Women's Lives* (Minneapolis: University of Minnesota Press, 2003). Rushdy takes the feminist critique to heart in *Remembering Generations: Race and Family in Contemporary African American Fiction* (Chapel Hill: University of North Carolina Press, 2001), which can be read as a supplement to and revision of his earlier study.

47 See Robin Marantz Henig, "In Vitro Revelation," *New York Times*, October 5, 2010.

48 Most famously Gena Corea and members of FINNRAGE called for a moratorium on the use of all reproductive technologies and all forms of baby selling. See Corea, *The Mother Machine: Reproductive Technologies from Artificial Insemination to Artificial Wombs* (New York: Harper and Row, 1985); Rita Arditti, Renate Duelli-Klein, and

Shelley Minden, eds., *Test-Tube Women: What Future for Motherhood?* (London: Pandora, 1984).

49 Angela Y. Davis, "Surrogates and Outcast Mothers: Racism and Reproductive Politics in the Nineties," in Joy James, *The Angela Y. Davis Reader*, 212; hereafter cited parenthetically.

50 See my discussion of outsourced and transnational surrogacy in chapter 1.

51 See Roberts, *Killing the Black Body*, 278. I examine this observation fully in the previous chapter, which takes Roberts's passage as its epigraph.

52 Of the hundreds of critical articles and chapters on *Beloved*, two make the connection between *Beloved* and the Baby M case: Mark R. Patterson, "Surrogacy and Slavery: The Problematics of Consent in Baby M, *Romance of the Republic*, and *Pudd'nhead Wilson*," *American Literary History* 8.3 (1996): 448–70; Elizabeth Tobin, "Imagining the Mother's Text: Toni Morrison's *Beloved* and Contemporary Law," *Harvard Women's Law Journal* 16 (1993): 233–73. I thank Mark Patterson for bringing his essay to my attention. Notably Davis makes a related argument when she recommends that misguided historians of slavery "would do well to read Gayl Jones' *Corregidora*" ("The Legacy of Slavery," 26). Like Morrison, Davis was an early promoter of Jones's work.

3. Violent Insurgency, or "Power to the Ice Pick"

1 See Toni Morrison, foreword to *Beloved* (New York: Vintage, 2004), xvii; hereafter cited parenthetically. *Beloved* was first published in 1987, the year after the Baby M case became a national sensation.

2 See Jennifer Nelson, *Women of Color and the Reproductive Rights Movement* (New York: New York University Press, 2003); Deborah R. Grayson, "'Necessity Was the Midwife of Our Politics': Black Women's Health Activism in the 'Post'–Civil Rights Era (1980–1996)," in *Still Lifting, Still Climbing: African American Women's Contemporary Activism*, ed. Kimberly Springer (New York: New York University Press, 1999), 131–48; Byllye Y. Avery, "Breathing Life into Ourselves: The Evolution of the National Black Women's Health Project," in *The Black Women's Health Book: Speaking for Ourselves*, ed. Evelyn C. White (Seattle: Seal Press, 1990), 4–10; Angela Y. Davis, "Sick and Tired of Being Sick and Tired: The Politics of Black Women's Health," in White, *The Black Women's Health Book*, 18–26; African American Women Are for Reproductive Freedom, "We Remember," in Springer, *Still Lifting*, 38–41; Wahneema Lubiano, "Black Ladies, Welfare Queens, and State Minstrels: Ideological War by Narrative Means," in *Race-ing Justice, En-gendering Power: Essays on Anita Hill, Clarence Thomas, and the Construction of Social Reality*, ed. Toni Morrison (New York: Pantheon, 1992), 323–63.

3 Toni Morrison, "The Site of Memory," in *Out There: Marginalization and Contemporary Cultures*, ed. Russell Ferguson (Cambridge, MA: MIT Press, 1990), 302; hereafter cited parenthetically.

4 Barbara Christian notes that "Morrison has said that she did not inquire further into Garner's life other than to note the event for which this slave woman became famous." She further observes that Morrison frequently stated her interest in writing about events "too horrible" or "too dangerous . . . to recall" by slave narrators. "Beloved, She's Ours," *Narrative* 5.1 (1997): 39, 40.

5 Christian writes, "Morrison allows her character to be 'freed' so that she must confront her own act" ("Beloved, She's Ours," 41).

6 Paul Gilroy, *The Black Atlantic: Modernity and Double Consciousness* (Cambridge, MA: Harvard University Press, 1993), 63–69, quotes 63 and 66. Gilroy concludes of his observations about Garner, "It is impossible to explore these important matters here" (68).

7 In "Love and Violence/Maternity and Death: Black Feminism and the Politics of Reading (Un)representability," *Black Women, Gender and Families* 1.1 (2007): 94–124, Sara Clarke Kaplan argues that to retrieve women's violent agency, we must treat infanticide as a form of radical resistance that has a long tradition among female slaves who were engaged in undoing the philosophical foundations of slavery and the liberal humanist project more generally. Also see Carole Boyce Davies, "Mobility, Embodiment and Resistance: Black Women's Writings in the US," in *Black Women, Writing, and Identity: Migrations of the Subject* (New York: Routledge, 1994), 130–51; Amanda Putnam, "Mothering Violence: Ferocious Female Resistance in Toni Morrison's *The Bluest Eye*, *Sula*, *Beloved*, and *A Mercy*," *Black Women, Gender and Families* 5.2 (2011): 25–43.

8 Clarke Kaplan takes up *Beloved* to expose the difficulty that historical scholarship on slavery has had in grappling with enslaved women as instigators of "counter-hegemonic fatal violence" ("Love and Violence," 101). Employing Orlando Patterson's conceptual terminology, she argues that Sethe's "choice of death is . . . an embodied political refusal to live under the conditions of . . . 'Social Death,' the status of social nonentity produced and maintained by the material and discursive structures of slavery" (99).

9 Valerie Smith argues thus in *Toni Morrison: Writing the Moral Imagination* (Chichester, UK: Wiley-Blackwell, 2012), 61–63. Smith identifies James Berger and Dennis Childs as critics who explore how *Beloved* operates within the discursive contexts of the 1980s and thus in relation to President Ronald Reagan's denials of systemic racism and black incarceration. I add to this list Kathryn Stockton's work on *Beloved* and AIDS and Darieck Scott's work on *Beloved* and black queer studies. James Berger, "Ghosts of Liberalisms: Morrison's *Beloved* and the Moynihan Report," PMLA 111.3 (1996): 408–20; Dennis Childs, "'You Ain't Seen Nothin' Yet': *Beloved*, the American Chain Gang, and the Middle Passage Remix," *American Quarterly* 61.2 (2009): 271–97; Kathryn Bond Stockton, "Prophylactics and Brains: *Beloved* in the Cybernetic Age of AIDS," *Studies in the Novel* 28.3 (1996): 435–65; Darieck Scott, *Extravagant Abjection: Blackness, Power, and Sexuality in the African American Literary Imagination* (New York: New York University Press, 2010), especially 1–32.

10 Mae G. Henderson, "Toni Morrison's *Beloved*: Re-membering the Body as Historical Text," in *Comparative American Identities: Race, Sex, and Nationality in the Modern Text*, ed. Hortense J. Spillers (New York: Routledge, 1991), 82. Henderson points out that "Sethe" recalls the Old Testament figure Seth, the prophetic soothsayer, and that Morrison offers Sethe's actions as prophesy (78).

11 While originally intended as a group escape (like Garner's), Morrison highlights Sethe's individual agency when she escapes Sweet Home alone.

12 W. E. B. Du Bois, "Of the Passing of the First Born," in *The Souls of Black Folk* (1903), ed. John Edgar Wideman (New York: Vintage, 1990), 155. The theme of maternal sacrifice of the slave child as merciful is reworked in *A Mercy*, which can thus be read as a rejoinder to *Beloved*.

13 Saidiya Hartman, *Scenes of Subjection: Terror, Slavery, and Self-Making in Nineteenth-Century America* (New York: Oxford University Press, 1997), 108.

14 Dean Franco argues (employing Spillers) that Sethe stakes a property claim when she murders *Beloved*, effectively turning the "discourse [of property] against itself, from the inside out." "What We Talk about When We Talk about *Beloved*," *Modern Fiction Studies* 52.2 (2006): 423.

15 Hortense Spillers, "Mama's Baby, Papa's Maybe: An American Grammar Book," *Diacritics* 17.2 (1987): 79.

16 The Nephew, who is wedded to Manichaean oppositions and racial science's pseudo-rationality, remains flummoxed. As he tellingly repeats, each time evincing the distortion that characterizes his (il)logic, "What she go and do that for?" (*Beloved*, 177).

17 Linda Krumholz asserts that Baby Suggs "represents an epistemological and discursive philosophy" that shapes Morrison's work. "The Ghosts of Slavery: Historical Recovery in Toni Morrison's *Beloved*," *African American Review* 26.3 (1992): quote 398. I would add that it is because Baby Suggs never judges Sethe that Sethe longs for her as she rememories her mother.

18 Morrison produces an image of insurgent rationality by preserving the image of Garner's decisiveness in Sethe's. In contrast to media portraits of Mary Beth Whitehead and Anna Johnson as pathologically confused, Morrison refuses to represent women forced to surrogate as unduly emotional, unscrupulous, or in any way unfit for motherhood. McDaniels-Wilson suggests that one manifestation of posttraumatic stress in incarcerated women who have been victims of racialized sexual violence—women whom she treats in her clinical practice and whom she compares to Garner—is "dissemblance" (as opposed to "dissociation"), "a façade of calm as a way of coping . . . and resisting stigmatization." See Cathy McDaniels-Wilson, "The Psychological Aftereffects of Racialized Sexual Violence," in *Gendered Resistance: Women, Slavery, and the Legacy of Margaret Garner*, ed. Mary E. Frederickson and Delores M. Walters (Urbana: University of Illinois Press, 2013), 201.

19 Stuart Hall et al., *Policing the Crisis: Mugging, the State, and Law and Order* (London: Macmillan, 1978), 181–217.

20 For instance, see Krumholz, "The Ghosts of Slavery," 395: "History-making becomes a healing process for characters, the reader, and the author." Krumholz also suggests that Morrison constructs a parallel such that Sethe's psychological recovery is tantamount to historical and national recovery. This idea has been further developed by trauma studies scholars. See Naomi Morgenstern, "Mother's Milk and Sister's Blood: Trauma and the Neoslave Narrative," *Differences* 8.2 (1996): 101–26; Jean Wyatt, "Giving Body to the Word: The Maternal Symbolic in Toni Morrison's *Beloved*," PMLA 108.3 (1993): 474–88, and "Identification with the Trauma of Others: Slavery, Collective Trauma, and the Difficulties of Representation in Toni Morrison's *Beloved*," in *Risking Difference: Identification, Race, and Community in Contemporary Fiction and Feminism* (New York: State University of New York Press, 2004), 66–84. Avery F. Gordon offers a robust refutation of what I shorthand "the healing argument": "Not Only the Footprints but the Water Too and What Is Down There," in *Ghostly Matters: Haunting and the Sociological Imagination* (Minneapolis: University of Minnesota Press, 1997), 137–92. For additional critique of the trauma studies approach to the novel, see Franco, "What We Talk about When We Talk about *Beloved*."

21 Kathi Weeks, *The Problem with Work: Feminism, Marxism, Antiwork Politics and Postwork Imaginaries* (Durham: Duke University Press, 2011), 96–101, 113–37. I am indebted to an anonymous reader of my manuscript for noting the relevance to my argument of Silvia Federici's and Leopoldina Fortunati's ideas. Feminist autonomists view women calling for recognition of their reproductive labor as capitalism's truest antagonists. As Weeks observes, although the "wages for housework" movement to which Federici and Fortunati were dedicated has been too readily discredited, it contains political insights useful in crafting a robust feminist politics that disavows normative work discourse and effete ideas of equality (as opposed to substantive freedom). The refusal of housework and the demand for wages for the reproductive labor unacknowledged as labor by other Marxists is performative and demands both self-valorization and the radical invention of power. I take this chapter's epigraph from Federici's interview with Matthew Carlin. Silvia Federici, "The Exploitation of Women, Social Reproduction, and the Struggle against Global Capitalism," interview by Matthew Carlin, *Theory & Event* 17.3 (2014), http://muse.jhu.edu/article/553382. Also see Federici, *Revolution at Point Zero: Housework, Reproduction, and Feminist Struggle* (New York: Autonomedia, 2012); Leopoldina Fortunati, *The Arcane of Reproduction: Housework, Prostitution, Labor and Capital* (1981; New York: Autonomedia, 1995).

Autonomists share some of the concerns voiced by subaltern studies scholars who examine insurgency and refusal from below, and who have prodded historians to recognize politics whose forms of materialization and mobilization differ from and are relatively independent of elite modes of organization and politics and may have distinct aims. This is not surprising given the indebtedness of both autonomist theory and subaltern studies to Antonio Gramsci. For instance, in *Provincializing Europe: Postcolonial Thought and Historical Difference*

(Princeton: Princeton University Press, 2000), Dipesh Chakrabarty influentially discusses how heterogeneous political forms of subaltern resistance elude available or hegemonic tools and methods and calls for attentiveness to "History 2," the history that he associates with the subaltern. History 2 interrupts the universalizing thrust of History 1 (the history associated with capitalist hegemony) and reveals the bearer of labor power as a human being living a life that is filled with meaning beyond the capacity to (re)produce value for capitalism.

22 Weeks, *The Problem with Work*, 26.

23 Rachel Lee notes that Sethe's rememory of Nan's words is prefaced by Sethe's observation that Nan spoke in a language that she no longer understands. For this reason, Lee suggests that Nan's meaning is as much fabricated by Sethe as spoken by Nan. This suggestion strengthens my claim that Sethe *constructs* rather than finds in Nan's words a connection to her mother. See Rachel C. Lee, "Missing Peace in Toni Morrison's *Sula* and *Beloved*," in *Understanding Toni Morrison's Beloved and Sula: Selected Essays and Criticisms of the Works by the Nobel Prize–Winning Author*, ed. Solomon Ogbede Iyasẹre and Marla W. Iyasẹre (Troy, NY: Whitston, 2000), 277–96.

24 Christian, "*Beloved*, She's Ours," 42.

25 This is another way in which Morrison revises the Garner story. As others suggest, the pale faces of Garner's children intimate that they are her master's. Morrison differentiates Sethe from Garner by refusing to question Halle's paternity. See Mark Reinhardt, *Who Speaks for Margaret Garner? The True Story That Inspired Toni Morrison's Beloved* (Minneapolis: University of Minnesota Press, 2010), 40–41; Steven Weisenburger, *Modern Medea: A Family Story of Slavery and Child-Murder from the Old South* (New York: Hill and Wang, 1998), 48.

26 Williams writes that structures of feeling are akin to "undeniable experiences of the present," but that the difficulty of the term *experience* (and thus his preference for *feeling*) is that *experience* implies the past tense while feeling conveys the immediacy and indeterminacy of the formation in question. Raymond Williams, *Marxism and Literature* (Oxford: Oxford University Press, 1977), 128–35.

27 It is possible to read *Beloved* as a response to Gayl Jones's *Corregidora*, a novel that Morrison edited as she worked on *The Black Book*. In an interview with Robert Stepto, Morrison claims that Jones's stories are without joy or pleasure. By contrast, in *Beloved* she sought to express both amid exploitation and violence. See Morrison, "Intimate Things in Place: A Conversation with Toni Morrison," interview by Robert B. Stepto, *Massachusetts Review* 18.3 (1977): 485. Thanks to Habiba Ibrahim for directing me to this interview.

28 This neologism is akin to *rememory* in its combination and reappropriation of common components to say something new. *Disremember* expresses neither failure to remember nor mistaken recollection. Rather it connotes refusal to share memory.

29 When Ella first meets Sethe and her newborn on the banks of the Ohio River she admonishes Sethe, upon seeing Denver's face "poke out of the wool blanket,"

that Sethe should not "love anything" (108), a sentiment that foreshadows her identification with Sethe.

30 Psychoanalytically oriented criticism has the unfortunate if unintentional effect of casting Sethe's relationship with her children as pathological. As a mother, critics argue, she must learn that her progeny are separate (rather than a "part" of herself). As a consequence, psychoanalytic readings of the novel inadvertently duplicate some aspects of Moynihan's pathologization of the black family.

31 It is also argued, if less often, that the alliance between Sethe and Amy Denver constitutes an optimistic form of interracial solidarity that signals the possibility for alliance (if not community) between white and black women. Krumholz explains, "The similarity between the two women's situations supercedes their mutual, racially based mistrust" ("The Ghosts of Slavery," 399).

32 Gordon predicates her reading on "The Story of a Hat," the actual hat belonging to the abolitionist Levi Coffin, and on recognition of the many hats that catalyze Sethe's response: Coffin's, School Teacher's, and Bodwin's. Gordon, "Not Only the Footprints," especially 143–64.

33 As has been argued, the scene reveals liberalism's inability to eviscerate the property system that sustained slavery and made it possible to commodify human beings in the first place (Berger, "Ghosts of Liberalism," 416; Gordon, "Not Only the Footprints"). Berger believes "Bodwin shares with twentieth-century liberals the features that led the civil rights moments of the late 1960s to reject the Moynihan Report and the tradition of Frazier and Myrdal" (417). For Gordon, Sethe's attack on Bodwin materializes a critique of the abolitionist project and of liberal modes of redress in general.

34 This reading of the complicity of liberalism and slavery resonates with Lisa Lowe's account in The Intimacies of Four Continents (Durham: Duke University Press, 2015) of how liberalism manifests the persistence of the property relation forged in the crucible of slavery, colonialism, and imperialism. As Lowe explains, because liberalism is wedded to the property relation, we continue to grapple with a shabby notion of freedom, or what Stephanie Smallwood labels "commodified freedom." "Commodified Freedom: Interrogating the Limits of Anti-Slavery Ideology in the Early Republic," Journal of the Early Republic 24.2 (2004): 289–98.

35 Given Morrison's involvement with Davis as an editor of her work we can speculate that Morrison read Davis's essay on Little and was aware of her activism on Little's behalf. See Davis, "JoAnne Little: The Dialectics of Rape," Ms. Magazine, June 1975, 74–77, 106–8, reprinted in The Angela Y. Davis Reader, ed. Joy James (Malden, MA: Blackwell, 1998), 141–60. On Morrison's editorial work see Cheryl A. Wall, "Toni Morrison, Editor and Teacher," in The Cambridge Companion to Toni Morrison, ed. Justine Tally (New York: Cambridge University Press, 2007), 142–43.

36 Danielle L. McGuire offers a comprehensive account of the Little case and of the organizing against sexual abuse and rape that grew out of it. See At the Dark End of the Street: Black Women, Rape, and Resistance—A New History of the Civil Rights Movement from Rosa Parks to the Rise of Black Power (New York: Knopf, 2010), 202–28. In "Les-

sons in Self-Defense: Gender Violence, Racial Criminalization, and Anticarceral Feminism," *Women's Studies Quarterly* 43.3–4 (2015): 52–71, and chapter 2 in *All Our Trials: Prisons, Policing, and the Feminist Fight to End Violence* (Chicago: University of Illinois Press, 2019), Emily Thuma examines the response to the case and its role in the formation of multiracial alliances that drew attention to the problem of racialized incarceration as an answer to sexual violence. I am indebted to Thuma for sharing her ongoing work on the case, and for alerting me to the political slogan that Little's supporters emblazoned on a T-shirt Thuma found preserved in an archival box at the Sophia Smith Collection at Smith College (see fig. 3.1). In "'I'm Gonna Get You': Black Womanhood and Jim Crow Justice in the Post–Civil Rights South," in *U.S. Women's History: Untangling the Threads of Sisterhood*, ed. Leslie Brown, Jacqueline Castledine, and Anne Valk (New Brunswick, NJ: Rutgers University Press, 2017), 98–123, Christina Greene explores the excessive sentencing to which Little was subject (fourteen to twenty years in a five-by-seven-foot cell for a nonviolent property offense) and the danger of allowing triumphalist accounts of the case's outcome to direct our attention away from examination of the Little case as a representative story about widespread abuse in policing, sentencing, and imprisonment of black women.

37 Davis, "JoAnne Little: The Dialectics of Rape," 74–77, 106–8; 149–60 in the reprint. All further citations are to the reprint and will be made parenthetically. A range of national groups rallied around Little, including the Women's Legal Defense Fund, the Feminist Alliance against Rape, the Rape Crisis Center, the National Black Feminist Organization, and the National Organization for Women. See McGuire, *At the Dark End of the Street*, 214.

38 In "'Joanne Is You and Joanne Is Me': A Consideration of African American Women and the 'Free Joan Little' Movement, 1974–75," in *Sisters in the Struggle: African American Women in the Civil Rights–Black Power Movement*, ed. Bettye Collier-Thomas and V. P. Franklin (New York: New York University Press, 2001), 259–79, Genna Rae McNeil offers an analysis of the Little case that is based on interviews with several of the figures in the Free Joan Little campaign, including Davis. McNeil observes that Davis committed to the campaign "because of her sense of gratitude to those who had championed her cause as a political prisoner only a few years before" (268–69), and because she saw activism on behalf of Little as an opportunity to connect her antiracist work to her feminism in a manner that was distinct from the direction then being pursued by the white middle-class women's movement.

39 For discussion of Johnson Reagon's involvement in the Free Joan Little campaign, see McNeil, "'Joanne Is You and Joanne Is Me,'" 270–71.

40 Most critics analyze the final page in *Beloved* and Morrison's repeated and multivalent declaration that "this is not a story to pass on." Here I weigh in on the meaning of "pass on" by affirming those readings that regard the declaration as prescriptive rather than descriptive: this is not a story to pass on in that it is not a story that we can *refuse* to tell and retell to future generations.

41 "'Joanne Is You and Joanne Is Me,'" 260–61.

42 Toni Morrison, "Author Toni Morrison Discusses Her Latest Novel *Beloved*," interview by Gail Caldwell, *Boston Globe*, October 6, 1987, 67–68, reprinted in *Conversations with Toni Morrison*, ed. Danielle Kathleen Taylor-Guthrie (Jackson: University of Mississippi Press, 1994), 239–45.

4. The Problem of Reproductive Freedom in Neoliberalism

1 Dorothy E. Roberts, "Race, Gender, and Genetic Technologies: A New Reproductive Dystopia," *Signs* 34.4 (2009): 783–84.

2 Roberts, "Race, Gender, and Genetic Technologies," 784–85.

3 Roberts, "Race, Gender, and Genetic Technologies," 791. Roberts recognizes that in the new dystopia "the biological definition of race is stronger than ever," but she argues that in the supposedly postracial context of neoliberalism, class rather than race structures consumption of reprogenetics, leaving "the masses" to "suffer most" (799–800). Also see Dorothy E. Roberts, "Privatization and Punishment in the New Age of Reprogenetics," *Emory Law Journal* 54.3 (2005): 1343–60, and her update of the argument in *Fatal Invention: How Science, Politics, and Big Business Recreate Race in the Twenty-First Century* (New York: New Press, 2011).

4 Walter Benjamin, "Theses on the Philosophy of History" (1940), in *Illuminations*, trans. Harry Zohn, ed. Hannah Arendt (New York: Schocken Books, 1968), 253–64; hereafter cited parenthetically.

5 In "On Failing to Make the Past Present," *Modern Language Quarterly* 73:3 (2012): 453–74, Stephen Best critiques "melancholic historicism" that roots the unresolved loss of the present in the slave past and is thus able to view the past in the present only as a wound. To think the past as resource he turns to Benjamin's "Theses." Like Best, I argue that Benjamin's observations allow historical inquiry to animate hope, or, as Best expresses it, "to rouse the dead from their sleep" so that our dialogue with them might inflect our understanding of what is to be done, not only what has been done (464). Also see Lisa Lowe's related argument in *The Intimacies of Four Continents* (Durham: Duke University Press, 2015), 135–75.

6 Foucault suggests that biopower began to gain a hold in the late seventeenth century, became consistently visible through the emergence of a discourse on population in the eighteenth century, and flowered in the form of nineteenth-century governance. Michel Foucault, *The History of Sexuality, Volume 1: An Introduction* (1978), trans. Robert Hurley (New York: Vintage, 1990); *Society Must Be Defended: Lectures at the Collège de France, 1975–76*, trans. David Macey, ed. Mauro Bertani and Alessandro Fontana (New York: Picador, 2003); and *The Birth of Biopolitics: Lectures at the Collège de France, 1978–79*, trans. Graham Burchell, ed. Michel Senellart (New York: Palgrave Macmillan, 2008).

7 Foucault, *The History of Sexuality*, 135–59. Notably Foucault does not treat slavery as a form of biopower.

8   Madhu Dubey also argues that slavery is defamiliarized through a process of mutation that operates across Butler's novels. As a consequence it comes to refer to a wide range of abusive practices that are no longer "reducible to race . . . even when race does operate as a central axis of inequality." Dubey suggests reading these mutations as a meditation on the "perplexities surrounding the category of race in the post–civil rights decades." "Octavia Butler's Novels of Enslavement," *Novel* 46.3 (2013): 346. Here I suggest reading them as a meditation on the afterlife of reproductive slavery in biocapitalism and neoliberalism.

9   On the persistence of racist and geneticized racial projects in supposedly postracial times, see Alys Eve Weinbaum, "Racial Aura: Walter Benjamin and the Work of Art in a Biotechnological Age," *Literature and Medicine* 26.1 (2007): 207–39; Michael Omi, "'Slippin' into Darkness': The (Re)Biologization of Race," *Journal of Asian American Studies* 13.3 (2010): 343–58; Roberts, *Fatal Invention*.

10 Raymond Williams, *Marxism and Literature* (Oxford: Oxford University Press, 1977), 4, 121–27; hereafter cited parenthetically.

11 I take the concept of articulation from Stuart Hall, who writes, "The object of analysis is always the specificity of this 'structure-superstructure' complex— though as a historically concrete articulation." "Race Articulation, and Societies Structured in Dominance," in *Sociological Theories: Race and Colonialism* (Paris: UNESCO, 1980), 332.

12 Benjamin, "Theses," 255.

13 Saidiya Hartman treats *Kindred* as feminist theory. As in the previous chapter, I find inspiration in Hartman's call for "critical fabulation" in the face of the historical archive's silences. See "Venus in Two Acts," *Small Axe* 12.2 (2008): 12. On *Kindred* see Dubey, "Octavia Butler's Novels of Enslavement"; Linh U. Hua, "Reproducing Time, Reproducing History: Love and Black Feminist Sentimentality in Octavia Butler's *Kindred*," *African American Review* 44.3 (2011): 391–407; Christine Levecq, "Power and Repetition: Philosophies of (Literary) History in Octavia E. Butler's *Kindred*," *Contemporary Literature* 41.3 (2000): 525–53; Philip Miletic, "Octavia Butler's Response to Black Arts/Black Power Literature and Rhetoric in *Kindred*," *African American Review* 49.3 (2016): 261–275; Angelyn Mitchell, *The Freedom to Remember: Narrative, Slavery, and Gender in Contemporary Black Women's Fiction* (New Brunswick, NJ: Rutgers University Press, 2002), 42–63; Marisa Parham, "Saying 'Yes': Textual Trauma in Octavia Butler's *Kindred*," *Callaloo* 32.4 (2009): 1315–31; Ahsraf H. A. Rushdy, *Remembering Generations: Race and Family in Contemporary African American Fiction* (Chapel Hill: University of North Carolina Press, 2001), 99–127; Sarah Eden Schiff, "Recovering (from) the Double: Fiction as Historical Revision in Octavia Butler's *Kindred*," *Arizona Quarterly* 65.1 (2009): 107–36; Marc Steinberg, "Inverting History in Octavia Butler's Postmodern Slave Narrative," *African American Review* 38.3 (2004): 467–76; Lisa Yaszek, "'A Grim Fantasy': Remaking American History in Octavia Butler's *Kindred*," *Signs* 28.4 (2003): 1053–66.

14 Stephanie Turner, "'What Actually Is': The Insistence of Genre in Octavia Butler's *Kindred*," FEMSPEC 4.2 (2004): 259–80, and Nadine Flagel, "'It's Almost Like Being

There': Speculative Fiction, Slave Narrative, and the Crisis of Representation in Octavia Butler's Kindred," *Canadian Review of American Studies* 42.2 (2012): 217–45, argue that *Kindred* ought to be read as generically hybrid (as what Turner calls "historiographic metafiction"). Both seek to liberate it from the genre straightjacket.

15 Dubey makes a similar point in "Octavia Butler's Novels of Enslavement."

16 Octavia Butler, *Kindred* (Boston: Beacon, 1979), *Wild Seed* (New York: Warner, 1980), and "Bloodchild" (1984) in *Bloodchild and Other Stories* (New York: Four Walls Eight Windows, 1995); hereafter all three are cited parenthetically. As in chapter 1, here I follow scholars of biocapitalism who argue for its emergence in the 1970s and its synergy with neoliberalism.

17 The series includes *Patternmaster* (New York: Warner, 1976), *Mind of My Mind* (New York: Warner, 1977), and *Clay's Ark* (New York: Warner, 1984).

18 Achille Mbembe, "Necropolitics," trans. Libby Meintjes, *Public Culture* 15.1 (2003): 11–40.

19 Jared Sexton, "People-of-Color-Blindness: Notes on the Afterlife of Slavery," *Social Text* 28.2 (2010): 31–56. Ladelle McWhorter, "Sex, Race and Biopower: A Foucauldian Genealogy," *Hypatia* 19.3 (2004): 39–62, critiques extension of the analysis of biopower to slavery.

20 Sarah Wood, "Subversion through Inclusion: Octavia Butler's Interrogation of Religion in *Xenogenesis* and *Wild Seed*," FEMSPEC 6.1 (2005): 93; Ingrid Thaler, *Black Atlantic Speculative Fictions: Octavia Butler, Jewelle Gomez, and Nalo Hopkinson* (New York: Routledge, 2010), 19–43. Wood suggests that Anyanwu is based on Atagbusi, an Onitsha Igbo healer and shapeshifter.

21 Grace Kyungwon Hong, *Death beyond Disavowal: The Impossible Politics of Difference* (Minneapolis: University of Minnesota Press, 2015), 15, 63–64.

22 See Orlando Patterson, *Slavery and Social Death: A Comparative Study* (Cambridge, MA: Harvard University Press, 1982), 1–14.

23 Dubey argues that Butler critiques the alignment of black women with nature and animality through depiction of Anyanwu's capacity to become animal. In the process, Butler impugns scientific rationality for its predatory exploitation of black women's bodies. "Becoming Animal in Black Women's Science Fiction," in *Afro-Future Females: Black Writers Chart Science Fiction's Newest New-Wave Trajectory*, ed. Marleen S. Barr (Columbus: Ohio State University Press, 2008), 31–51.

24 Lauren J. Lacey, "Octavia E. Butler on Coping with Power in *Parable of the Sower*, *Parable of the Talents*, and *Fledgling*," *Critique* 49.4 (2008): 383.

25 Thomas is enslaved by Doro because his mind-reading abilities represent a genetic resource. They also make it impossible for Thomas to exist in proximity to other human beings, though not Doro, whose mind Thomas cannot open and destroy.

26 As Anyanwu explains, these kindred feel "more comfortable" masquerading as slaves on her plantation "than they had ever [felt] . . . elsewhere" (235).

27 Butler challenges the idea of Canaanites found in the Old Testament. These are not cursed children of Ham; they are blessed. See Thaler, *Black Atlantic Speculative*

Fictions, 29–34. Prior struggles temper Doro's initial impulse to destroy Anyanwu's Canaan. In implicit recognition of Anyanwu's capacity for resistance, Doro wages a war of position, rechanneling his desire to kill into temporary alliance. Although a lull results, war is reignited when the toxic progeny Doro sets upon Canaan destroy its exceptional residents.

28 It is worth observing the partial anagram embedded in the protagonist's and antagonist's names—Anyanwu, "a new way," and Doro, "door" or portal—and speculating about the narrative irresolution these names portend.

29 Darko Suvin, *Metamorphoses of Science Fiction: On the Poetics and History of a Literary Genre* (New Haven: Yale University Press, 1979), 3–15. Here I extend the discussion of science fiction to sf.

30 Fredric Jameson, *Archaeologies of the Future: The Desire Called Utopia and Other Science Fictions* (New York: Verso, 2005), and "Reification and Utopia in Mass Culture," *Social Text* 1.1 (1979): 130–48; Carl Freedman, *Critical Theory and Science Fiction* (Hanover, NH: Wesleyan University Press, 2000); Tom Moylan, *Scraps of the Untainted Sky: Science Fiction, Utopia, Dystopia* (Boulder, CO: Westview Press, 2000).

31 See Foucault, *The Birth of Biopolitics*; Melinda Cooper, *Life as Surplus: Biotechnology and Capitalism in the Neoliberal Era* (Seattle: University of Washington Press, 2008).

32 In this sense Dana refuses to raise the question that Audre Lorde first posed: "In what way do I contribute to the subjugation of *any part of those who I call my people?*" Grace Kyungwon Hong suggests that in raising this question Lorde advances a politics of difference that "pushes past the limits of the political as it is conventionally defined." Such a politics "holds in suspension the conflicting goals of the preservation or protection of the political subject *and* the recognition of the others at whose expense that subject is protected" (*Death and Disavowal*, 15).

33 There are two exceptions: Dubey, "Octavia Butler's Novels of Enslavement," and Hua, "Reproducing Time, Reproducing History." Both explore Dana's complicity in perpetuation of Alice's enslavement. In Hua's reading, as in the one I offer here, Dana's inability to imagine that the call to travel back in time emanates from Alice (as opposed to Rufus) is of paramount importance and represents a failure of political imagination that is repeated rather than corrected in the criticism on the novel.

34 Instructively, this scene lies at the center of the novel and thus in the same structural position as the scene in which Doro brings Anyanwu to Thomas. In both novels, sexual exploitation targeted at reproductive engineering constitutes the pivot around which the plot turns. Hua argues, as I do here, that Dana and Alice ought to be read as antagonists. See Hua, "Reproducing Time, Reproducing History."

35 In readings focused on the master-slave relationship, Rufus and Dana's white husband are frequently paired and the modern interracial relationships read as mired in slavery. See, for example, Carlyle Van Thompson, "Moving Past the Present: Racialized Sexual Violence and Miscegenous Consumption in Octavia Butler's *Kindred*," in *Eating the Black Body: Miscegenation as Sexual Consumption in African American Literature and*

Culture (New York: Peter Lang, 2006), 107–44; Diana R. Paulin, "De-Essentializing Interracial Representations: Black and White Border-Crossings in Spike Lee's *Jungle Fever* and Octavia Butler's *Kindred*," *Cultural Critique* 36 (1997): 165–93.

36 On the uncritical embrace of forms of futurity moored in heterosexual reproduction see Lee Edelman, *No Future: Queer Theory and the Death Drive* (Durham: Duke University Press, 2004), 1–32; Gillian Harkins, *Everybody's Family Romance: Reading Incest in Neoliberal America* (Minneapolis: University of Minnesota Press, 2009); Chandan Reddy, *Freedom with Violence: Race, Sexuality, and the US State* (Durham: Duke University Press, 2011).

37 On choice and agency in neoliberalism, see Jane Elliott, "Suffering Agency: Imagining Neoliberal Personhood in North America and Britain," *Social Text* 31.2 (2013): 83–101; Nikolas S. Rose, *Powers of Freedom: Reframing Political Thought* (New York: Cambridge University Press, 1999).

38 See Rushdy, *Remembering Generations*, 107–8; and Lawrie Balfour, "Vexed Genealogy: Octavia Butler and Political Memories of Slavery," in *Democracy's Literature: Politics and Fiction in America*, ed. Patrick Deneen and Joseph Romance (Lanham, MD: Rowman and Littlefield, 2005), 178–79.

39 For discussion of autonomists' ideas of freedom, see Kathi Weeks, *The Problem with Work: Feminism, Marxism, Antiwork Politics, and Postwork Imaginaries* (Durham: Duke University Press, 2011), especially 22.

40 See Delores Williams, *Sisters in the Wilderness: The Challenge of Womanist God-Talk* (Maryknoll, NY: Orbis Books, 1993), hereafter cited parenthetically; Renita J. Weems, *Just a Sister Away: A Womanist Vision of Women's Relationships in the Bible* (San Diego: LuraMedia, 1988), 1–24; Wilma Ann Bailey, "Black and Jewish Women Consider Hagar," *Encounter* 63.1–2 (2002): 37–44; Phyllis Trible and Letty M. Russel, eds., *Hagar, Sarah, and Their Children: Jewish, Christian, and Muslim Perspectives* (Louisville, KY: Westminster John Knox, 2006). The list of Hagar's trials is Williams's in *Sisters in the Wilderness*, 4.

41 Numerous writers before and after Butler have invoked Hagar as a heroine. See, for instance, Pauline Hopkins, *Hagar's Daughter: A Story of Southern Caste Prejudice* (1902), in *The Magazine Novels of Pauline Hopkins* (New York: Oxford University Press, 1988), 1–284; Mary Johnston, *Hagar* (Boston: Houghton Mifflin, 1913); Margaret Laurence, *The Stone Angel* (New York: Knopf, 1964); Charlotte Gordon, *The Woman Who Named God: Abraham's Dilemma and the Birth of Three Faiths* (New York: Little, Brown, 2009).

42 Much criticism on "Bloodchild" finds redemption in its story of interspecies relations, or what some regard as collaborations. See, for instance, Kristin Lillvis, "Mama's Baby, Papa's Slavery? The Problem and Promise of Mothering in Octavia E. Butler's 'Bloodchild,'" MELUS 39.4 (2014): 7–22; John Carlo Pasco, Camille Anderson, and Sayatani DasGupta, "Visionary Medicine: Speculative Fiction, Racial Justice and Octavia Butler's 'Bloodchild,'" *Science Fiction and Medical Humanities* 42 (2016): 246–251; Stephanie A. Smith, "Octavia Butler: A Retro-

spective," *Feminist Studies* 33.2 (2007): 385–92; Amanda Thibodeau, "Alien Bodies and a Queer Future: Sexual Revision in Octavia Butler's 'Bloodchild' and James Tiptree, Jr.'s 'With Delicate Mad Hands,'" *Science Fiction Studies* 39.2 (2012): 262–82. Less often scholars interpret the text as a critical meditation on capitalism, the exploitation of labor, and the treatment of the human body in property law. See Eva Cherniavsky, *Incorporations: Race, Nation, and the Body Politics of Capital* (Minneapolis: University of Minnesota Press, 2006), 41–47; Karla F. C. Holloway, *Private Bodies, Public Texts: Race, Gender, and a Cultural Bioethics* (Durham: Duke University Press, 2011), 32–36.

43 For a redemptive reading of Butler's aliens as "queer" beings see Thibodeau, "Alien Bodies and a Queer Future." By contrast, I read Tlic queerness as readily incorporated into Tlic hegemony.

44 As Louis Althusser observes, ideology is "not the system of the real relations which govern the existence of individuals, but the imaginary relation of those individuals to the real relations in which they live." "Ideology and Ideological State Apparatuses (Notes towards an Investigation)," in *Lenin and Philosophy and Other Essays*, trans. Ben Brewster (New York: Monthly Review, 1971), 165. Althusser also argues that "ideology has no history" (159), an ideological proposition about ideology that accounts for the erasure of the history of slavery by the Tlic and the humans living among them.

45 On the use of love in defining and legitimizing political actors of various stripes see Sara Ahmed, *The Cultural Politics of Emotion* (New York: Routledge, 2004), 122–41.

46 Douglass observes that in the moment in which he elected to move into direct battle with Mr. Covey he found both his sense of freedom and his manhood rekindled and revived. *Narrative of the Life of Frederick Douglass, an African Slave* (1845), in *The Classic Slave Narratives*, ed. Henry Louis Gates Jr. (New York: Signet Classics, 2002), 394.

47 Here I again take inspiration from Benjamin: "To articulate the past historically does not mean to recognize it 'the way it really was.' . . . It means to seize hold of a memory as it flashes up at a moment of danger" ("Theses," 255).

5. A Slave Narrative for Postracial Times

1 These include the Booker, Arthur C. Clarke, and National Book Critics Circle awards. *Never Let Me Go* was named best novel of 2005 by *Time* magazine and adapted for film by Mark Romanek in 2010. Kazuo Ishiguro, *Never Let Me Go* (New York: Vintage, 2005), hereafter cited parenthetically; Mark Romanek, director, *Never Let Me Go*, DVD (Century City, CA: Fox Searchlight Pictures, 2010); Michael Bay, director, *The Island*, DVD (Universal City, CA: DreamWorks Pictures, 2005).

2 These events are routinely invoked to mark the emergence of popular concern with and intensified media attention to cloning. Dolly was cloned in 1996 and

her birth announced in 1997. Her birth is widely thought to herald human cloning. In *Clones and Clones: Facts and Fantasies about Human Cloning* (New York: Norton,
1998), 11, Martha C. Nussbaum and Cass R. Sunstein explain, "The arrival of Dolly
made it clear that human beings would soon have to face the possibility of human
cloning—and it has been this idea . . . that has caused public anxiety. To many,
if not most of us, cloning represents a possible turning point in the history of humanity." Prime Minister Tony Blair and President Bill Clinton lauded the completion of the map of the human genome as a monumental accomplishment in 2000.
The article announcing cloning of thirty human embryos was quickly followed
by an article on the creation of eleven stem cell lines from adult human skin cells.
A report disclaiming both accomplishments as fraudulent was published in 2006,
at which time legal actions were taken against Hwang Woo-Suk, the leader of
the Seoul University team responsible. Although less well publicized, cloning for
purposes of research was legalized in the United States in 2002. See Joan Haran
et al., eds., *Human Cloning in the Media: From Science Fiction to Science Practice* (New
York: Routledge, 2008), 13–43, 67–92; Sarah Franklin, *Dolly Mixtures: The Remaking
of Genealogy* (Durham: Duke University Press, 2007); Gina Kolata, *Clone: The Road
to Dolly and the Path Ahead* (New York: William Morrow, 1998).

3 In *Never Let Me Go* individuals from whom clones are derived are known as
"originals" or "normals." In *The Island* they are called "sponsors," and clones are
referred to as "life insurance policies," falsely represented to "sponsors" as unconscious, vegetative beings or "agnates."

4 On rupture of distinctions between natural and technological reproduction see
Sarah Franklin, *Biological Relatives: IVF, Stem Cells, and the Future of Kinship* (Durham:
Duke University Press, 2013), and "Life Itself: Global Nature and the Genetic
Imaginary," in *Global Nature, Global Culture*, ed. Sarah Franklin, Celia Lury, and
Jackie Stacey (London: Sage, 2000), 188–227. On organ scarcity see Lawrence
Cohen, "The Other Kidney: Biopolitics beyond Recognition," *Body & Society* 7.2–3
(2001): 9–29; Nancy Scheper-Hughes, "Commodity Fetishism in Organs Traffick-
ing," *Body & Society* 7.2–3 (2001): 31–62, and "Rotten Trade: Millennial Capitalism,
Human Values and Global Justice in Organs Trafficking," *Journal of Human Rights*
2.2 (2003): 197–226.

5 *The Island* can be regarded as representative of a range of popular depictions of
cloning, including *Boys from Brazil* (based on Ira Levin's novel), *Where Late the Sweet
Birds Sang*, *Parts: The Clonus Horror*, *The 6th Day*, *Alien Resurrection*, *Cloud Atlas* (based
on David Mitchell's novel of the same name), *Code 46*, *Moon*, and *Orphan Black*. For
discussion see Haran et al., *Human Cloning in the Media*. See Franklin J. Schaffner, director, *Boys from Brazil*, DVD (Los Angeles: 20th Century Fox, 1978); Levin, *Boys from
Brazil* (New York: Random House, 1976); Kate Wilhelm, *Where Late the Sweet Birds
Sang* (New York: Harper and Row, 1976); Robert S. Fiveson, director, *Parts: The Clonus Horror*, DVD (Los Angeles: Group 1 International Distribution Organization,
1979); Roger Spottiswoode, director, *The 6th Day*, DVD (Los Angeles: Columbia
Pictures, 2000); Jean-Pierre Jeunet, director, *Alien Resurrection*, DVD (Los Angeles:

20th Century Fox, 1997); Lana Wachowski, Tom Tykwer, and Andy Wachowski, directors, *Cloud Atlas*, DVD (Burbank: Warner Bros. Pictures, 2012); David Mitchell, *Cloud Atlas* (New York: Random House, 2004); Michael Winterbottom, director, *Code 46*, DVD (Beverly Hills: MGM, 2003); Duncan Jones, director, *Moon*, DVD (New York: Sony Pictures Classics, 2009); Graeme Manson and John Fawcett, *Orphan Black: Season 1–Season 4*, DVD (New York: BBC America Home Entertainment, 2016).

6   This reading accords with the overview of popular representations of cloning offered by Haran et al., *Human Cloning in the Media*, 56, 64.

7   In Foucault's conceptualization of biopolitics death enters the deployment of power as state racism. Mbembe deepens Foucault's point by developing the concept of necropolitics, a form of power in which racism divides the population into those whose lives may be sustained and (re)produced by killing others with impunity, and those who are subjected to premature death, effectively creating a state of permanent war. See Achille Mbembe, "Necropolitics," trans. Libby Meintjes, *Public Culture* 15.1 (2003): 11–40. Several scholars engage Foucault and Agamben in relation to Ishiguro's novel; to my knowledge no other treatment of the novel takes up racial slavery. See Shameem Black, "Ishiguro's Inhuman Aesthetics," *Modern Fiction Studies* 55.4 (2009): 785–807; Arne De Boever, "Bare Life and the Camps in Kazuo Ishiguro's *Never Let Me Go*," in *Narrative Care: Biopolitics and the Novel* (London: Bloomsbury, 2013), 59–91; Sara Wasson, "'A Butcher's Shop Where the Meat Still Moved': Gothic Doubles, Organ Harvesting, and Human Cloning," in *Gothic Science Fiction, 1980–2010*, ed. Sara Wasson and Emily Alder (Liverpool, UK: Liverpool University Press, 2011), 73–86; Gabriele Griffin, "Science and the Cultural Imaginary: The Case of Kazuo Ishiguro's *Never Let Me Go*," *Textual Practice* 23.4 (2009): 645–63.

8   Notably cloning was made illegal in the UK under the Human Reproductive Cloning Act of 2001. Although there is a national embargo on federal funding for research involving human cloning in the US, there is no legal prohibition. While some states ban cloning and gestation of cloned embryos, others allow it. See Haran et al., *Human Cloning in the Media*, 37.

9   Romanek cinematically reinforces the presumptive whiteness of clones by casting all characters as white. To my knowledge, Rachel Lee offers the only other reading focused on the novel's racial formation. As she explains, "The clones' 'species-being' is not commensurate with race read off the body's surface—the 'old raciology' tied to the visual scale of epidermal phenotype." As in the present analysis, Lee argues that the clones' difference is tied to their "manner of reproduction" rather than to gross morphology. What she describes as a continuum of "minoritizing patterns" that moves from racial phenotype to biopolitical technique, I describe as "the flickering off of blackness." Whereas Lee's analysis views the clones as akin to Asians, the "model minority" that complies with the performance demands made on them, I seek to underscore the historical connections between visible blackness and racial difference (visible or invisible) and the clones' enslavability. The fact that both readings are made available by the same

text suggests the complexity of the overlapping processes of racialization that operate in and through biocapitalism and neoliberalism. See *The Exquisite Corpse of Asian America: Biopolitics, Biosociality, and Posthuman Ecologies* (New York: New York University Press, 2014), 59–64, quote 61. I thank Rachel for her feedback on an early version of this chapter.

10 On reader complicity see Anne Whitehead, "Writing with Care: Kazuo Ishiguro's *Never Let Me Go*," *Contemporary Literature* 52.1 (2011): 54–83.

11 Following M. I. Finlay, Sandra Joshel, "Ancient Roman Slavery and American History" lecture, University of Washington, Seattle, October 23, 2013 (delivered as part of the Slavery and Freedom in the Making of America public lecture series), distinguishes "societies with slavery" from "slave societies" in the ancient world. In the former, slaves are owned as property and work alongside other laborers. In the latter, 20 to 30 percent of the population is enslaved and produces the bulk of the income. In a slave society, slavery is economic, social, cultural, and ideological. As Joshel argues, Romans thought with slaves; they defined themselves, their social relations, and their ideas of freedom in relation to slaves and their ideas about slaves and slavery. I follow Joshel in making this distinction and here extend it to the world of the novel—which, I argue, is a biocapitalist society with slavery.

12 My use of *constellation* throughout this chapter builds on my reading of Benjamin's "Theses" in chapter 4. Walter Benjamin, "Theses on the Philosophy of History" (1940), in *Illuminations*, trans. Harry Zohn, ed. Hannah Arendt (New York: Schocken Books, 1968), 253–64; hereafter cited parenthetically.

13 Rereading inevitably alters the novel's impact. Each textual encounter is increasingly self-reflexive in that readers know in advance that the narrative obscures the truth. Consequently rereading leads to a perception of complicity in banalization of violence that is, on first reading, more obscure. On banalization of the evisceration of the welfare state in the novel, see Bruce Robbins, "Cruelty Is Bad: Banality and Proximity in *Never Let Me Go*," *Novel* 40.3 (2007): 289–302. Also see Hannah Arendt, *Eichmann in Jerusalem: A Report on the Banality of Evil* (1963; New York: Penguin, 1994).

14 See Martin Puchner, "When We Were Clones," *Raritan* 24.7 (2008): 36; Louis Menand, "Something about Kathy," *New Yorker* 81.6 (2005): 78–79; Claire Messud, "Love's Body," *The Nation*, May 16, 2005, 28; Justine Burley, "A Braver, Newer World," *Nature* 425.7041 (2005): 427; Valerie Sayers, "Spare Parts," *Commonweal* 132.13 (2005): 27; Joseph O'Neill, "Never Let Me Go," *Atlantic Monthly* 295.4 (2005): 123.

15 Thanks to Alexandra Deem for feedback on this chapter and to the many undergraduate students who have taken up this text in my Marxist Theory class and shared their responses to it.

16 For present purposes, the most important distinction between novel and film is that in the latter clones wear identification bracelets that make surveillance possible. No such repressive apparatus exists in the novel; the clones simply self-govern.

17 De Boever argues that Hailsham is a world "that can only exist on the condition that one does not ask too many questions," an idea that resonates with the present argument ("Bare Life and the Camps," 63).

18 Karl Marx, *Capital: A Critique of Political Economy*, vol. 1 (1867), trans. Ben Fowkes (New York: Vintage, 1977); hereafter cited parenthetically.

19 In *Provincializing Europe: Postcolonial Thought and Historical Difference* (Princeton: Princeton University Press, 2000), 47–71, Dipesh Chakrabarty notes that Marx mistranslated (from Greek) and replaced "shoes" with "beds," a mistake that renders operations of equivalence still more mysterious. My reading of the passage is influenced by Chakrabarty's.

20 Aristotle lived in what Joshel, "Ancient Roman Slavery and American History," calls a society with slavery. A so-called slave society did not come into existence until the first century BCE, nearly two hundred years after Aristotle lived. See note 11.

21 Marx writes, "The mode of production of material life conditions the general process of social, political, and intellectual life. It is not the consciousness of men that determines their existence, but their social existence that determines their consciousness." Preface to *A Contribution to the Critique of Political Economy* (1859), in *Early Writings*, trans. Rodney Livingstone and Gregor Benton, ed. Quintin Hoare (New York: Vintage, 1974), 425.

22 Arguments in favor of the organ trade are made by free-market economists and physicians who profit from harvests and transplants. Quote is from Scott Carney, *The Red Market: On the Trail of the World's Organ Brokers, Bone Thieves, Blood Farmers, and Child Traffickers* (New York: William Morrow, 2011), 3. Also see Melinda Cooper and Catherine Waldby, *Clinical Labor: Tissue Donors and Research Subjects in the Global Bioeconomy* (Durham: Duke University Press, 2014); Donna Dickenson, *Body Shopping: The Economy Fuelled by Flesh and Blood* (Oxford: Oneworld, 2008); Catherine Waldby and Robert Mitchell, *Tissue Economies: Blood, Organs, and Cell Lines in Late Capitalism* (Durham: Duke University Press, 2006); Lori Andrews and Dorothy Nelkin, *Body Bazaar: The Market for Human Tissue in the Biotechnology Age* (New York: Crown, 2001); Stephen Wilkinson, *Bodies for Sale: Ethics and Exploitation in the Human Body Trade* (New York: Routledge, 2003); Andrew Kimbrell, *The Human Body Shop: The Engineering and Marketing of Life* (San Francisco: HarperCollins, 1994); and Nancy Scheper-Hughes's pioneering work: "The Tyranny of the Gift: Sacrificial Violence in Living Donor Transplants," *American Journal of Transplantation* 7.3 (2007): 507–11; "Organs Trafficking: The Real, the Unreal and the Uncanny," *Annals of Transplantation* 11.3 (2006): 16–30; "Parts Unknown: Undercover Ethnography of the Organs-Trafficking Underworld," *Ethnography* 5.1 (2004): 29–73; and "Rotten Trade."

23 Marx, *Capital*, 152.

24 Although theorists of racial capitalism previously discussed do not treat biocapitalism, formulations advanced by Cedric Robinson and others implicitly suggest that biocapitalism, like all iterations of capitalism, ought to be recognized as

a form of racial capitalism that necessarily bears a relationship to slavery. See Cedric J. Robinson, *Black Marxism: The Making of the Black Radical Tradition* (Chapel Hill: University of North Carolina Press, 1983); Barbara Fields, "Ideology and Race in American History," in *Region, Race and Reconstruction: Essays in Honor of C. Vann Woodward*, ed. J. Morgan Kousser and James M. McPherson (New York: Oxford University Press, 1982), 143–78; Stuart Hall, "Race, Articulation, and Societies Structured in Dominance," in *Sociological Theories: Race and Colonialism* (Paris: UNESCO, 1980), 305–45; Walter Johnson, *River of Dark Dreams: Slavery and Empire in the Cotton Kingdom* (Cambridge, MA: Harvard University Press, 2013); Stephanie Smallwood, *Saltwater Slavery: A Middle Passage from Africa to American Diaspora* (Cambridge, MA: Harvard University Press, 2007); Moon-Ho Jung, *Coolies and Cane: Race, Labor, and Sugar in the Age of Emancipation* (Baltimore: Johns Hopkins University Press, 2006); Lisa Lowe, *The Intimacies of Four Continents* (Durham: Duke University Press, 2015); Edward Baptist, *The Half Has Never Been Told: Slavery and the Making of American Capitalism* (New York: Basic Books, 2014).

25 In this way, the neglect of slavery reduplicates that already noted in scholarship on biocapitalism. See chapter 1.

26 On contemporary slavery and trafficking, see Kevin Bales, *Disposable People: New Slavery in the Global Economy* (Berkeley: University of California Press, 1999), hereafter cited parenthetically; Alison Brysk and Austin Choi-Fitzpatrick, eds., *From Human Trafficking to Human Rights: Reframing Contemporary Slavery* (Philadelphia: University of Pennsylvania Press, 2012); Joel Quirk, *The Anti-Slavery Project: From the Slave Trade to Human Trafficking* (Philadelphia: University of Pennsylvania Press, 2011); Siddharth Kara, *Sex Trafficking: Inside the Business of Modern Slavery* (New York: Columbia University Press, 2009); Christien van den Anker, ed., *The Political Economy of New Slavery* (New York: Palgrave Macmillan, 2004); Denise Brennan, *Life Interrupted: Trafficking into Forced Labor in the United States* (Durham: Duke University Press, 2014). Quirk challenges Bales's division between new and old slavery, and Brennan rejects the use of the term altogether. In so doing Brennan joins African activists who have argued for restricted use of slavery in the contemporary context.

27 Apparently Bales overlooks Caribbean slavery. Ishiguro's portrait of clones' extermination through repeated donation necessarily recalls the slaves who were worked to death, especially on Caribbean sugar plantations.

28 The New UN Protocol to Prevent, Suppress and Punish Trafficking in Persons, Especially Women and Children is one of two supplements to the UN Convention against Transnational Organized Crime, adopted in November 2000. It constitutes the first internationally agreed upon definition of trafficking and was expressly adopted to make international law more successful in combating transnational organized crime involving organ theft. The new definition of trafficking it puts forth includes "recruitment, transportation, transfer, harboring or receipt of persons . . . for the purpose of slavery or practices similar to slavery, servitude or removal of organs." See Christien van den Anker, "Introduction: Combatting Contemporary Slavery," in *The Political Economy of New Slavery*, 5, and "Con-

temporary Slavery, Global Justice and Globalization," in *The Political Economy of New Slavery*, 30; David Ould, "Trafficking and International Law," in Anker, *The Political Economy of New Slavery*, 55–74.

29 The other argument that can be made against Bales is that almost all the new slaves whom he discusses are people of color, most from the Global South. While slaveholders are no longer necessarily white, slaves are Thai, Filipino, Brazilian, Pakistani, Indian, Turkish, Chinese, and so on.

30 Benjamin, "Theses," 261.

31 It is argued that depth reading developed in response to the combined hegemony of Marxist and psychoanalytic frameworks in literary criticism. See Eve Kosofsky Sedgwick, "Paranoid Reading and Reparative Reading, or You're So Paranoid You Probably Think This Essay Is about You," in *Touching Feeling: Affect, Pedagogy, Performativity* (Durham: Duke University Press, 2003), 123–51; Stephen Best and Sharon Marcus, eds., "The Way We Read Now," special issue, *Representations* 108 (2009); Heather Love, "Close but Not Deep: Literary Ethics and the Descriptive Turn," *New Literary History* 41.2 (2010): 371–91.

32 Best and Marcus, "Surface Reading: An Introduction," in "The Way We Read Now," 3, 9.

33 Best and Marcus implicitly invoke the criticism on *Beloved* here. See also Love, "Close but Not Deep." For a reading of *Beloved* that insists on engagement with ghosts and haunting and thus resonates with the present argument see Avery Gordon, "Not Only the Footprints but the Water Too and What Is Down There," in *Ghostly Matters: Haunting and the Sociological Imagination* (Minneapolis: University of Minnesota Press, 1997), 137–92. Notably, slavery is one of the historically repressed contexts most frequently uncovered when scholars read symptomatically. This begs the question: Which histories go missing when we opt for surface reading?

34 Ishiguro has explicitly said this about his own fiction. In a 2015 interview he observed, "You have to leave a lot of meaning underneath the surface." Alexandra Alter and Dan Bilefsky, "Genre-Spanning Author of *The Remains of the Day* Wins Noble," *New York Times*, October 6, 2017.

35 See Orlando Patterson, *Slavery and Social Death: A Comparative Study* (Cambridge, MA: Harvard University Press, 1982).

36 Significantly the clones never discuss birth or parentage. Instead they seek out their "originals"—those from whom they have been derived. I treat the clones' provenance and motherlessness in my epilogue.

37 Here I follow Louis Althusser in arguing that literature allows us to see, perceive, and feel ideology. "A Letter on Art in Reply to André Daspre," in *Lenin and Philosophy and Other Essays* (New York: Monthly Review, 1971), 151–56.

38 See Jane Elliott and Gillian Harkins, "Introduction: Genres of Neoliberalism," special issue, *Social Text* 31.2 (2013): 1–17; hereafter cited parenthetically.

39 Jane Elliott, "Suffering Agency: Imagining Neoliberal Personhood in North America and Britain," *Social Text* 31.2 (2013): 84; hereafter cited parenthetically.

40 See Jodi Melamed, *Represent and Destroy: Rationalizing Violence in the New Racial Capitalism* (Minneapolis: University of Minnesota Press, 2011). Melamed argues that the postwar period is characterized by "race liberal projects," including "neoliberal multiculturalism"; here I suggest that the postwar world of the novel is more aptly characterized by neoliberal postracialism.

41 See Mbembe, "Necropolitics"; Jared Sexton, "People-of-Color-Blindness: Notes on the Afterlife of Slavery," *Social Text* 28.2 (2010): 31–56; Alexander G. Weheliye, *Habeas Viscus: Racializing Assemblages, Biopolitics, and Black Feminist Theories of the Human* (Durham: Duke University Press, 2014). The idea of a multicentury continuum stretching back to slavery and colonialism and forward to fascist totalitarianism has been theorized by others. In *The Origins of Nazi Violence*, trans. Janet Lloyd (New York: New Press, 2003), Enzo Traverso examines the origins of Nazi violence, locating the racism that animated National Socialism in the history of colonization in Africa. For Traverso the concentration camp is not anomalous but rather the logical outcome of a Western colonial mind-set capable of orchestrating mass extermination and industrialized killing. Paul Gilroy examines "the camp" and argues that "camp mentality" informs contemporary racism: *Against Race: Imagining Political Culture beyond the Color Line* (Cambridge, MA: Harvard University Press, 2000). Several sf scholars argue similarly. For Maria Varsam, all dystopian worlds strip away individual freedom, especially women's reproductive freedom. For this reason, depictions of slavery constitute "living memory" and may be used to catalyze realization of "the present as history." "Concrete Dystopia: Slavery and Its Others," in *Dark Horizons: Science Fiction and the Dystopian Imagination*, ed. Raffaella Baccolini and Tom Moylan (New York: Routledge, 2003), 203–24.

42 Weheliye, *Habeas Viscus*, 37.

43 Foucault's work on biopolitics is arguably the most influential, and thus its focus on the Holocaust and its omission of slavery and the practice of slave breeding are instructive in relation to this argument. In the 1975–76 lectures given at the Collège de France and collected in *Society Must Be Defended* and the 1978–79 lectures collected in *The Birth of Biopolitics*, as well as in *The History of Sexuality, Volume I* (1976), Foucault describes the emergence of biopolitical governance. Biopolitical statecraft took root as early as the late eighteenth century; however, it is not until the mid-twentieth century that biopower reaches its apotheosis. Foucault writes that "the entry of the phenomena peculiar to the life of the human species into the order of knowledge and power, into the sphere of political techniques" signaled a decisive historical conjuncture. During World War II, "for the first time in history . . . biological existence was reflected in political existence," and "the life of the species . . . wagered on its own political strategies" (*Society Must Be Defended: Lectures at the Collège de France, 1975–76*, trans. David Macey, ed. Mauro Bertani and Alessandro Fontana [New York: Picador, 2003], 254–55, quotes 142–43; hereafter cited parenthetically as SD). Biopolitics targets the population, through

the individual, who is, in turn, abstracted and managed through deployment of norms, standards, and values—the precise forms of governance that Miss Emily describes as emergent in the wake of the Morningdale scandal. As the new methods of statistics, epidemiology, and the biological sciences (including genetics) develop, governance through correction, normalization, and health optimization supersedes discipline and punishment (read: sovereign power), and allows for division of the population into those whose lives are protected and those whose lives may be taken with impunity. This division, was and remains fundamentally racial in character.

In an oft-traversed passage, Foucault explains that racism allows for the entrance of death into biopolitics by "introducing a break into the domain of life that is under power's control." Racism fragments the field of the biological that power controls, as "it is a way of separating out the groups that exist within a population . . . a way of establishing a biological type caesura within a population that appears to be a biological domain" (SD, 255). For this reason, Foucault concludes, racism, above all else, justifies "the relationship of war" by distinguishing the "enemy" biologically: "The death of the bad race, of the inferior race (or the degenerate, or the abnormal) is something that will make life in general healthier: healthier and purer" (SD, 255). In short, in a biopolitical society, "racism is the precondition that makes killing acceptable" and that justifies "the murderous function of the State" (SD, 256). Notably, Foucault pinpoints fascist totalitarianism as the historical formation through which older forms of power have passed on their way to becoming racist: "If the power of normalization wishes to exercise the old sovereign right to kill, it must become racist. And if, conversely, a power of sovereignty . . . that has the right of life and death, wishes to work with the instruments, mechanisms, and technology of normalization, it too must become racist" (SD, 256). Underscoring the centrality of the Nazi example, Foucault observes that "no state could have more disciplinary power than the Nazi regime," as no other state has "so tightly, so insistently, regulated [the biological]" (SD, 259).

As others have pointed out, Foucault never considers four hundred years of racial slavery in the Americas and the Caribbean within the geotemporality of modern biopolitics and his discussion of racism. This omission reifies a Eurocentric worldview, and is enabled by Foucault's complete neglect of the science of slave management and breeding in the new world, the form of plantation governance necessitated by the closure of the transatlantic slave trade and the subsequent transition from continuous importation of new slaves to slave breeding. Although the historians of slavery discussed in chapter 1 do not use Foucauldian language, their research suggests that maximization of life for the master class was exercised through imposition of a "biological caesura" (SD, 255) that was racial in character, and that governance of the slave population was orchestrated through reproductive controls that resulted in the extraction of reproductive labor and its living products from slaves whose labor was racialized and racializing.

44 On "transvaluation" see Michel Foucault, "Nietzsche, Genealogy, History" (1977), in *The Foucault Reader*, ed. Paul Rabinow (New York: Pantheon Books, 1984), 76–100.

45 The question of the engineered being's capacity to love is a motif rooted in romantic fiction (i.e., *Frankenstein*) and reproduced in modern classics (e.g., *Blade Runner*). See Nussbaum and Sunstein, *Clones and Clones*; Haran et al., *Human Cloning in the Media*.

46 Although Tommy does not produce deferral-worthy art when at Hailsham, he later creates miniature animal portraits in the hope of making a strong case for deferral. The equation of clone art with humanness rings changes on the equation of human ingenuity with patentability. In contemporary patent law, establishment of property in the body is dependent on demonstration of human invention. See Donna Dickenson, "Genomes Up for Grabs: or, Could Dr. Frankenstein Have Patented His Monster?," in *Body Shopping*, 90–114.

47 Stephanie Smallwood, "Commodified Freedom: Interrogating the Limits of Anti-Slavery Ideology in the Early Republic," *Journal of the Early Republic* 24.2 (2004): 289–98.

48 Patterson makes a similar observation from the vantage point of the slave: "Freedom is born, not in the consciousness of the master, but in the reality of the slave's condition" (*Slavery and Social Death*, 98).

49 On choice in neoliberalism, see Nikolas S. Rose, *Powers of Freedom: Reframing Political Thought* (New York: Cambridge University Press, 1999); Elliott, "Suffering Agency." On the irrelevance of rational choice theory to understanding the global organ trade see Scheper-Hughes, "Parts Unknown."

50 Other scholars have examined the adaptation of the slave narrative in speculative or postmodern fiction. What distinguishes the present analysis is the idea that the slave narrative need not be populated by phenotypically black bodies, nor need it expressly depict the historical enslavement of Africans. See A. Timothy Spaulding, *Re-forming the Past: History, the Fantastic, and the Postmodern Slave Narrative* (Columbus: Ohio State University Press, 2005); Madhu Dubey, "Speculative Fictions of Slavery," *American Literature* 82.4 (2010): 779–805. Also see Isiah Lavender III, *Race in American Science Fiction* (Bloomington: Indiana University Press, 2011). Lavender advances the universal claim that race need not be expressly depicted for racial difference to impose the principal structuring effect on the genre's narrative strategies. I do not wish to go so far here.

51 See John Sekora, "Black Message/White Envelope: Genre, Authenticity, and Authority in the Antebellum Slave Narrative," *Callaloo* 10.3 (1987): 482–515. Notably, contemporary slave narratives are often curated, as they were in the nineteenth century, by abolitionists. See Kevin Bales and Zoe Trodd, eds., *To Plead Our Own Cause: Personal Stories by Today's Slaves* (Ithaca, NY: Cornell University Press, 2008).

52 Georg Lukács, "Reification and the Consciousness of the Proletariat," in *History and Class Consciousness: Studies in Marxist Dialectics* (Cambridge, MA: MIT Press, 1971), 83–222.

53 I follow Benjamin in using the term apperception—the perception of our materially altered perception—thus.

54 The song to which Kathy listens was created by Luther Dixon and Jane Monheit for Mark Romanek's and Alex Garland's filmic adaption of the book. The fictional album from which it is taken, *Songs after Dark*, appears to be inspired by the work of Julie London, though some speculate that "Judy Bridgewater" is a clever amalgam of Judy Garland and Dee Dee Bridgewater, and others that Bridgewater is a cover for Ishiguro's real-life musical collaborator, the London-based songwriter Stacey Kent. Ishiguro cowrote four songs for Kent's 2007 album, *Breakfast on the Morning Train*. Though interviews with Ishiguro deny the Kent-Bridgewater connection, she includes an old jazz favorite entitled "Never Let Me Go" on her album.

    Jane Monheit's vocal performance of "Never Let Me Go" was released September 14, 2010, on *Never Let Me Go: Original Motion Picture Soundtrack*, by Rachel Portman, Varèse Sarabande, compact disc. See Peter Howell, "The Hunt for the Elusive Judy Bridgewater," *The Star*, September 30, 2010. Thanks to Christina Walter for alerting me to the song's provenance.

55 Benjamin's description resonates powerfully: "A Klee painting . . . shows an angel looking as though he is about to move away from something he is fixedly contemplating. . . . This is how one pictures the angel of history. His face is turned toward the past. Where we perceive a chain of events, he sees one single catastrophe which keeps piling wreckage upon wreckage and hurls it in front of his feet. The angel would like to stay, awaken the dead, and make whole what has been smashed. But a storm is blowing from paradise; it has got caught in his wings with such violence that the angel can no longer close them. This storm irresistibly propels him into the future to which his back is turned, while the pile of debris before him grows skyward. This storm is what we call progress" ("Theses," 257–58).

Epilogue

1 Aldous Huxley, *Brave New World* (1932; New York: Harper Perennial, 1946).

2 At the time of writing, two types of cloning, therapeutic and reproductive, are possible. In the former, cell lines and pluripotent stem cells are reproduced through cloning techniques and multiplied outside of the human body for use in various regenerative therapies. In the latter, gestation of cloned embryos *inside* a female body is the only existent means by which a living organism can come into the world.

3 This requires qualification: unlike the sterile clones in Ishiguro's novel, the clones in *The Island* provide wombs, among other organs. In one pivotal scene, a woman uses her cloned self to deliver a child; as soon as the child is born, the clone is euthanized.

4 Lee Edelman, *No Future: Queer Theory and the Death Drive* (Durham: Duke University Press, 2004). In contrast to Edelman, who focuses on "the Child" in discourses of reproductive futurism to the exclusion of the reproductive body, I seek to restore the reproductive body (though not heterosexuality) to the center of the discussion of futurity.

5 See Slavoj Žižek, "Children of Men Comments," *Children of Men*, directed by Alfonso Cuarón, DVD (Hollywood: Universal Pictures, 2007); "The Clash of Civilizations at the End of History," Scribd, accessed January 21, 2017, https://www.scribd.com /document/19133296/Zizek-The-Clash-of-Civilizations-at-the-End-of-History. Žižek claims that "the background persists," becoming the real text. For him the story of infertility as a biological problem is merely an extended metaphor for the crisis of Western civilization. Also see Zahid Chaudhary, "Humanity Adrift: Race, Materiality, and Allegory in Alfonso Cuarón's *Children of Men*," *Camera Obscura* 24.3 (2009): 73–109. Chaudhary offers a reading of the background text as a post-9/11 text, one that constitutes a dialectical image and messianic prophesy.

6 On the film as post-9/11 commentary see Žižek, "Children of Men Comments"; Chaudhary, "Humanity Adrift"; Jayna Brown, "The Human Project: Utopia, Dystopia, and the Black Heroine in *Children of Men* and *28 Days Later*," *Transitions* 110 (2013): 120–35. On the centrality of reproductive dispossession see Heather Latimer, "Bio-Reproductive Futurism: Bare Life and the Pregnant Refugee in Alfonso Cuarón's *Children of Men*," *Social Text* 29.3 (2011): 51–72; Sayantani DasGupta, "(Re)Conceiving the Surrogate: Maternity, Race, and Reproductive Technologies in Alfonso Cuarón's *Children of Men*," in *Gender Scripts in Medicine and Narrative*, ed. Marcelline Block and Angela Lafler (Newcastle upon Tyne, UK: Cambridge Scholars, 2010), 178–211; Sarah Trimble, "Maternal Back/grounds in *Children of Men*: Notes Toward an Arendtian Biopolitics," *Science Fiction Film and Television*, 4.2 (2011): 249–70. Brown and Trimble root Kee's reproductive dispossession in slavery; DasGupta roots it in colonial violence against "Third World women," including Indian surrogates.

7 As critics who take up the novel in relation to the film point out, the main distinction between the two is the racialization of the mother of the future. See DasGupta, "(Re)Conceiving the Surrogate"; Soo Darcy, "Power, Surveillance and Reproductive Technology in P. D. James' *The Children of Men*," in *Women's Utopian and Dystopian Fiction*, ed. Sharon R. Wilson (Newcastle upon Tyne: Cambridge Scholars, 2013), 88–111.

8 See Barbara Korte, "Envisioning a Black Tomorrow? Black Mother Figures and the Issue of Representation in *28 Days Later* (2003) and *Children of Men* (2006)," in *Multi-Ethnic Britain 2000+: New Perspectives in Literature, Film and the Arts*, ed. Lars Eckstein et al. (Amsterdam: Rodopi, 2008), 315–25; Jonathan Romney, "Green and Pleasant Land," *Film Comment* 43.1 (2007): 32–35; Žižek, "Children of Men Comments." Other readings see multivalent possibilities at film's end. Sara Ahmed argues that the bleak and promising are conjoined through the haptic nature of the narrative: "Happy Futures, Perhaps," in *Queer Times, Queer Becom-*

ings, ed. E. L. McCallum and Mikko Tuhkanen (Albany: State University of New York Press, 2011), 159–82.

9 Toni Morrison, *Playing in the Dark: Whiteness and the Literary Imagination* (New York: Vintage Books, 1992), 51–52.

10 Jennifer Morgan, *Laboring Women: Reproduction and Gender in New World Slavery* (Philadelphia: University of Pennsylvania Press, 2004), 12–49.

11 Terryl Bacon and Govinda Dickman, "'Who's the Daddy?' The Aesthetics and Politics of Representation in Alfonso Cuarón's Adaptation of P. D. James's *Children of Men*," in *Adaptation in Contemporary Culture: Textual Infidelities*, ed. Rachel Carroll (New York: Continuum, 2009), 147–59.

12 See DasGutpa, "(Re)Conceiving the Surrogate"; Latimer, "Bio-Reproductive Futurism"; Korte, "Envisioning a Black Tomorrow?" DasGupta argues that Theo's ex-wife may be likened to Elizabeth Stern, the intending mother in the Baby M case. Korte regards Theo as the biblical Joseph and thus as a "surrogate father."

BIBLIOGRAPHY

African American Women Are for Reproductive Freedom. "We Remember." 1984. In *Still Lifting, Still Climbing: African American Women's Contemporary Activism*, edited by Kimberly Springer, 38–41. New York: New York University Press, 1999.

Agamben, Giorgio. *Homo Sacer: Sovereign Power and Bare Life*. Translated by Daniel Heller-Roazen. Stanford: Stanford University Press, 1998.

Ahmed, Sara. *The Cultural Politics of Emotion*. New York: Routledge, 2004.

———. "Happy Futures, Perhaps." In *Queer Times, Queer Becomings*, edited by E. L. McCallum and Mikko Tuhkanen, 159–82. Albany: State University of New York Press, 2011.

Allen, Anita. "The Black Surrogate Mother." *Harvard Blackletter Journal* 8 (1991): 17–31.

———. "Surrogacy, Slavery, and the Ownership of Life." *Harvard Journal of Law & Public Policy* 13.1 (1990): 139–49.

Allen, Theodore W. *The Invention of the White Race*. Vol. 1: *Racial Oppression and Social Control*. New York: Verso, 1994.

Almeling, Rene. *Sex Cells: The Medical Market for Eggs and Sperm*. Berkeley: University of California Press, 2011.

Alter, Alexandra, and Dan Bilefsky. "Genre-Spanning Author of *The Remains of the Day* Wins Nobel." *New York Times*, October 6, 2017.

Althusser, Louis. "Ideology and Ideological State Apparatuses (Notes towards an Investigation)." In *Lenin and Philosophy and Other Essays*, translated by Ben Brewster, 127–86. New York: Monthly Review, 1971.

———. "A Letter on Art in Reply to André Daspre." In *Lenin and Philosophy and Other Essays*, translated by Ben Brewster, 151–56. New York: Monthly Review, 1971.

Andrews, Lindsey. "Black Feminism's Minor Empiricism: Hurston, Combahee, and the Experience of Evidence." *Catalyst* 1.1 (2015): 1–37.

Andrews, Lori, and Dorothy Nelkin. *Body Bazaar: The Market for Human Tissue in the Biotechnology Age*. New York: Crown, 2001.

Andrews, William L., and Nellie Y. McKay. *Toni Morrison's Beloved: A Casebook*. New York: Oxford University Press, 1999.

Anker, Christien van den, ed. *The Political Economy of New Slavery*. New York: Palgrave Macmillan, 2004.

Aptheker, Herbert. *American Negro Slave Revolts*. New York: International Publishers, 1943.

Arditti, Rita, Renate Duelli-Klein, and Shelley Minden, eds. *Test-Tube Women: What Future for Motherhood?* London: Pandora, 1984.

Arendt, Hannah. *Eichmann in Jerusalem: A Report on the Banality of Evil.* 1963. New York: Penguin, 1994.

Aristarkhova, Irina. *Hospitality of the Matrix: Philosophy, Biomedicine, and Culture.* New York: Columbia University Press, 2012.

Armstrong, Scott. "California Surrogacy Case Raises New Questions about Parenthood: Mother Seeks Custody, but She Has No Genetic Link to Child." *Christian Science Monitor*, September 25, 1990.

Audi, Tamara, and Arlene Chang. "Assembling the Global Baby." *Wall Street Journal*, December 10, 2010.

Avery, Byllye Y. "Breathing Life into Ourselves: The Evolution of the National Black Women's Health Project." In *The Black Women's Health Book: Speaking for Ourselves*, edited by Evelyn C. White, 4–10. Seattle: Seal Press, 1990.

"Baby M: Groping for Right and Law." *New York Times*, April 2, 1987.

Bacon, Terryl, and Govinda Dickman. "'Who's the Daddy?' The Aesthetics and Politics of Representation in Alfonso Cuarón's Adaptation of P. D. James's *Children of Men*." In *Adaptation in Contemporary Culture: Textual Infidelities*, edited by Rachel Carroll, 147–59. New York: Continuum, 2009.

Bailey, Alison. "Reconceiving Surrogacy: Toward a Reproductive Justice Account of Indian Surrogacy." *Hypatia* 26.4 (2011): 715–41.

Bailey, Wilma Ann. "Black and Jewish Women Consider Hagar." *Encounter* 63.1–2 (2002): 37–44.

Baker, Brenda. "A Case for Permitting Altruistic Surrogacy." *Hypatia* 11.2 (1996): 34–49.

Bales, Kevin. *Disposable People: New Slavery in the Global Economy.* Berkeley: University of California Press, 1999.

Bales, Kevin, and Zoe Trodd, eds. *To Plead Our Own Cause: Personal Stories by Today's Slaves.* Ithaca, NY: Cornell University Press, 2008.

Balfour, Lawrie. "Vexed Genealogy: Octavia Butler and Political Memories of Slavery." In *Democracy's Literature: Politics and Fiction in America*, edited by Patrick Deneen and Joseph Romance, 171–90. Lanham, MD: Rowman and Littlefield, 2005.

Balibar, Étienne, and Immanuel Wallerstein. *Race, Nation, Class: Ambiguous Identities.* New York: Verso, 1991.

Bambara, Toni Cade. *The Black Woman: An Anthology.* New York: New American Library, 1970.

Baptist, Edward. *The Half Has Never Been Told: Slavery and the Making of American Capitalism.* New York: Basic Books, 2014.

Baptist, Edward E., and Stephanie H. M. Camp. *New Studies in the History of American Slavery.* Athens: University of Georgia Press, 2006.

Barrett, Michèle. *Women's Oppression Today: Problems in Marxist Feminist Analysis.* London: Verso, 1980.

Barron, James. "Views on Surrogacy Harden after Baby M Ruling." *New York Times*, April 2, 1987.

Bay, Mia. *The White Image in the Black Mind: African American Ideas about White People, 1830–1925*. New York: Oxford University Press, 2000.

Bay, Michael, director. *The Island*. DVD. Universal City, CA: DreamWorks Pictures, 2005.

Beaulieu, Elizabeth Ann. *Black Women Writers and the American Neo-Slave Narrative: Femininity Unfettered*. Westport, CT: Greenwood, 1999.

Becker, Gary. *A Treatise on the Family*. Cambridge, MA: Harvard University Press, 1981.

Beckles, Hilary McD. *Natural Rebels: A Social History of Enslaved Women in Barbados*. New Brunswick, NJ: Rutgers University Press, 1989.

Bedore, Pamela. "Slavery and Symbiosis in Octavia Butler's *Kindred*." *Foundation* 31.84 (2002): 73–81.

Bell, Bernard W. *The Afro-American Novel and Its Tradition*. Amherst: University of Massachusetts Press, 1987.

———. "*Beloved*: A Womanist Neo-Slave Narrative; Or Multivocal Remembrances of Things Past." *African American Review* 26.1 (1992): 7–15.

Belliotti, Raymond A. "Marxism, Feminism, and Surrogate Motherhood." *Social Theory and Practice* 14.3 (1988): 389–417.

Benjamin, Walter. "Theses on the Philosophy of History." 1940. In *Illuminations*, translated by Harry Zohn, edited by Hannah Arendt, 253–64. New York: Schocken Books, 1968.

———. "The Work of Art in the Age of Mechanical Reproduction." 1936. In *Illuminations*, translated by Harry Zohn, edited by Hannah Arendt, 217–52. New York: Schocken Books, 1968.

Berger, James. "Ghosts of Liberalism: Morrison's *Beloved* and the Moynihan Report." *PMLA* 111.3 (1996): 408–20.

Bergmann, Sven. "Fertility Tourism: Circumventive Routes That Enable Access to Reproductive Technologies and Substances." *Signs* 36.2 (2011): 280–89.

Best, Stephen M. *The Fugitive's Properties: Law and the Poetics of Possession*. Chicago: University of Chicago Press, 2004.

———. "On Failing to Make the Past Present." *Modern Language Quarterly* 73:3 (2012): 453–74.

Best, Stephen, and Sharon Marcus. "Surface Reading: An Introduction." *Representations* 108 (2009): 1–21.

Bettanin, Giuliano. "Defining a Genre: Octavia Butler's *Kindred* and Women's Neo-Slave Narrative." *49th Parallel* 14 (2004): 1–10.

Bettenhausen, Elizabeth. "Hagar Revisited: Surrogacy, Alienation, and Motherhood." *Christianity and Crisis* 47.7 (1987): 157–59.

Bianchi, Emanuela. *The Feminine Symptom: Aleatory Matter in the Aristotelian Cosmos*. New York: Fordham University Press, 2014.

Birch, Kean, and David Tyfield. "Theorizing the Bioeconomy: Biovalue, Biocapital, Bioeconomics or . . . What?" *Science, Technology, & Human Values* 38.3 (2012): 299–327.

Black, Shameem. "Ishiguro's Inhuman Aesthetics." *Modern Fiction Studies* 55.4 (2009): 785–807.

Blassingame, John W. *The Slave Community: Plantation Life in the Antebellum South*. New York: Oxford University Press, 1972.

Bliss, Catherine. *Race Decoded: The Genomic Fight for Social Justice*. Stanford: Stanford University Press, 2012.

Bond Stockton, Kathryn. "Prophylactics and Brains: *Beloved* in the Cybernetic Age of AIDS." *Studies in the Novel* 28.3 (1996): 434–65.

Boris, Eileen. *Home to Work: Motherhood and the Politics of Industrial Homework in the United States*. New York: Cambridge University Press, 1994.

Boris, Eileen, and Jennifer Klein. *Caring for America: Home Health Workers in the Shadow of the Welfare State*. New York: Oxford University Press, 2012.

Boris, Eileen, and Elisabeth Prügl, eds. *Homeworkers in Global Perspective: Invisible No More*. New York: Routledge, 1996.

Boris, Eileen, and Rhacel Salazar Parreñas, eds. *Intimate Labors: Cultures, Technologies, and the Politics of Care*. Stanford: Stanford University Press, 2010.

Boyce Davies, Carole. "Mobility, Embodiment, and Resistance: Black Women's Writing in the US." In *Black Women, Writing, and Identity: Migrations of the Subject*, 130–51. New York: Routledge, 1994.

———. "Mother Right/Write Revisited: *Beloved* and *Dessa Rose* and the Construction of Motherhood in Black Women's Fiction." In *Narrating Mothers: Theorizing Maternal Subjectivities*, edited by Brenda O. Daly and Maureen T. Reddy, 44–57. Knoxville: University of Tennessee Press, 1991.

Brennan, Denise. *Life Interrupted: Trafficking into Forced Labor in the United States*. Durham: Duke University Press, 2014.

Brewer, Rose M. "Theorizing Race, Class, Gender: The New Scholarship of Black Feminist Intellectuals and Black Women's Labor." In *Theorizing Black Feminisms: The Visionary Pragmatism of Black Women*, edited by Stanlie M. James and Abena P. A. Busia, 13–30. London: Routledge, 1993.

Briggs, Laura. *Somebody's Children: The Politics of Transracial and Transnational Adoption*. Durham: Duke University Press, 2012.

Brown, Jayna. "The Human Project: Utopia, Dystopia, and the Black Heroine in *Children of Men* and *28 Days Later*." *Transitions* 110 (2013): 120–35.

Brown, Kathleen M. *Good Wives, Nasty Wenches, and Anxious Patriarchs: Gender, Race, and Power in Colonial Virginia*. Chapel Hill: University of North Carolina Press, 1996.

Brown, Kimberly Juanita. *The Repeating Body: Slavery's Visual Resonance in the Contemporary*. Durham: Duke University Press, 2015.

———. "Slavery's Afterlife in Text and Image." *Criticism* 56.4 (2014): 837–40.

Brown, Malaika. "Surrogate Mothers: Are We Creating a Class of Breeders?" *Los Angeles Sentinel*, September 9, 1993.

Brown, Wendy. "American Nightmare: Neoliberalism, Neoconservatism, and De-Democratization." *Political Theory* 34.6 (2006): 690–714.

———. "Neo-liberalism and the End of Liberal Democracy." *Theory & Event* 7.1 (2003). https://muse.jhu.edu/article/48659.

Browne, Simone. *Dark Matters: On the Surveillance of Blackness.* Durham: Duke University Press, 2015.

Brysk, Alison, and Austin Choi-Fitzpatrick, eds. *From Human Trafficking to Human Rights: Reframing Contemporary Slavery.* Philadelphia: University of Pennsylvania Press, 2012.

Buia, Carolina. "The Booming Market for Breast Milk." *Newsweek,* May 23, 2015.

Burley, Justine. "A Braver, Newer World." *Nature* 435.7041 (2005): 427.

Bush, Barbara. "Hard Labor: Women, Childbirth, and Resistance in British Caribbean Slave Societies." In *More than Chattel: Black Women and Slavery in the Americas,* edited by David Barry Gaspar and Darlene Clark Hine, 193–217. Bloomington: Indiana University Press, 1996.

———. *Slave Women in Caribbean Society, 1650–1838.* Bloomington: Indiana University Press, 1990.

Butler, Octavia E. "Bloodchild." 1984. In *Bloodchild and Other Stories.* New York: Four Walls Eight Windows, 1995.

———. *Clay's Ark.* New York: Warner, 1984.

———. *Dawn.* New York: Warner, 1987.

———. *Kindred.* Boston: Beacon, 1979.

———. *Mind of My Mind.* New York: Warner, 1977.

———. *Patternmaster.* New York: Warner, 1976.

———. *Wild Seed.* New York: Warner, 1980.

Cacho, Lisa Marie. *Social Death: Racialized Rightlessness and the Criminalization of the Unprotected.* New York: New York University Press, 2012.

Camp, Stephanie M. H. *Closer to Freedom: Enslaved Women and Everyday Resistance in the Plantation South.* Chapel Hill: University of North Carolina Press, 2004.

Carby, Hazel V. *Reconstructing Womanhood: The Emergence of the Afro-American Woman Novelist.* New York: Oxford University Press, 1987.

———. "The Souls of Black Men." In *Next to the Color Line: Gender, Sexuality, and W. E. B. Du Bois,* edited by Susan Gillman and Alys Eve Weinbaum, 234–68. Minneapolis: University of Minnesota Press, 2007.

Carney, Scott. *The Red Market: On the Trail of the World's Organ Brokers, Bone Thieves, Blood Farmers, and Child Traffickers.* New York: William Morrow, 2011.

Cary, Lorene. *The Price of a Child: A Novel.* New York: Knopf, 1995.

Centers for Disease Control and Prevention. "Pregnancy Mortality Surveillance System." Last updated December 13, 2016. https://www.cdc.gov/reproductivehealth /maternalinfanthealth/pmss.html.

Chakrabarty, Dipesh. *Provincializing Europe: Postcolonial Thought and Historical Difference.* Princeton: Princeton University Press, 2000.

Chang, Grace. *Disposable Domestics: Immigrant Women Workers in the Global Economy.* Cambridge, MA: South End, 2000.

Chatterjee, Indrani. *Gender, Slavery, and Law in Colonial India.* London: Oxford University Press, 1999.

Chatterjee, Indrani, and Richard M. Eaton, eds. *Slavery and South Asian History*. Bloomington: Indiana University Press, 2006.

Chaudhary, Zahid R. "Humanity Adrift: Race, Materiality, and Allegory in Alfonso Cuarón's *Children of Men*." *Camera Obscura* 24.3 (2009): 73–109.

Cherniavsky, Eva. *Incorporations: Race, Nation, and the Body Politics of Capital*. Minneapolis: University of Minnesota Press, 2006.

Cherry, April L. "Nurturing in the Service of White Culture: Racial Subordination, Gestational Surrogacy, and the Ideology of Motherhood." *Texas Journal of Women and the Law* 10.2 (2001): 83–128.

Childs, Dennis. *Slaves of the State: Black Incarceration from the Chain Gang to the Penitentiary*. Minneapolis: University of Minnesota Press, 2015.

———. "'You Ain't Seen Nothin' Yet': *Beloved*, the American Chain Gang, and the Middle Passage Remix." *American Quarterly* 61.2 (2009): 271–97.

Christian, Barbara. "*Beloved*, She's Ours." *Narrative* 5.1 (1997): 36–49.

———. *Black Feminist Criticism: Perspectives on Black Women Writers*. New York: Pergamon, 1985.

———. *Black Women Novelists: The Development of a Tradition, 1892–1976*. Westport, CT: Greenwood, 1980.

———. "But What Do We Think We're Doing Anyway: The State of Black Feminist Criticism(s) or My Version of a Little Bit of History." In *Changing Our Own Words: Essays on Criticism, Theory, and Writing by Black Women*, edited by Cheryl A. Wall, 58–74. New Brunswick, NJ: Rutgers University Press, 1989.

———. "Diminishing Returns: Can Black Feminism(s) Survive the Academy?" In *Multiculturalism: A Critical Reader*, edited by David Theo Goldberg, 168–79. Cambridge, MA: Blackwell, 1994.

———. "The Race for Theory." *Cultural Critique* 6 (1987): 51–63.

Chu, Dan. "A Judge Ends a Wrenching Surrogacy Dispute, Ruling That Three Parents for One Baby Is One Mom Too Many." *People*, November 5, 1990.

Clarke Kaplan, Sara. "Love and Violence/Maternity and Death: Black Feminism and the Politics of Reading (Un)representability." *Black Women, Gender, and Families* 1.1 (2007): 94–124.

Cliff, Michelle. *Abeng*. New York: Plume, 1984.

———. *Free Enterprise*. New York: Dutton, 1993.

———. *No Telephone to Heaven*. New York: Dutton, 1987.

Cohen, Lawrence. "The Other Kidney: Biopolitics beyond Recognition." *Body & Society* 7.2–3 (2001): 9–29.

Colen, Shellee. "'Like a Mother to Them': Stratified Reproduction and West Indian Childcare Workers and Employers in New York." In *Conceiving the New World Order: The Global Politics of Reproduction*, edited by Faye Ginsburg and Rayna Rapp, 78–102. Berkeley: University of California Press, 1995.

Collier-Thomas, Bettye, and V. P. Franklin, eds. *Sisters in Struggle: African American Women in the Civil Rights–Black Power Movement*. New York: New York University Press, 2001.

Collins, Patricia Hill. *Black Feminist Thought: Knowledge, Consciousness, and the Politics of Empowerment*. Boston: Unwin Hyman, 1990.

———. "Shifting the Center: Race, Class, and Feminist Theorizing about Motherhood." In *Mothering: Ideology, Experience, and Agency*, edited by Evelyn Nakano Glenn, Grace Chang, and Linda Rennie Forcey, 45–65. New York: Routledge, 1994.

Cooper, California J. *Family: A Novel*. New York: Doubleday, 1991.

Cooper, Melinda. *Life as Surplus: Biotechnology and Capitalism in the Neoliberal Era*. Seattle: University of Washington Press, 2008.

Cooper, Melinda, and Catherine Waldby. *Clinical Labor: Tissue Donors and Research Subjects in the Global Bioeconomy*. Durham: Duke University Press, 2014.

Corea, Gena. *The Mother Machine: Reproductive Technologies from Artificial Insemination to Artificial Wombs*. New York: Harper and Row, 1985.

Coward, Rosalind. *Patriarchal Precedents: Sexuality and Social Relations*. Boston: Routledge Kegan & Paul, 1983.

Cuarón, Alfonso, director. *Children of Men*. DVD. Hollywood: Universal Studios, 2006.

Dalla Costa, Mariarosa. "Capitalism and Reproduction." *Capitalism, Nature, Socialism* 7:4 (1996): 111–20.

Dalla Costa, Mariarosa, and Selma Jones. *The Power of Women and the Subversion of Community*. Bristol, UK: Falling Wall, 1973.

Darcy, Soo. "Power, Surveillance and Reproductive Technology in P. D. James' *The Children of Men*." In *Women's Utopian and Dystopian Fiction*, edited by Sharon R. Wilson, 88–111. Newcastle upon Tyne, UK: Cambridge Scholars, 2013.

DasGupta, Sayantani. "(Re)Conceiving the Surrogate: Maternity, Race, and Reproductive Technologies in Alfonso Cuarón's *Children of Men*." In *Gender Scripts in Medicine and Narrative*, edited by Marcelline Block and Angela Lafler, 178–211. Newcastle upon Tyne, UK: Cambridge Scholars, 2010.

DasGupta, Sayantani, and Shamita Das Dasgupta, eds. *Globalization and Transnational Surrogacy in India: Outsourcing Life*. Lanham, MD: Lexington Books, 2014.

Davis, Angela Y. *The Angela Y. Davis Reader*, edited by Joy James. Malden, MA: Blackwell, 1998.

———. *Are Prisons Obsolete?* New York: Seven Stories, 2003.

———. "JoAnne Little: The Dialectics of Rape." *Ms. Magazine*, June 1975, 74–77, 106–8. Reprinted in *The Angela Y. Davis Reader*, edited by Joy James, 141–60. Malden, MA: Blackwell, 1998.

———. "Reflections on the Black Woman's Role in the Community of Slaves." *Black Scholar* 3.4 (1971): 2–15.

———. "Sick and Tired of Being Sick and Tired: The Politics of Black Women's Health." In *The Black Women's Health Book: Speaking for Ourselves*, edited by Evelyn C. White, 18–26. Seattle: Seal Press, 1990.

———. *Women, Race, and Class*. New York: Vintage, 1981.

De Boever, Arne. "Bare Life and the Camps in Kazuo Ishiguro's *Never Let Me Go*." In *Narrative Care: Biopolitics and the Novel*, 59–91. London: Bloomsbury, 2013.

Deming, Barbara. *We Cannot Live without Our Lives*. New York: Grossman, 1974.

Deomampo, Daisy. "Gendered Geographies of Reproductive Tourism." *Gender & Society* 27.4 (2013): 514–37.

———. *Transnational Reproduction: Race, Kinship, and Commercial Surrogacy in India*. New York: New York University Press, 2016.

———. "Transnational Surrogacy in India: Interrogating Power and Women's Agency." *Frontiers* 34.3 (2013): 167–88.

Derrida, Jacques. "The Law of Genre." Translated by Avital Ronell. *Critical Inquiry* 7.1 (1980): 55–81.

———. *The Post Card: From Socrates to Freud and Beyond*. Translated by Alan Bass. Chicago: University of Chicago Press, 1987.

Dickenson, Donna. *Body Shopping: The Economy Fuelled by Flesh and Blood*. Oxford: Oneworld, 2008.

———. *Property in the Body: Feminist Perspectives*. New York: Cambridge University Press, 2007.

Diedrich, Maria, Henry Louis Gates Jr., and Carl Pedersen, eds. *Black Imagination and the Middle Passage*. New York: Oxford University Press, 1999.

Dillaway, Heather E. "Mothers for Others: A Race, Class, and Gender Analysis of Surrogacy." *International Journal of Sociology of the Family* 34.2 (2008): 301–26.

Dorsey, Joseph C. "Women without History: Slavery and the International Politics of Partus Sequitur Ventrem in the Spanish Caribbean." *Journal of Caribbean History* 28.2 (1994): 165–207.

Douglass, Frederick. *Narrative of the Life of Frederick Douglass, an African Slave*. 1845. In *The Classic Slave Narratives*, edited by Henry Louis Gates Jr., 323–426. New York: Signet Classics, 2002.

———. "What to the Slave Is the Fourth of July?" In *The Oxford Frederick Douglass Reader*, edited by William A. Andrews, 108–30. New York: Oxford University Press, 1996.

Du Bois, W. E. B. *Black Reconstruction in America, 1860–1880*. 1935. New York: Free Press, 1998.

———. *The Souls of Black Folk*. 1903. Edited by John Edgar Wideman. New York: Vintage, 1990.

Dubey, Madhu. "Becoming Animal in Black Women's Science Fiction." In *Afro-Future Females: Black Writers Chart Science Fiction's Newest New-Wave Trajectory*, edited by Marleen S. Barr, 31–51. Columbus: Ohio State University Press, 2008.

———. "Octavia Butler's Novels of Enslavement." *Novel* 46.3 (2013): 345–63.

———. "The Politics of Genre in *Beloved*." *Novel* 32.2 (1999): 187–206.

———. *Signs and Cities: Black Literary Postmodernism*. Chicago: University of Chicago Press, 2003.

———. "Speculative Fictions of Slavery." *American Literature* 82.4 (2010): 779–805.

duCille, Ann. "The Occult of True Black Womanhood: Critical Demeanor and Black Feminist Studies." *Signs* 19.3 (1994): 591–630.

Edelman, Lee. *No Future: Queer Theory and the Death Drive*. Durham: Duke University Press, 2004.

Edmond, Wendy, and Suzie Fleming, eds. *All Work and No Pay: Women, Housework, and the Wages Due*. Bristol, UK: Falling Wall, 1975.

Eisenstein, Zillah R., ed. *Capitalist Patriarchy and the Case for Socialist Feminism*. New York: Monthly Review Press, 1978.

Elliott, Jane. "Suffering Agency: Imagining Neoliberal Personhood in North America and Britain." *Social Text* 31.2 (2013): 83–101.

Elliott, Jane, and Gillian Harkins. "Introduction: Genres of Neoliberalism." *Social Text* 31.2 (2013): 1–17.

Farmer-Kaiser, Mary. *Freedwomen and the Freedmen's Bureau: Race, Gender, and Public Policy in the Age of Emancipation*. New York: Fordham University Press, 2010.

Faulkner, Ellen. "The Case of 'Baby M.'" *Canadian Journal of Women and the Law* 3.1 (1989): 239–45.

Federici, Silvia. *Caliban and the Witch: Women, the Body, and Primitive Accumulation*. New York: Autonomedia, 2004.

———. "The Exploitation of Women, Social Reproduction, and the Struggle against Global Capital." Interview by Matthew Carlin. *Theory & Event* 17.3 (2014). http://muse.jhu.edu/article/553382.

———. Foreword to *Patriarchy and Accumulation on a World Scale: Women in the International Division of Labor*, by Maria Mies, ix–xii. London: Zed Books, 2014.

———. *Revolution at Point Zero: Housework, Reproduction, and Feminist Struggle*. New York: Autonomedia, 2012.

———. "'We Have Seen Other Countries and Have Another Culture': Migrant Domestic Workers and the International Production and Circulation of Feminist Knowledge and Organization." *Working USA* 19.1 (2016): 9–23.

Ferguson, Roderick A. *Aberrations in Black: Toward a Queer of Color Critique*. Minneapolis: University of Minnesota Press, 2004.

Fernandes, Leela. *Transnational Feminism in the United States: Knowledge, Ethics, and Power*. New York: New York University Press, 2013.

Fett, Sharla M. *Working Cures: Healing, Health, and Power on Southern Slave Plantations*. Chapel Hill: University of North Carolina Press, 2002.

Field, Martha A. *Surrogate Motherhood: The Legal and Human Issues*. Cambridge, MA: Harvard University Press, 1988.

Fields, Barbara. "Ideology and Race in American History." In *Region, Race, and Reconstruction: Essays in Honor of C. Vann Woodward*, edited by J. Morgan Kousser and James M. McPherson, 143–78. New York: Oxford University Press, 1982.

Firestone, Shulamith. *The Dialectic of Sex: The Case for Feminist Revolution*. New York: Farrar, Straus and Giroux, 1970.

Fiveson, Robert S., director. *Parts: The Clonus Horror*. DVD. Los Angeles: Group 1 International Distribution Organization, 1979.

Fixmer-Oraiz, Natalie. "Speaking of Solidarity: Transnational Gestational Surrogacy and the Rhetorics of Reproductive (In)Justice." *Frontiers* 34.3 (2013): 126–63.

Flagel, Nadine. "'It's Almost Like Being There': Speculative Fiction, Slave Narrative, and the Crisis of Representation in Octavia Butler's Kindred." *Canadian Review of American Studies* 42.2 (2012): 216–45.

Flavin, Jeanne. *Our Bodies, Our Crimes: The Policing of Women's Reproduction in America.* New York: New York University Press, 2009.

Follett, Richard. "Gloomy Melancholy: Sexual Reproduction among Louisiana Slave Women, 1840–60." In *Women and Slavery: The Modern Atlantic.* Vol. 2 of *Women and Slavery,* edited by Gwyn Campbell, Suzanne Miers, and Joseph C. Miller, 54–75. Athens: Ohio University Press, 2007.

Fontanella-Khan, Amana. "India, the Rent-a-Womb Capital of the World: The Country's Booming Market for Surrogacy." *Slate,* August 23, 2010. http://www .slate.com/articles/double_x/doublex/2010/08/india_the_rentawomb_capital_of _the_world.html.

Fortunati, Leopoldina. *The Arcane of Reproduction: Housework, Prostitution, Labor and Capital.* 1981. Translated by Hilary Creek. New York: Autonomedia, 1995.

Foster, Guy Mark. "'Do I Look Like Someone You Can Come Home to from Where You May Be Going?' Re-mapping Interracial Anxiety in Octavia Butler's Kindred." *African American Review* 41.1 (2007): 143–64.

Foucault, Michel. *The Birth of Biopolitics: Lectures at the Collège de France, 1978–79.* Translated by Graham Burchell. Edited by Michel Senellart. New York: Palgrave Macmillan, 2008.

———. *The History of Sexuality, Volume 1: An Introduction.* 1978. Translated by Robert Hurley. New York: Vintage, 1990.

———. "Nietzsche, Genealogy, History." 1977. In *The Foucault Reader,* edited by Paul Rabinow, 76–100. New York: Pantheon Books, 1984.

———. *Society Must Be Defended: Lectures at the Collège de France, 1975–76.* Translated by David Macey. Edited by Mauro Bertani and Alessandro Fontana. New York: Picador, 2003.

Fraad, Harriet, Stephen Resnick, and Richard Wolff. *Bringing It All Back Home: Class, Gender, and Power in the Modern Household.* London: Pluto, 1994.

Franco, Dean. "What We Talk about When We Talk about Beloved." *Modern Fiction Studies* 52:2 (2006): 415–39.

Franklin, John Hope, and Loren Schweninger. *Runaway Slaves: Rebels on the Plantation.* New York: Oxford University Press, 1999.

Franklin, Sarah. *Biological Relatives: IVF, Stem Cells, and the Future of Kinship.* Durham: Duke University Press, 2013.

———. "Deconstructing 'Desperateness': The Social Construction of Infertility in Popular Representations of New Reproductive Technologies." In *The New Reproductive Technologies,* edited by Maureen McNeil, Ian Varcoe, and Steven Yearley, 220–29. London: Macmillan, 1990.

———. *Dolly Mixtures: The Remaking of Genealogy.* Durham: Duke University Press, 2007.

———. *Embodied Progress: A Cultural Account of Assisted Conception*. London: Routledge, 1997.

———. "Life Itself: Global Nature and the Genetic Imaginary." In *Global Nature, Global Culture*, edited by Sarah Franklin, Celia Lury, and Jackie Stacey, 188–227. London: Sage, 2000.

Franklin, Sarah, and Margaret Lock, eds. *Remaking Life and Death: Toward an Anthropology of Biosciences*. Santa Fe, NM: School of American Research Press, 2003.

Franklin, Sarah, and Heléna Ragoné, eds. *Reproducing Reproduction: Kinship, Power, and Technological Innovation*. Philadelphia: University of Pennsylvania Press, 1998.

Frazier, E. Franklin. *The Negro Family in the United States*. Chicago: University of Chicago Press, 1939.

Frederickson, Mary E., and Delores M. Walters. Preface to *Gendered Resistance: Women, Slavery, and the Legacy of Margaret Garner*, edited by Mary E. Frederickson and Delores M. Walters, xi–xvii. Urbana: University of Illinois Press, 2013.

Freedman, Carl. *Critical Theory and Science Fiction*. Hanover, NH: Wesleyan University Press, 2000.

Gabler-Hover, Janet. *Dreaming Black/Writing White: The Hagar Myth in American Cultural History*. Lexington: University of Kentucky Press, 2000.

Gabriel, Abram. "A Biologist's Perspective on DNA and Race in the Genomics Era." In *Genetics and the Unsettled Past: The Collision of DNA, Race, and History*, edited by Keith Wailoo, Alondra Nelson, and Catherine Lee, 43–66. New Brunswick, NJ: Rutgers University Press, 2012.

Gates, Henry Louis, Jr., ed. *Reading Black, Reading Feminist: A Critical Anthology*. New York: Meridian Books, 1990.

Genovese, Eugene D. *Roll, Jordan, Roll: The World the Slaves Made*. New York: Vintage, 1972.

Giddings, Paula. *When and Where I Enter: The Impact of Black Women on Race and Sex in America*. New York: William Morrow, 1984.

Gillman, Susan, and Alys Eve Weinbaum, eds. *Next to the Color Line: Gender, Sexuality, and W. E. B. Du Bois*. Minneapolis: University of Minnesota Press, 2007.

Gilroy, Paul. *Against Race: Imagining Political Culture beyond the Color Line*. Cambridge, MA: Harvard University Press, 2000.

———. *The Black Atlantic: Modernity and Double Consciousness*. Cambridge, MA: Harvard University Press, 1993.

Gimenez, Martha E. "The Mode of Reproduction in Transition: A Marxist-Feminist Analysis of the Effects of Reproductive Technologies." *Gender and Society* 5.3 (1991): 334–50.

Glass, Marvin. "Reproduction for Money: Marxist Feminism and Surrogate Motherhood." *Nature, Society, and Thought* 7.3 (1994): 281–97.

Glenn, Evelyn Nakano. *Forced to Care: Coercion and Caregiving in America*. Cambridge, MA: Harvard University Press, 2010.

———. "From Servitude to Service Work: Historical Continuities in the Racial Division of Paid Reproductive Labor." *Signs* 18.1 (1992): 1–43.

Glenn, Evelyn Nakano, Grace Chang, and Linda Rennie Forcey, eds. *Mothering: Ideology, Experience, and Agency*. New York: Routledge, 1994.

Glymph, Thavolia. *Out of the House of Bondage: The Transformation of the Plantation Household*. New York: Cambridge University Press, 2003.

Goldman, Anne E. "'I Made the Ink': (Literary) Production and Reproduction in *Dessa Rose* and *Beloved*." *Feminist Studies* 16.2 (1990): 313–30.

Gomez, Jewelle. *The Gilda Stories: A Novel*. Ithaca, NY: Firebrand Books, 1991.

Gordon, Avery. "Not Only the Footprints but the Water Too and What Is down There." In *Ghostly Matters: Haunting and the Sociological Imagination*, 137–92. Minneapolis: University of Minnesota Press, 1997.

Gordon, Charlotte. *The Woman Who Named God: Abraham's Dilemma and the Birth of Three Faiths*. New York: Little, Brown, 2009.

Grayson, Deborah R. "Mediating Intimacy: Black Surrogate Mothers and the Law." *Critical Inquiry* 24.2 (1998): 525–46.

———. "'Necessity Was the Midwife of Our Politics': Black Women's Health Activism in the 'Post'–Civil Rights Era (1980–1996)." In *Still Lifting, Still Climbing: African American Women's Contemporary Activism*, edited by Kimberly Springer, 131–48. New York: New York University Press, 1999.

Greene, Christina. "'I'm Gonna Get You': Black Womanhood and Jim Crow Justice in the Post–Civil Rights South." In *U.S. Women's History: Untangling the Threads of Sisterhood*, edited by Leslie Brown, Jacqueline Castledine, and Anne Valk, 98–123. New Brunswick, NJ: Rutgers University Press, 2017.

Griffin, Farah Jasmine. "Textual Healing: Claiming Black Women's Bodies, the Erotic and Resistance in Contemporary Novels of Slavery." *Callaloo* 19.2 (1996): 519–36.

Griffin, Gabriele. "Science and the Cultural Imaginary: The Case of Kazuo Ishiguro's *Never Let Me Go*." *Textual Practice* 23.4 (2009): 645–63.

Gupta, Jyotsna Agnihotri. "Parenthood in the Era of Reproductive Outsourcing and Global Assemblages." *AJWS* 18.1 (2012): 7–29.

Gutman, Herbert. *The Black Family in Slavery and Freedom, 1750–1925*. New York: Pantheon, 1976.

Haley, Sarah. *No Mercy Here: Gender, Punishment, and the Making of Jim Crow Modernity*. Chapel Hill: University of North Carolina Press, 2016.

Hall, Stuart. "Race, Articulation, and Societies Structured in Dominance." In *Sociological Theories: Race and Colonialism*, 305–45. Paris: UNESCO, 1980.

Hall, Stuart, Chas Critcher, Tony Jefferson, John Clarke, and Brian Roberts. *Policing the Crisis: Mugging, the State, and Law and Order*. London: Macmillan, 1978.

Hanley, Robert. "Baby M's Mother Wins Broad Visiting Rights." *New York Times*, April 7, 1988.

———. "Bonding Is Described at Baby M Hearing." *New York Times*, February 28, 1987.

———. "Court Restores Baby M Visits by Whitehead." *New York Times*, April 11, 1987.

———. "Father of Baby M Granted Custody; Contract Upheld; Surrogacy Is Legal." *New York Times*, April 1, 1987.

———. "Father of Baby M Thought Mother Had Been Screened." *New York Times*, January 14, 1987.

———. "Reporter's Notebook: Grief over Baby M." *New York Times*, January 12, 1987.

———. "Testimony Ends at Baby M Hearing." *New York Times*, March 10, 1987.

———. "Wife in Baby M Dispute Recalls Tearful Appeal." *New York Times*, January 7, 1987.

Haran, Joan, Jenny Kitzinger, Maureen McNeil, and Kate O'Riordan, eds. *Human Cloning in the Media: From Science Fiction to Science Practice*. New York: Routledge, 2008.

Harkins, Gillian. *Everybody's Family Romance: Reading Incest in Neoliberal America*. Minneapolis: University of Minnesota Press, 2009.

Harris, Cheryl I. "Whiteness as Property." *Harvard Law Review* 106.8 (1994): 1709–91.

Harris, M. A., Bill Cosby, and Toni Morrison, eds. *The Black Book*. New York: Random House, 1974.

Harrison, Laura. *Brown Bodies, White Babies: The Politics of Cross-Racial Surrogacy*. New York: New York University Press, 2016.

Hartman, Saidiya. "The Belly of the World: A Note on Black Women's Labors." *Souls* 18.1 (2016): 166–73.

———. *Lose Your Mother: A Journey along the Atlantic Slave Route*. New York: Farrar, Straus and Giroux, 2007.

———. *Scenes of Subjection: Terror, Slavery, and Self-Making in Nineteenth-Century America*. New York: Oxford University Press, 1997.

———. "Venus in Two Acts." *Small Axe* 12.2 (2008): 1–14.

Hartmann, Heidi, and Lydia Sargent, eds. *The Unhappy Marriage of Marxism and Feminism: A Debate on Class and Patriarchy*. London: Pluto Press, 1981.

Hartouni, Valerie. "Breached Birth: Reflections on Race, Gender, and Reproductive Discourse in the 1980s." *Configurations* 2.1 (1994): 73–88.

———. "Containing Women: Reproductive Discourse in the 1980s." In *Technoculture*, edited by Constance Penley and Andrew Ross, 27–58. Minneapolis: University of Minnesota Press, 1991.

———. "Reproductive Technologies and the Negotiation of Public Meanings: The Case of Baby M." In *Provoking Agents: Gender and Agency in Theory and Practice*, edited by Judith Kegan Gardiner, 115–32. Urbana: University of Illinois Press, 1995.

Harvey, David. *A Brief History of Neoliberalism*. New York: Oxford University Press, 2005.

Haworth, Abigail. "Surrogate Mothers: Womb for Rent." *Marie Claire*, July 29, 2007.

Helmreich, Stefan. "Species of Biocapital." *Science as Culture* 17.4 (2008): 463–78.

Henderson, Mae G. "The Stories of O(Dessa): Stories of Complicity and Resistance." In *Female Subjects in Black and White: Race, Psychoanalysis, Feminism*, edited by Elizabeth Abel, Barbara Christian, and Helene Moglen, 285–304. Berkeley: University of California Press, 1997.

————. "Toni Morrison's *Beloved*: Re-membering the Body as Historical Text." In *Comparative American Identities: Race, Sex, and Nationality in the Modern Text*, edited by Hortense J. Spillers, 62–86. New York: Routledge, 1991.

Henig, Robin Marantz. "In Vitro Revelation." *New York Times*, October 5, 2010.

Hine, Darlene C. "Female Slave Resistance: The Economics of Sex." *Western Journal of Black Studies* 3.2 (1979): 123–27.

————. "Foreword: Gendered Resistance Now." In *Gendered Resistance: Women, Slavery, and the Legacy of Margaret Garner*, edited by Mary E. Frederickson and Delores M. Walters, ix–x. Urbana: University of Illinois Press, 2013.

————. *Hine Sight: Black Women and the Reconstruction of American History*. Bloomington: Indiana University Press, 1994.

Hoang, Kimberly Kay, and Rhacel Salazar Parreñas, eds. *Human Trafficking Reconsidered: Rethinking the Problem, Envisioning New Solutions*. New York: Debate Education Association, 2014.

Hochschild, Arlie Russell. *The Outsourced Self: Intimate Life in Market Times*. New York: Metropolitan Books, 2012.

Holloway, Karla F. C. "*Beloved*: A Spiritual." *Callaloo* 13.3 (1990): 516–25.

————. *Private Bodies, Public Texts: Race, Gender, and a Cultural Bioethics*. Durham: Duke University Press, 2011.

Holmes, Kristine. "'This Is Flesh I'm Talking about Here': Embodiment in Toni Morrison's *Beloved* and Sherley Anne Williams' *Dessa Rose*." *LIT* 6.1–2 (1995): 133–48.

Hong, Grace Kyungwon. *Death beyond Disavowal: The Impossible Politics of Difference*. Minneapolis: University of Minnesota Press, 2015.

————. *The Ruptures of American Capital: Women of Color Feminism and the Culture of Immigrant Labor*. Minneapolis: University of Minnesota Press, 2006.

Hopkins, Pauline. *Hagar's Daughter: A Story of Southern Caste Prejudice*. 1902. In *The Magazine Novels of Pauline Hopkins*, 1–284. New York: Oxford University Press, 1988.

Hopkinson, Nalo. *The Salt Roads*. New York: Warner Books, 2003.

Howell, Peter. "The Hunt for the Elusive Judy Bridgewater." *The Star*, September 30, 2010.

Hua, Linh U. "Reproducing Time, Reproducing History: Love and Black Feminist Sentimentality in Octavia Butler's *Kindred*." *African American Review* 44.3 (2011): 391–407.

Hunter, Tera W. *To 'Joy My Freedom: Southern Black Women's Lives and Labors after the Civil War*. Cambridge, MA: Harvard University Press, 1997.

Huxley, Aldous. *Brave New World*. 1932. New York: Harper Perennial, 1946.

Ikemoto, Lisa C. "Destabilizing Thoughts on Surrogacy Legislation." *University of San Francisco Law Review* 28.3 (1994): 633–45.

————. "Eggs as Capital: Human Egg Procurement in the Fertility Industry and the Stem Cell Research Enterprise." *Signs* 34.4 (2009): 763–81.

Imarisha, Walidah, and adrienne maree brown, eds. *Octavia's Brood: Science Fiction Stories from Social Justice Movements*. New York: AK Press, 2015.

Ishiguro, Kazuo. *Never Let Me Go*. New York: Knopf, 2005.

Iyasẹre, Solomon O., and Marla W. Iyasẹre, eds. *Understanding Toni Morrison's Beloved and Sula: Selected Essays and Criticisms of the Works by the Nobel Prize–Winning Author.* Troy, NY: Whitston, 2000.

Jacobson, Heather. *Labor of Love: Gestational Surrogacy and the Work of Making Babies.* New Brunswick, NJ: Rutgers University Press, 2016.

James, Joy. "Profeminism and Gender Elites: W. E. B. Du Bois, Anna Julia Cooper, and Ida B. Wells-Barnett." In *Next to the Color Line: Gender, Sexuality, and W. E. B. Du Bois,* edited by Susan Gillman and Alys Eve Weinbaum, 69–95. Minneapolis: University of Minnesota Press, 2007.

James, P. D. *Children of Men.* New York: Knopf, 1992.

Jameson, Fredric. *Archaeologies of the Future: The Desire Called Utopia and Other Science Fictions.* New York: Verso, 2005.

———. "Reification and Utopia in Mass Culture." *Social Text* 1.1 (1979): 130–48.

Jerng, Mark. "Giving Form to Life: Cloning and Narrative Expectations of the Human." *Partial Answers* 6.2 (2008): 369–93.

Jesser, Nancy. "Blood, Genes and Gender in Octavia Butler's *Kindred* and *Dawn.*" *Extrapolation* 43.1 (2002): 36–61.

Jeunet, Jean-Pierre, director. *Alien Resurrection.* DVD. Los Angeles: 20th Century Fox, 1997.

Johnson, Charles. *Middle Passage.* New York: Atheneum, 1990.

———. *Oxherding Tale.* Bloomington: Indiana University Press, 1982.

Johnson, Ian, and Cao Li. "China Experiences Booming Underground Market in Child Surrogacy." *New York Times,* August 3, 2014.

Johnson, Walter. "On Agency." *Journal of Social History* 37.1 (2003): 113–24.

———. *River of Dark Dreams: Slavery and Empire in the Cotton Kingdom.* Cambridge, MA: Harvard University Press, 2013.

———. *Soul by Soul: Life inside the Antebellum Slave Market.* Cambridge, MA: Harvard University Press, 1999.

Johnston, Mary. *Hagar.* Boston: Houghton Mifflin, 1913.

Jones, Ashby, "Putting a Price on a Human Egg." *Wall Street Journal,* July 27, 2015, Eastern edition.

Jones, Duncan, director. *Moon.* DVD. New York: Sony Pictures Classics, 2009.

Jones, Gayl. *Corregidora.* New York: Random House, 1975.

Jones, Jacqueline. *Labor of Love, Labor of Sorrow: Black Women, Work, and the Family from Slavery to the Present.* New York: Basic Books, 1985.

———. *A Social History of the Laboring Classes from Colonial Times to the Present.* Malden, MA: Blackwell, 1999.

Joshel, Sandra. "Ancient Roman Slavery and American History." Lecture. University of Washington, Seattle, October 23, 2013.

Jung, Moon-Ho. "Black Reconstruction and Empire." *South Atlantic Quarterly* 112.3 (2013): 465–71.

———. *Coolies and Cane: Race, Labor, and Sugar in the Age of Emancipation.* Baltimore: Johns Hopkins University Press, 2006.

Kahn, Susan Martha. *Reproducing Jews: A Cultural Account of Assisted Conception in Israel.* Durham: Duke University Press, 2000.

Kandel, Randy Frances. "Which Came First: The Mother or the Egg? A Kinship Solution to Gestational Surrogacy." *Rutgers Law Review* 47.1 (1994): 165–239.

Kaplan, Ann E. "The Politics of Surrogacy Narratives: Notes toward a Research Project." In *Feminist Nightmares: Women at Odds: Feminism and the Problem of Sisterhood,* edited by Susan Ostrov Weisser and Jennifer Fleischner, 189–205. New York: New York University Press, 1994.

Kapsalis, Terri. "Mastering the Female Pelvis: Race and the Tools of Reproduction." In *Skin Deep, Spirit Strong: The Black Female Body,* edited by Kimberly Wallace-Sanders, 263–300. Ann Arbor: University of Michigan Press, 2002.

Kara, Siddharth. *Sex Trafficking: Inside the Business of Modern Slavery.* New York: Columbia University Press, 2009.

Kasindorf, Martin. "And Baby Makes Four: *Johnson v. Calvert* Illustrates Just about Everything That Can Go Wrong in Surrogate Births." *Los Angeles Times Magazine,* January 20, 1991, 10–34.

Katz Rothman, Barbara. *Recreating Motherhood: Ideology and Technology in Patriarchal Society.* New York: Norton, 1989.

———. "Reproductive Technology and the Commodification of Life." In *Embryos, Ethics, and Women's Rights: Exploring the New Reproductive Technologies,* edited by Elaine Hoffman Baruch, Amadeo F. D'Adamo, and Joni Seager, 95–100. New York: Harrington Park, 1988.

———. "Surrogacy: A Question of Values." In *Beyond Baby M: Ethical Issues in New Reproductive Technologies,* edited by Dianne M. Bartels, Reinhard Priester, Dorothy E. Vawter, and Arthur L. Caplan, 235–42. Clifton, NJ: Humana, 1990.

Keizer, Arlene R. *Black Subjects: Identity Formation in the Contemporary Narrative of Slavery.* Ithaca, NY: Cornell University Press, 2004.

Keller, Catherine. "Delores Williams: Survival, Surrogacy, Sisterhood, Spirit." *Union Seminary Quarterly Review* 58.3–4 (2004): 84–94.

Kelley, Robin D. G. *Freedom Dreams: The Black Radical Imagination.* Boston: Beacon, 2002.

Ketchum, Sara Ann. "Selling Babies and Selling Bodies." *Hypatia* 4.3 (1989): 116–27.

Kimbrell, Andrew. *The Human Body Shop: The Engineering and Marketing of Life.* San Francisco: HarperCollins, 1994.

Kolata, Gina. *Clone: The Road to Dolly and the Path Ahead.* New York: William Morrow, 1998.

Kolbert, Elizabeth. "A Dispute on Baby M." *New York Times,* October 6, 1986.

Korte, Barbara. "Envisioning a Black Tomorrow? Black Mother Figures and the Issue of Representation in *28 Days Later* (2003) and *Children of Men* (2006)." In *Multi-Ethnic Britain 2000+: New Perspectives in Literature, Film and the Arts,* edited by Lars Eckstein, Barbara Korte, Eva Ulrike Pirker, and Christoph Reinfandt, 315–25. Amsterdam: Rodopi, 2008.

Krauthamer, Barbara. "A Particular Kind of Freedom: Black Women, Slavery, Kinship, and Freedom in the American Southeast." In *Women and Slavery: The Modern*

Atlantic. Vol. 2 of *Women and Slavery*, edited by Gwyn Campbell, Suzanne Miers, and Joseph C. Miller, 100–127. Athens: Ohio University Press, 2007.

Krumholz, Linda. "The Ghosts of Slavery: Historical Recovery in Toni Morrison's *Beloved*." *African American Review* 26.3 (1992): 395–408.

Lacey, Lauren J. "Octavia E. Butler on Coping with Power in *Parable of the Sower*, *Parable of the Talents*, and *Fledgling*." *Critique* 49.4 (2008): 379–94.

Landes, Elizabeth M., and Richard A. Posner. "The Economics of the Baby Shortage." *Journal of Legal Studies* 7.2 (1978): 323–48.

LaRoche, Cheryl Janifer. "Coerced but Not Subdued: The Gendered Resistance of Women Escaping Slavery." In *Gendered Resistance: Women, Slavery, and the Legacy of Margaret Garner*, edited by Mary E. Frederickson and Delores M. Walters, 49–76. Urbana: University of Illinois Press, 2013.

Latimer, Heather. "Bio-Reproductive Futurism: Bare Life and the Pregnant Refugee in Alfonso Cuarón's *Children of Men*." *Social Text* 29.3 (2011): 51–72.

Laurence, Margaret. *The Stone Angel*. New York: Alfred Knopf, 1964.

Lavender, Isiah. *Race in American Science Fiction*. Bloomington: Indiana University Press, 2011.

Lawson, Erica. "Black Women's Mothering in a Historical and Contemporary Perspective." In *Mother Outlaws: Theories and Practices of Empowered Mothering*, edited by Andrea O'Reilly, 193–202. Toronto: Women's Press, 2004.

Lee, Rachel C. *The Exquisite Corpse of Asian America: Biopolitics, Biosociality, and Posthuman Ecologies*. New York: New York University Press, 2014.

———. "Missing Peace in Toni Morrison's *Sula* and *Beloved*." In *Understanding Toni Morrison's Beloved and Sula: Selected Essays and Criticisms of the Works by the Nobel Prize–Winning Author*, edited by Solomon Ogbede Iyasẹre and Marla W. Iyasẹre. 277–96. Troy, NY: Whitston, 2000.

Lemert, Charles. "The Race of Time: Du Bois and Reconstruction." *Boundary 2* 27.3 (2000): 215–48.

Lemke, Thomas. *Biopolitics: An Advanced Introduction*. New York: New York University Press, 2011.

Levecq, Christine. "Power and Repetition: Philosophies of (Literary) History in Octavia E. Butler's *Kindred*." *Contemporary Literature* 41.3 (2000): 525–53.

Levin, Ira. *Boys from Brazil*. New York: Random House, 1976.

Lewin, Tamar. "Coming to U.S. for Baby, and Womb to Carry It." *New York Times*, July 6, 2014.

Lewis, David Levering. Introduction to *Black Reconstruction in America, 1860–1880*, by W. E. B. Du Bois, vii–xvii. New York: Free Press, 1998.

———. *W. E. B. Du Bois: The Fight for Equality and the American Century, 1919–1963*. New York: Henry Holt, 2000.

Li, Stephanie. "Love and the Trauma of Resistance in Gayl Jones's *Corregidora*." *Callaloo* 29.1 (2006): 131–50.

Lillvis, Kristen. "Mama's Baby, Papa's Slavery? The Problem and Promise of Mothering in Octavia E. Butler's 'Bloodchild.'" MELUS 39.4 (2014): 7–22.

Love, Heather. "Close but Not Deep: Literary Ethics and the Descriptive Turn." *New Literary History* 41.2 (2010): 371–91.

Lowe, Lisa. *The Intimacies of Four Continents.* Durham: Duke University Press, 2015.

Lubiano, Wahneema. "Black Ladies, Welfare Queens, and State Minstrels: Ideological War by Narrative Means." In *Race-ing Justice, En-gendering Power: Essays on Anita Hill, Clarence Thomas, and the Construction of Social Reality,* edited by Toni Morrison, 323–63. New York: Pantheon, 1992.

Lukács, Georg. *History and Class Consciousness: Studies in Marxist Dialectics.* Cambridge, MA: MIT Press, 1971.

Mamo, Laura. *Queering Reproduction: Achieving Pregnancy in the Age of Technoscience.* Durham: Duke University Press, 2007.

Manson, Graeme, and John Fawcett. *Orphan Black: Season 1–Season 4.* DVD. New York: BBC America Home Entertainment, 2016.

Markens, Susan. "Interrogating Narratives about the Global Surrogacy Market." *S&F Online* 9.1–9.2 (2010–2011). http://sfonline.barnard.edu/reprotech/markens_01.htm.

———. *Surrogate Motherhood and the Politics of Reproduction.* Berkeley: University of California Press, 2007.

Martin, Emily. *The Woman in the Body: A Cultural Analysis of Reproduction.* Boston: Beacon, 1987.

Marx, Karl. *Capital: A Critique of Political Economy.* Vol. 1. 1867. Translated by Ben Fowkes. New York: Vintage, 1977.

———. Preface to *A Contribution to the Critique of Political Economy.* 1859. In *Early Writings,* translated by Rodney Livingstone and Gregor Benton, edited by Quintin Hoare, 424–28. New York: Vintage, 1974.

Marx, Karl, and Friedrich Engels. *The Communist Manifesto.* 1848. Translated by Samuel Moore. New York: Oxford University Press, 1992.

Mbembe, Achille. "Necropolitics." Translated by Libby Meintjes. *Public Culture* 15.1 (2003): 11–40.

McDaniels-Wilson, Cathy. "The Psychological Aftereffects of Racialized Sexual Violence." In *Gendered Resistance: Women, Slavery, and the Legacy of Margaret Garner,* edited by Mary E. Frederickson and Delores M. Walters, 191–205. Urbana: University of Illinois Press, 2013.

McDowell, Deborah E. *The Changing Same: Black Women's Literature, Criticism, and Theory.* Bloomington: Indiana University Press, 1995.

McElroy, Ruth. "Whose Body, Whose Nation? Surrogate Motherhood and Its Representation." *European Journal of Cultural Studies* 5.3 (2002): 325–42.

McGuire, Danielle L. *At the Dark End of the Street: Black Women, Rape, and Resistance—A New History of the Civil Rights Movement from Rosa Parks to the Rise of Black Power.* New York: Knopf, 2010.

McKittrick, Katherine. *Demonic Grounds: Black Women and the Cartographies of Struggle.* Minneapolis: University of Minnesota Press, 2006.

McMillan, Uri. *Embodied Avatars: Genealogies of Black Feminist Art and Performance*. New York: New York University Press, 2015.

McNeil, Genna Rae. "'Joanne Is You and Joanne Is Me': A Consideration of African American Women and the 'Free Joan Little' Movement, 1974–75." In *Sisters in the Struggle: African American Women in the Civil Rights–Black Power Movement*, edited by Bettye Collier-Thomas and V. P. Franklin, 259–79. New York: New York University Press, 2001.

McWilliams, Carey. *Brothers under the Skin: African Americans and Other Minorities*. Boston: Little, Brown, 1943.

McWhorter, Ladelle. "Sex, Race, and Biopower: A Foucauldian Genealogy." *Hypatia* 19.3 (2004): 38–62.

Mehta, Uday Singh. *Liberalism and Empire: A Study in Nineteenth-Century British Liberal Thought*. Chicago: University of Chicago Press, 1999.

Melamed, Jodi. "Racial Capitalism." *Critical Ethnic Studies* 1.1 (2015): 76–85.

———. *Represent and Destroy: Rationalizing Violence in the New Racial Capitalism*. Minneapolis: University of Minnesota Press, 2011.

Menand, Louis. "Something about Kathy." *New Yorker* 81.6 (2005): 78–79.

Messud, Claire. "Love's Body." *The Nation*, May 16, 2005, 28.

Michaels, Meredith W. "Other Mothers: Toward an Ethic of Postmaternal Practice." *Hypatia* 11.2 (1996): 49–70.

Mies, Maria. *Patriarchy and Accumulation on a World Scale: Women in the International Division of Labour*. London: Zed Books, 1986.

———. "Preface to the Critique Influence Change Edition." In *Patriarchy and Accumulation on a World Scale: Women in the International Division of Labor*, xiii–xxiv. London: Zed Books, 2014.

Miletic, Philip. "Octavia E. Butler's Response to Black Arts/Black Power Literature and Rhetoric in *Kindred*." *African American Review* 49.3 (2016): 261–75.

Mitchell, Angelyn. *The Freedom to Remember: Narrative, Slavery, and Gender in Contemporary Black Women's Fiction*. New Brunswick, NJ: Rutgers University Press, 2002.

Mitchell, David. *Cloud Atlas*. New York: Random House, 2004.

Mitter, Swasti. *Common Fate, Common Bond: Women in the Global Economy*. London: Pluto Press, 1986.

Moglen, Helene. "Redeeming History: Toni Morrison's *Beloved*." In *Female Subjects in Black and White: Race, Psychoanalysis, Feminism*, edited by Elizabeth Abel, Barbara Christian, and Helene Moglen, 201–20. Berkeley: University of California Press, 1997.

Mohapatra, Seema. "Achieving Reproductive Justice in the International Surrogacy Market." *Annals of Health Law* 21 (2012): 191–200.

———. "Stateless Babies and Adoption Scams: A Bioethical Analysis of International Commercial Surrogacy." *Berkeley Journal of International Law* 30.2 (2012): 412–50.

Moitt, Bernard. *Women and Slavery in the French Antilles, 1635–1848*. Bloomington: Indiana University Press, 2001.

Monheit, Jane. "Never Let Me Go," written by Luther Dixon. *Never Let Me Go: Original Motion Picture Soundtrack*, by Rachel Portman. Varèse Sarabande, compact disc. Released September 14, 2010.

Morgan, Jennifer L. "Archives and Histories of Racial Capitalism: An Afterword." *Social Text* 33.4 (2015): 153–61.

———. *Laboring Women: Reproduction and Gender in New World Slavery*. Philadelphia: University of Pennsylvania Press, 2004.

———. "*Partus Sequitur Ventrem*: Law, Race, and Reproduction in Colonial Slavery." *Small Axe* 55 22.1 (March 2018): 1–17.

Morgan, Kenneth. "Slave Women and Reproduction in Jamaica, ca. 1176–1834." In *Women and Slavery: The Modern Atlantic*. Vol. 2 of *Women and Slavery*, edited by Gwyn Campbell, Suzanne Miers, and Joseph C. Miller, 27–53. Athens: Ohio University Press, 2007.

Morgenstern, Naomi. "Mother's Milk and Sister's Blood: Trauma and the Neoslave Narrative." *Differences* 8.2 (1996): 101–26.

Morrison, Toni. "The Art of Fiction: 134." Interview by Elissa Schappell and Claudia Brodsky Lacour. *Paris Review* 128 (1993): 82–125.

———. "Author Toni Morrison Discusses Her Latest Novel *Beloved*." Interview by Gail Caldwell. *Boston Globe*, October 6, 1987. Reprinted in *Conversations with Toni Morrison*, edited by Danielle Kathleen Taylor-Guthrie, 239–45. Jackson: University of Mississippi Press, 1994.

———. *Beloved*. New York: Knopf, 1987.

———. Foreword to *Beloved*, xv–xix. New York: Vintage, 2004.

———. "In the Realm of Responsibility: A Conversation with Toni Morrison." Interview by Marsha Darling. *Women's Review of Books* 5.6 (1988): 5–6.

———. "Intimate Things in Place: A Conversation with Toni Morrison." Interview by Robert B. Stepto. *Massachusetts Review* 18.3 (1977): 473–89.

———. "Living History: A Meeting with Toni Morrison." Interview by Paul Gilroy. In *Small Acts: Thoughts on the Politics of Black Cultures*, edited by Paul Gilroy, 175–82. London: Serpent's Tail, 1993.

———. "Memory, Creation, and Writing." *Thought* 59.235 (1984): 385–90.

———. *A Mercy*. New York: Knopf, 2008.

———. "Nobel Lecture 1993." *World Literature Today* 68.1 (1994): 4–8.

———. *Playing in the Dark: Whiteness and the Literary Imagination*. New York: Vintage, 1992.

———. "Rediscovering Black History: It's Like Growing Up Black One More Time." *New York Times Magazine*, August 11, 1974, 14, 16, 18, 20, 22, 24.

———. "Rootedness: The Ancestor as Foundation." In *Black Women Writers (1950–1980): A Critical Evaluation*, edited by Mari Evans, 339–45. New York: Anchor, 1984.

———. "The Site of Memory." In *Out There: Marginalization and Contemporary Cultures*, edited by Russell Ferguson, 299–305. Cambridge, MA: MIT Press, 1990.

Morrissey, Marietta. *Slave Women in the New World: Gender Stratification in the Caribbean*. Lawrence: University of Kansas Press, 1989.

Moylan, Tom. *Demand the Impossible: Science Fiction and the Utopian Imagination*. New York: Methuen, 1986.

———. *Scraps of the Untainted Sky: Science Fiction, Utopia, Dystopia*. Boulder, CO: Westview Press, 2000.

Moynihan, Daniel Patrick. *The Negro Family: The Case for National Action*. 1965. In *The Moynihan Report and the Politics of Controversy*, edited by Lee Rainwater and William L. Yancey, 47–94. Cambridge, MA: MIT Press, 1967.

Mullen, Harryette. "Runaway Tongue: Resistant Orality in *Uncle Tom's Cabin, Our Nig, Incidents in the Life of a Slave Girl*, and *Beloved*." In *The Culture of Sentiment: Race, Gender, and Sentimentality in Nineteenth-Century America*, edited by Shirley Samuels, 244–64. New York: Oxford University Press, 1992.

Murakawa, Naomi. *First Civil Right: How Liberals Built Prison America*. New York: Oxford University Press, 2014.

Mydans, Seth. "Science and the Courts Take a New Look at Motherhood." *New York Times*, November 4, 1990.

———. "Surrogate Denied Custody of Child: Judge in California Rules for Genetic Parents and Bars Two-Mother Situation." *New York Times*, October 23, 1990.

Nelson, Alondra. *The Social Life of DNA: Race, Reparations, and Reconciliation after the Genome*. Boston: Beacon, 2016.

Nelson, Jennifer. *Women of Color and the Reproductive Rights Movement*. New York: New York University Press, 2003.

Neuhaus, Richard John. "Renting Women, Buying Babies and Class Struggles." *Transaction/Society* 25.3 (1988): 8–10.

"Noel Keane, 58, Lawyer in Surrogate Mother Cases, Is Dead." *New York Times*, January 28, 1997.

Nordstrom, Carolyn. *Global Outlaws: Crime, Money, and Power in the Contemporary World*. Berkeley: University of California Press, 2007.

Nsiah-Jefferson, Laurie. "Reproductive Laws, Women of Color, and Low-Income Women." *Women's Rights Law Reporter* 11.1 (1989): 15–38.

Nussbaum, Martha C., and Cass R. Sunstein. *Clones and Clones: Facts and Fantasies about Human Cloning*. New York: Norton, 1998.

Oliver, Kelly. "Marxism and Surrogacy." *Hypatia* 4.3 (1989): 95–116.

Omi, Michael. "'Slippin' into Darkness': The (Re)Biologization of Race." *Journal of Asian American Studies* 13.3 (2010): 343–58.

O'Neill, Joseph. "Never Let Me Go." *The Atlantic* 295.4 (2005): 123.

Oparah, Julia Chinyere, and Alicia D. Bonaparte. *Birthing Justice: Black Women, Pregnancy, and Childbirth*. Boulder, CO: Paradigm, 2015.

Ortiz, Ana Teresa, and Laura Briggs. "The Culture of Poverty, Crack Babies, and Welfare Cheats: The Making of the 'Healthy White Baby Crisis.'" *Social Text* 21.3 (2003): 39–57.

Ould, David. "Trafficking and International Law." In *The Political Economy of New Slavery*, edited by Christien van den Anker, 55–74. New York: Palgrave Macmillan, 2004.

Painter, Nell Irvin. *Sojourner Truth: A Life, a Symbol*. New York: Norton, 1996.

———. *Soul Murder and Slavery.* Waco, TX: Baylor University Press, 1995.

———. *Southern History across the Color Line.* Chapel Hill: University of North Carolina Press, 2002.

Pande, Amrita. "'At Least I Am Not Sleeping with Anyone': Resisting the Stigma of Commercial Surrogacy in India." *Feminist Studies* 36.2 (2010): 292–312.

———. "Commercial Surrogacy in India: Manufacturing a Perfect Mother Worker." *Signs* 35.4 (2010): 969–92.

———. "'It May Be Her Eggs but It's My Blood': Surrogates and Everyday Forms of Kinship in India." *Qualitative Sociology* 32.4 (2009): 379–97.

———. "Not an 'Angel,' Not a 'Whore': Surrogates as 'Dirty' Workers in India." *Indian Journal of Gender Studies* 16.2 (2009): 141–73.

———. *Wombs in Labor: Transnational Commercial Surrogacy in India.* New York: Columbia University Press, 2014.

"Parental Rights Denied to a Surrogate Mother." *New York Times*, May 22, 1993.

Parham, Marisa. "Saying 'Yes': Textual Trauma in Octavia Butler's *Kindred.*" *Callaloo* 32.4 (2009): 1315–31.

Parreñas, Rhacel Salazar. *The Force of Domesticity: Filipina Migrants and Globalization.* New York: New York University Press, 2008.

———. "The Reproductive Labour of Migrant Workers." *Global Networks* 12.2 (2012): 269–75.

———. *Servants of Globalization: Women, Migration, and Domestic Work.* Stanford: Stanford University Press, 2001.

Pasco, John Carlo, Camille Anderson, and Sayantani Dasgupta. "Visionary Medicine: Speculative Fiction, Racial Justice and Octavia Butler's 'Bloodchild.'" *Medical Humanities* 42.4 (2016): 246–51.

Pateman, Carole. *The Sexual Contract.* Stanford: Stanford University Press, 1988.

Patterson, Mark. "Surrogacy and Slavery: The Problematics of Consent in Baby M, *Romance of Republic*, and *Pudd'nhead Wilson.*" *American Literary History* 8.3 (1996): 448–70.

Patterson, Orlando. *Slavery and Social Death: A Comparative Study.* Cambridge, MA: Harvard University Press, 1982.

Paulin, Diana R. "De-essentializing Interracial Representations: Black and White Border-Crossings in Spike Lee's *Jungle Fever* and Octavia Butler's *Kindred.*" *Cultural Critique* 36 (1997): 165–93.

Perrin, Liese M. "Resisting Reproduction: Reconsidering Slave Contraception in the Old South." *Journal of American Studies* 35.2 (2001): 255–74.

Peterson, Christopher. "Beloved's Claim." *Modern Fiction Studies* 52.3 (2006): 548–69.

Peterson, Iver. "Baby M and Controversy over Fertility." *New York Times*, January 31, 1987.

———. "Baby M, Ethics and the Law." *New York Times*, January 18, 1987.

———. "Baby M Trial Splits Ranks of Feminists." *New York Times*, February 24, 1987.

Pollitt, Katha. "The Strange Case of Baby M." *The Nation*, May 23, 1987, 667–88.

————. "When Is a Mother Not a Mother?" *The Nation*, December 31, 1990, 1, 840, 842–45, 846.

Price, Kimala. "What Is Reproductive Justice? How Women of Color Activists Are Redefining the Pro-Choice Paradigm," *Meridians* 10.2 (2010): 42–65.

"Psychiatrist Testifies in Surrogate Birth Case." *New York Times*, October 11, 1990.

Puchner, Martin. "When We Were Clones." *Raritan* 27.4 (2008): 34–49.

Putnam, Amanda. "Mothering Violence: Ferocious Female Resistance in Toni Morrison's *The Bluest Eye, Sula, Beloved*, and *A Mercy*." *Black Women, Gender and Families* 5.2 (2011): 25–43.

Quirk, Joel. *The Anti-Slavery Project: From the Slave Trade to Human Trafficking*. Philadelphia: University of Pennsylvania Press, 2011.

Radin, Margaret Jane. *Contested Commodities*. Cambridge, MA: Harvard University Press, 1996.

Ragoné, Heléna. "Of Likeness and Difference: How Race Is Being Transfigured by Gestational Surrogacy." In *Ideologies and Technologies of Motherhood: Race, Class, Sexuality, Nationalism*, edited by Heléna Ragoné and France Winddance Twine, 56–75. New York: Routledge, 2000.

————. *Surrogate Motherhood: Conception in the Heart*. Boulder, CO: Westview, 1994.

Randall, Alice. *The Wind Done Gone*. Boston: Houghton Mifflin, 2001.

Reardon, Jenny. *Race to the Finish: Identity and Governance in an Age of Genomics*. Princeton: Princeton University Press, 2005.

Reddy, Chandan. *Freedom with Violence: Race, Sexuality, and the US State*. Durham: Duke University Press, 2011.

Reed, Ishmael. *Flight to Canada*. New York: Random House, 1976.

Reinhardt, Mark. *Who Speaks for Margaret Garner? The True Story That Inspired Toni Morrison's Beloved*. Minneapolis: University of Minnesota Press, 2010.

Rifkin, Jeremy, and Andrew Kimbrell. "Put a Stop to Surrogate Parenting Now." *USA Today*, August 20, 1990.

Robbins, Bruce. "Cruelty Is Bad: Banality and Proximity in *Never Let Me Go*." *Novel* 40.3 (2007): 289–302.

Robbins, Sonia Jaffe. "When Is a Mother Not a Mother? The Baby M Case." *Women and Language* 13.1 (1990): 41–46.

Roberts, Dorothy. *Fatal Invention: How Science, Politics, and Big Business Re-create Race in the Twenty-First Century*. New York: New Press, 2011.

————. *Killing the Black Body: Race, Reproduction, and the Meaning of Liberty*. New York: Pantheon, 1997.

————. "Privatization and Punishment in the Age of Reprogenetics." *Emory Law Journal* 54.3 (2005): 1343–60.

————. "Race, Gender, and Genetic Technologies: A New Reproductive Dystopia." *Signs* 34.4 (2009): 783–804.

Roberts, Elizabeth F. S. "Examining Surrogacy Discourses between Feminine Power and Exploitation." In *Small Wars: The Cultural Politics of Childhood*, edited by Nancy

Scheper-Hughes and Carolyn Sargent, 93–110. Berkeley: University of California Press, 1998.

Robinson, Cedric J. *Black Marxism: The Making of the Black Radical Tradition*. 1983. Chapel Hill: University of North Carolina Press, 2000.

———. "A Critique of W. E. B. Du Bois's Black Reconstruction." *Black Scholar* 8.7 (1977): 44–50.

Rody, Caroline. *The Daughter's Return: African-American and Caribbean Women's Fictions of History*. New York: Oxford University Press, 2001.

———. "Toni Morrison's *Beloved*: History, 'Rememory,' and a 'Clamor for a Kiss.'" In *Understanding Toni Morrison's Beloved and Sula: Selected Essays and Criticisms of the Works by the Nobel Prize–Winning Author*, edited by Solomon Ogbede Iyasẹre and Marla W. Iyasẹre, 83–112. Troy, NY: Whitston, 2000.

Roediger, David R. *The Wages of Whiteness: Race and the Making of the American Working Class*. New York: Verso, 1991.

Romanek, Mark, director. *Never Let Me Go*. DVD. Century City, CA: Fox Searchlight Pictures, 2010.

Romney, Jonathan. "Green and Pleasant Land." *Film Comment* 43.1 (2007): 32–35.

Rose, Mark. "Mothers and Authors: *Johnson v. Calvert* and the New Children of Our Imaginations." *Critical Inquiry* 22.4 (1996): 613–33.

Rose, Nikolas S. *Powers of Freedom: Reframing Political Thought*. New York: Cambridge University Press, 1999.

Ross, Loretta J. "The Color of Choice: White Supremacy and Reproductive Justice." In *Color of Violence: The Incite! Anthology*, edited by INCITE! Women of Color against Violence, 53–65. Cambridge, MA: South End Press, 2006.

———. "Re-enslaving African American Women." *On the Issues*, November 24, 2008. https://www.trustblackwomen.org/2011-05-10-03-28-12/publications-a-articles /african-americans-and-abortion-articles/27-re-enslaving-african-american -women.

Roth, Sarah N. "'The Blade Was in My Own Breast': Slave Infanticide in 1850s Fiction." *American Nineteenth Century History* 8.2 (2007): 169–85.

Rudrappa, Sharmila. *Discounted Life: The Price of Global Surrogacy in India*. New York: New York University Press, 2015.

Rushdy, Ashraf H. A. *Neo-Slave Narratives: Studies in the Social Logic of a Literary Form*. New York: Oxford University Press, 1999.

———. *Remembering Generations: Race and Family in Contemporary African American Fiction*. Chapel Hill: University of North Carolina Press, 2001.

Rutherford, Charlotte. "Reproductive Freedoms and African American Women." *Yale Journal of Law and Feminism* 4 (1992): 255–90.

Sachs, Andrea. "And Baby Makes Four." *Time*, August 27, 1990, 53.

Sama—Resource Group for Women and Health. *Birthing a Market: A Study on Commercial Surrogacy*. New Delhi: Sama, 2012.

Sanders, Cheryl J. "Surrogate Motherhood and Reproductive Technologies: An African American Perspective." *Creighton Law Review* 25.5 (1992): 1707–23.

Sanger, Carol. "(Baby) M Is for the Many Things: Why I Start with Baby M." *Saint Louis University Law Journal* 44.4 (2000): 1443–64.

———. "Developing Markets in Baby-Making: In the Matter of Baby M." *Harvard Journal of Law and Gender* 30.1 (2007): 67–97.

Sargent, Lydia, ed. *Women and Revolution: A Discussion of the Unhappy Marriage of Marxism and Feminism*. Boston: South End Press, 1981.

Saung, Jey. "Reproducing the Nation-State: Surrogate 'Gaybies,' Queer Family, and Biopolitics of Colonialism." Paper presented at the Biopower and Biopolitics Graduate Seminar, Seattle, Washington, March 3, 2016.

Sayers, Valerie. "Spare Parts." *Commonweal* 132.13 (2005): 27.

Schaffner, Franklin J., director. *Boys from Brazil*. DVD. Los Angeles: 20th Century Fox, 1978.

Scheper-Hughes, Nancy. "Commodity Fetishism in Organs Trafficking." *Body & Society* 7.2–3 (2001): 31–62.

———. "Organs Trafficking: The Real, the Unreal and the Uncanny." *Annals of Transplantation* 11.3 (2006): 16–30.

———. "Parts Unknown: Undercover Ethnography of the Organs-Trafficking Underworld." *Ethnography* 5.1 (2004): 29–73.

———. "Rotten Trade: Millennial Capitalism, Human Values and Global Justice in Organs Trafficking." *Journal of Human Rights* 2.2 (2003): 197–226.

———. "The Tyranny of the Gift: Sacrificial Violence in Living Donor Transplants." *American Journal of Transplantation* 7.3 (2007): 507–11.

Schiff, Sarah Eden. "Recovering (from) the Double: Fiction as Historical Revision in Octavia E. Butler's Kindred." *Arizona Quarterly* 65.1 (2009): 107–36.

Schwartz, Marie Jenkins. *Birthing a Slave: Motherhood and Medicine in the Antebellum South*. Cambridge, MA: Harvard University Press, 2006.

Scott, Darieck. *Extravagant Abjection: Blackness, Power, and Sexuality in the African American Literary Imagination*. New York: New York University Press, 2010.

Sedgwick, Eve Kosofsky. "Paranoid Reading and Reparative Reading, or You're So Paranoid You Probably Think This Essay Is about You." In *Touching Feeling: Affect, Pedagogy, Performativity*, 123–51. Durham: Duke University Press, 2003.

Sekora, John. "Black Message/White Envelope: Genre, Authenticity, and Authority in the Antebellum Slave Narrative." *Callaloo* 10.3 (1987): 482–515.

Sexton, Jared. "People-of-Color-Blindness: Notes on the Afterlife of Slavery." *Social Text* 28.2 (2010): 31–56.

Shalev, Carmel. *Birth Power: The Case for Surrogacy*. New Haven: Yale University Press, 1989.

Sharp, Lesley A. "The Commodification of the Body and Its Parts." *Annual Review of Anthropology* 29 (2000): 287–328.

Sharpe, Christina. "In the Wake." *Black Scholar* 44.2 (2014): 59–69.

———. *In the Wake: On Blackness and Being*. Durham: Duke University Press, 2016.

———. *Monstrous Intimacies: The Making of Post-Slavery Subjects*. Durham: Duke University Press, 2010.

Sharpe, Jenny. *Ghosts of Slavery: A Literary Archaeology of Black Women's Lives.* Minneapolis: University of Minnesota Press, 2003.

Shaw, Stephanie J. "Mothering under Slavery in the Antebellum South." In *Mothering: Ideology, Experience, and Agency,* edited by Evelyn Nakano Glenn, Grace Chang, and Linda Rennie Forcey, 237–58. New York: Routledge, 1994.

Shipp, E. R. "Parental Rights Law: New Jersey Supreme Court Will Examine If Standard Rules Affect Baby M Case." *New York Times,* April 8, 1987.

Shon, Sue. "Making Sense: Race and Modern Vision." PhD diss., University of Washington, 2015.

Silliman, Jael, Marlene Gerber Fried, Loretta Ross, and Elena Gutiérrez, eds. *Undivided Rights: Women of Color Organize for Reproductive Justice.* Cambridge, MA: South End Press, 2004.

Smallwood, Stephanie E. "Commodified Freedom: Interrogating the Limits of Anti-Slavery Ideology in the Early Republic." *Journal of the Early Republic* 24.2 (2004): 289–98.

———. *Saltwater Slavery: A Middle Passage from Africa to American Diaspora.* Cambridge, MA: Harvard University Press, 2007.

Smith, Stephanie A. "Octavia Butler: A Retrospective." *Feminist Studies* 33.2 (2007): 385–93.

Smith, Valerie. *Not Just Race, Not Just Gender: Black Feminist Readings.* New York: Routledge, 1998.

———. *Self-Discovery and Authority in Afro-American Narrative.* Cambridge, MA: Harvard University Press, 1987.

———. *Toni Morrison: Writing the Moral Imagination.* Chichester, UK: Wiley-Blackwell, 2012.

Spar, Debora. *The Baby Business: How Money, Science, and Politics Drive the Commerce of Conception.* Boston: Harvard Business School, 2006.

Spartaco: Schiavi e Padrona a Roma. Multimedia exhibit. Museo dell'Ara Pacis, Rome. March 31–September 17, 2017.

Spaulding, Timothy. *Re-forming the Past: History, the Fantastic, and the Postmodern Slave Narrative.* Columbus: Ohio State University Press, 2005.

Spillers, Hortense J. *Black, White, and in Color: Essays on American Literature and Culture.* Chicago: University of Chicago Press, 2003.

———. "Mama's Baby, Papa's Maybe: An American Grammar Book." *Diacritics* 17.2 (1987): 65–81.

Spivack, Carla. "The Law of Surrogate Motherhood in the United States." *American Journal of Comparative Law* 58 (2010): 97–114.

Spivak, Gayatri. "Diasporas Old and New: Women in the Transnational World." *Textual Practice* 10.2 (1996): 245–69.

———. "In a Word: An Interview." Interview by Ellen Rooney. *Differences* 1.2 (1989): 124–56.

———. *Outside in the Teaching Machine.* New York: Routledge, 1993.

Spottiswoode, Roger, director. *The 6th Day.* DVD. Los Angeles: Columbia Pictures, 2000.

Springer, Kimberly. *Living for the Revolution: Black Feminist Organizations 1968–1980.* Durham: Duke University Press, 2005.

————, ed. *Still Climbing, Still Lifting: African American Women's Contemporary Activism.* New York: New York University Press, 1999.

Stanley, Amy Dru. *From Bondage to Contract: Wage Labor, Marriage, and the Market in the Age of Slave Emancipation.* New York: Cambridge University Press, 1998.

Steinberg, Marc. "Inverting History in Octavia Butler's Postmodern Slave Narrative." *African American Review* 38.3 (2004): 467–76.

Stetson, Erlene. "Studying Slavery: Some Literary and Pedagogical Considerations on the Black Female Slave." In *All the Women Are White, All the Blacks Are Men, but Some of Us Are Brave: Black Women's Studies,* edited by Gloria T. Hull, Patricia Bell Scott, and Barbara Smith, 62–84. Old Westbury, CT: Feminist Press, 1982.

Stone, Lorraine. "Neoslavery—'Surrogate' Motherhood Contracts v. the Thirteenth Amendment." *Law & Inequality: A Journal of Theory and Practice* 6.2–3 (1988): 63–73.

Stowe, Harriet Beecher. *Uncle Tom's Cabin.* 1852. Edited by Henry Louis Gates Jr. and Hollis Robbins. New York: Norton, 2007.

Strathern, Marilyn. "Potential Property: Intellectual Rights and Property in Persons." *Social Anthropology* 4.1 (1996): 17–32.

Stumpf, Andrea E. "Redefining Mother: A Legal Matrix for New Reproductive Technologies." *Yale Law Journal* 96.1 (1986): 187–208.

Styron, William. *The Confessions of Nat Turner.* New York: Random House, 1967.

Sunder Rajan, Kaushik. *Biocapital: The Constitution of Postgenomic Life.* Durham: Duke University Press, 2006.

————, ed. *Lively Capital: Biotechnologies, Ethics, and Governance in Global Markets.* Durham: Duke University Press, 2012.

"Surrogate Is Denied Custody." *New York Times,* September 22, 1990.

"Surrogate Mother Sues for Baby's Custody." *New York Times,* August 15, 1990.

Suvin, Darko. *Metamorphoses of Science Fiction: On the Poetics and History of a Literary Genre.* New Haven: Yale University Press, 1979.

Tadiar, Neferti Xina M. *Things Fall Away: Philippine Historical Experience and the Makings of Globalization.* Durham: Duke University Press, 2009.

Tate, Claudia. *Domestic Allegories of Political Desire: The Black Heroine's Text at the Turn of the Century.* New York: Oxford University Press, 1992.

Teman, Elly. *Birthing a Mother: The Surrogate Body and the Pregnant Self.* Berkeley: University of California Press, 2010.

Thaler, Ingrid. *Black Atlantic Speculative Fictions: Octavia Butler, Jewelle Gomez, and Nalo Hopkinson.* New York: Routledge, 2010.

Thibodeau, Amanda. "Alien Bodies and a Queer Future: Sexual Revision in Octavia Butler's 'Bloodchild' and James Tiptree, Jr.'s 'With Delicate Mad Hands.'" *Science Fiction Studies* 39.2 (2012): 262–82.

Thompson, Carlyle Van. "Moving Past the Present: Racialized Sexual Violence and Miscegenous Consumption in Octavia Butler's *Kindred*." In *Eating the Black Body: Miscegenation as Sexual Consumption in African American Literature and Culture*, 107–44. New York: Peter Lang, 2006.

Thompson, Charis. *Making Parents: The Ontological Choreography of Reproductive Technologies*. Cambridge, MA: MIT Press, 2005.

———. "Skin Tone and the Persistence of Biological Race in Egg Donation for Assisted Reproduction." In *Shades of Difference: Why Skin Color Matters*, edited by Evelyn Nakano Glenn, 131–47. Stanford: Stanford University Press, 2009.

Thuma, Emily. "Lessons in Self-Defense: Gender Violence, Racial Criminalization, and Anticarceral Feminism." *Women's Studies Quarterly* 43.3–4 (2015): 52–71.

———. *All Our Trials: Prisons, Policing, and the Feminist Fight to End Violence*. Chicago: University of Illinois Press, 2019.

Tifft, Susan. "It's All in the (Parental) Genes." *Time*, November 5, 1990, 77.

Tillet, Salamishah. *Sites of Slavery: Citizenship and Racial Democracy in the Post–Civil Rights Imagination*. Durham: Duke University Press, 2012.

Tobin, Elizabeth. "Imagining the Mother's Text: Toni Morrison's *Beloved* and Contemporary Law." *Harvard Women's Law Journal* 16 (1993): 233–73.

Tong, Rosemarie. "Surrogate Motherhood." In *A Companion to Applied Ethics*, edited by R. G. Frey and Christopher Heath Wellman, 369–81. Malden, MA: Blackwell, 2003.

Traverso, Enzo. *The Origins of Nazi Violence*. Translated by Janet Lloyd. New York: New Press, 2003.

"Trends in Maternal Mortality: 1990 to 2015: Estimates by WHO, UNICEF, UNFPA, World Bank Group and the United Nations Population Division." Geneva: WHO Document Production, 2015.

Trible, Phyllis, and Letty M. Russell, eds. *Hagar, Sarah, and Their Children: Jewish, Christian, and Muslim Perspectives*. Louisville, KY: Westminster John Knox, 2006.

Trimble, Sarah. "Maternal Back/grounds in *Children of Men*: Notes toward an Arendtian Biopolitics." *Science Fiction Film and Television* 4.2 (2011): 249–70.

Turner, Sasha. *Contested Bodies: Pregnancy, Childrearing, and Slavery in Jamaica*. Philadelphia: University of Pennsylvania Press, 2017.

Turner, Stephanie S. "'What Actually Is': The Insistence of Genre in Octavia Butler's *Kindred*." FEMSPEC 4.2 (2004): 259–80.

Twine, France Winddance. *Outsourcing the Womb: Race, Class, and Gestational Surrogacy in a Global Market*. New York: Routledge, 2011.

U.S. Embassy and Consulates in India. "Report Birth Abroad: Surrogacy, ART, and IVF." Accessed January 22, 2016. https://in.usembassy.gov/u-s-citizen-services/birth/report-birth-abroad/.

Varsam, Maria. "Concrete Dystopia: Slavery and Its Others." In *Dark Horizons: Science Fiction and the Dystopian Imagination*, edited by Raffaella Baccolini and Tom Moylan, 203–24. New York: Routledge, 2003.

Vora, Kalindi. "Indian Transnational Surrogacy and the Commodification of Vital Energy." *Subjectivity* 28.1 (2009): 266–78.

———. *Life Support: Biocapital and the New History of Outsourced Labor*. Minneapolis: University of Minnesota Press, 2015.

———. "Re-imagining Reproduction: Unsettling Metaphors in the History of Imperial Science and Commercial Surrogacy in India." *Somatechnics* 5.1 (2015): 88–103.

Wachowski, Lana, Tom Tykwer, and Andy Wachowski, directors. *Cloud Atlas*. DVD. Burbank, CA: Warner Bros. Pictures, 2012.

Wacquant, Loïc. "Deadly Symbiosis: When Ghetto and Prison Meet and Merge." *Punishment and Society* 3.1 (2001): 95–134.

Waldby, Catherine, and Melinda Cooper. "The Biopolitics of Reproduction: Post-Fordist Biotechnology and Women's Clinical Labor." *Australian Feminist Studies* 23.55 (2008): 57–73.

Waldby, Catherine, and Robert Mitchell. *Tissue Economies: Blood, Organs, and Cell Lines in Late Capitalism*. Durham: Duke University Press, 2006.

Walker, Alice. *The Color Purple: A Novel*. New York: Harcourt Brace Jovanovich, 1982.

Wall, Cheryl A. "Toni Morrison, Editor and Teacher." In *The Cambridge Companion to Toni Morrison*, edited by Justine Tally, 139–50. New York: Cambridge University Press, 2007.

Wallerstein, Immanuel. *After Liberalism*. New York: New Press, 1995.

Walters, Delores M. "Introduction: Re(dis)covering and Recreating the Cultural Milieu of Margaret Garner." In *Gendered Resistance: Women, Slavery, and the Legacy of Margaret Garner*, edited by Mary E. Frederickson and Delores M. Walters, 1–24. Urbana: University of Illinois Press, 2013.

Warner, Judith. "Outsourced Wombs." *New York Times*, January 3, 2008.

Wasson, Sara. "'A Butcher's Shop Where the Meat Still Moved': Gothic Doubles, Organ Harvesting, and Human Cloning." In *Gothic Science Fiction, 1980–2010*, edited by Sara Wasson and Emily Alder, 73–86. Liverpool, UK: Liverpool University Press, 2011.

Weeks, Kathi. *The Problem with Work: Feminism, Marxism, Antiwork Politics, and Postwork Imaginaries*. Durham: Duke University Press, 2011.

Weems, Renita J. *Just a Sister Away: A Womanist Vision of Women's Relationships in the Bible*. San Diego: LuraMedia, 1988.

Weheliye, Alexander G. *Habeas Viscus: Racializing Assemblages, Biopolitics, and Black Feminist Theories of the Human*. Durham: Duke University Press, 2014.

Weinbaum, Alys Eve. "Interracial Romance and Black Internationalism." In *Next to the Color Line: Gender, Sexuality, and W. E. B. Du Bois*, edited by Susan Gillman and Alys Eve Weinbaum, 96–123. Minneapolis: University of Minnesota Press, 2007.

———. "Marx, Irigaray, and the Politics of Reproduction." *Differences* 6.1 (1994): 98–128.

———. "Racial Aura: Walter Benjamin and the Work of Art in a Biotechnological Age." *Literature and Medicine* 26.1 (2007): 207–39.

———. *Wayward Reproductions: Genealogies of Race and Nation in Transatlantic Modern Thought*. Durham: Duke University Press, 2004.

Weisenburger, Steven. *Modern Medea: A Family Story of Slavery and Child-Murder from the Old South*. New York: Hill and Wang, 1998.

White, Deborah Gray. *Ar'n't I a Woman? Female Slaves in the Plantation South*. New York: Norton, 1985.

———. *Too Heavy a Load: Black Women in Defense of Themselves, 1894–1994*. New York: Norton, 1999.

Whitehead, Anne. "Writing with Care: Kazuo Ishiguro's *Never Let Me Go*." *Contemporary Literature* 52.1 (2011): 54–83.

Wiegman, Robyn. "Intimate Publics: Race, Property, and Personhood." *American Literature* 74.4 (2002): 859–85.

Wilder, Bruce L. "Surrogate Exploitation." *New York Times*, November 22, 1990.

Wilhelm, Kate. *Where Late the Sweet Birds Sang*. New York: Harper and Row, 1976.

Wilkinson, Stephen. *Bodies for Sale: Ethics and Exploitation in the Human Body Trade*. New York: Routledge, 2003.

Williams, Delores S. *Sisters in the Wilderness: The Challenge of Womanist God-Talk*. Maryknoll, NY: Orbis Books, 1993.

Williams, Eric. *Capitalism and Slavery*. Chapel Hill: University of North Carolina Press, 1944.

Williams, Patricia J. *The Alchemy of Race and Rights: Diary of a Law Professor*. Cambridge, MA: Harvard University Press, 1991.

———. "On Being the Object of Property." *Signs* 14.1 (1988): 5–24.

———. *The Rooster's Egg: On the Persistence of Prejudice*. Cambridge, MA: Harvard University Press, 1995.

Williams, Raymond. *Keywords: A Vocabulary of Culture and Society*. Oxford: Oxford University Press, 1976.

———. *Marxism and Literature*. Oxford: Oxford University Press, 1977.

Williams, Sherley Anne. *Dessa Rose*. New York: William Morrow, 1986.

Winant, Howard. *The New Politics of Race: Globalism, Difference, Justice*. Minneapolis: University of Minnesota Press, 2004.

———. "Race and Racism: Towards a Global Future." *Ethnic and Racial Studies* 29.5 (2006): 986–1003.

Winterbottom, Michael, director. *Code 46*. DVD. Beverly Hills: MGM, 2003.

Wolff, Cynthia Griffin. "'Margaret Garner': A Cincinnati Story." *Massachusetts Review* 32.3 (1991): 417–40.

Wood, Sarah. "Subversion through Inclusion: Octavia Butler's Interrogation of Religion in *Xenogenesis* and *Wild Seed*." FEMSPEC 6.1 (2005): 87–99.

Wyatt, Jean. "Giving Body to the Word: The Maternal Symbolic in Toni Morrison's *Beloved*." PMLA 108.3 (1993): 474–88.

———. "Identification with the Trauma of Others: Slavery, Collective Trauma, and the Difficulties of Representation in Toni Morrison's *Beloved*." In *Risking Difference: Identification, Race, and Community in Contemporary Fiction and Feminism*, 66–84. New York: State University of New York Press, 2004.

Yanuck, Julius. "The Garner Fugitive Slave Case." *Mississippi Valley Historical Review* 40.1 (1953): 47–66.

Yaszek, Lisa. "'A Grim Fantasy': Remaking American History in Octavia Butler's Kindred." *Signs* 28.4 (2003): 1053–66.

Younger, Judith T. "What the Baby M Case Is Really All About." *Law & Inequality: A Journal of Theory and Practice* 6.2–3 (1988): 75–82.

Žižek, Slavoj. "*Children of Men* Comments." *Children of Men*. Directed by Alfonso Cuarón. DVD. Hollywood: Universal Pictures, 2007.

———. "The Clash of Civilizations at the End of History." Scribd. Accessed January 21, 2017. https://www.scribd.com/document/19133296/Zizek-The-Clash-of -Civilizations-at-the-End-of-History.

INDEX

biocapitalism, 4–17; assisted reproductive technologies and, 39–44, 83–84; *Beloved* and, 83–84, 88–90; black feminism and, 22–25, 108–10; Butler's fiction and, 114–19, 139–46; childbirth metaphor and, 30–33; *Children of Men* and, 182–86; cloning and, 147–52; contract labor vs. slavery and, 19–25; exchange relationships in, 157–60; genealogy of concept, 4–17, 39–44, 196n25; *Never Let Me Go* and, 157–64; organ trade and, 27–28, 148–52; racial capitalism and, 4–17, 33, 35–36, 104–10, 151–52, 231n9, 234n24; reproductive labor and, 5–17, 42, 180, 196n28; slave episteme and, 157–60; slavery and, 16–17, 39–44, 116–46; surrogacy/slavery nexus and, 54–60, 84–86; terminology, 195n15

Biocapital: The Constitution of Postgenomic Life (Sunder Rajan), 39–41

biopolitics: Butler's fiction and, 121–34, 136–46; eugenics and, 166–67; neoliberalism and, 128–29; slavery as, 117–27. *See also* biopower

biopower: black studies scholarship on, 12, 231n7; Butler's fiction and, 127–34; eugenics and, 166–67; eurocentrism of, 205n76, 237n43; Foucault's theory of, 114–15, 120, 128, 224n6; racial capitalism and, 167–72; slavery and, 237n43. *See also* biopolitics

Birth of Biopolitics, The (Foucault), 128

Black Atlantic, The (Gilroy), 90–91

black body: in Butler's fiction, 115, 125–27, 139–46; in *Children of Men*, 184–86; Roberts's discussion of, 47–49, 112. *See also* blackness; female body

Black Book, The (anthology), 90, 107, 221n27

black feminism: Baby M case and, 8–9, 21, 33, 41, 44–49, 84–85, 197n35; biocapitalism and, 55–60; Butler's

fiction and, 113–46; Du Bois and, 67–71; fragility of, 247n53; and freedom, 88–89, 109–10; general strike and, 71–83; historical context for, 23–26; history of slavery and, 61–66; insurgency of slave women and, 64–66; *Johnson v. Calvert* case and, 33, 49–54; Little case and, 104–10; neo-slave narratives and, 80–87; as propaganda, 71–80; scholarship on fugitive slaves, 68, 212n20; surrogacy/slavery nexus and, 8–9, 26, 31, 46–49, 53–54, 85, 199n48; theology, 22–23. *See also* black Marxism

black feminist philosophy of history, 3–4, 61–87; *Beloved* as contribution to, 89, 109–10; biocapitalism and, 26; black feminist fiction and, 15–16, 80–87; Butler's fiction and, 113–16; *Children of Men* and, 185–86; Davis's contributions to, 74–77; surrogacy/slavery nexus and, 8–9, 18–25, 136

black liberation movement, sexism of, 74–77

black Marxism, 3–4, 34–39, 59–60, 65–66, 79–80; black feminism and, 62–63, 123; Ishiguro and, 159; masculinism of, 65–66

Black Marxism (Robinson), 34–39, 65–66

black nationalism, 23

blackness: and genetics, 190n21; in *Johnson v. Calvert*, 50–54; and legal status, 53–54; national belonging and, 184; reproduction of, 36–38, 51, 185; slavery and, 162–63, 167; of surrogates, 52, 55; visibility of, 10–13, 168, 190n21, 231n9; of women slaves, 38. *See also* whiteness

Black Power, 23

black radical tradition, 3–4; biocapitalism and, 233n24; black feminism and, 3–4, 26, 44, 62, 65, 79, 108–10;

masculinism of, 65–67, 73; racial capitalism and, 34; Robinson and, 34–39, 65–66, 96–97; slavery in, 3–4, 42–44. *See also* black Marxism

Black Reconstruction (Du Bois): gender and sexuality in, 66–71, 76–77; "general strike," 67–71, 83, 89–90, 108–9, 216n44; historical truth, 71–80; "propaganda of history," 71–80, 108–9; slaves as "black workers," 67–71, 78–79

black women's health movement, 47–48, 88–89

"Bloodchild" (Butler), 118–27, 136–46, 150; biocapitalism and, 143–46; biopolitics and, 136–46; interspecies relationships in, 137–46, 226n23; racial capitalism and, 141–42

bondage, contract and, 3, 15 19–20, 31–33. *See also* slavery

Boris, Eileen, 6

Brave New World (Huxley), 178

Brown, Louise, 83–84

Bush, Barbara (author of *Slave Women in Caribbean Society*), 36

Butler, Octavia, 24–25, 27, 81–84, 110; on biopolitics and biopower, 121–34, 136–46; and black Marxism, 123; dystopian fiction of, 112–45; on hegemony, 117–18; on kinship, 127–34; on slavery, 117–27; and surrogacy/slavery nexus, 134–46. *See also individual works*

Calvert, Crispina, 49–54, 201n57, 204n72

Calvert, Mark, 49–54

Camp, Stephanie, 36

Capital (Marx), 154–56, 170

capitalism: Butler's approach to, 123–27; crisis of, 96; exchange value in, 155–56; exploitation of female body in, 47–49, 196n29; freedom and, 20–25; Marx's characterization of, 29–30; racial character of, 34–39, 194n7; refusal

of rationality of, 97–98; slavery and, 2–3, 66, 211n16. *See also* biocapitalism; racial capitalism

capital punishment, 89

Carby, Hazel, 4

care work: devaluation of, 6–7; slave women and, 213n32; as violence, in *Never Let Me Go*, 153–56

Caribbean slavery, 36–37

Cary, Lorene, 81

Chakrabarty, Dipesh, 222n19

childbirth: as Marx's metaphor, 29–30; slavery and, 30; surrogacy and, 31–33. *See also* reproductive labor; surrogacy; surrogacy/slavery nexus

Children of Men, The (film), 25, 28, 179–86

Childs, Dennis, 20, 218n9

choice: in Butler's fiction, 117–27, 127–34, 134–46; neoliberalism and, 111, 113; in *Never Let Me Go*, 152–54, 164–66; and slavery, 162–64

Christian, Barbara, 4, 90, 100

civil rights movement: black feminism and, 23, 65–66; neoliberalism and, 166

Civil War, 63–64, 70–71

Clarke Kaplan, Sara, 91, 218nn7–8

Cliff, Michelle, 81

Clinical Labor (Cooper and Waldby), 42–43

cloning, 27–28, 41; bans on, 231n8; biocapitalism and, 166–72; bodily dispossession and, 148–52, 177–78; dystopian visions of, 147–52; eugenics and, 164–72; exchange relationships and, 157–60; "natal alienation" and "social death" and, 162–63; neoslavery and, 172–76; racial capitalism and, 231n9; representation in film and literature, 147–76; representation in media, 229n2; slavery and, 161–64; surrogacy/slavery nexus and, 177–78; therapeutic and reproductive uses of, 239n2

emancipation, deferral of freedom and, 32–33

embryonic stem cell banking, 41

Engels, Friedrich, 3, 6, 34–35, 79, 194n9

enslavability, reproduction and, 38–39, 93–94. See also *partus sequitur ventrem*

eugenics: assisted reproductive technologies and, 111–12, 204n75; in *Never Let Me Go*, 164–72; in *Wild Seed*, 119–27

exchange relationship: biocapitalism and slavery and, 157–60; in *Never Let Me Go*, 154–56, 174–76; transnational surrogacy as, 56–60

Federici, Silvia, 6, 88, 220n21

female body: Aristotelian view of, 202n60; in *Beloved*, 29, 95; in Butler's fiction, 121–34; capitalism and exploitation of, 47–49, 196n29; cloning and dispossession of, 177–78, 240n4; surrogacy/slavery nexus and, 179–86. See also black body

"Female Slave Resistance: The Economics of Sex" (Hine), 77

feminist scholarship: Baby M case and, 45–49; biocapitalism and, 4–17, 41–44; on science and technology, 40–41; on surrogacy, 25–26, 33; transnational/outsourced surrogacy and, 54–60. See also black feminism; black feminist philosophy of history

Ferguson, Roderick, 191n29

Fett, Sharla, 36

Fifteenth Amendment, 52

FINNRAGE, 216n48

Fortunati, Leopoldina, 6, 220n21

Foucault, Michel: biopower, 12, 114–15, 120, 128, 224n6, 231n7; on history, 71; on racism, 205n76, 237n43; slavery and, 237n43; surrogacy and, 58

Fourteenth Amendment, 52

Franklin, Sarah, 40–41

Freedman, Carl, 127

freedom: autonomism and, 97–98; black feminism and, 88–89, 109–10; capitalism and, 19–20; of clones, 147–52; commodification of, 19–20, 35, 170; insurgent rationality and, 92–93; in *Never Let Me Go*, 164–72; slavery and, 88–89, 91–92. See also choice; violent insurgency

"freedom dreams": black feminism and, 23–25; in *Never Let Me Go*, 175; of women slaves, 108–9

Free Joan Little campaign, 106–10

Fugitive Slave Act, 63–64, 95, 210n4

Garner, Margaret, 26, 61–66, 86–87, 210n4, 210n8, 210n10; *Beloved* and, 88–90, 92, 211n12, 219n18, 221n25; *The Black Book* and, 107–8; historical legacy of, 90–91; trial of, 92–93

Gendered Resistance (anthology), 62

general strike: *Beloved* and, 89–90, 98, 106; black feminism and, 71–72, 77–78, 108–9; Davis and, 73–76; Du Bois and, 16, 26, 66–72, 216n44; gender of, 67–72, 83; and neo-slave narratives, 91–93. See also violent insurgency

genomics: biocapitalism and, 39–41; Butler's fiction and, 115, 119–27; cloning and, 229n2; race and, 204n74, 224n3; white entitlement and, 53–54

geopolitics: biocapitalism and, 60; outsourced and transnational surrogacy and, 204n75

gestational surrogacy, 18–25, 55, 196n21, 206nn77–78; "natural" motherhood and, 198n37; "rescue narrative" and, 208n84. See also *Johnson v. Calvert*; surrogacy; surrogacy/slavery nexus

Gilroy, Paul, 90–91, 236n41

Glenn, Evelyn Nakano, 6

Pande, Amrita, 56–58, 208n84
Parslow, Richard (Judge), 50–54
partus sequitur ventrem, 6, 10, 47, 50–54, 94; and *Beloved*, 94; and surrogacy, 48, 50–51, 200n52
Pateman, Carole, 20
Patterson, Orlando, 19, 122, 162–63, 218n8
Perkins-Valdez, Dolen, 81
"philosophy of history." *See* Benjamin, Walter; black feminist philosophy of history
Playing in the Dark (Morrison), 30–31
Plessy v. Ferguson, 53
Pollitt, Katha, 46
polygenesis discourse, 196n21
post-Fordism, 7
postracial ideology and postracialism: Butler's fiction and, 4, 113, 115–16; neoliberalism and, 27–28, 35, 104, 112, 114, 161–64, 185–86; in *Never Let Me Go*, 5, 172–76; reproductive extraction and, 177–78,
prenatal property, 48–49
primitive accumulation: black Marxism and, 34–39; Marx and Engels on, 29–30
propaganda: black feminism as, 71–75, 109; Du Bois on, 71, 109, 213n26; neo-slave narratives as, 81; surrogacy and, 22

racial capitalism, 2–3; biocapitalism as, 4–17, 33, 35–36, 104–10, 151–52, 232n9, 233n24; black feminism and, 8–9, 108–10; in Butler's fiction, 114, 141–46; insurgency against, 15–16, 26, 61–66, 72–77, 89; in *Never Let Me Go*, 160–64, 231n9; (re)production and, 34–41; slavery and, 88–90, 95–110; surrogacy and, 10, 25–26, 199n47
racialization: gestational surrogacy and, 18–25, 43–54, 55–60, 196n21, 206nn77–78; Indian surrogacy and, 209n92, 209n94; of reproductive

labor and laborer, 6–9, 13–17, 51–54, 240n7; slave breeding and, 31–33. *See also partus sequitur ventrem*
racism: biopolitics and, 12–13, 166–72; of disparities in capital punishment and sentencing, 89; Holocaust and, 166–72, 236n41; Marxism and, 34, 194n9
Radical Republicanism, 63
Ragoné, Heléna, 193n46, 206n77
Randall, Alice, 81
rape: of black women prisoners, 104–5; as counterinsurgency, 75–77, 214n33, 214n35; Davis on, 75–77; Du Bois on, 68; in *Kindred*, 121–33; slave women's resistance to, 15–16, 26, 61–66, 72–77, 89
rationality: in *Beloved*, 95–96, 219n18; and irrationality of slavery, 90, 95–96; of violent insurgency, 92–110
Reagan, Ronald, 218n9
Reagon, Bernice Johnson, 107–8
recombinant DNA technology, 40
Reconstruction, 53, 64–66
Reddy, Chandan, 190n21
Reed, Ishmael, 80
"Reflections on the Black Woman's Role in the Community of Slaves" (Davis), 72–77
refusal of dispossession: autonomist feminism and, 97, 220n21; in *Beloved*, 89–90, 94, 97–98, 103–10; black feminism and, 24–25, 64, 79; in Butler's fiction, 124–27; cloning and organ trade and, 148–52; Davis on, 74–77; Garner and, 86–87; general strike as, 61–67; in *Kindred*, 122–34; Little case and, 105–10; neo-slave narratives and, 81–83, 87; slave women and, 15–16, 23, 26, 61–66, 72–77. *See also* general strike; violent insurgency
Reinhardt, Mark, 63
rememory in *Beloved*, 98–101, 221n28